Option for the Poor

A HUNDRED YEARS OF
VATICAN SOCIAL TEACHING

Revised Edition

Also by the author
   Spirituality and Justice
   Integral Spirituality
   The Social Justice Agenda

Option for the Poor

A HUNDRED YEARS OF
VATICAN SOCIAL TEACHING

Revised Edition

Donal Dorr

ORBIS BOOKS
Maryknoll, New York 10545

Fourth printing, March 2001

The Catholic Foreign Mission Society of America (Maryknoll) recruits and trains
people for overseas missionary service. Through Orbis Books, Maryknoll aims to
foster the international dialogue that is essential to mission. The books published,
however, reflect the opinions of their authors and are not meant to represent the
official position of the society.

Published in the USA and Canada
by Orbis Books
Maryknoll, New York 10545

Published in Ireland by
Gill and Macmillan Ltd
Goldenbridge
Dublin 8
with associated companies in
Auckland, Budapest, Gaborone, Harare, Hong Kong,
Kampala, Kuala Lumpur, Lagos, London, Madras,
Manzini, Melbourne, Mexico City, Nairobi,
New York, Singapore, Sydney, Tokyo, Windhoek

First published 1983
Revised and expanded edition 1992

Typeset in Ireland
Printed in the United States of America

Library of Congress Cataloging-in-Publication Data

Dorr, Donal.
    Option for the poor : a hundred years of Vatican social teaching /
Donal Dorr. — Rev. ed.
      p. cm.
    Includes bibliographical references.
    ISBN 0-88344-827-0 (pbk.)
    1. Sociology, Christian (Catholic)—History. 2. Catholic Church—
Doctrines—History. I. Title.
BX1753.D66   1992
261.8—dc20
                                          92-20785
                                             CIP

Table of Contents

Preface

The first edition of this book was published nine years ago and it has been reprinted several times. In this revised and up-dated edition there are thousands of changes, ranging from minor stylistic points to very substantial additions or corrections.

For the benefit of those who may be familiar with the first edition, the following is a summary of the major changes I have made. The introductory chapter has been substantially altered. The second half of Chapter 3 (on colonialism) and the second half of Chapter 5 (on decolonisation) are new. The last few pages of Chapter 7 and the first few pages of Chapter 8 (on the concept of development) are new. Some of the material of Chapter 12 has been changed significantly and the chapter has been expanded. Chapter 13 is entirely new; it covers the period 1982–92 and includes an extended treatment of two social encyclicals (*Sollicitudo Rei Socialis* and *Centesimus Annus*) as well as a shorter account of the encyclical *Redemptoris Missio*, the two Vatican documents on Liberation Theology, the papal documents on ecology and women, and a variety of other material. The final chapter is almost entirely new, but it incorporates a little of the material from the last chapter of the first edition. Smaller changes have been made in the other chapters to take account of more recent research and my own 'second thoughts' about important issues, or simply to clarify what I intended to say. I have expanded the bibliography of secondary sources considerably and have added a separate comprehensive bibliography of the Church documents to which I refer in the book.

Because this is a 'study edition', for use by individuals or groups, I have endeavoured to make it more 'user friendly' in a number of ways. In the first edition there were over 800 end-notes, taking up 44 pages. In this edition I have incorporated most of the references into the main body of the text. In this way the number of notes has been reduced by four fifths. At the end of each chapter I have added the following materials:

— a summary of the material covered in the chapter;

— a few 'questions for review' which may help readers to check whether they have understood the main points;

— one or two 'questions for reflection' which are intended to stimulate readers to relate what has been said in the chapter to the wider world and to their own experience;

— one or two 'issues for further study' which indicate related subjects which might be suitable topics for essays, term papers, or personal study.

I take this opportunity to thank some of those who have helped me to write the book. I am grateful to Bishop Eamonn Casey, former chairman of Trócaire, the Irish Catholic Agency for World Development, and to Brian McKeown, its director, for their vision and support. Trócaire, in conjunction with the theology faculty of Maynooth College, established the Cardinal Conway Research Fellowship in the Theology of Development; the original edition of this book was written while I was the holder of this fellowship. I wish to thank the members of the staff and committees of Trócaire for their inspiration and encouragement; and the president and staff of Maynooth College, who welcomed me and provided an ambience which encouraged me to study.

The research for this new edition was carried out partly under the sponsorship of the Irish Missionary Union and of Trócaire. I am grateful to Enda Watters, Jenny Doolin, John O'Connell and Anne Reilly of the IMU and to Colm Regan of Trócaire for encouragement and support. This edition was written while I lived in the community of priest and student members of St Patrick's Missionary Society in Kiltegan House, Maynooth. I am thankful to all of them for their exceptional kindness and inspiration and I dedicate this work to them.

I am indebted to Padraig Ó Maille, and to my brother Noel, for helping me to clarify what I wanted to say. I would like also to thank Michael Gill and Bridget Lunn of Gill and Macmillan, and Robert Ellsberg, Sue Perry and John Eagleson of Orbis Books for their encouragement and advice.

During the years while I was doing the research for both the original and the revised editions of this book, I was able to spend a good deal of time learning at first hand what it means for Church people to make an 'option for the poor'. I am deeply grateful to many friends and fellow-workers—in East, West,

Central, and Southern Africa, as well as in Brazil, Ireland, England, Scotland, the USA and Australia—who took part with me in workshops or courses about justice, development, and human liberation; they gave me new life and helped me to grow in understanding and commitment during these years. These interludes were as much part of my theological research as the study of Church documents—and a lot more exciting! This book is written not just for scholars and students but also for those fellow-workers and for people like them in many parts of the world—Christians who feel called to work for justice and who turn to Church social teaching for inspiration and for guidance about how to answer the call.

Earlier drafts of Chapter 4 and of part of Chapter 6 were published in *Doctrine and Life* and *The Irish Theological Quarterly* respectively; some passages of Chapter 12 were published in *The Furrow*; and an earlier version of some pages of Chapter 13 was published in Gregory Baum (ed.), *The Logic of Solidarity* (Orbis: 1989).

Donal Dorr,
Ash Wednesday 1992

Introduction

This book is a study of Catholic social teaching over the past hundred years—or, to be more precise, over the period 1878 to early 1992. The general aim is to examine how this teaching developed over that time and to determine in what sense, and to what extent, a consistent, organic tradition has been developed. The more specific aim is examine the extent to which, during this period, the official teaching of the Church was a defence of the poor and powerless in society and an encouragement to them in the struggle for justice.

I have used the phrase 'option for the poor' as a convenient way to focus these questions. This term only came into common usage during the 1970s. Since it is relatively new, it would of course be anachronistic to expect to find a clear expression of it in the earlier stages of the teaching of the past hundred years. But it is important to get behind the *term* 'option for the poor', so as to look at the *reality* that is designated by the term. That is what I have tried to do throughout this book. I have examined the stances taken by different popes in relation to issues of poverty, injustice and oppression in society. To what extent were they on the side of the poor and the powerless in the struggle against injustice? That is the key issue—and it arose long before the term 'option for the poor' was coined. The advantage of using the concept of an option for the poor is that it provides a standard by which one can assess the reality and thoroughness of the official Church's frequently expressed concern for the poor.

A Response to Structural Injustice

The term 'option for the poor' burst on to the ecclesiastical scene only about twenty years ago. Since then it has become the most controversial religious term since the Reformers' cry, 'Salvation through faith alone'. Hostile critics dismiss the notion as an unlikely cross between Latin American Catholicism and Marxism. But most of those who are in favour of the idea believe that the Church is called to make an 'option for the poor' not merely in Latin America but everywhere else as well. Furthermore, they find the basis for such an option in the Bible rather than in Marx—and, fortunately for them, they were saying this long before the collapse of the Marxist-inspired governments of Eastern Europe.

The notion of an option for the poor developed in Latin America as Church leaders there began to implement the renewal sparked off by Vatican II. At the heart of this option were three basic elements:

— Firstly, there was a commitment by Church leaders not to collude with oppressive regimes but to campaign actively for structural justice in society and to take the risk of throwing the authority of the official Church behind efforts to resist oppression and exploitation.

— Secondly, there was a belief that the key agents in bringing about such change must be the poor, the oppressed and the marginalised themselves; and therefore a commitment to work 'from below' for and with these groups, actively supporting and empowering them.

— Thirdly, there was a commitment to make the Church itself more just and participative; in this way poor and oppressed groups and individuals could have their dignity and value recognised by being listened to, and could have a practical experience of being empowered by participating in decision-making.

Some people reject the notion of an option for the poor on the grounds that it implies a rejection of the rich and is therefore incompatible with the Christian message which is intended for all. But, as Albert Nolan points out:

> The option for the poor is not a choice about the *recipients* of the gospel message, *to whom* we must preach the gospel; it is a matter of *what gospel* we preach to anyone at all. It is concerned with the *content* of the gospel message itself. (Nolan 18)*

To make an option for the poor is simply to commit oneself to justice and therefore to take up the cause of the poor in their struggle for justice.

---

* For details of references given thus, by author and page no., see Biobliography of Secondary Sources, p. 412, for full details. Where more than one work by the same author is listed, the year of publication will appear in the text reference in square brackets.

An option for the poor is a commitment by individual Christians and the Christian community at every level to engage actively in a struggle to overcome the social injustices which mar our world. To be genuine it must come from a real experience of solidarity with the victims of our society. This means that one aspect of an option for the poor has to do with sharing in some degree in the lives, sorrows, joys, hopes, and fears of those who are on the margins of society. Without this, the attempt to serve the interests of 'the poor' will be patronising—and it will make them feel more powerless and dependent than ever. But an option for the poor is not primarily the choice of a less affluent life-style by individuals or groups. It is a commitment to resist the structural injustice which marks our world. The person who makes such an option is undertaking to work to change the unjust economic, social and political structures which determine how power and resources are shared out in the world—and also in the Church. The aim is to bring about a more just society.

The word 'option' suggests a personal choice. While continuing to put emphasis on this personal aspect, I would want to insist that the choice in question is not essentially an act of private asceticism or even of face-to-face compassion for a poor person. It is specifically a response at the level of the wider society as a whole, a response to the unjust ordering of society. Therefore it makes sense only in the context of an awareness of how society is in fact structured.

We live in a stratified society where certain economic, political, cultural, and religious structures maintain and promote the dominance of the rich and powerful over the mass of ordinary people and peoples. These structures operate through agencies and institutions that are staffed mainly by middle-class people—those who provide the professional and commercial services of society. Whatever their private loyalties and values, these service people contribute to structural injustice through the kind of work they are doing. The possibility of making an 'option for the poor' arises for such people and it is mainly to them that the challenge is issued. Some of the services provided by the Churches are an integral part of the institutions of society—for instance of the educational or medical system of the country. Those who are working in, or responsible for, Church services of this kind are asking themselves whether their work, however good it may be in itself, is an adequate embodiment of the Church's commitment to justice in society.

An 'option for the poor', in the sense in which it is intended here, means a series of choices, personal or communal, made by individuals, by communities, or even by corporate entities such as a religious congregation, a diocese, or a Church (as represented by its central administration, and, in varying degrees, by its ordinary members). It is the choice to disentangle themselves from serving the interests of those at the 'top' of society and to begin instead to come into solidarity with those at or near the bottom. Such solidarity means commitment to working and living within structures and agencies that promote the interests of the less favoured sectors of society. These would include those who are economically poor, the groups that are politically marginalised or oppressed, people discriminated against on sexual grounds, peoples that have been culturally silenced or oppressed, and those who have been religiously disinherited or deprived.

It is not my intention in this book to give a detailed and systematic explanation of what an 'option for the poor' means. Certain aspects of the question are touched on in an incidental way, in the course of this study of Church teaching. I have written more extensively on the topic elsewhere, with special reference to how the more experiential aspect of such an option (sharing the life of 'the poor') might be fitted together with the more organisational aspects (building alternative structures) (Dorr 1984, 1990 and 1991).

In recent years many earnest Christians who have been trying to discern 'the signs of the times' in renewal courses and assemblies find themselves challenged to make an 'option for the poor'. Yet, having worked with many groups of this kind, I have come to believe that many of those who are faced with this challenge do not really know what it involves. Some find the term 'option for the poor' both confusing and threatening, for it puts a question mark over their present way of life and previous commitments. Fears and guilt create an aura of ambiguity around the term, as well as some selective blindness. People demand 'a simple explanation' of the term. When that is given they often respond with questions that begin: 'But surely . . . ?' These 'but surely' questions are an indication that the questioner has reached the point of resistance. Too direct a response to such questions may arouse defensiveness. Frequently it is more useful to provide some kind of biblical background and to trace the recent development in Church action, reflection, and teaching. This allows people space to answer the questions for themselves.

Since the first edition of this book was issued in 1983 I have come to see more clearly how close is the link between the concept of an option for the poor and the new style of doing theology which is called liberation theology. It is no coincidence that both emerged twenty years ago in the same Latin American milieu. One of the main reasons why many Church people in the West have difficulties in relation to option for the poor is that they have no real sympathy with the whole project of liberation theology. This applies to three different categories of Christians in the West:

— The first of these are people who see such an option as a version of the Marxist class option, or are opposed to it on the grounds that it is a politicisation of the Faith. These people are not at all opposed to helping the poor. But they see liberation theology as a dangerous threat to the stability of society and to the teaching authority of Church leaders.

— In the second category are religious communities or individual Christians who feel guilty about the poverty all round them and want to share the life of the poor. They may revise their Constitutions or their personal ideals by undertaking 'an option for the poor'. But they may have very little understanding of the political aspects of such an option. They may also fail to advert to the fact that what is in question is not just living poorly but an empowering of 'the poor' through searching *with* them for the meaning of Christian faith in our world. If such individuals or groups are to come to a more authentic understanding of what is meant by an option for the poor they need to get some sense of the whole project that is liberation theology—not as a set of theories but as a way of exploring with 'ordinary' people the relevance of Jesus to our daily lives. This can soon lead on to effective challenges to the power structures of State or Church.

— The third category of Church people in the West who have difficulties with the notion of an option for the poor include many of those who feel called to struggle for justice in the economic and political spheres. They see this as part of their Christian vocation, but they assume that it is to be carried out according to the usual Western model of political organisation or lobbying. Frequently, then, they end up organising on *behalf* of the poor but not really working very effectively *with* them. For them, too, the project that is liberation theology can open up an entirely new way of being with 'ordinary' or marginalised people; out of this comes a better understanding of what is meant by an option for the poor.

The Biblical Concept of Poverty

In view of the particular importance of the biblical basis for making an 'option for the poor' I propose here to give a very brief outline of what the Bible has to say on the subject of poverty and oppression.

In the Old Testament the term 'the poor' refers especially to those groups of people who are economically deprived, who have no social status, who are treated unjustly by foreign rulers or by the authorities in their own land. These people are oppressed because they are poor, and are therefore at the mercy of the unscrupulous. Furthermore, they are poor because they are oppressed: they have been further impoverished by being cheated and deprived of their rights.

Some groups of 'the poor' are doubly oppressed. They are the people who are at risk not only because they are economically poor but also because they happen to be widows, orphans, or resident aliens—categories of people who have nobody to defend them against exploitation. The Old Testament leaves us in no doubt that God has a special care for the poor. The oppression of God's people in Egypt moved Yahweh to save them, as the Book of Exodus recounts. After the Israelites had settled in 'the Promised Land' the poor among them found themselves oppressed by the wealthy and powerful of their own people. Time after time God sent the prophets to protest against this injustice and to proclaim God's care for the poor.

The New Testament deepens our understanding of what it means to be poor. In some important respects, Jesus himself should be seen as one of 'the poor'. Having 'emptied himself' to share our humanity (Phil. 2:7), he became a native of a despised village (Jn. 1:46) and was known as a carpenter's son

(Mat. 13:55). He resisted the temptation to carry out his mission through the use of glory and power (Mat. 4:5–10). He was the innocent victim of persecution and was executed as a criminal after an unjust trial.

The Bible makes it clear that there can be an unjust use of power by religious leaders as well as by civil authorities. The reaction of Christ to the scribes and pharisees, as portrayed in the New Testament, suggests that he sees them as oppressors, imposing their will on the mass of ordinary believers (e.g. Mat. 15:3–20; 23:4–38). In challenging this abuse of power, Christ was standing in the tradition of Moses and the prophets who cried out against economic injustice and political oppression. Defence of the poor includes standing up for those who are powerless before religious authorities who abuse their power.

Some Christians today hold that the Bible—especially the New Testament—is more concerned about 'poverty of spirit' than about material poverty. However, a study of the theme of poverty in the Bible suggests that it is not helpful to make too sharp a distinction between 'the poor' and those who are 'poor in spirit'. The Scriptures indicate that those who are poor and defenceless have nobody to turn to but God. God has a special care for the victims of injustice and those who are poor; and they in turn can more easily accept the divine care and protection. Of course, poor people can also turn away from God—through bitterness and lack of hope. But in general it is more likely that those who are economically and politically poor will also be 'poor in spirit', dependent on and open to God. On the other hand the rich and powerful tend to rely on themselves and therefore to close themselves off from God. Of course rich people may also turn to God; but so long as they remain attached to wealth and rely on their own power it is almost impossible for them to be 'poor in spirit' and to enter God's realm (cf. Mat. 19: 24).

These brief points from Scripture go some way towards clarifying what an 'option for the poor' means—and what it does not mean. Such an option, seen in a biblical perspective, would mean some special care or preference for people or groups who are marginalised in human society. It is quite true that there is a sense in which *everybody* is 'poor before God'. But this idea can be invoked as a way of evading the central thrust of the biblical teaching about poverty. The meaning of the word 'poor' can be extended and redefined to a point where the challenge of the scriptural position gets lost. In Chapter 12 of this book the question of the meaning of the word 'poor' is treated in a little more detail; and there I examine the different senses in which one might speak of the 'poverty' of rich people.

Catholic Social Teaching

The subtitle of this book is intended to limit and qualify the main title, by indicating that I am dealing here only with one aspect of the topic 'option for the poor'. The focus of my attention here is the social teaching of the Roman Catholic Church over the past hundred and thirteen years. (I have written elsewhere about the approach of other Churches to the question—see Dorr [1991] 63–82.) Furthermore, I have not tried to give an exhaustive treatment of the topic even within the Catholic Church but have confined my attention mainly to Vatican teaching. I have not attempted to give a full account of the official documents of regional groups of bishops. But I do pay some attention to such teaching where it is of significance for the Church as a whole and especially where it has had an impact on Vatican teaching. For instance, I have given some account of the Medellín and Puebla documents from Latin America, and referred more briefly to the pastoral letters on social issues issued by the US Bishops' Conference and to the Basel document issued in 1989 by the Conference of European Churches.

This study is not confined to the most formal Church documents such as papal encyclicals. In order to present the teaching of some popes, especially Pius XII and John Paul II, I found it necessary to take account of many of the more important addresses which these popes saw as being in some sense authoritative.

I take it that the various documents and statements represent the considered views of their official authors, no matter who may have prepared the drafts. So I have not devoted much attention to the question of who drafted the various documents. But where information on this matter is available I have taken account of it.

Until twenty years ago most Catholic commentaries on the social encyclicals treated them as quite beyond any overt criticism—though in practice each commentator interpreted them in the light of his or her own viewpoint. Nowadays papal teaching is no longer assured of a welcome even from Catholics. Some liberal theologians and commentators criticise it harshly and at times unfairly. On the other hand, many of the conservatives comment on it with a certain sycophantic fund-amentalism, while at the same time emphasising the parts which fit in with their own viewpoint. The result, of course, is that the real message of these important documents never reaches very many ordinary Christians. There is need for a serious and objective evaluation of these documents and my hope is that this book will contribute to such a study.

In evaluating the views and actions of Church leaders I have tried to take account of their historical situation. In this way I hope to provide a background to present-day issues and to throw light on the overall pattern of the Church's teaching. But the book is intended to be theology as much as history. I do not think it is possible to write history from some totally detached or uncommitted point of view. Objectivity is not attained by abandoning all commitment; and commitment to social justice is part of the Christian faith in the light of which I have done this theological study. This faith has affected my choice of data and my understanding and evaluation of the material.

My faith has even had an effect on the way I have written the book. I have tried to take account of the fact that the social teaching of the Church is a personal challenge to each of us. This challenge can get lost if the presentation is unduly academic. Academic accounts of Catholic social teaching can easily give the impression of complacency, as though the Church were outside history, sitting in judgment on various social systems (e.g. Charles, Herr). I know from experience that many Christians who are working for justice are eager to study the Church's social teaching. But they want it presented in a way that relates it to practical commitment. And they would like the presentation to be not only objective but also challenging and even inspirational.

In the subtitle of this book I use the phrase 'social teaching'. This calls for a brief comment. Up to the 1960s the term 'Catholic social doctrine' was commonly used. However, towards the end of Vatican II this term fell into theological disrepute. Some theologians felt it smacked of a timeless dogmatism which would be particularly inappropriate in matters of social morality where the emphasis of Church teaching has changed so much over the years. Others objected to the notion of a 'Catholic social doctrine' or even a 'Catholic social teaching' on the grounds that this phrase suggests that the Church has a body of principles and a model of society that amount to a 'third way', that is, an alternative to the capitalist and socialist models; this they considered unacceptable.

In the course of Chapters 11 and 14 of the book I have discussed these issues. Here in the introduction it suffices to say that Pope John Paul II has succeeded to some extent in reinstating the term 'social doctrine', using it alongside 'social teaching' and similar terms. But this does not mean a return to the situation of the 1930s when many Catholics thought the Church had a blueprint for society. It is clear that, for John Paul, social 'doctrine' or teaching does not mean an immutable set of truths. He sees it as an organic tradition of teaching by the Church on social issues. This tradition is open to development; and the pope believes that he himself has made his own contribution to it. It is not primarily a question of laying down rules for how society should be organised; but he believes that the Church has a duty to teach and witness to certain basic truths about the human person and certain fundamental human values which ought to be respected in society. It is within the context of such an organic tradition of social teaching that the notion of an 'option for the poor' can best be understood.

SUMMARY

This study of Catholic social teaching examines the extent to which the Church's teaching is an effective defence of the poor and powerless in society and an encouragement to them in the struggle for justice. The concept of an 'option for the poor' is a standard by which one can assess the depth and effectiveness of the Church's concern for the poor.

An option for the poor is a commitment to struggle against structural injustice. Those who make such an option are in solidarity with the victims of our society, and with them they set out to work for a more equitable sharing of power and resources in society and in the Church. This commitment has a solid base in the biblical teaching about the attitude of God towards injustice, oppression and poverty.

The notion of an option for the poor gives rise to confusion or a sense of threat in those who do not have a sympathetic understanding of the approach of the liberation theologians. These theologians try to be with 'ordinary' people (especially the poor) in their struggle to make the world and the Church more just and more humane. A crucial aspect of an option for the poor is a commitment to work with people who are poor or oppressed, helping them explore and articulate the relation between their faith and the reality of their lives.

This study of the Church's teaching seeks to interpret our history in the light of a faith commitment and to combine objectivity with challenge.

Questions for review:

1. What is the political aspect of an option for the poor?
2. What more is involved in an option for the poor over and above political action in the usual sense?
3. To whom does the term 'the poor' apply in the Bible?
4. Is it anachronistic to examine the social teaching of a hundred years ago in the light of the concept of an option for the poor?

Questions for reflection:

1. What would it mean to engage in a project of liberation theology in your country? Who are attempting such a project?
2. Who are 'the poor' and who are 'the powerful' in the world today, in your own country, in the Church?

Issues for further study:

1. The poor and the oppressed in the Bible. (Read Tamez.)
2. Jesus and liberation theology. (Read Sobrino.)

1

Rerum Novarum: *A Call for Justice*

The first of the great social encyclicals, *Rerum Novarum*, was issued by Leo XIII in 1891.[1] In it the pope protested strongly against the harsh conditions which industrial workers had to endure. It is sometimes cynically suggested that Leo was moved to issue it more by the loss to the Church of the working classes of Europe than by their exploitation and suffering. No doubt he was anxious to ensure that the Church should not be rejected by the mass of the new urban poor. But that is no reason to cast doubt on the genuineness of his protest about their treatment. This protest did not spring from Leo's own first-hand experience. For he had not previously been very actively involved in a campaign on behalf of workers; he was more of a scholar and diplomat than an activist. The encyclical was written in response to a strong and constantly growing pressure from many sources, including distinguished Church leaders in Europe and America whose views were respected by Leo. They wanted an authoritative statement from the pope partly because it would be a powerful support to all who were protesting against the exploitation of workers, and partly because it would make Catholics less likely to adopt the more 'extreme' views put forward by various champions of the working classes (for background see Molony 8–63).

Anybody who reads *Rerum Novarum* today, more than ninety years after it was written, may feel that the changes it calls for are not very radical, and that it is rather vague in regard to how they should be brought about. Clearly, it does not go nearly as far as the encyclicals of more recent popes in articulating the requirements of social justice, and in offering specific criticisms of the structures and practices which lead to poverty and oppression. Nevertheless, it lays a solid foundation on which the later social encyclicals and other Church documents could build.

Though the content of Leo's encyclical was important and remains important, what was perhaps even more important was the character of the document as a cry of protest against the exploitation of poor workers. It is not so much the detail of what Leo had to say that was significant but the fact that he chose to speak out at that time, intervening in a most solemn way in a burning issue of the day. His intervention meant that the Church could not be taken to be indifferent to the injustices of the time. Rather, it was seen to be taking a stand on behalf of the poor.

The fact that Catholic Church leaders since that time have frequently spoken out strongly on issues of social injustice makes it difficult to appreciate just how significant it was that Pope Leo should issue his encyclical at that time. An analogy may help. Suppose the present pope were to issue an encyclical maintaining that it is quite immoral for any nation or individual to make or handle nuclear weapons. Commentators might say that this was simply an application of known principles of morality. But the document would have enormous significance as an intervention which committed the Vatican firmly to a specific practical application of general moral principles. It would put the pope firmly on the side of the nuclear disarmers, and against those who hold that nuclear weapons are necessary. In a somewhat similar way, *Rerum Novarum* represents a definite moral stance by the pope. It committed the Catholic Church officially to a rejection of a central thesis of the liberal capitalism of the Western world, namely, that labour is a commodity to be bought at market prices determined by the law of supply and demand rather than by the human needs of the worker (e.g. RN 16–17; 33–4).* So already in this first of the social encyclicals there was a strong protest against the prevailing order.

It is clear that Leo XIII *intended* his encyclical to be a major intervention in defence of the poor. He solemnly and firmly proposed his teaching as a remedy for the social problems of the time (RN 13), at the heart of which was 'the misery and

* For details of all references to Vatican documents see Biobliography of Church Documents p. 397.

wretchedness pressing so unjustly on the majority of the working class' (RN 2); and he saw such an intervention as necessary in view of the fact that 'a small number of very rich people have been able to lay upon the teeming masses of the labouring poor a yoke little better than that of slavery itself' (RN 2).

Looked at from the point of view of its effect, this first of the social encyclicals must be seen as a very significant move of the Church towards the side of the poor. It ensured that social issues could no longer be treated as marginal or secondary to the mission of the Church, or as an 'optional extra'. This applied not merely in the sphere of official teaching but also in practical commitment. *Rerum Novarum* gave great encouragement to those of the clergy and laity who had been working for years to get the Catholic Church more involved in social issues; and it had the long-term effect of greatly increasing the numbers of such committed activists. So, if one judges in terms of the effects over a considerable period of years, it is correct to say with Vidler that the encyclical 'had a truly epoch-making effect in driving home the idea that Catholics must have a social conscience' (Vidler 127). But this did not happen over-night. There were practical and theological obstacles which made for a progress that was uneven and very slow in some sectors of society. In fact the encyclical was at first largely ignored by many of the people with whom it was most directly concerned—employers, industrial workers, and even some Churchmen. In some places, such as Latin America, it was scarcely read at all. Where it was read it was not always accepted. It gave rise to some scandal, not only in society but even within the Church itself (cf. Chenu 15, 18; Molony 123–9; Murray [1953] 551; McGovern 99; Pius XI QA 14).

The reason for this shocked reaction and the resistance that accompanied it was not so much any specific course of action proposed by the pope. It was rather the much more fundamental point that he challenged the current assumption that the 'laws' of economics should be treated as though they were laws of nature, and therefore the basis for morality. Pope Leo issued this challenge at the most obvious point of all, which is also the most sensitive point: he questioned the sacrosanctness of the wage contract. He rejected the assumption that the employer's obligations in justice can be taken to have been fulfilled once the agreed wage has been paid. Leo insisted that 'there underlies a dictate of natural justice more imperious and ancient than any bargain between one person and another, namely that wages ought not to be insufficient to support a frugal and well-behaved wage-earner' (RN 34). He drew the conclusion that if, 'through necessity or fear of a worse evil' the worker accepts a wage less than that required for frugal living then 'that person is made the victim of force and injustice' (RN 34). None of this involved any radical new departure in Catholic moral theology. For instance, the same general principles were applied by moral theologians of that period in their assessment of the morality of 'secret compensation': they judged that it was morally acceptable for workers to supplement an unjust wage by petty pilfering. Nevertheless, in the atmosphere of the time, it was really quite shocking that Leo should bluntly apply these general principles to a situation that was so widespread. It amounted to a clear and outspoken contradiction of the taken-for-granted views of those who held power in the Western world.

The basic principle behind Leo's stance is that human labour cannot be treated simply as a commodity, because to do so is a denial of human dignity and a reduction of the worker to the status of a thing. Needless to say, there is nothing startling in Leo's assertion that it is shameful and inhuman to treat people as though they were things. But for a pope to invoke this principle in defence of underpaid workers was quite startling—shocking for some and inspiring for others. That is why it can be claimed that the importance of *Rerum Novarum* is to be measured not merely in terms of its contribution to the body of teaching (or 'doctrine') of the Catholic Church but also in terms of its impact as an *intervention* on the side of the poor: that is what we may call the 'effective' meaning of the document in contrast to its 'doctrinal' meaning.

It is only in the context of this overriding purpose and effective meaning of *Rerum Novarum* that we can understand properly the point of the fairly lengthy section of the encyclical which is devoted to a treatment of socialism (RN 16). It is sometimes assumed that the main purpose of *Rerum Novarum* was to condemn socialism, and that the encyclical is 'the Church's answer to socialism'. This view was given a particular credibility in the English-speaking world by the fact that the standard English translation gave a rather free rendering of the very first words of the encyclical. It spoke of 'a desire for revolutionary change'. This phrase evoked fears of the turmoil of revolution and could convey the impression that the main aim of the pope was to speak out against the revolutionary ideas of Marx. In fact, the Italian text makes it clear that, in using the words '*rerum novarum*', the pope was speaking of the 'burning desire for change' which was characteristic of the period (cf. Molony 102–3). Leo's main purpose was to speak out, not against Marxist revolution but against the exploitation of workers carried out in the name of liberal capitalism. As the historian John Molony (103) says:

> Then or later, to caricature the encyclical by a free translation of its first line as merely another condemnation of socialism was to cast a gloss on its meaning which Leo never intended, despite the trenchant criticism of socialism which it contained.

Leo was undoubtedly concerned about socialism. This is evident from the fact that he had already condemned it on a number of occasions. In *Rerum Novarum* he set out not merely to reject it but also to refute it (RN 3–12); but it must be said that his account does scant justice to the views of the more moderate socialists of the time. It is clear that Leo considered this part of the encyclical to have an importance in its own right: it warned off the small but significant number of radical Catholics who were flirting with socialist ideas. However, his formal rejection of socialism also served a different and wider purpose. It gave Leo the freedom to condemn the abuses within the existing capitalist system without leaving himself open to the accusation that he favoured socialism.

In spite of its strong rejection of socialism the encyclical must have appeared to many to be tainted with socialist principles on one vital issue—the question of intervention by the State. Leo was already radically challenging the principles of liberal capitalism by his insistence on the need for the State to intervene at times in economic affairs (cf. Molony 123); to many of the people of his time, his adoption of this stance meant that he had already gone over to socialism. It is true that in the early part of the document the pope lays down very strict limits to the right of the State to intervene in the affairs of the individual and the family (RN 6, 9, 10, 11).[2] But later on in the encyclical he makes particular mention of the duty of the State to be concerned for the interests of the working classes i.e. the poor (RN 27). He explains his position as follows:

> . . . when there is question of defending the rights of individuals, the poor and badly-off have a claim to especial consideration. The richer class have many ways of shielding themselves . . . whereas the mass of the poor . . . must chiefly depend upon the assistance of the State (RN 29)

In later paragraphs the pope specifies various ways in which the State should protect workers from abuse and exploitation (RN 32–4). This whole approach involved a rejection of the principles of *laissez faire* capitalism, especially as expounded by the Manchester school.

From the point of view of its 'doctrine', *Rerum Novarum* can be seen as a balanced statement of general principles which rejects the two extremes—socialism on the one hand and uncontrolled capitalism on the other. But when one considers its effective meaning as an intervention by the pope in the social issues of the time it is clear that it is an attempt to place the Catholic Church on the side of the poor—or of the working class, which at that time was more or less the same thing.[3] It succeeded in doing so to a considerable extent—at least in so far as it was the first major official step in a long process which has been continuing, with some 'ups and downs', up to the present.

However, a clarification is called for at once: the encyclical did not attempt to put the Church on the side of the working class over against another class. What it was against was not a group or class but simply the reality of exploitation. So it did not represent a 'class option' in the usual sense of the term. In fact a major concern of the pope was to bridge the gap between the classes of society.[4] Nevertheless, this in no way detracts from the fact that in this encyclical Leo XIII took a firm stand on the side of the mass of exploited workers in the society of the time. It would be overstating the case to claim that *Rerum Novarum* represents or calls for 'an option for the poor' in the sense in which that term is generally understood today; but it indicates that the pope had a particular concern for the poor and it can now be seen as a major step on the road which eventually led to such an option.

I must add at once that the spirituality enshrined in *Rerum Novarum* is quite different to that which is associated with the making of an option for the poor. A clue to Leo's spirituality is to be found in the changes that were made to the text of *Rerum Novarum* while it was being composed. In the first draft of the encyclical the opening words presented the pope as speaking on behalf of 'the God who wants to be present in the poor'. But this was edited out in later versions and the tone was changed so that the pope was presented instead as the one who puts before the world the truth that has been entrusted to the Church. Furthermore, the later drafts included a strong insistence on Christian resignation, absent from the first draft (cf. Molony 67, 79, 81). As I shall point out in the next chapter, Pope Leo advocated a spirituality which would now be seen as 'escapist': he encouraged the poor to put up with their lot by reminding them of the rewards of the life to come.

The Proposed Remedy

In *Rerum Novarum* Leo XIII proposed the Church's 'remedy' (RN 12) for the social problem, a remedy which he believed would, if applied, eliminate the grave injustices of the existing system and bring harmony to the social and economic order. But how realistic was this solution? Granted that the pope was seeking to defend the poor against exploitation, was he also proposing a coherent programme which could bring this about in practice? Or was there a gap between the aim he wished to attain and the means he proposed?

What kind of changes does Leo XIII have in mind? As already noted, *Rerum Novarum* insists on the duty of the State to protect the poor (RN 29). This amounts to a call for a major change in the role which the State had been playing in society in Leo's time. In order to understand and assess the pope's call, it is helpful to consider an issue frequently overlooked by moralists—the relation between economic power and political power.

We can look briefly at two contrasting views of the role of the State in society. (By 'the State' I understand here the apparatus of government that has power to control the way people act in society.) First, there is the classical theory of liberal capitalism. It held that the State should mainly confine itself to 'political' matters such as defending society from external aggression and ensuring internal order and stability; normally the government should not 'interfere' in the economic sphere, but should rather allow private enterprise, open competition, and the forces of the market to operate freely. The assumption here is that the State and its agencies (the judiciary, the security forces, the civil service, etc.) are 'neutral' and independent in relation to any economic rivalries or conflicts that take place in society; their task is to provide the framework within which economic activity can take place peacefully and effectively.

In sharp contrast to this is the Marxist theory. It holds that in fact the State is not neutral; political power is normally held by those with economic power—and, as one might expect, they use the apparatus of the State to further their own interests; the lower classes find that the laws and the security forces are being used to oppress them and to ensure that they cannot escape from the economic exploitation practised by those who control the wealth.

What was the view of Leo XIII? He disagreed with both of the above views. But in speaking about the role of the State in *Rerum Novarum* he comes fairly close to each of the two views at different times. His ideal of what the State ought to be, though it differs significantly from that of liberal capitalism, nevertheless shares with the latter the assumption that the State is neutral and 'above' economics. But, on the other hand, Leo's account of what happens *in practice* is closer to the Marxist view.

According to the principles laid down by Leo, economic power ought not to overlap with political power. In society as it ought to be, the wealthy would not control the apparatus of the State. Instead, the State would be above the interests of all classes and would keep a balance between them (RN 26–7). Leo maintains that cooperation rather than conflict is to be the basis of the social order: 'The great mistake . . . is to take up the notion that class is naturally hostile to class, and that the wealthy and working-classes are intended by nature to live in mutual conflict' (RN 15). The reason this mistaken view was held, the pope believed, lay in the failure to appreciate the design of nature for the body politic:

> Just as the symmetry of the human frame is the result of the suitable arrangement of the different parts of the body, so in a State is it ordained by nature that these two classes should dwell in harmony and agreement, so as to maintain the balance of the body politic. Each needs the other: Capital cannot do without Labour, nor Labour without Capital (RN 15).

The institutions of the State have the task of preserving and fostering the cooperation of the different classes. This means that, in principle, the State is neutral; it is not the instrument of the richer class.

However, a quite different account of the State is suggested by the actual situation as it had evolved up to the time at which the encyclical was written. Looking at what had taken place all around him, Pope Leo did not gloss over the obvious fact that in practice the rich were the ones who held the effective power, a power that extended into the apparatus of the State:

> On the one side there is the party which holds power because it holds wealth; . . . which manipulates for its own benefit . . . all the sources of supply, and which is even represented in the councils of the State itself. On the other side there is the needy and powerless multitude. . . . (RN 35).

Faced with this reality, Leo proposed his long-term solution: the gulf between the classes should be narrowed by enabling as many workers as possible to become owners of property (RN 35). This indicates that he recognised that, in practice, so long as wealth is concentrated in the hands of the few, these few are likely to have undue political power and will use this power for their own benefit. In other words, so long as most of the wealth of the nation is in the hands of one sector of society, the State will be hindered in playing its proper role of protecting the rights of the poor. Leo was well aware that this was actually happening; that is why he insisted so strongly on the need for the State to protect the rights of workers, and why he went on to list several of these rights (RN 26–34).

We have now noted two of the key changes which Leo proposed as a remedy for the social problem: immediate action by the State to protect the interests of the working classes and a more long-term effort to distribute ownership of property much more widely. The next question is, who or what are to be the agents of change that can ensure that the remedy is really applied and the changes take place? How can one make sure that those who have the power to make the changes have the will to do so—and that those who want the changes are in a position to bring them about?

Leo XIII gives a double answer to this question. Firstly, he insists on the vital role which the Church has to play in society. Secondly, he defends the right of workers to band together in trade unions or other associations for their own protection (RN 36). Unfortunately, however, each of these two sources or agents of change is open to serious challenge in the form in which it is presented in *Rerum Novarum*. In the following two sections of this chapter, I shall consider each of these points in turn.

How Prophetic can the Church dare to be?

First of all, Leo insists strongly on the right of the Church to play a major role in shaping society; in fact this is one of the vital points on which he challenges the assumptions of liberal capitalism (cf. Molony 123). The 'liberal' view was that religion is largely a private affair. Leo, in contrast, held that religion is the most powerful intermediary of all in drawing the rich and the working class together; and he saw the Church as the spokesperson for religion in reminding each class of its duties to the other and especially of the obligations of justice (RN 16). In Leo's view the Church has a task which would nowadays be called 'prophetic'—that of challenging each of the classes of society to meet its obligations in justice to the others. But how can the Church best promote cooperation and respect, combined with justice, in the relations between the classes? Leo's view—and his difficulties—can best be understood by looking at two contrasting strategies. One possible approach is to call the rich and powerful to conversion, while exhorting the poor and powerless to be patient—and especially to respect public order in the way they seek their rights. In this approach those who hold power would be encouraged not merely to change their hearts but also to change the structures of society so that injustice would be eliminated.

A very different strategy would be to animate the poor to demand their rights. They would be encouraged not simply to wait patiently for justice but rather to confront the rich and powerful when this proves necessary. The Church could assure them that God is the God of the poor, who supports those who feel called to act like Moses in challenging the injustice of the powerful.

Are the two policies mutually exclusive? Partly, but not entirely. It is possible for Church leaders to appeal to the rich while animating the poor. But the two strategies differ fundamentally on one major point—whether the poor ought to be encouraged to wait patiently or, on the other hand, to engage where necessary in active confrontation. The difference between the two approaches is based above all on the different degree of importance each gives to the value of stability in society. In the first approach stability is seen as a very high value, so indispensable that one dare not put it at risk. In the second approach, stability is seen as an important value but one that must at times be risked in order to ensure justice in society; furthermore, it is considered that the best guarantee of long-term stability is to ensure that society is just.

How does Leo's approach relate to these two possible strategies? It must be said that he adopted a position much nearer to the first approach than to the second—and this was because he was so convinced of the importance of stability in society. There is no doubt that he wanted major changes. But what he had in mind was change 'from the top down' rather than 'from the bottom up'. He issued a ringing call to conversion to the people who held economic power. But what if this call goes largely unheeded? Then it appears that, for Leo, the poor working class have little option but to put up with their sad situation.

Various encyclicals issued by Leo XIII give indications that for him the changes in society that would make for social justice depended to a very considerable degree on a change of heart by those who held economic and political power. In the next chapter I shall make a detailed study of various writings of Leo in order to provide a background against which his approach in *Rerum Novarum* can be understood more clearly. But *Rerum Novarum* itself throws quite a lot of light on the pope's attitude, both in what it says and in what it fails to say.

A central paragraph in the encyclical lists the reciprocal duties of employers and workers, duties of which the Church reminds them in order to promote harmony and justice. First, those of the employers:

> The following duties bind the wealthy owner and the employer: not to look upon their work-people as their bondsmen but to respect in every person his or her dignity and worth. . . . They are reminded that . . . to misuse people as though they were things in the pursuit of gain . . . is truly shameful and inhuman. . . . Furthermore, employers must never tax their work-people beyond their strength, or employ them in work unsuited to their sex and age. Their great and principal duty is to give every one what is just. . . . to gather one's profit out of the need of another, is condemned by all laws human and divine. . . . Lastly, the rich must religiously refrain from cutting down the workers' earnings, whether by force, by fraud, or by usurious dealing . . . (RN 16–7).

The whole passage constitutes a very moving call for conversion—and not just a change of heart but significant changes in business practice and standards of behaviour in the economic world. But there is an element of unrealism in it. For, unfortunately, Leo is making a rhetorical statement rather than one that is literally true when he says that, 'all laws human and divine' condemn those who gather their profit out of the need of another. There are some human laws which allow such exploitation. It is precisely at this point that a wide gap exists between the laws governing business in an unbridled liberal capitalist society and what the Church sees as the divine law.

What if this gap still remains, in spite of Pope Leo's eloquent appeal? What is the pope's response if employers continue to neglect the duties he has listed, if they fail to respect their workers, if they still fail to pay a just wage and if they tax them beyond their strength? What if the wealthy continue to make a profit out of the need of the poor? Above all, what if the laws of the State continue to allow this exploitation to take place and if the law-courts and security forces fail to offer the poor adequate protection against these injustices? These are not hypothetical questions. The pope was well aware that injustices of this kind were a permanent feature of the social situation of his time. One is entitled, therefore, to ask what action he recommends to workers in the face of such abuses.

The following is a list of some of the duties which *Rerum Novarum* lays down for workers:

> . . . fully and faithfully to perform the work which has been freely and equitably agreed upon; never to injure the property, nor outrage the person, of an employer; never to resort to violence in defending their own cause, nor to engage in riot or disorder; and to have nothing to do with people of evil principles, who . . . excite foolish hopes . . . (RN 16).

This catalogue gives very little encouragement to activism on the part of workers in the struggle for rights. Not merely does it not give any guidelines by which workers might determine how far they could go in a situation of confrontation, but it does not appear to envisage that they might be entitled to engage in serious confrontation. For instance, workers are told that they must not injure the property of an employer. But it is not clear whether Leo adverted to the implications of this teaching. If taken strictly it would seem to imply that a strike is wrong whenever it causes damage to the property of an employer. Did the pope really want to go as far as that?

In a later paragraph of the encyclical he says that when a strike poses an imminent threat of public disturbance the law may be invoked to protect the peace (RN 29); this implies, of course, that a strike may be lawful where it does not pose such a threat. But it is significant that Leo's main emphasis is on circumstances which would make a strike wrong rather than on those which would justify it. Two paragraphs later he acknowledges that strikes occur, points out their causes and consequences, but does not make an explicit judgment about their morality (RN 31).

Leo XIII was well aware that insistence by workers on their rights in the economic sphere could quickly spill over into the political area and give rise to a threat to public order. His reluctance to encourage the working class to press militantly for their rights stems from his belief that nothing should be done that might cause such a 'disturbance'. The pope wanted to preserve a clear line of distinction between the socio-economic sphere and the political sphere,[5] so that his challenge to the *status quo* in the economic order would not be taken as an incitement to confrontation in the political field.

Was Leo entitled to rely on this distinction between the economic sphere and the political sphere? Perhaps the best answer is to say that the distinction is very useful in principle but that in the late nineteenth century it could be used to evade the more difficult social issues. It is certainly very useful to carve out a clearly defined area called 'the economic' as distinct from the area called 'the political'. Within this economic area a certain clash of interest and a struggle between competing groups can then be accepted and 'contained'. But this presupposes that the richer classes are not allowed to use their economic power to exert political pressure on others. A limited degree of struggle in the economic area is tolerable if the State can ensure that its laws and institutions remain neutral, so as to serve all classes with impartial justice. In the time of Leo XIII this political impartiality was not maintained. As he himself pointed out, the wealthy exercised undue political power (RN 35). In practice this meant that key institutions of the State—its laws, its courts, and the police—showed a greater or lesser degree of bias against the poor. Such a bias is not merely something personal but a structural imbalance.

In this situation only *political* changes could ensure that the *economic* rights of the poor were protected. To confine the struggle of workers to the purely economic order would very frequently mean condemning them to futility. For as soon as a really effective economic weapon was developed—for instance a general strike—it could at once be countered by political means. For instance, if the wealthy classes found that their dominant position was under threat as a result of a general strike they could use their power over the institutions of the State to ensure that such a strike was banned by law or was made subject to crippling restrictions.

Suppose Church authorities in these circumstances were to say that the poor are not entitled to work for major political changes, structural changes. This would amount to an option *against* the poor. It would be giving ideological support to those who were oppressing the poor. Leo XIII did not make such an option—at least not explicitly. But he failed to give clear guidelines for political and quasi-political action by the working class; and this was the only kind of action which was likely to bring about the changes that would make society just. He allowed such words and phrases as 'disorder' (RN 16) and 'danger of disturbance to the public peace' (RN 29) to remain vague in meaning and therefore capable of being invoked to cover almost any situation which threatened the interests of the rich and powerful. He did not distinguish clearly between, on the one hand, an altogether unacceptable level of violent or disruptive action and, on the other hand, a certain level of disturbance and instability which may be necessary if structural injustices are to be overcome despite the resistance of powerful groups. In other words, he failed to develop guidelines for confrontation.

Pope Leo set up an ideal of harmony in society that was so exalted and perfect that it remained abstract and unreal. Instead of envisaging a whole series of possible situations, approximating in a greater or lesser degree to the ideal, he seemed to consider only two alternatives to his ideal. The first of these was 'disorder' or 'disturbance'; and this was something he felt he had to condemn. The second alternative was the existing state of what would now be called 'structural injustice'. This was the situation where the institutions of the State supported and reinforced the gap between rich and poor. This too was something that he had to condemn. But when this condemnation had little or no practical effect, then it seemed as though the Church would have to acquiesce reluctantly in the existing unjust situation rather than opt for 'disorder'. This acquiescence, reluctant though it was, gave a considerable degree of religious support to a society that was structurally unjust. It undoubtedly diminished the effectiveness of *Rerum Novarum* as a cry of protest and a call for justice on behalf of the poor.

To understand why Leo XIII found himself in this awkward position we must look beyond *Rerum Novarum* to the writings in which he presented his teaching on political questions. This will be the subject of the next chapter. But before moving on to that study there is one further important point in *Rerum Novarum* which needs to be looked at.

Workers' Organisations

In the previous section we have been considering religion and the Church as a possible agent of change in society, a force that might be able to bring about the transformation required to make it a structurally just society. In this final section we go on to examine more closely the teaching of *Rerum Novarum* on the other possible agent of major social change which has to be considered in the present context, namely, the trade union movement. (For the pope entirely ruled out revolutionary movements as accept-able agents of change; and in *Rerum Novarum* he did not consider the question of political change brought about by democratic action—that did not enter into the socio-economic question with which he was concerned in this encyclical.)[6] We have already noted that the pope was reluctant to encourage workers to take organised militant action to secure their rights. What then was his teaching in regard to trade unions or other associations which could give some power to the workers?

At the beginning of *Rerum Novarum* there is a perceptive passage in which the pope points to one of the basic reasons why workers at that time could be so exploited. He says: ' . . . the ancient workers' guilds were abolished in the last century, and no other protective organisation took their place' (RN 2). This statement has sometimes been dismissed as a pointless pining for an out-dated social order. No doubt there is a certain nostalgia there. But what the pope says immediately afterwards shows that this passage contains one of the most important insights in the whole encyclical.[7] The pope adverts to the fact that, partly as a result of the abolition of the guilds, 'workers have been surrendered, isolated and helpless, to the hard-heartedness of employers and the greed of unchecked competition' (RN 2). The point to note here is that the plight of the workers is not attributed simply to the hard-heartedness and greed of employers and their unchecked competition against each other. Rather the problem arises because the workers no longer have protective organisations or other defences. It is this lack of protection which has now left them 'isolated and helpless' at the mercy of employers. Greed and competition remain 'unchecked' precisely because the workers lack any organisation to defend their interests. At this point the pope is not saying whether he considers that employers are more hard-hearted and greedy nowadays than they were in the past. Instead, he is focusing attention on the safeguards which society offers, or fails to offer, to workers; and this is a question of the *structures* of society, rather than a purely *moral* matter, such as how virtuous the employers are.

This passage indicates that Leo XIII had gone some way towards analysing the structures of the society of his time and pinpointing the relationship between poverty and the power-lessness of workers. So it would not be quite fair to suggest, as Chenu does, that *Rerum Novarum* fails entirely to offer a 'structural analysis' of the causes of poverty (Chenu 25). What is true, however, is that there is little coherent development of the basic insight about the need for protective organisations for workers. Perhaps even more important is the fact that Leo's prophetic voice seemed to falter when it came to drawing practical conclusions from his insight about the importance of trade unions.

The history of Western countries over the past 150 years shows how major changes can be brought about in society by an effective trade union movement. Through the unions, workers have been able to bargain with employers from a position of some strength. The trade unions have often ensured that the solidarity of workers is not weakened by the use of non-union labour to break strikes. More recently, trade unions have also had some involvement in the shaping of government policy. This quasi-political role is a necessary check on the political influence which can be exerted on government by the employers. The result is that there is a somewhat better chance that the State will protect the interests of workers, as Pope Leo wished (RN 29). The result, so far, of all this leaves much to be desired, both with regard to the internal organisation of Western countries and in their relationship with the poor countries of the Third World. But it represents a considerable advance on the society of Leo's time in so far as the internal structures of these countries are concerned; it goes some way towards having that balance in the body politic which Leo considered to be essential (RN 15).

The central point that emerges from this brief look at the role of trade unions is that major social injustices can be overcome

even if the rich and powerful are not 'converted'. The greed
and hard-heartedness of employers may still be present. But
now they are no longer 'unchecked', to use Leo's word (RN 2).
Workers are no longer 'isolated and helpless'. They have a
structure that protects them. It is a good example of what is
meant when people say that social injustice must be dealt with
at the *structural level*, not merely by working for the moral
conversion of the oppressors.

Since Leo had noted the disastrous effect of the loss of the
workers' guilds, one might have expected that he would go on
to point out the need for strong and united movements of
workers. One would expect him to recommend such organisations in order to ensure adequate protection against the hard-
heartedness and greed of employers, and particularly to protect
workers in the face of that cut-throat competition which often
'forces' employers to treat their workers unjustly. Despite the
obvious advantages of such an approach, *Rerum Novarum* does
not come out clearly in favour it. This may have been partly
due to an inability of Leo XIII and his advisers to anticipate
how the trade union movement would develop. But it would
appear that it was at least partly due to hesitation about giving
encouragement to any kind of movement that could bring
about significant structural change. The practical proposals
put forward by the pope fall far short of recommending a
strong and united workers' movement which would confront
employers and actively campaign for a more just society.

The pope defends the basic right of workers to form associations. The most important of these, he says, are 'Working-
people's Unions' (RN 36). But the encyclical goes on to speak
about associations in such vague and general terms that what
he says could scarcely be applied to trade unions in the modern
sense. These paragraphs (RN 36–44) refer to a wide variety of
associations ranging from sodalities to trade unions; and it is
difficult if not impossible to know which of Leo's remarks are
intended to refer to which type of organisation.[8] Having said
that working-people's unions are the most important form of
association the pope immediately goes on to speak in very
general terms about unions or associations some of which are
open in their membership to employers as well as workers (RN
36). When he goes on to speak of organisations which aim to

promote the cause of workers, he carefully avoids the use of such militant phrases as 'struggling for rights'; his main emphasis is on self-restraint and harmony. Working-people's associations, he says, must give their 'chief attention to the duties of religion and morality' and their concept of social betterment should have this chiefly in view (RN 42). Indeed there is no clear evidence in the encyclical that the pope approved of the idea of a trade union as presently understood, namely, an organisation which has limited goals of a secular nature and is confined in its membership to 'workers' as distinct from employers (or top management).

The reluctance of the pope to dissociate spiritual from temporal welfare is very important. He wanted to ensure that Catholic workers would not be 'led astray' by associations that were not explicitly Catholic. So he encouraged Catholic workers to form their own associations as an alternative to those which might expose their religion to peril (RN 40).[9] There were two unfortunate results of this policy. In the first place it contributed notably to a fragmentation of the trade union movement. Instead of uniting with other activists in a strong united workers' movement, very many socially-oriented Catholics, in various European countries, formed Catholic trade unions. This had the effect of greatly weakening the solidarity of workers; for, inevitably, the different unions began to compete with each other and adopted different policies and strategies on particular issues. A second result of Leo's policy was that it diminished the influence that Catholic social activists could have on those of other Churches, or of no Church, and vice versa; so the Catholic social movement remained rather cut off from similar movements outside the Church, while the emerging 'secular' trade unions tended to become secularist and even at times anti-Catholic.

There was, then, a clear disparity between the kind of workers' associations that Leo XIII was actually recommending and the kind of workers' movement that would have a real chance of bringing about the major structural changes required if society were to become just. The main reason for this seems to be that Leo XIII was not prepared to take the risks involved in calling for, and actively supporting, a united militant workers' movement. The encyclical itself indicates some of the pope's reservations. He believed that many of the existing unions were 'in the hands of secret leaders and . . . managed on principles ill-according with Christianity and the public well-being' (RN 40). Furthermore, he was convinced that these unions and their leaders were trying to bring about what would now be called a 'closed shop'—a situation where only those who joined that union would be able to get a job. The combination of these two features was seen by the pope as posing a very grave danger for Catholic workers; for he felt that for them to be forced to join such unions would put their faith, and therefore their salvation, at risk (RN 40). There can be little doubt that the principles which he saw as incompatible with Christianity were socialist and revolutionary ones—the two being, for Leo, more or less inseparable.

The attitude of Leo XIII to trade unions was largely determined by two of his major concerns. On the one hand he wanted to vindicate the right of the individual to free association in the protection of personal interests; so he affirmed the basic right of the worker to join a union or form a new one. But on the other hand the pope had an overriding concern for public order. It was this which led him to oppose any movement that sought to change the social structures of society by vigorous action 'from below'. If an assessment of *Rerum Novarum* is to be fair it must take account of both these points. It must not play down the importance of the pope's vindication of the right to form trade unions. But it must also acknowledge that Leo was a very long way from encouraging militant action by workers to reconstruct society. The reason for this will emerge more clearly in the next chapter which sets out to examine his socio-political teaching as enunciated in a wide variety of documents issued prior to, and subsequent to, *Rerum Novarum*.

SUMMARY

Leo XIII's *Rerum Novarum* was the first major step by the Vatican towards putting the Church on the side of the poor and the working class. Its impact came not so much from its content as from the fact that by issuing an encyclical on this topic the pope was seen to be coming to the defence of the poor. The encyclical expresses deep concern for the plight of the poor, makes a strong protest on their behalf, and calls for changes in society. But Leo failed to make a clear option for the poor in the formal sense. However, the encyclical can be seen as the beginning of a process which eventually led Church leaders to approve of the notion of an 'option for the poor'. The crucial point is the pope's insistence that the worker as a person must take precedence over the so-called laws of economics. By asserting this principle Pope Leo was challenging the dominant liberal capitalist ideology of the time. He also strongly attacked the socialist position and in this way sought to find a middle way between individualism and collectivism.

Leo called for major changes in the socio-economic order. He maintained that the State has a duty in the short term to protect workers against exploitation, and in the long term to ensure that the ownership of property is much more widely distributed. But Leo wanted these changes to be initiated 'from the top down', that is, by the very people or classes who were benefiting from the existing liberal-capitalist order. If they failed to introduce a more equitable society, Leo was not prepared to encourage the poor or workers to engage in confrontation. He defended the right of workers to form trade unions, but he did not want the unions to play a political role in changing society. Nor did he want Catholics to join with other workers in the kind of strong united trade union movement that could bring about major social changes.

Questions for review:

1. What aspects of capitalism was Leo opposed to and what aspects did he approve of?
2. What was Leo's position about the role of trade unions? about strikes?
3. What did Leo hold about the role of the Church in society?

Questions for reflection:

1. Is capitalism today worse or better than in the time of Leo XIII?
2. If *Rerum Novarum* were being re-written today what categories of people should it focus on as being the poorest and most oppressed? Why has this change occurred?
3. What is the role of the trade union movement in your own country today? What is the relationship between the Church and the trade unions?

Issues for further study:

1. Leo's position about the worker's right to a *family* wage. (Read Molony.)
2. Why did the Church lose the working classes in Europe and not in America or Australia? (Read Church histories of the period.)

2

Leo XIII and Allegiance to the State

A nineteenth-century industrialist is reported to have said that the best way to prevent strikes would be to establish an association of St Francis Xavier (Vidler 91). The implication is that the Catholic Church and its associations served the function, whether deliberately or not, of making workers less likely to take militant action in pursuit of better pay and conditions. To what extent was this true? No simple answer can be given to the question, since, as we saw in the last chapter, even the pope felt himself pulled in two directions. He certainly wanted to defend the rights of exploited workers. But he was also reluctant to sanction any activity that could disturb public order. In this chapter I shall look more closely at Leo XIII's teaching on allegiance to the civil authorities, in order to understand why he laid so much stress on public order. The pope's teaching on these matters is to be found only peripherally in *Rerum Novarum*; the main sources are a series of other encyclicals and documents issued by the pope at various times during his long pontificate. A study of the teaching in these sources will help one to see *Rerum Novarum* in context.

Authority is from God

There are good reasons for saying that in the mind of Leo XIII one of the purposes of Catholic associations was to discourage militancy on the part of workers. The following passage from his 1978 encyclical, *Quod Apostolici Muneris*, provides evidence for this:

> ... it seems expedient to encourage associations for handicraft workers and labourers, which, placed under the sheltering care of religion, may render the members content with their lot and resigned to toil, inducing them to lead a peaceful and tranquil life (BP I, 40; *Great Ency* 33)[1].

One can distinguish three very different kinds of reason why the pope laid so much emphasis on workers being content with their lot:

— At the practical level he was anxious to have close co-operation between Church and State, so he offered the support of the Church to governments so far as possible.

— At the more philosophical-theological level he had a conception of civil authority which required that he stress the duty of obedience and submission.

— At the psychological level, he was personally very perturbed about the danger of revolution.

In Leo XIII these three levels of motivation interlock and support each other; so it would be pointless to focus exclusively on one or other as the primary reason for a particular statement or action. Nevertheless, it is useful to make the distinction because the earnestness with which the pope pursued his policy of practical cooperation with governments, and the tirelessness with which he propounded his philosophy on the nature of authority, can be understood more clearly and sympathetically in the light of his real anxiety about the danger of anarchy and the disintegration of society.

In the encyclical *Inscrutabili*, issued in 1878 just two months after he became pope, Leo XIII made a strong appeal to civil authorities that they should cooperate with the Church and accept the support the Church offered them:

> We address ourselves to princes and chief rulers of the nations and earnestly beseech them . . . not to refuse the Church's aid . . . but with united and friendly aims to join themselves to her as the source of authority and salvation . . . considering that their own peace and safety, as well as that of their people, is bound up with the safety of the Church and the reverence due to her . . . (BP I, 16–18.)[2]

Some months later, in the encyclical *Quod Apostolici Muneris*, he indicated the kind of support the Church can give to rulers of the State: the Church teaches that the authority of civil rulers must be accepted because it comes from God himself: 'From the heads of States, to whom as the Apostle admonishes, all owe submission, and on whom the rights of authority are bestowed by God Himself, these sectaries withhold obedience

. . . ' (BP I, 28; *Great Ency* 23). So he maintains that it is 'impious' to rise up against one's rulers. Later in the same encyclical he says that the Church constantly urges on everybody the apostolic precept that one should obey rulers as a matter of conscience (BP I, 32; *Great Ency* 27). Two and a half years later, in 1881, Leo issued an encyclical, *Diuturnum*, devoted to the specific question of the origin of civil power. Rejecting the 'modern' view that it comes from a mandate of the people, he insisted that civil power has its source in God. In support of this position he invokes the Old Testament, the New Testament, the Fathers of the Church, and arguments from reason (BP I, 144–6). Central to his case is his claim that a purely human origin for civil authority is too weak and fragile a basis for it (BP I, 154). The authority of rulers requires a religious foundation. Leo points out that the Church had recognised this, even in early Christian times when believers were being persecuted; even then they saw the power of the rulers as coming from God (BP I, 150–2).

The pope goes on to note that once states came to have Christian rulers the Church redoubled its efforts to promote the awareness of the sacredness of authority; in this way people were drawn to reverence and love their rulers by the aura of religious majesty that surrounded them (BP I, 154). Leo maintains that reliance on force provided rulers with an insecure basis for obedience; what is required is something loftier—and more effective. Strict laws will not have the desired effect unless people are motivated by a sense of obligation and a salutary fear of God (BP I, 156). It is not surprising, then, to find Leo saying, later in the encyclical, that the Church strengthens the authority of rulers and helps it in many ways (BP I, 158). As he pointed out in the following year, in the encyclical *Auspicato Concessum*, 'those who are imbued with the Christian religion know with certainty that they are bound in conscience to submit to those who lawfully rule them'; and he concluded that religion is the most effective way to root out violence, envy between different classes, and the desire for a new order in society (BP I, 176).[3]

In 1885, in his classical encyclical *Immortale Dei*, on the Christian constitution of states, Pope Leo covered much the same ground, with some additional nuances:

> . . . every civilised community must have a ruling authority
> and this authority, no less than society itself, has its source
> in nature, and has, consequently, God for its author. Hence
> it follows that all public power must proceed from God . . .
> (BP II, 18; *Great Ency* 109)

He goes on to draw the conclusions. It is a matter of justice and
duty to obey rulers. To despise legitimate authority, in whom-
soever invested, is a rebellion against the divine will. To cast
aside obedience, and by popular violence to incite revolt, is
treason not merely against a human person but against God (BP
II, 20). Later in the same encyclical he remarks that the order of
the commonwealth should be maintained as sacred; obedience
to rulers is submission to God, because God is exercising
sovereignty through the medium of humans (BP II, 30).

Four years later, in the encyclical *Quemquam Pluries*, Leo
remarked that while it is true that the poor and manual workers
have the right to escape from their poverty to a better condition
by lawful means, nevertheless reason and justice require that
they should not overturn the order established by God's
providence (BP II, 256–8). This is an important statement. It
suggests that not only is God the source of political power in a
general way but also that God gives support to whatever
particular form of government has emerged in a given country—
for this is attributed to God's providence.

In the encyclical *Quod Multum*, which Leo XIII wrote in
1886 to the bishops of Hungary, there is a passage which not
only sums up several of the points already noted but also
conveys a sense of the *spirituality* which the pope was promoting:

> The best and most effective way of avoiding the horrors of
> socialism . . . is for the citizens to be completely imbued
> with religion . . . . For just as religion requires the worship
> and fear of God so also it demands submission and obedience
> to lawful authority; it forbids any kind of seditious activity
> and wills that the property and the rights of everybody be
> safeguarded; and those who are more wealthy should magnan-
> imously help the poor masses. Religion cares for the poor
> with every form of charity; it fills the stricken with the sweetest
> comfort by offering them the hope of very great and immortal
> good things which are all the more plentiful in the future in

proportion to the extent to which one has been weighed down more heavily or for a longer time (BP II, 88).[4]

Perhaps the most significant feature of Leo's approach here is the way in which he quite consciously links economics and politics with life after death. He recognises that it is those who are economically deprived who pose a threat to political stability. And he spells out the role of religion in helping to meet and overcome that threat by placating the poor. This is done most effectively by promising them rewards in heaven proportionate to the miseries they have endured patiently on earth.

This spirituality was applied by Pope Leo even in situations where rulers abuse their God-given authority. In his early encyclical *Quod Apostolici Muneris*, directed against socialism, communism and nihilism, the pope makes it clear that abuses by rulers give subjects no right to rebel:

> Should it, however, happen at any time, that in the public exercise of authority rulers act rashly and arbitrarily, the teaching of the Catholic Church does not allow subjects to rise against them without further warranty, lest peace and order become more and more disturbed, and society run the risk of greater detriment. And when things have come to such a pass as to hold out no further hope, she teaches that a remedy is to be sought in the virtue of Christian patience and in urgent prayer to God. (BP I, 34; *Great Ency* 28)

This passage not merely forbids rebellion but reinforces the prohibition by offering what would now be called an escapist answer to problems of injustice: prayer is presented as an alternative to the kind of action that might change the unjust situation. Further on, Pope Leo unashamedly speaks of how the Church cheers and comforts the hearts of the poor by setting before them the example of Christ, or by reminding them that Jesus called them 'blessed' and told them to hope for the reward of eternal happiness. The pope adds that this is obviously the best way to lessen the undying struggle between rich and poor (BP I, 36–8).

All this adds up to a comprehensive spirituality which damps down any inclination the poor might have to put up active resistance to situations of injustice. Three forms of religious argument or persuasion are involved:

— First, they are told that resistance is sinful because the authority exercised by the government comes from God, and to resist is to disobey God.

— Secondly, the promise of reward in the next life is offered to those who suffer patiently under unjust rulers in this life.

— Thirdly, the example of the patient suffering Christ is held up as a model to the poor.

To reinforce these arguments the Church contributes to the lessening of tension between rich and poor in two other ways—by urging the rich to be generous in helping the poor, and by itself engaging in charitable activity to ease the misery of the poor.

To sum up, then, there can be no doubt that Leo was quite correct when he claimed that the Church offers invaluable support to State governments. This support comes partly from the theology of civil authority which Pope Leo so clearly propounded. It comes partly from the escapist spirituality which he proposed. And, finally, it comes from the deliberate action of the Church in easing the suffering of the poor with a view to lessening the likelihood that they would rebel against the established order.

Some Qualifications

Does all this mean that according to Leo's teaching the Church gives unqualified support to all governments, and condemns every instance of disobedience and every attempt to bring about change? By no means. There are certain qualifications to be made. These constitute a quite significant feature of the theoretical synthesis presented by the pope. In the practical sphere they also have a certain importance, though they are rather severely limited in the area to which they apply.

The first qualification concerns a situation where a ruler commands something that is evidently wrong, opposed to the law of God or the will of God. One is then entitled—and indeed obliged—not to obey the command (BP I, 148).[5] This apparent exception fits into the overall pattern of Leo's teaching because, as he says in *Libertas Praestantissimum*, 'the right to command and to require obedience exists only so far as it is in accordance with the authority of God, and is within the measure that God has laid down'; and in the situation now envisaged 'there is a wide departure from this divinely constituted order and at the same time a direct conflict with the divine authority' (BP II, 202; *Great Ency* 156). Strictly speaking this is not an exception at all, not really a case of disobedience in the proper sense. For, as Leo explains in *Diuturnum*, those rulers whose will is in opposition to the will and law of God have gone beyond the limits of their authority. Leo adds an interesting remark which brings out the relationship which he sees between authority and justice. Such rulers, he says, have contravened justice; therefore their authority can no longer have validity, since there is no authority where there is no justice (BP I, 148).

It may be noted in passing that this 'exception' has a somewhat different connotation to that of the modern understanding of conscientious objection—although the two obviously have a common basis and they overlap to some extent. The pope's presentation, which is the traditional Catholic one, puts less emphasis on the rights of the individual (subjective) conscience and more on the objective will and law of God. It would appear that Leo was not thinking primarily of the isolated individual. The kind of situation he would have had mostly in mind was that of Christians assured by Church authorities that certain kinds of action are contrary to the objective law of God.

The case just described seems to envisage a certain passive resistance on a specific issue; it is simply a refusal to obey a particular command or law. But is there room for any more active form of resistance, for some positive line of action which could bring about a change in the situation? Leo's answer is 'yes'. He gives it quite strongly. But he gives it with a significant lack of concrete indications about how such active resistance can take place. The pope's teaching on this matter came in an important encyclical written in 1892 and entitled *Au milieu des sollicitudes*. This encyclical was his response to a very delicate political situation where he had to be quite circumspect in what he said. At this time some royalists in France were suggesting that the French Republic of the time was 'animated by such anti-Christian sentiments that honest people, Catholics particularly, could not conscientiously accept it' (BP III, 119; *Great Ency* 258). The pope did not accept this argument. He drew a careful distinction between the 'constituted powers' of the State on the one hand, and 'legislation' on the other. The fact that odious legislation is passed by a regime does not prove that it is not a duly constituted political authority. One owes respect to such authorities. But this does not mean that one is bound to give unlimited respect—and, still less, unlimited obedience—to all legislative measures, of whatever kind, enacted by those who hold lawful political authority. The pope concluded that one should never approve of those points of legislation which are hostile to religion and to God; in fact one's duty is to condemn them (BP III, 119–20).

So far Pope Leo was simply giving a somewhat more elaborate version of the general principle that one must obey God above all. But he also says to the French of the time: 'good people should put aside all political dissensions and unite as one to combat, by all legal and upright means, progressive abuses of legislation' (BP III, 119). This is an exhortation to something much more than mere passive refusal to obey evil laws. It recommends active resistance. But the significant point is that this resistance is to employ only 'legal and upright means'. In other circumstances the phrase 'legal means' might be understood to include ways of acting that are lawful in the eyes of God even though they are unjustly decreed to be illegal by a particular government. But the context here, and the other statements of Leo which I have quoted, show that he approved only of those forms of political representation or activity that do not challenge the legitimacy of the authority of those in power.

The next question is whether there are any circumstances in which one would be entitled to go even further: to engage in a kind of political planning and action that would aim at replacing the existing rulers by new rulers or by a different structure of government. Clearly there is no difficulty about seeking to replace one government by another through the process of a free election in a state which is constituted in such a way as to allow such elections; for in that situation there is an agreed and orderly transfer of authority from one group of office-holders to another. But is this the only kind of situation in which it is legitimate to seek to oust one's rulers? To answer this question it is necessary to sift very carefully through the teaching of the pope in regard to the relationship between authority and 'social need', as well as the relation between the moral right to exercise political authority and the actual possession of political power.

In 1881 Pope Leo taught (in *Diuturnum*) that people are not forbidden to choose for themselves the type of government that is appropriate to their nature and traditions—provided justice is preserved (BP I, 142–4).[6] At that time, and again in *Immortale Dei* (1885), he held that the right to rule is not tied to any particular form of government (BP II, 18). But when and how are people entitled to choose for themselves a particular form of government? This question has to be made more specific in order to apply it to the real world where people normally live under some existing form of government. The question becomes: when and how—if at all—are people entitled to *change* their existing form of government? In 1888 (in *Libertas Praestantissimum*) Leo XIII said that it is lawful to seek a different constitution or structure of government 'where there exists, or there is reason to fear, an unjust oppression of the people . . . or a deprivation of the liberty of the Church'; and a few lines further on he added that 'it is not of itself wrong to prefer a democratic form of government' (BP II, 210). The vague Latin phrase translated here as 'a different constitution or structure of government' seems to mean more than the normal replacement through elections of one democratic government by another.[7] This teaching raises considerable difficulties in regard to the coherence of Leo's teaching. For if the situation is one of 'unjust oppression of the people' it must be presumed that those who hold the political power and are guilty of this oppression will be most unwilling to relinquish their power. How then is the person who seeks a different structure of government to avoid being guilty of subversion? To answer this one must find out what is the precise nature of subversion and, in particular, whether there is any way in which a new form of government can replace an old one without the intervention of any subversive activity.

Social Need in a Revolutionary Situation

The French political situation of 1892 pushed Pope Leo to a very deep analysis of the issues of legitimacy and allegiance. In his encyclical *Au milieu des sollicitudes* of that year to the Church in France, he offered a very carefully nuanced political philosophy (BP III, 112–22; *Great Ency* 249–62). It included the general principles which he had already laid down in earlier encyclicals. But it set them within a wider theoretical framework and it also applied his overall vision to the specific situation in France.

First of all the pope recalls that over the preceding century a variety of different political systems have existed in France. He maintains that in 'the sphere of speculative ideas' a person is free to prefer one political form or structure to another. But as a matter of contingent historical fact each nation has a part-icular form of government. Then the pope says: 'It is hardly necessary to repeat that all individuals are bound to accept these governments and not to attempt to overthrow them or change their form.' (BP III, 117—my translation). He goes on to recall that the Church has always condemned those who rebelled against legitimate authority. Next he points out that 'whatever be the form of civil power in a nation it cannot be considered so definitive as to have the right to remain immutable' (BP III, 117, *Great Ency* 256). Time, he says, brings fundamental changes in the political institutions of human societies (BP III, 118). Then he comes to the crucial question: 'How do these political changes come about?' His answer deserves to be quoted at some length:

> They sometimes follow in the wake of violent crises, too often of a bloody character, in the midst of which preexisting governments totally disappear; then anarchy holds sway, and soon public order is shaken to its foundations and finally overthrown. From that time onward a *social need* obtrudes itself upon the nation; it must provide for itself without delay . . . . Now this social need justifies the creation and the existence of new governments, whatever form they take; since, in the hypothesis wherein we reason, these new governments are a requisite to public order, all public order being impossible without a government. (BP III, 118, *Great Ency* 258).

This is a very significant passage, both in what it says and in what it omits. Leo does not claim to be speaking of all situations where the structures of government have undergone major change. He concentrates on one particular 'scenario' which, he says, sometimes happens. It is the situation in which a regime dissolves into anarchy and out of this anarchy a new regime emerges; the pope sets out to show how such a regime can have legitimacy. The crucial point is this: *the legitimacy of the new government does not depend on the legitimacy of the rebellion against the previous regime.* The new rulers are now entitled to demand obedience from the people; but that does not imply that the previous rulers had already lost this right prior to their downfall. Quite the contrary. They never lost the right to rule until they lost the power to rule—that is, until their government collapsed. So long as the previous government retained power to govern, all attempts to overthrow it were unlawful and sinful.

The neatness of Leo's teaching is that it explains how there can be a transition of lawful authority from the old regime to the new one—but it does so without offering any moral justification or support to attempts to bring about such a transition! It explains the legitimacy of post-revolutionary governments without conceding anything to those who seek to bring about a revolution. Presumably Leo XIII felt entitled to limit himself to the kind of situation he outlined because he considered that it was exemplified in France at least in the case of the original French Revolution. (Its application to changes of regime in France during the nineteenth century may be more doubtful.) The pope did not consider other kinds of situation—ones where existing governments were forced out and were replaced by fundamentally different regimes without any intervening period of anarchy. Nevertheless, it appears that one could extend the application of Leo's principles to cover such situations as well. Suppose a particular government is losing its power to rule, either gradually or quite suddenly. Suppose this loss of ability to govern is, practically speaking, irreversible. There comes a point in the process where anarchy, though not yet a reality, has become an imminent likelihood. Presumably the 'social need' of the people (of which the pope speaks) would at that point require the emergence of an alternative ruling power. The acceptance of this new form of government would then be 'not only permissible but even obligatory', to use Leo's own phrase (BP III, 118).

Pragmatism or Principle?

The key to the whole argument presented by Leo XIII on this issue lies in his conception of the source of political authority. He insists always that authority comes from God. 'Social need' merely determines who is to exercise this authority and the form the government is to take.[8] What gives the new regime the moral right to exact obedience from the citizens is the fact that God is supporting it, exercising sovereignty through it. But why has God now given this moral authority to the new regime? Not because its structures are better, or its office-holders more just, than those of the previous regime, but simply because it now holds effective power. To put it very crudely one might say: 'God backs only the winners.' God gives the right to demand allegiance and obedience only to those who successfully retain or gain actual control. The determining factor is not justice but power.

Now at last we are in a position to answer the question posed a few pages back, namely, when and how—if at all—are people entitled to seek a change in their existing form of government. Putting together the various elements in Pope Leo's teaching (and its implications) the answer comes out as follows:

1. *When* is a change justified?—When there is abuse of power by the rulers over some time, to a point where unjust oppression exists or can reasonably be feared.

2. *How* may such a change be sought?—By 'legal and upright means'. And who decides whether a given means is legal? Apparently it is the existing regime. At this point one must envisage two possible situations. The first case is one where people, using whatever means the regime permits, succeed in compelling the rulers either to abandon their injustice or to yield power in an orderly way to a different government. The second case is where the regime resists all such pressures; when those who hold power find the pressure becoming intolerable they simply pass a law banning the use of whatever effective means is being used against them. If the regime is a really unjust and corrupt one it is most likely that it will refuse to bow to purely moral pressures and that it will declare illegal any activity that threatens its existence. In this extreme case the answer to the question, 'How can people work for change?'

amounts to, 'Only by ineffective means'! That is precisely why the pope had to include as part of his teaching the point that in the last resort oppressed people have to endure evil and turn to prayer, rather than seek to oust the regime.

Does this mean that concern for justice can never entitle one to seek political change? No, because, as noted earlier, Leo teaches that citizens may and must exert pressure to get evil legislation changed.[9] But the presupposition here is that they are working within the existing system, continuing to give it their allegiance. If citizens cannot obtain justice within the existing system they may not take the further step of trying to topple it by means declared illegal by the regime itself. At that point the limit has been reached; injustice must then be endured. For to challenge the system, even in defence of justice, is to challenge the authority of God. Questions about the injustice of the regime are not relevant at this point, for injustices do not entitle one to rebel. It would appear that according to the teaching of Leo XIII there can be no such thing as a justified revolution.[10]

It is interesting to note that one of Pope Leo's own advisers, the noted philosopher and theologian Cardinal Zigliara, followed the scholastic tradition in accepting that active resistance to tyrannical abuse of power could sometimes be justified. He argued that this was resistance not to authority but to violence, not to the ruler but to an unjust aggressor who was in the very act of violating a genuine right (Zigliara, 266–7).[11] Leo XIII, in his carefully constructed teaching on political authority, does not invoke these nice distinctions; it seems that he decided not to follow Zigliara's view. It is possible, of course, that he accepted it at the level of abstract theory; but, if so, he must have decided that the argument was not applicable to the kind of situations he faced. The traditional theory itself included the notion that there should be a proportion between the evil to be corrected and the means used to correct it. It seems that Leo held that a revolution would cause so much damage to society that it would certainly be a greater evil than the injustices that provoked it. Holding such a view, Leo did not need to reject formally the traditional teaching about justified rebellion; he could simply maintain that in the world of his time no revolution could be justified.

One important implication of Leo's position needs to be noted. According to the pope's argument the wrongness of sub-version is not due solely to the violence which those involved in it may practice. Its evil is more basic. It is the fact that the order of society is being overturned and its stability disrupted; and this damage inflicted on the common good is at the same time a flouting of God's authority, since the existing authorities are God's agents. It follows that to seek to overthrow a regime even by *non-violent* means would also be fundamentally wrong. Questions about just means do not arise, since there can be no just means by which one could reject God's authority as embodied in the regime. This is the logic of Leo's position. It is true that he speaks of citizens uniting to combat abuses and of the lawfulness of seeking a different form of government (BP III, 119–20; BP II, 210). But this allows only such questioning of the system as the system itself tolerates. It appears then that those who accept Pope Leo's teaching on political authority are morally obliged to avoid planning or organising any serious attempt to replace the regime under which they live, or at least any attempt which is forbidden by that regime. They cannot give support to revolutionaries, however non-violent, until these have actually succeeded in undermining the regime; and at that point they must suddenly transfer their allegiance since they are then bound to support the new regime!

When spelled out in this blunt fashion Pope Leo's teaching on political authority may seem shockingly pragmatic. Does this mean that the pope subordinated the value of justice to the values of order and stability? To put the question in this way is hardly fair to the pattern of his thinking. As he would see it, public order is not an alternative to justice in society. Rather, stability and order are a fundamental precondition for justice, and might even be called an integral part of the just society. This explains why they have an overriding importance in his teaching, so much so that other instances of injustice have to be tolerated rather than have the order of society disturbed.

Leo XIII's desire to promote stability in society fitted well with his commitment to presenting a body of socio-political teaching which would clearly demonstrate how useful the Church could be to civil authorities and how unjustified were any accusations that the Church promoted disloyalty. His teaching served this purpose admirably:

— It showed how the Church could recognise the legitimacy of any and every regime and could negotiate with any government, even when disapproving of particular legislation which such a government might have enacted.

— It established the neutrality of the Church vis-à-vis any particular political party,[12] and even in relation to different political systems—monarchy, democracy, etc.

— It explained how individual Christians or the local Church could dissent from particular laws or edicts which they found unacceptable, and could even exert pressure on the government to have them changed—but using only whatever means were allowed by the laws of the regime.

— It provided a convincing answer to those who accused the Church of undermining the loyalty of citizens; for it gave to every existing regime the highest level of legitimation and support, namely, the assurance that the rulers derived their authority from God and were to be obeyed for this reason; and it unequivocally condemned all revolutionary activity and seditious plotting.

— While giving no support to political movements for radical change, it left Leo room to express deep concern about the plight of the poor and to voice serious misgivings about the capitalist order, which he held responsible for much of their suffering; and it left him free to call for changes in the socio-economic order; in this way he could hope to bridge the wide gap between the Church and the industrial workers.

Pope Leo's effort to establish the credibility of the Church as a force for stability was not made merely to promote the Church itself but also because he was passionately concerned that order should be preserved or restored in society. He believed the world had been seriously damaged by anarchy, revolution and a spirit of licence. He was convinced, as he said in a letter to his Secretary of State in 1887, that there was 'grave need for society to return to the true principles of order, so imprudently abandoned and neglected' (BP VIII, 73). The Church, he believed, had an important role to play in restoring public order. It could teach each group in society its proper obligations (RN 13–6). It could be a mediating influence between the rulers and the people in cases of excess by either side (*Diuturnum*, BP I, 154). But above all it could throw the full weight of its authority—and of God's authority—behind existing regimes and against subversion and revolution. This task was the high moral purpose which rescued Leo from any taint of mere pragmatism in his political teaching. His sincerity is shown by the fact that he insisted on the duty of allegiance even to regimes that were harassing the Church. The promotion of public order was for Leo a major service to humanity, a fundamental element in the task of the Church.

There has always been a certain pragmatic element in the teaching of the Church on political questions, particularly in regard to issues relating to a just war and to obedience to civil authority. At first sight it may seem that the Church adopts and inculcates an attitude of compromise—a readiness to tolerate injustice rather than challenge those who hold power. But in fact what the Church proposes is a healthy pragmatism, a rejection of the kind of romantic idealism that would want to pull down a whole society rather than endure any injustice. What the Church's traditional teaching insists on is that there should be some proportion between the evil and the proposed remedy; the harm done to society by the attempt to correct injustices must be less than that done by the original abuses. Leo XIII is therefore quite within the tradition when he gives a high priority to order and stability in society. He is not going beyond the traditional outlook in giving a certain moral weight to the fact that a particular individual or group actually holds political power; that is not pragmatism in the bad sense but realistic concern for the common good. The question that needs to be asked is not, 'Why does Leo set a high importance on stability in society and stress the value of loyalty to existing governments?'; rather the question is, 'Why does he give *overriding* importance to stability and order, so that resistance beyond the bounds of the laws of the regime can never be countenanced, no matter how unjust the regime may be?' For it is on this issue that Leo XIII departs from the traditional teaching worked out by the scholastics. To understand his attitude one has to look more closely at the political and social situation of Leo's time and the kind of concerns and fears the situation aroused in him—above all, his anxiety about revolution.

Fear of Revolution

Pope Leo XIII's teaching on political issues was not worked out in an academic environment where his thinking might be protected in some degree from the pressures of practical political affairs. His teaching was immediately related to actual situations and was intended to be a major part of his pastoral ministry. So his perceptions of the political situation—and of the role of the Church in it—had a considerable influence on his political philosophy.

In this, Leo XIII was by no means unique. Many other Churchmen of the late nineteenth century were genuinely shocked by the poverty and defencelessness of the working class. A considerable number of them became deeply involved in the efforts of voluntary agencies to relieve distress and give some help to the victims of social injustice. A rather smaller number were prepared, like Leo XIII, to go so far as to be quite outspoken in condemning the causes of such injustice. But very few Churchmen were prepared to give support or approval to efforts to bring about radical changes in the order of society. It was widely accepted by leaders of the Christian Churches that loyalty to the existing State authorities and structures was a fundamental Christian obligation. The Churches played a conservative role in society by propounding a theology and a spirituality that discouraged any radical questioning in the political sphere.

It should, however, be noted that in the second half of the nineteenth century significant groups of Christians in several European countries were proposing alternative models of society. Some Christians were flirting with socialist notions. But the ideal favoured most widely by socially aware groups of Christians was that of a society organised along corporatist lines (cf. Vidler 126, 144–5). Pope Leo XIII had some sympathy with certain Catholic social reformers with leanings in this direction; indeed he was influenced by them in writing *Rerum Novarum*. But it would probably be fair to say that their influence on him was more in causing him to write the encyclical than in the actual content of it. He agreed with them that the abolition of the guilds was a major cause of the social problem (RN 2). But he did not endorse their proposals for a corporatist state. He probably felt that these were unrealisable at that time. He must also have felt that they were too radical: the proposals involved a major reconstruction of the social and political order. And the last thing Leo wanted was that the Catholic Church should be identified in any degree with something that might smack of revolutionary change.

So, leaving aside theoretical dreams of a new kind of society, in practice the Catholic Church, led by the Vatican, was firmly against any significant attempts to bring about radical changes in the structures of society. The Protestant and Orthodox Churches were also socially conservative. Some of the factors influencing the Churches were common to all of them; others were specific to particular Churches. My intention here is to consider briefly some particular reasons why the Catholic Church (and, more specifically, the Vatican) was especially resistant at that time to radical social change. The central point to be noted is what the word 'revolution' conjured up for the pope and the Vatican. The previous hundred years had inflicted on the Catholic Church two wounds so serious that they called in question its self-understanding and seemed like a threat to its very existence; both of them were associated with the word 'revolution'.

The first of these happenings was the French revolution which overthrew the old order in France; it was followed by major social and political changes in other European countries, changes that were less sudden and perhaps less profound but which affected the Church in a very serious way. The second happening was the loss by the papacy of its temporal power, a process in which a key psychological moment was the establishment of the Roman Republic of 1848, the memory of which caused shudders in the Vatican.[13] The Catholic Church, and particularly the papacy, had made a remarkable come-back with the growth of what might be called a cult of the pope, and the development of Catholic institutions and new forms of spirituality. But this growth in new directions had by no means numbed the pain of the political-social wounds associated with 'revolution'. There was an almost neurotic fear of social disorder—so much so that nearly every other social value was in practice subordinated to the values of stability and harmony in society.

One effect of this conservative stance was that many of those who worked for radical change in society perceived the Church as part of the established order; so they tended to be anti-Christian, or at least anti-Church. The effect of the sharp polarisation was that each side lived up to the worst expectations of the other. The revolutionaries fulfilled the fears of Church leaders that their aims were anti-Christian. And the Churchmen lived up to the Marxist accusation that they were allies of the dominant class, using religion to inhibit radical social change.

Against this background one can begin to understand Pope Leo's concern for stability and public order, leading to his support for existing regimes. The priority he gave to order in society left him in the ironic position of giving moral support and religious legitimation to regimes that were quite hostile to much of what the Church stood for. The Vatican still felt itself to be manning the defences of the old order (despite the significantly new elements in the approach of Leo XIII, as compared with that of Pius IX).[14] But in fact the old order had largely been swept away. The new regimes had taken away from the Church almost everything they could take: the position of Rome as an independent state; the Church's establishment position in some 'Catholic' states; many of the traditional institutions and rights of the Church. Furthermore, the new economic order (with its social consequences) had cost the Church the allegiance of the industrial working class. Meanwhile the new middle class were more willing to 'use' the Church than to share the pope's concern about the plight of the poor. The new elite had a 'liberal' ideology which was hostile to the influence of the Church and indifferent to many traditional Christian values. Nevertheless this new elite had succeeded not merely in gaining power but in presenting themselves as the representatives of 'order', the only realistic alternative to the utter lawlessness of revolution. So the pope's concern to promote social stability and public order made it almost impossible for him to offer an effective challenge to the new order—even though he recognised and condemned the gross injustices within it.

A lot of the difficulty stemmed from a failure by the pope to make adequate distinctions between various kinds of left–wing thinking and various levels of challenge to the existing structures of society. Leo seems to have thought of socialism as the summit and source of practically every social evil one could imagine. In the document *Auspicato Concessum* he painted a lurid picture: ' . . . the beginning and the instruments of "Socialism" are violence, violations of injustice, the craze for a new order and envy between the different classes of society' (BP I, 176). He generally linked socialism with revolution. He traced the two to a common origin in the Reformation, which, he said, led to rationalism and so to the exclusion of God from public life; the notion of reward and punishment in the future life was eliminated, so it was not surprising that the poor should become discontented and should covet the wealth of the rich (*Quod Apostol*, BP I, 30).[15] From the same roots, in Leo's view, there sprang the idea that government arises only from the will of the people (*Immortale Dei*, BP II, 34). To him this suggested not just democracy but anarchism and nihilism— and so he bracketed these theories with socialism (*Quod Apostol*, BP I, 26).[16] For good measure he added in Freemasonry, which he saw as favouring the same aim, namely, the overthrow of the order of society (*Humanum Genus*, BP I, 264–6).[17]

It would seem, then, that 'socialism' became for Pope Leo XIII a kind of short-hand word whose meaning included all kinds of political extremism. That is why he could say in 1901 that he saw in the growing power of the socialist movement a threat of 'the most disastrous national upheavals' (BPVI, 220). When he spoke of socialism he probably had in mind the Paris Commune of 1871 and the violence that attended its brief life and bloody death. He was genuinely fearful that the vast majority of humankind would fall back into a 'most abject condition of bondage', or else that human society would be 'agitated by constant outbreaks and ravaged by plunder and rapine'; that is why he wanted the Church to appease the conflict between rich and poor, by warning the rich of eternal punishment if they refused 'to give of their superfluity to the poor', and by comforting the hearts of the poor with the hope of reward in heaven (*Quod Apostol* BP I, 36–8; *Quod Multum* BP II, 88).

The pope's fear of 'socialism' led him to modify an earlier draft of *Rerum Novarum* in which the right to private property had been subordinated to the wider principle that the goods of the earth are for the common good (Chenu 22; cf. Molony 69).[18] He felt, it seems, that a statement of this kind would be, or would appear to be, too close to the socialist view. So he gave a very restrictive interpretation to the traditional teaching that 'God has granted the earth to humankind in general'; this simply means, he says, 'that no part of it was assigned to anyone in particular, and that the limits of private possession have been left to be fixed by people's own industry, and by the laws of individual races' (RN 7). This was quite a different emphasis from that of traditional scholastic teaching. Another departure from the scholastic tradition has already been noted—the refusal to accept that rebellion could ever be justified. It too came from Leo's concern for stability and fear of revolution.

The horror evoked by 'socialism' in many Church leaders in the late nineteenth century might be compared to the almost paranoid fear of 'communism' that pervaded the ruling strata of society in Latin America in the 1960s and 1970s. There was the same failure to make distinctions, to avoid being limited to just two alternatives—either total revolution or support for existing unjust regimes. Under Leo XIII the Catholic Church was just beginning to take the first steps towards extricating itself from this awkward dilemma. In the political sphere the Church was coming to terms with democracy. And in the economic sphere the publication of *Rerum Novarum* represented a major advance. For this encyclical was a strong challenge to the *status quo*. I hope I have shown, however, that Pope Leo's political philosophy, his spirituality, and his fear of revolution, all imposed severe limits to the extent to which he could carry through that challenge. Leo XIII called for a change of attitude by the rich and the acceptance of practices and laws that would protect the poor. But if such changes 'from the top' were not introduced, the pope had no very effective way in which he could promote fundamental changes in society. In the last resort he felt that the Church was obliged to encourage allegiance to the liberal capitalist regimes of the time, even while speaking out against the injustices that were so evident in them.

Inadequate Solution—but a Major Advance

Leo XIII did not experience any contradiction in his approach.

For him there was a clear distinction between, on the one hand, the existing socio-economic order, whose abuses he condemned, and, on the other hand, the political order, which he felt obliged to support. Where he failed was in not paying sufficient attention to the crucial question of who was exercising effective power in society. He noted the fact that the wealthy had gained power in the State (RN 35). But he did not advert to the consequent inconsistency in his own position. He was defending the existing political order while condemning the existing economic order—despite his acknowledgment of the fact that the two were so closely interlinked that the rich could use the machinery of the State to promote their interests at the expense of the poor.

For the most part, Leo XIII seems to have forgotten that his ideal conception of the State was not realised in practice. Apart from the passing remark in *Rerum Novarum* which I have just referred to, he seems to assume that the government, in exercising its political function, is not unduly biased in favour of the rich. Leo wanted governments to protect the poor in various ways which he did not specify in detail. Nevertheless, he did not want them to 'interfere' very much in economic affairs. So what he wanted was a 'middle way' between socialism and liberal capitalism. The main difficulty with this does not lie in the proposal itself but in the assumption that the governments of Leo's time would be willing to implement it in practice. For, as he himself acknowledged, the rich had gained control of the governments, and therefore of the apparatus of the State.

In the civil and criminal law enacted and enforced by most, if not all, of the states of the time there was a bias in favour of the people of property. This bias in favour of the rich extended also into the day-to-day administration of 'justice' by police, law-courts, and other branches of government. Like any other bias, this was of course largely imperceptible to those who benefited from it. They were convinced that the State, and especially 'the Law' were embodiments of justice and quite impartial. They did not realise what was really implied in their demand that the State should 'interfere' only minimally in economic affairs. What it really meant was a demand that their privileged position be preserved, that the structural inequality between rich and poor be maintained and supported by political means. One example of this has already been noted in the previous chapter: when poor workers found really effective means to defend their economic rights (for instance, a general strike), these could be labelled 'subversive' and declared illegal.

Pope Leo XIII seems to have presumed that socio-economic reform could come about without significant political changes and even without major challenge to existing political structures. This presumption helps to explain how he could combine the real concern for the poor expressed in *Rerum Novarum* with a total rejection of anything that might be considered subversive. But it was rather unrealistic to expect that the rich and powerful could be persuaded by moral exhortations to relinquish their privileged position. If they chose to be intransigent, Leo's teaching offered little by way of remedy for this. I would therefore conclude that what Leo XIII presented as the official Church teaching on socio-political questions did not measure up to the deeply Christian instinct that led him to cry out against mistreatment of the poor. I would go further and say that the attitudes and spirituality that were linked to, and reflected, his teaching contributed to the failure of the Church to gain the confidence of the mass of industrial workers.

On the other hand it must not be forgotten that *Rerum Novarum* was a major intervention by the pope in defence of the poor. As such it helped to put the Church firmly on their side. The effect was two-fold. The encyclical led Church people to make a deeper study of the causes of poverty and to seek more effective means of overcoming them. And at the same time it gave heart to those of the workers and the poor who were able and willing to hear its message; this inspirational effect was quite important, especially when over the years it became apparent that many Church leaders were taking the encyclical seriously.

A further reason for saying that *Rerum Novarum* was an important step towards putting the Church on the side of the poor has to do with its teaching, its 'doctrine'. It laid a solid basis for the emergence of the concept of 'social justice'. This term was not used regularly in papal documents until much later. But what it eventually came to mean was largely what Pope Leo wrote about in his encyclical. He specified a range of obligations quite different from those that fall under the category of commutative justice. It is true that he did not neatly specify all the different categories of obligation (see RN 19, 25–40; cf. also his encyclical *Graves de Communi*, BP VI, 218–20). But what seems to emerge is that it is a matter of justice (not 'merely' of charity) to ensure that the social order does not facilitate the exploitation of the poor. This teaching of Leo XIII had a basis in the past—in the moral teaching of the scholastics. It was an important contribution to the Church of Leo's own time. For it widened the whole concept of justice in theology and Church teaching and helped to rescue it from a narrow individualism and 'privatisation'. In doing so it laid a foundation for the eventual development of the notion of an 'option for the poor'—and a spirituality that would embody such an option.

Taken as a whole, the economic, social, and political teaching of Leo XIII represents a major achievement. Despite the weaknesses or inadequacies that have been noted, it is a powerful synthesis, comprehensive and systematic. While rooted in tradition, it offers an opening to the new situation, a situation which included the emergence of democratic governments, the reality or threat of political revolution, and the development of an industrial proletariat ground down by poverty. It is not surprising, then, that Leo's teaching has remained the basis of the official Catholic position on social issues. Later popes constantly referred back to the teachings of Leo XIII and seldom attempted to change them. Indeed for a long time *Rerum Novarum* was seen not just as the foundation for the Church's teaching on 'the social question' but as the more or less definitive statement of that teaching; and on political issues Leo's other encyclicals, notably *Immortale Dei*, were given a similar definitive position. Forty years were to pass before any pope set out even to up-date the teaching of Pope Leo XIII on social questions.

SUMMARY

Pope Leo wished for changes in the economic order of society. But he was not prepared to approve of the kind of political activity that would be likely to bring such changes about. He was so convinced of the importance of order in society, and so concerned about the evil effects of revolution, that he built his political theology around stability as the key value. He insisted that political power derives from God and that to disobey civil authority is to rebel against God. He did not follow the older Catholic tradition which held that it is lawful to resist a tyrannical abuse of power. He refused to accept that rebellion could sometimes be justified.

In certain circumstances (mainly where the rights of the Church were interfered with) Pope Leo encouraged Catholics to seek political change; but only by legal means. In the last analysis, where changes could not be brought about without a threat to social order, he expected Christians to put up with injustice.

Leo's spirituality was in line with his theology. It was of a kind that actively discouraged the poor from confronting the wealthy to claim their rights; he asked the victims of oppression and injustice to put up with their suffering in the hope of a reward in the next life.

Questions for review:

1. Why was Pope Leo so fearful of anarchy and instability?
2. What kind of resistance to injustice did Leo approve of and what kind did he forbid?
3. What was Leo's attitude to democracy?

Questions for reflection:

1. Contrast your own spirituality with that of Leo in relation to social and political activity.
2. Are there times when it is better to endure injustice than to resist it?

Issues for further study:
1. Leo's conception of Church and State as each a 'perfect society'. (Read Murray [1952–3])
2. The effects on the Church of the loss of overt political power. (Read Aubert [1978].)

3

Transitions

I have entitled this chapter 'Transitions' because in it I propose to examine two important transitional periods in the life of the Church. The first is the interval of about thirty years between the death of Leo XIII and the publication by Pius XI in 1931 of the second of the great social encyclicals, *Quadragesimo Anno*. I shall look at the social teaching of Pius X and Benedict XV. The second transition is the much longer one from the colonial age to the age of decolonisation. This was a process that received very little attention in the late eighteenth and early nineteenth centuries. But it is important that we take some account of at it this stage, in order to fill in the background to the later teaching of the Church; for more recent social teaching focuses a great deal of attention on the issue of the relationship between the wealthy nations and the poor ones (which are mostly the former colonies).

SECTION I: PIUS X AND BENEDICT XV

The social question was not very high on the agenda of Pope Pius X. Though he did not entirely ignore it (e.g. his 1905 encyclical *Il fermo proposto* ASS 37, 741–67), he was more concerned with practical religious reform (cf. Camp 14) and with the crisis of modernism. The British author Alec Vidler remarks that Pius X was determined to stamp out social as well as doctrinal modernism (Vidler 139–40). What this meant in practice was mostly that he wanted to ensure hierarchical and clerical control over all kinds of 'Catholic Action' concerned with social reform (cf. Camp 117 on 'integrism'; and Chenu 29–30). Richard Camp claims that the call of Leo XIII for social and economic reform was 'supported in word but stifled in deed' by Pius X (Camp 14). This claim may be somewhat exaggerated but it has in it an element of truth. It is an overstatement to the extent that Pius was not opposed to a slow and cautious movement towards economic reform and an overcoming of the misery of the poor, and certainly he did not want to lend support to social injustice. But on the other hand it is true that he was instrumental in stifling two social reform movements, one in Italy in 1903 and one in France in 1910. His opposition was largely aroused by the relative independence which the lay leadership had achieved in these movements; this gave rise to practical problems about obedience to ecclesiastical authority. But there was also an issue that had more to do with theory and official teaching: the question of the equality of human beings. On this matter Pius spoke out sharply:

> . . . it is in accordance with the pattern established by God that human society should have rulers and subjects, employers and employees, rich and poor, wise and ignorant, nobles and common people . . . (*Fin dalla prima*, ASS 36, 341).[1]

The French movement which Pius condemned was in favour of a system of cooperatives which would enable every worker to become in some sense an owner-employer. Even though *Rerum Novarum* had explicitly called for a widening of ownership (RN 35), Pius X was not happy with the co-operative proposal. He felt it was inspired by the ideal of levelling out the differences between different classes in society—and he seems to have considered this ideal to be too utopian (Letter on *Le Sillon*, AAS 2, 613–33). One can only conclude that, for a variety of reasons, Pius was in practice opposed to a movement which might have been able to put into effect in some degree one of the most important proposals of *Rerum Novarum*.

The most notable document issued by Pius X on social questions was the *Motu Proprio* of 1903 called *Fin dalla prima*. It consists mainly of a schematic summary of major points from the teaching of Leo XIII, with references to Pope Leo's documents. The style of *Fin dalla prima*, as well as the points which Pius X chose to emphasise, gives the document the character of a manual of discipline. Notably absent is any sense of Leo's passionate concern for the plight of the working classes; the concern of Pius X seemed to be to ensure unity within the Church and stability in society.

Fin dalla prima differs subtly but significantly from *Rerum Novarum* on one important point, which it mentions twice:

> VI. To calm the strife between rich and poor, it is necessary to distinguish between justice and charity. Only when justice has been violated is there a right to make a claim, in the strict sense of the word.
>
> XIX. Finally, let Catholic writers, while upholding the cause of the people and of the poor, beware of using language which may inspire the masses with hatred of the upper classes of society. Let them not talk of claims and of justice, when it is a question of mere charity . . . (AAS 341–2, 344; *Pope and People* 184, 187—translation slightly emended).

In the first of these passages a reference is given to the text of *Rerum Novarum*. But the fact is that while the latter encyclical undoubtedly speaks both of obligations of justice and of obligations of charity it does not by any means draw the same conclusions as Pope Pius X.[2]

The way in which Pius applies the distinction between justice and charity is unfortunate. He says that there is a 'claim, in the strict sense of the word' only when justice has been violated. When this is put together with the second quotation, the effect is to suggest that it is 'merely' an obligation of charity to bring about an equitable social order. This set back the emerging concept of 'social justice' to which *Rerum Novarum* had made such a notable contribution. It gave the impression that any social obligation which could not be specified in the strict interpersonal terms of commutative justice was not really a matter of justice at all and was for that reason less compelling or could be ignored with greater impunity.

Benedict XV

From the point of view of the general history of the Church there was a major difference between Pius X and his successor, Benedict XV. The latter was much more liberal in approach than Pius; indeed it is even said that Benedict had been suspected by his predecessor of being tainted with modernism! Certainly, when he took over as pope, Benedict curbed the excesses of anti-modernism and began to open up the Catholic Church to a cautious dialogue with the modern world. In the field of socio-political activity, Benedict was much more advanced in his approach than Pius. For instance, he allowed Catholics to play a more active role in Italian political life, thus opening the way for a rapprochement between Church and State. Benedict was also very concerned about the problems of war and peace. The First World War dominated his pontificate and he spent a good deal of his energy in working for peace and in trying to have the Church accepted as a mediator. His concern with national and international political matters meant that he paid less attention to the socio-economic aspects of 'the social question'.

My concern here with Benedict XV is not with his general impact on the life of the papacy and the Church but with the much more limited question of his *teaching* on social issues. In this regard the difference between himself and his predecessor is much less striking than in the area of practical action and policy. He did not speak very often about socio-economic matters; and when he did so his statements were conservative in tone and content. This may have been partly due to a lingering anti-modernism and suspicion of new thinking on social issues. Perhaps also it suited Benedict to sound rather more conservative than he was in practice.

In the encyclical *Ad Beatissimi*, issued in 1914, Benedict insists that since political power has its source in God, it is to be obeyed as a matter of conscience (AAS 6, 570–1). He adds that experience shows that when rulers despise divine authority, their people tend to despise human authority; therefore governments ought not to divorce their governing of the country and the education of the young from the teaching of the Church (AAS 6, 571).

In a letter written in 1920 to the Bishop of Bergamo, Pope Benedict also insisted that a diversity of classes in society was part of the natural order and was willed by God (AAS 12, 111). Although he encouraged Catholics to help the poor, at the same time he wanted the poor to be imbued with a spirituality that would discourage them from seeking vainly for a higher situation than they could reach and from trying to escape from evils they could not avoid; they should rather be encouraged to put up with their troubles peacefully in the hope of the good things of heaven (AAS 12, 111).

Benedict held that envy and hatred between the classes in society was fomented by socialist agitators whose fallacies led the proletariat to forget that though people are equal by nature this does not mean that they must all occupy an equal place in the community. Having given this legitimation for the inequalities in society, Benedict went on to make the following revealing remarks:

> . . . who will ever make them see that the position of each one is that which each by use of his or her own natural gifts—unless prevented by force of circumstances—is able to make for himself or herself? And so the poor who strive against the rich as though they had taken part of the goods of others, not merely act contrary to justice and charity but also act irrationally, particularly as they themselves by honest industry can improve their fortunes if they choose (*Ad Beatissimi*, AAS 6, 571–2; *Pope and People* 208—translation emended).

This passage shows the extent to which the pope had come to accept the belief which, more than anything else, gives a moral legitimation to the capitalist system. This is the belief that under such a system everybody, or at least nearly everybody, has a reasonable chance to 'make good'. In fact there is frequently the suggestion that everybody has more or less an equal chance, at least in principle. Of course those who hold this view then add on some such qualifying phrase as that used by the pope—'unless prevented by force of circumstances'. This makes the statement technically true. But there is a complete failure to note that the 'circumstances' in which poor people find themselves are such that they can seldom escape their poverty. In fact, then, the main cause of poverty is not the failure by people to make use of their personal talents but rather the situation in which they are trapped. In other words, the system itself is biased against the poor, so that they seldom get the opportunity to develop and use their talents to the extent that would enable them to escape their poverty. It was this bias which Pope Leo XIII had seen, and which he had spoken out against in *Rerum Novarum*. So it is rather unfortunate that Benedict XV should have lent his authority as pope to what might be called 'the mythological basis of the capitalist order'. This looks like a backward step from *Rerum Novarum.*

SECTION II

COLONIALISM AND DECOLONISATION

In the first section of this chapter I have been examining the extent to which the main thrust of Pope Leo's teaching was accepted or adapted by the two popes who followed him. In this section I move on to take up a quite different issue of social justice. This is the question of the stance of the Catholic Church in relation to the whole process of colonisation and decolonisation. That this is an important topic is obvious, since world history over the past four hundred years has largely been the history of the colonial expansion of Europe into other continents and the story of the attempt in more recent times of the nations of Latin America, Asia, Africa, the Caribbean and the Pacific to gain their independence.

Yet this whole issue was given very little attention in the social teaching of the Catholic Church in the late nineteenth and early twentieth century. Indeed it was so passed over that it is quite difficult to integrate this theme with the rest of the Catholic social teaching of the time. For this reason I said very little about the subject in the first edition of this book, since I felt it would be easier to write about it elsewhere. But I now believe that such a two-track approach is unsatisfactory. Over the past fifty years the question of the relationship between 'The North' and 'The South' (or, in older terminology, between 'The First World' and 'The Third World') has been moving more and more to the very centre of the social justice agenda of the Churches. In order to have a proper grasp of this present-day issue it is essential to have some understanding of how the Church saw colonialism and what it had to say about the early stages of the process of decolonisation.

The Colonial Period

Five hundred years ago Europe 'discovered' the Americas and

at about the same time the sea route between Europe and East Asia was opened up. There followed a major commercial and political expansion of European nations into Asia, Africa and Latin America. The popes saw this as an opportunity for the Church to bring the Gospel to other continents. But this expansion took place at a time when the papacy was in no position to send out ships of its own. The only way in which Catholic missionaries could reach out to these distant lands was to travel along with the merchants, the soldiers and the colonists from Portugal and Spain. The colonial powers were quite happy to bring Church people along. But the papacy paid a heavy price for this favour. The popes were forced to concede to the Portuguese and Spanish authorities the right to nominate bishops and in this way to exercise effective control over much of the institutional life of the Church. This *padrõado* or power of patronage was conceded through a number of papal decrees between the years 1460 and 1515 (cf. Alix 55–7).

From the start, this caused considerable difficulties for the Vatican authorities who found that they had conceded so much to the colonial powers that they had little control over ecclesiastical affairs in Latin America. Before long they began the long and difficult process of disengaging the papacy from what they saw as too close an association with the colonial powers. Their objections to the power of 'patronage' arose from abuses in the ecclesiastical and humanitarian spheres rather than from any fundamental disapproval of the principle of colonialism.

At this time the Church as a whole accepted a theology which could justify colonisation under certain circumstances. Colonisers could be seen as performing a service to humankind in so far as they were understood to be occupying uninhabited or underpopulated areas and tapping unused resources of the Earth (Alix, 19).[3] However, the reality of European conquest and colonisation was far removed from anything that could be justified by such a theology—though most Church leaders seemed to be nearly as blind to this fact as the colonists themselves.

There were a few prophetic figures like Bishop Bartholomew de las Casas who were so outraged that they could not be silenced when they cried out against the exploitation that was taking place under the guise of colonisation and evangelisation (cf. Williamson). And so, for a fairly brief period in the sixteenth and seventeenth centuries the treatment of the colonised peoples became a burning issue in the Church. Responding to the protests, the popes denounced abuses. Papal briefs issued in 1547 by Paul III and in 1567–8 by Pius V condemned the enslavement of people and forced 'conversions' as well as the waging of unjust war against the indigenous inhabitants of the newly 'discovered' lands (cf. Alix 73). But such denunciations were quite ineffective; so the popes got on with the task of trying to ensure that the Church was established in the colonies. They tried to concentrate on ecclesiastical affairs and not to get too entangled in politics.

Despite the occasional protests of Church leaders against abuses and the attempt by the Vatican to maintain a certain distance from purely political affairs in the new colonies, there can be no doubt that the Church gave a certain legitimacy to political and economic colonialism by its day-to-day cooperation with the occupying powers. It should be noted, however, that the Vatican soon developed an official policy which strongly insisted that political colonialism should not be accompanied by cultural and religious colonialism. In 1659 Pope Alexander VII issued an important 'Instruction' about missionary work. He maintained that what missionaries should bring from Europe was only the faith—and they should reject only what was clearly contrary to the faith (Alix 20–1, 73–4).

So the Vatican did not accept that the way to evangelise the 'pagans' was to westernise them. In practice, of course, there was a serious divergence of views about which elements in the local cultures should be judged to be contrary to the faith. This is evident from the controversies surrounding the attempts of the Jesuits to incarnate the Christian faith in Indian and Chinese culture—and the strong opposition to their approach. (See, for instance, von Pastor 166–170 for some background on the issue of the cult of ancestors.)

In his 'Instruction' about missionary work Alexander VII did not make any judgment about the rightness or wrongness of political conquest in the colonies. But he linked colonial expansion to a mission of spiritual education. This understanding of colonialism has important implications: if the coloniser is seen as an educator then the role of the colonial power is a temporary one, since it must be presumed that the period of education will come to an end. However, Pope Alexander's document has nothing to say either about the duration of the 'educational' process or about the political conditions attached to it.

Over the next two centuries the Vatican seems to have acquiesced in the colonisation policy of Portugal and Spain. There were occasional protests by Church authorities against particular barbarities or gross injustices. But there seems to have been little or no suggestion that the whole process of European colonisation was morally repugnant. In fact the question of the morality of the colonial process had ceased to arouse much interest in the theologians and Church leaders of Europe. Though Leo XIII was the author of the first great social encyclical and of several other encyclicals on political matters, he and his immediate successors scarcely adverted to the issue of the morality of colonialism; this, despite the fact that almost all the countries of Latin America had become independent in the nineteenth century; and, by the early twentieth century, Poland, Ireland, and several Baltic and Balkan States had all got out from under the great European empires.

First Steps in Decolonisation

During the first half of the nineteenth century various Latin American countries struggled for autonomy and eventually won their independence from the European 'mother-lands' of Spain and Portugal. The Vatican handled this whole process with great caution. It sought to stay aloof from the political struggles. But once each new nation had irreversibly won its independence the Vatican recognised it.

The emergence of independent nations in Latin America led the Vatican to envisage the possibility (though not the probability) that Africa and Asia might at some stage undergo a process of decolonisation. In an Apostolic Letter of 1893 Pope Leo XIII referred to the fact that at some future date the foreign clergy might be obliged to leave India or the Indies. He considered this extremely unlikely, but nevertheless felt it was an eventuality which ought to be prepared for (Alix 75). The concern of the pope was not about the legitimacy of a struggle for independence by India or other nations, but about the future of the Church in such a situation.

This document of Pope Leo gives a good insight into how Rome saw the situation at that time. It indicates that one of the main reasons why the pope did not speak out against colonialism was precisely because he, like most of his contemporaries, could hardly imagine an end to the colonial era. The late nineteenth century was a time when 'the West' had gained political dominance over much of the world. European nations were busy carving up Africa between them and intervening crudely in Asian countries. Matching this reality of political ascendancy was the myth of European cultural superiority which at this time was at its height.

The myth of Western superiority was not seriously undermined by the fact that many Latin American nations had become independent. For their struggle for independence was not, for the most part, led by the indigenous peoples of Latin America. It was led rather by people of European stock, the descendants of the colonists—or by people of racially mixed stock who had been culturally assimilated, at least to the extent of adopting Spanish or Portuguese as their mother-tongue. Even the very phrase 'Latin America' is revealing. It indicates that the southern part of the American continent had, like its northern neighbour, been assimilated in some sense into the Western world.

The extent to which Latin America was really westernised is of course a delicate and controversial topic—particularly in the context of the fairly recent emergence of liberation theology, which makes much of the differences between Latin America and 'the Western powers'. For our present purposes it is not necessary to discuss this issue. It suffices to note that at the end of the nineteenth century Latin America was ruled by people who saw themselves as the descendants of the colonists. This meant that the achievement of independence of Latin American countries would hardly be seen at that time as setting a precedent which could be followed in other continents; for in Africa and Asia the process of colonisation had not progressed to the point where indigenous peoples were largely exterminated or 'assimilated' and where local languages were eliminated or marginalised. (There are, however, some exceptions:

one could argue that Latin America set a precedent for the ill-fated attempt of the white minority in South Africa—and later in Rhodesia/Zimbabwe—to gain independence from Britain and establish States that would be permanently ruled by the descendants of the original colonists.)

An important reason why the Vatican in the early part of the present century did not take a clear stand against colonialism was that it had recently lost its direct political power and was trying to find a new role in the political world as a mediator and arbitrator between the great powers. From shortly before the turn of the century the popes began to put themselves forward in the role of peace-makers. Benedict XV tried to play this role at the time of World War I, but was given little recognition by the great powers. During the 1920s he and Pius XI continued the effort to have the papacy accepted as an 'honest broker' in international political life. The signing in 1929 of the Lateran Treaty with the Italian government provided the popes with a firm basis in international law for such a role, for this Treaty gave international recognition to the political neutrality of the Vatican. The text of the treaty included a declaration by the Holy See that it would remain 'extraneous to all temporal disputes between nations . . . ' (Flannery 34). The Vatican's commitment to neutrality in political affairs made it difficult for the popes to challenge the European powers on the issue of their colonial policies.

Behind these political and cultural stances lay a theology and spirituality quite different to those which prevail at the present time. Having lost its overt political power, the Church was concentrating on religious and spiritual matters. But unfortunately the current understanding of what was 'religious' or 'spiritual' was marred by a dualism which greatly exaggerated the gap between secular matters and the religious sphere.

Ecclesiastical leaders whose thinking was infected with this kind of dualism almost invariably wanted to keep the Church out of politics. But, in attempting to be neutral or 'above politics,' they often, in practice, condoned social and political injustices and can even be accused of colluding with those who practised them. In the case of the Vatican during the end of the last century and the early part of the present century this problem was compounded by a great fear of political instability—as I pointed out in Chapter 2 above. The result was that the popes threw the Church's authority behind the existing regimes. They made little attempt to challenge the policies of the imperial powers—except in cases where these clashed with the rights or interests of the Church. This helps to explain why the Church seemed to 'go along with' colonialism so unquestioningly. Indeed, Pope Leo XIII did not even give backing to the independence struggles of Catholic peoples like the Poles and the Irish—even though the usual justification for colonialism could scarcely apply in these cases (cf. Alix 23, 80–1).

There is no indication that during the first forty years of the present century the popes showed any great concern about the injustice inherent in the maintenance of vast colonial empires. Instead, their attention continued to be focused almost entirely on the importance of building up a local clergy in these faraway lands. This was stressed by Benedict XV in his Apostolic Letter on the missions, *Maximum Illud*, issued in 1919 (AAS 7, 445–6). In 1926, Pius XI followed much the same line in his mission encyclical, *Rerum Ecclesiae* (AAS 18, 65–83). In it he referred to what he called the 'unlikely case' where a native population would seek to gain their freedom and drive out not only the colonial administration but also the foreign missionaries of the occupying power. He did not address the question of whether such a struggle for freedom would be justified; instead he confined himself to pointing out the disastrous position in which the Church would find itself in such a situation.

The theology behind this approach can be found in an instruction (*Quo Efficacius*) issued in 1920 by Benedict XV. In it he insisted that the sole concern of missionaries should be 'to gain souls and promote the glory of God'. He warned them that they should 'never get involved in any of the political or temporal interests of their own nation or any other nation'. He then went on to stress the duty of missionaries to exhort the people faithfully to obey the public authorities (cf. Alix 76–7).

In 1928 Pius XI sent a message to the bishops of China in which he stressed the importance of fully recognising the legitimate desires and rights of indigenous peoples (AAS 20, 245–6). By this time the struggle for independence was already well under way in India and in some African countries. So it is not surprising that the Vatican was at last beginning to call in question the political and cultural dominance of the West. But how could this be reconciled with the constant Vatican insistence on obedience to the ruling authorities? Perhaps by taking more seriously a principle which, as I noted above, had been alluded to by Pope Alexander VII back in 1659 but had never been fully worked out. This was the idea that colonialism could be justified as a *transitory* stage, destined to come to an end when the colonised peoples had 'come of age'. But there was no clear statement to this effect by Pius XI. There is no indication that he was moved by the growing cry being raised by poor and exploited peoples from many parts of the non-Western world. Like his predecessors he was content to follow the movement of history rather than trying to shape history by throwing the Church firmly on the side of the subject peoples who were making new or renewed efforts to shake off the oppressive and exploitative domination of the imperial powers.

SUMMARY

Pius X was much more conservative than Leo XIII on social issues; the result was that the Church moved backward from Leo's fairly advanced position. Pius insisted that the obligation to work for an equitable social order is not one of justice but merely of charity. This set back the emerging concept of social justice. Benedict XV, who followed Pius, was more liberal and flexible in his policies; but his *statements* on social issues were quite like those of Pius X. So there was little advance in social teaching during his papacy.

The Church acquiesced in, and gave religious support to, the colonial expansion of the European powers into other continents; but some outstanding Church people put up a strong resistance to exploitation and oppression by the colonial powers. After the first period, colonialism scarcely featured for 300 years as a social justice issue for the Church. In the late nineteenth and early twentieth centuries, the Church gave little or no support to indigenous peoples struggling for independence.

Questions for review:

1. In what ways did Pius X back-track on the social teaching of Leo?
2. What role did Benedict XV envisage for the Church in international society?
3. What spirituality did the Church expect its missionaries to live by during this period?

Question for reflection:

In what ways was the Church guilty of cultural and religious imperialism during the great missionary age; and in what ways did it resist this temptation? To what extent has it changed today in this regard?

Issue for further study:

To what extent did the Church collude in the oppression and exploitation of the peoples of Latin American, Asia and Africa? (Read Williamson, Boff and Elizondo, Pakenham.)

4

Piux XI and a New Social Order

The second of the great social encyclicals was issued by Pope Pius XI in 1931. It was written to commemorate the fortieth anniversary of Leo XIII's *Rerum Novarum* so it is known as *Quadragesimo Anno*; and the usual English title is 'The Social Order'.[1] In this chapter I shall examine the contribution to Catholic social teaching made by Pius XI in *Quadragesimo Anno* and some of his other encyclical letters. But I shall be doing this from a particular point of view. The main emphasis will not be on the point that is usually associated with Pius XI, namely, his proposal for a corporative or vocational ordering of society; though this question will of course have to be considered. The main concern of this study will be a prior question: did the pope commit the Church to supporting a radical transformation of the structures of society, an alternative to the capitalist or free enterprise model; and, if so, how far was he prepared to go in challenging the existing order?

Quadragesimo Anno is a worthy successor to *Rerum Novarum*. It has the same sense of moral outrage at the suffering of the poor (e.g. QA 59, 112) as one finds in Leo's encyclical; and the same kind of criticism of the economic liberalism which had caused that suffering (e.g. QA 10, 88). Moreover, Pius's encyclical, like that of his predecessor, rejects communism and socialism (QA 112, 117–20). Pius, like Leo, sees himself as presenting a 'middle way' between economic liberalism and socialism.

The new social encyclical sets out to vindicate and develop the teaching of *Rerum Novarum*. But then it goes on to look at current social issues in a radical way, with the aim of showing how they can be tackled according to Christian principles. Pius XI was very conscious that major changes had taken place over the previous forty years. He wanted to ensure that the Church's social teaching was fully up to date and clearly relevant to the actual situation of the time (QA 40, 117). In his view there were several particularly urgent reasons why the Church should be actively involved in social issues at that time:

— Wealth had come to be concentrated in the hands of a relatively small number of people (QA 105).[2]

— This concentration of wealth had led to a concentration of economic power and even of political power (QA 105–8).

— While the condition of the workers in the West had improved since the time of Leo, there was now, in the Americas and in the Far East, a vast increase in the number of very poor industrial workers 'whose groans rise from earth to heaven'; there was also 'the immense army of agricultural wage-earners whose condition is depressed in the extreme' (QA 59).

— There was the further problem of widespread unemployment at the time the encyclical was written (QA 74).[3]

Pius XI was not content merely to repeat, develop, and apply the teaching of Leo XIII. As the French theologian Chenu rightly remarks, he was concerned not just with the condition of workers but with the whole socio-economic order of society (Chenu 35).[4] He introduced into official Church teaching the term 'social justice' (QA 88) and gave general guidelines on how it should be realised in society.

Above all, he focused attention on the basic *causes* of injustice and poverty. He was prepared to go much further than Leo in doing what would now be called a 'structural analysis' of society, locating the inadequacies and built-in injustices in its structures. He avoided the mistake of adopting a purely 'moralising' approach, an attitude which explains social evils in terms of the sinfulness of individuals. On the other hand he also avoided the opposite mistake, namely, that of blaming the structures of society for all its ills. *Quadragesimo Anno* insists on the need for both 'a reform of social institutions' *and* 'the improvement of conduct' (QA 77; cf. QA 97, 98, 127). The encyclical treats these two aspects of the problem separately for the most part. But at one point it comes close to expressing an important insight about the relationship between the two, namely, that evil conduct can solidify into a set of practices and traditions which are themselves real 'structures' of society, affecting the more obvious political, social and economic structures. The pope does not quite say this. But he gives an impressive account of how moral standards tend to become eroded in the existing economic order (QA 132–5).

A New Spirituality

The main concern of this study is with what Pius had to say about the *structures* of society and the need for radical change in them. But before moving on to this question it is worthwhile considering one point about the reform of *conduct*. Perhaps the most effective way in which the Church can influence human behaviour is by promoting a particular kind of spirituality. Leo XIII had encouraged what might be termed 'a spirituality of stability': he laid emphasis on obedience to lawful authorities to a point where in the last analysis people were asked to endure gross injustices rather than overthrow the regimes that perpetrated them; and the promise of future reward was held out to those who were patient in this way. Pius XI seems to give less emphasis to this kind of spirituality. The author of *Quadragesimo Anno* is clearly aware of the Marxist accusation that the Church condones injustice by offering happiness in the next life as a reward for patience in the face of oppression in this life. He responds by denying that the Church in general does this, though he admits that some people in the Church do so. The pope condemns the conduct of those who 'abuse religion itself, trying to cloak their own unjust impositions under its name' (QA 125).

It is true that Pius XI maintains that workers should not feel 'discontent at the position assigned them by divine Providence in human society' (QA 137). But that comment should not be taken to indicate that he sees stability in society as something to be promoted at all costs. His remark is simply an expression of his concern that feelings of envy and hatred should be overcome through a theology and spirituality of human work (QA 137). In general, there is a slight but noticeable shift in emphasis from a more 'escapist' to a more 'worldly' spirituality, as one moves from *Rerum Novarum* to *Quadragesimo Anno*. This is a good example of how the 'doctrinal' continuity between Leo and Pius XI is combined with subtle but significant changes.

One can sense in *Quadragesimo Anno* the emergence of a new spirituality of justice; but it has not yet succeeded fully in maintaining its autonomy. On some occasions it almost seems as though concern for justice is little more than a means to the end of bringing workers into the Church, or ensuring that they are not led astray (cf. DR 61, 63, 70; *Firmissimum 22*). But *Quadragesimo Anno* shows that its author does see concern for justice as a fundamental value in its own right. It speaks, for instance, of choosing people who 'show themselves endowed with a keen sense of justice, ready to oppose with manly constancy unjust claims and unjust actions' (QA 142). The pope goes on to add that such people should show great prudence and should above all be filled with the charity of Christ (QA 142). Here we find linked together four major virtues—justice, courage, prudence and the love of Christ; for Pius XI these constitute the heart of a Christian spirituality of justice.

The Need for Structural Change

However important a change of heart and conduct may be, Pius XI was well aware that it is not sufficient on its own to overcome modern social problems. He believed that well-meaning employers were often trapped by the system, by structures in society that embodied injustice and created further injustice:

> We turn again in a special way to you, Christian employers and industrialists, whose problem is often so difficult for the reason that you are saddled with the heavy heritage of an unjust economic regime whose ruinous influence has been felt through many generations (DR 50).

One instance of the difficulty is the fact that competition may be so keen that individual employers know that any increase in their costs would put them out of business. Consequently they find themselves unable to pay their employees a just wage. The pope insisted that in these kinds of situations there is an obligation to establish structures or institutions designed to limit the competition which causes the injustice (DR 53). When Pius XI turns his attention in *Quadragesimo Anno* to the question of the reform of the structures of society he points out the key factor: *wealth gives power*. He goes much further than his predecessors in recognising that in a capitalist society the State is largely controlled by a wealthy group (cf. Calvez and Perrin 350), 'so that its resources and authority may be abused in economic struggles' (QA 108):

> The State which should be the supreme arbiter, ruling in regal fashion far above all party contention, intent only upon justice and the common good, has become instead a slave . . . (QA 109).[5]

At this point Pius makes his most radical criticism of the capitalist system as it has developed since the time of Leo XIII: 'Free competition has destroyed itself; economic domination has taken the place of the open market' (QA 109). Here the pope is pointing to a fatal weakness in capitalism, the point where it fails to be what it essentially claims to be. It begins as free enterprise; and this includes free competition. But a 'natural result' (QA 107) of the competition is that only the toughest survive. Before long the free competition is only a myth and an ideology; the reality is the elimination of competition and the securing of economic and even political domination by the most ruthless (cf. R. Miller 233). That is why Pius XI insists that 'the proper ordering of economic life cannot be left to free competition'; it must be 'subjected to and governed by a true and effective guiding principle' (QA 88). Public authorities must ensure that free competition is kept within just and definite limits and that economic power is kept under control (QA 110).[6] Such a degree of interference in 'the market' would amount to a radical change in the structures which had shaped the Western world.

In dealing with the question of the restructuring of society the pope is quite subtle. His encyclical cleverly combines the advantages of being broad and general with the advantages of being rather specific. Three paragraphs give a specific and fairly detailed account of the type of corporative State that was being introduced at that time in Italy by Mussolini (QA 92–4; for historical background see R. Miller 190–7). But the pope does not identify this as his own position. Instead he lists some of its advantages and disadvantages. In this way he succeeds in distancing himself somewhat from the model of society adopted by the Italian fascists; while at the same time he outlines its main features with a measure of what he himself called 'benevolent attention'.[7] On the other hand when Pius is making *his own* proposals he carefully avoids details and specific applications. Instead, he gives general norms such as the following:

— The aim of social policy must . . . be the re-establishment of vocational groups (QA 82).

— Professional corporations may take a variety of different forms (QA 86).

— Wages should be determined not with a view to private advantage but on the basis of providing employment for as many as possible (QA 74).

— No larger or higher association should 'arrogate to itself the functions which can be performed efficiently by smaller and lower societies' (QA 79). (This is the first clear articulation in papal teaching of the principle of subsidiarity which has become central to Catholic social thought.)

Pius XI reaffirmed the right of workers to form voluntary trade unions (QA 30, 34, 35, 87).[8] He even had strong words of criticism for those who were reluctant to acknowledge this right (QA 30–1; DR 50). A comparison of the descriptions of the role of trade unions in *Rerum Novarum* and *Quadragesimo Anno* shows an interesting shift of emphasis. There is an almost militant ring to what Pius says about unions, a tone quite different to that of Leo. Pius XI stresses the importance of unions as a means by which workers can protect themselves against oppression (QA 30, 34). He implies that the trade unions are the defenders and champions of the lowly and oppressed (QA 31). He even sees them as having what would now be called a conscientising role in so far is it was through unions that workers 'learned to defend their temporal rights and interests energetically and efficiently, retaining at the same time a due respect for justice' (QA 33).

In spite of all this, Pius XI did not envisage a solution to 'the social problem' as being reached through workers' organisations. The whole bent of his thinking was in a very different direction. He envisaged the elimination or at least the minimising of the division of society into classes (upper, middle and lower). This would be brought about by ensuring that the main divisions would be on the basis of the different sectors of society (e.g. agriculture, transport, various branches of industry) (QA 82–5). These 'vocational' structures would cut across class structures. Within each vocational sphere there could be opportunities for employers and employees to meet separately on occasion (QA 85). But the whole order of society would be designed in such a way as to ensure that there would be no opposition or confrontation between the whole class of workers and the class of employers as a whole. The division into vocational sectors would be a matter of organisational convenience; it would not be so rigid and total that it would itself give rise to the kind of destructive competition and group selfishness it was supposed to eliminate. In fact it was simply an application of the general principle of subsidiarity which Pius XI considered to be a 'fixed and unshaken' principle of social philosophy (QA 79).

A Rejection of Capitalism

Pope Pius XI, like Leo XIII, was very concerned to lessen hostility between the classes of society (QA 81–3; RN 15, 35, 41). His teaching, following that of Leo, proposed a conception of society as an ordered harmony, rather than a battleground where workers and employers confront each other (QA 83–4; RN 15). But Pius went much further than Leo in indicating how this was to be brought about. Leo had relied mainly on a reform of conduct rather than proposing any major change in the structures of society. Pius XI wanted structural as well as moral changes. A basic feature of the restructured society he proposed was that its main components would not be classes but vocational groups (QA 82). Such a society would, he believed, be more natural than one stratified into different classes (QA 83). Harmonious relationships could be expected to develop both *within* the vocational groups and *between* them (QA 85).

The pope did not go into detail about how these groupings should be organised or how their internal and external relationships should be structured. In fact he specifically said that people could choose for themselves the form they wished the professional groups to take (QA 86). But even though he does not give a blueprint covering such details, nevertheless it is clear that the type of society he was calling for represented a major change from the typical country where capitalism was in operation. The question therefore arises whether Pius was definitely rejecting the capitalist system. This calls for a nuanced answer.

When the encyclical insists that 'the proper ordering of economic life cannot be left to free competition' (QA 88), this is more than an objection to abuses of the system. It is a repudiation of the central principle of capitalism, its ideological foundation. At the heart of capitalist thinking is the belief that market forces should be the determining factor in the economic order, regulating prices, profits, and wages—as well as who succeeds and who fails. In rejecting this principle Pius rejects capitalism not just in its present form but in its essential nature. I cannot agree with the view of Villain that the Church 'does not condemn the principles of capitalism but condemns the liberalism which in fact has vitiated the working and evolution of capitalism, and consequently condemns "actual" capitalism' (Villain 233—my translation). This distinction between economic liberalism and the principles of capitalism is too strained; it cannot be maintained so long as the word 'capitalism' retains its proper meaning.

However, a certain qualification must be added at once. Capitalism has an attenuated meaning which might be summed up as 'a system in which individuals and groups have a right to own property and engage in business enterprises of various kinds'. In so far as the word is understood in this sense the pope was certainly not rejecting it.[9] Indeed he explicitly states that a system where capital and labour are normally provided by different people is not in itself to be condemned and certainly is not evil of its very nature (QA 100–1). Pius also held that free competition is 'justified and certainly useful provided it is kept within certain limits' (QA 88—Miller translation). He did not favour the extreme corporatist position which, paradoxically, had certain similarities to socialism, especially in the matter of restrictions on the use of private property (cf. Camp 65, 97).

Perhaps the attitude of Pius may be expressed by saying that he did not want capitalism in the strict sense, but he undoubtedly wanted a large measure of *free enterprise*. He wanted people to be free to own and use land, free to found and conduct businesses without undue interference by either public authorities or capitalistic monopolies. Furthermore, he believed that such regulation and control as was required should be carried out at a 'lower' rather than a 'higher' level; it should as far as possible be done through a vocational structure rather than by the State. All this is clear from the general principles he lays down (especially QA 61–90). It is supported by the tenor of the critical comments he makes about the fascist-corporatist system. (In fact he does not give this criticism as his own; instead he notes that some people consider the system to be excessively bureaucratic and see it as giving to the State a role that should be left to private initiative—QA 95).

Ambivalence

It has been said with some justification that Pius XI was ambivalent in regard to the capitalist system of his time (Camp 40). There is no doubt that some of his statements give the impression that he wanted a *reform* of the system while at other times it seems as though he wanted the system to be entirely *replaced*. A good deal of the confusion can be removed by invoking the distinction made above between 'free enterprise' and 'capitalism'; one might say that the pope wanted the former to be reformed and the latter to be replaced. But even this distinction does not clear up the sense of ambivalence entirely. However, such ambivalence is not necessarily a bad thing. If the pope had opted unambiguously in favour of one particular socio-economic system he would have been going beyond his proper role and his competence. Perhaps, then, the element of ambivalence should be seen as a virtue rather than a fault!

In order to clarify the issue further it is helpful to distinguish clearly between two different questions which have frequently been jumbled together. The first question is the one we have been considering, namely, did Pius XI reject capitalism—or, more accurately, in what sense did he reject it? The second question is: what economic system does *Quadragesimo Anno* propose? It has sometimes been assumed that one should answer this second question first; and in this way the first question will also be answered. But in fact there is no answer to the second question. An economic system would include 'technical' economic details which, according to Pius XI, are outside the competence and mission of the Church (QA 41). The reason he gives is that 'economic science' covers a sphere distinct from that of 'moral science', even though the two are closely related to each other (QA 42).[10] So the pope could not be expected to teach that a given economic system is *the* correct one. Rather he lays down general principles to which any system should conform; and he uses these principles to assess and criticise existing or proposed systems, namely, capitalism, communism, different varieties of socialism, and the fascist-corporatist system. Anybody who expects the encyclical to say definitely which is the correct system will certainly, like Camp, find its statements about capitalism a cause of 'bewilderment' and open to different interpretations (Camp 40). But to somebody who adopts another conception of the role and competence of the teaching authority of the Church, the apparent ambivalence of the encyclical will be simply an indication that Pius XI resisted the temptation to exceed that competence by making a pronouncement on a 'technical' issue of economics; not merely that, but he refused to be dogmatic on a matter where uncertainty and openness were the appropriate response.

It would be an exaggeration, however, to claim that all this was quite clear in the encyclical or even in the mind of the pope himself. In fact the way in which he treats the relationship between economic science and moral science (QA 42) is not entirely satisfactory. There is a suggestion of a kind of dualism and a reduction of economics to a purely instrumental role. The distinction Pius XI makes between the proper object of papal teaching and the 'technical aspects' of economics (QA 41)[11] is made only in passing and is not fully developed. It is only a first step, though an important one. It is important because it entitles the pope to refrain from giving specific teaching on 'technical' matters. But it is only a first step because its frame of reference is too static. It divides the issues too neatly into those which lie within the 'technical' sphere and those in the moral sphere where the pope sees himself as having the right and the duty to make pronouncements. The real life situation is by no means so amenable to such a clear distinction. Church leaders and the Church as a community have to assess concrete situations in the light of Christian experience and the principles which distil and express the wisdom of the past and the present. The distinction between 'technical' matters and moral issues, in so far as it exists, is itself an end-product of such assessment rather than a ready-made self-evident framework whose application is obvious and almost automatic. Furthermore, the dividing line between the two is a shifting one, since moral issues can open up in matters which had seemed to be purely 'technical'. Because of this complexity, Church authorities must recognise that it may be necessary to live with a good deal of uncertainty; at times the most they can do is commit themselves to searching for the best way forward.

Desire for Certainty

At the time of *Quadragesimo Anno*, and for thirty years afterwards, it was not easy for the Catholic community or its leaders to experience themselves as uncertain and searching on important social issues. There was considerable pressure on Church authorities to present themselves as 'having the answers'. A lot of this pressure came from the believing community who looked to the leadership for clear and authoritative teaching on all issues that had a moral dimension (QA 7, 8, 41, 117, 122). There were two good reasons why the pope should offer such authoritative teaching. Firstly, it gave the Catholic Church as a whole a clear sense that it had a message for the non-Catholic world. Secondly, it provided the Catholic laity and clergy with the assurance that they had a teaching authority to guide them. It is understandable then that many clergy and laity—and even the Vatican itself—came to speak about *Quadragesimo Anno* as though it had provided a definitive answer to 'the social question'.

If the encyclical is seen as 'the answer' or 'the solution' to the social problem it is a very short step to interpreting this to mean that it offers its readers 'the correct system'. The unanswered questions, the deliberate vagueness, and the slightly different emphases in different places are then no longer seen as indications of search and some uncertainty. No, the truth must be there. It has only to be brought forth by means of a careful exegesis of the text. Controversy then springs up on certain key issues—above all on the question of whether corporatism is being proposed as the Catholic solution (see, for instance, Nell-Breuning [1936] 21–32, 256). The controversy tends to centre not so much on the arguments for or against corporatism as on the proper interpretation of the text of the encyclical; for the text is presumed to contain the truth. In this way the prevailing theology and spirituality of authority and of the role of the Church led to a playing down of the fact that the pope did not commit himself on some important socio-economic issues.[12] The effect is that this reserve, which is an important feature of the encyclical, is not appreciated for what it is; instead it becomes the occasion for a rather fruitless exegetical controversy.

Why was Pius XI so Radical?

Quadragesimo Anno has been understood by some to be proposing an alternative socio-economic system, a replacement for the capitalist system. But in the light of what has just been said it seems more accurate to see the encyclical as laying down some fundamental principles of social morality, using these as a basis for evaluation, and concluding that they rule out the acceptance of socialism in any form, and of capitalism both in its basic ideological principle and in its actual historical development. If this account is true (and *a fortiori* if the encyclical is really proposing a specific socio-economic system, as some have assumed) then Pius XI is reacting against Western capitalism in a much more radical way than his predecessor (cf. O'Brien 19). Why was he less inhibited than Leo was forty years earlier, in calling for an abandonment of the system on which modern Europe and America had been built? Three factors may be mentioned as likely to have encouraged Pius XI to go much further than his predecessor:

— The economic collapse and 'the Great Depression' of the time had raised questions about the viability of an economic system which, whatever its moral weaknesses, had, until 1929, at least appeared to be extraordinarily successful in giving rise to 'progress' and a fair measure of stability, as well as meeting many human needs. Now the system seemed to have broken down; and unemployment was creating a great pool of disillusioned and alienated people, eagerly searching for some alternative to the system that had let them down.[13]

— Since the time of Leo XIII the inevitable and 'natural' consequences of the capitalist system had had the opportunity to emerge and develop further. Particularly significant was the fact noted earlier that the system had to a considerable extent ceased to be what it claimed to be, namely, one of free enterprise. Instead of giving most people a chance to become entrepreneurs, the system actually concentrated wealth and power in the hands of a privileged few (QA 105–9).

— The liberal capitalist system no longer seemed to be the only effective alternative to communism or socialism. Portugal and Italy were offering an approach that seemed as if it might be both more acceptable morally and also more successful. The corporatist-fascist model had one great advantage at this time: it still had the sparkle of newness. The problems intrinsic to it had not yet had time to develop fully. The difficulties the new system was encountering could plausibly be considered as 'teething troubles' which would soon be overcome.

Taken together these three factors constituted a powerful argument for envisaging radical change in the structures of society. For over a hundred years the popes had all experienced an overriding concern for political and social stability; the alternative had seemed to be some form of anarchy. But now the situation had changed in two respects. On the one hand there was no guarantee that the capitalist order as it had developed could in fact ensure social and political stability. On the other hand it seemed possible that there was an alternative socio-economic model which could ensure such stability, and could at the same time be more equitable. An added bonus was that there was at least some measure of resemblance between the corporatist model now being proposed and the ancient guild system so admired by both Leo and Pius XI (QA 78, 97; RN 2). And there was a much closer similarity between the new fascist-corporatist model of society and the version of corporatism that had been advocated for over fifty years by many Catholic social reformers. This lent some respectability to the new system and perhaps helped to offset the doubts that must have arisen as a result of the political philosophy and behaviour of the fascists. The effect of all this was that it could no longer be presumed that the Catholic Church would, in the last analysis, provide support for the *status quo* rather than take the risk of being an agent of major socio-political change.

Authority and Subversion

Although one can make a distinction between economics and politics, the two are closely interrelated. To seek to change the economic structures of society is itself a political action. So the question arises whether or to what extent Pius XI had thought through the political implications of his call for new socio-economic structures. How far was he prepared to go in supporting political activity designed to replace existing institutions? The question is not an abstract one. For it was during the pontificate of Pius XI that right-wing fascist movements overthrew the existing governments and came to power in a number of European countries; and in many other countries there were strong fascist movements struggling to seize power.

In the area of political philosophy Pius XI put forward nothing at all comparable to the comprehensive socio-economic principles which he had proposed in *Quadragesimo Anno*. It must be assumed that, in general, he adhered to the position worked out by Leo XIII. There is, however, one significant difference between Leo and Pius; it has to do with the matter of obedience to civil authority. The first thing to note is that, for the reasons just outlined, the question of accepting the *status quo* presented itself in a different light to Pius XI than to his predecessor. Leo's attitude was that existing regimes had to be supported even when their rulers' behaviour and policies were very unsatisfactory. The reason was that opposition to them meant lending support to the forces of communism and anarchy. Pius had an equal or even greater horror of communism (QA 112). But in the atmosphere of his time it was clear that communism was not the only alternative—or even the most likely one—to the political-economic structures that had developed in Western countries. This left him greater freedom in working out a theory about the boundary between subversion and legitimate opposition to injustice.

This issue scarcely arises in *Quadragesimo Anno*. But in three major encyclicals issued in March 1937 Pius XI confronted the question of obedience to civil authorities. In the first, *Mit brennender Sorge*, he made an outspoken attack on the Nazi regime in Germany. He repeated the Church's traditional teaching that the moral authority of the State has to be anchored in the authority of God (*Mit brennender Sorge*, 33). He protested strongly against the situation where young people and their parents were being called by the State to disobey God (*Mit brennender Sorge*, 41–2, 47). But the pope said nothing that could in any way be taken as an incitement to subversion. This is not too surprising, in view of the total dominance of the Nazis in Germany at that time, and the fact that the Church was already being severely harassed if not persecuted.

The second of the three encyclicals, *Divini Redemptoris*, is dated five days later than the first. This time the object of condemnation is communism. Here the pope repeats the traditional Catholic teaching that the human person has 'divinely-imposed obligations towards civil society' and civil authorities have the right to impose these duties (DR 30). He then goes on to insist that it is an 'unjust usurpation' for communism to seek to enforce its own programme instead of the divine law (DR 33). But he does not really address himself to the dilemma of allegiance faced by those who have to live under a communist government; for the pope's main concern was not with such people but with the threat of communism to the Western world.

The issue of allegiance was, however, taken up by Pius XI just nine days later in the third of these encyclicals. This was entitled *Firmissimum* and it dealt with the situation of Catholics in Mexico. Towards the end of it there are a few paragraphs where the pope bluntly faces the question of active resistance to the civil authorities. The central teaching runs as follows:

> . . . the Church . . . condemns every unjust rebellion or act of violence against the properly constituted civil power. On the other hand, . . . if the case arose where the civil power should so trample on justice and truth as to destroy even the very foundations of authority, there would appear no reason to condemn citizens for uniting to defend the nation and themselves by lawful and appropriate means against those who make use of the power of the State to drag the nation to ruin (*Firmissimum* 35).[14]

When Pius XI uses the phrase 'by lawful and appropriate means' (*'licita atque idonea auxilia'*) the context makes it clear that he is not leaving it to the oppressive regime itself to define what is 'lawful' or 'unlawful'.

This is indeed a notable departure from what had been taught by Leo XIII, Pius X, Benedict XV and by Pius XI himself up to that time. A departure, but not necessarily a total contradiction in teaching. It can be argued with some credibility that Pius XI believed he was dealing with a situation that had special features which made it morally different from the kind of situation faced by his predecessors; consequently he invoked aspects of traditional teaching which had not been mentioned by them simply because they were not relevant in the situations they confronted. If this argument is valid then it safeguards 'doctrinal' consistency between the teaching of Pius XI and that of Leo XIII. Such consistency has always been a high priority in the social teaching of the popes. It must be said, however, that in this case the consistency is, at best, somewhat strained. But whatever importance we give to coherence in the theory, there is another sense in which the statement of Pius XI represents a sharp break with the past. Its effect is to put 'on the agenda' of Catholics seeking social reform a question which Leo XIII and his successors had deliberately closed off. That question is whether a particular regime is so utterly unjust that the obligation of allegiance may be superseded by a more primordial obligation. Could it be legitimate to rebel? Could it even be a duty to do so, in order to replace an incorrigibly corrupt or unjust regime with one that would promote justice and the common good?

It might, perhaps, be claimed that the situation in Mexico at that time was morally unique and that therefore the pope's remarks in *Firmissimum* do not establish any precedent which could be invoked in other situations. But the way in which the pope's teaching is given rules out such an interpretation. Pius XI says, 'it is . . . Our duty to remind you of some general principles which must always be kept in mind'(*Firmissimum* 36); and twice he mentions that the way a person ought to act depends on circumstances (*Firmissimum* 34, 36). This indicates that he was judging the Mexican situation in the light of universal norms. In one sense every situation is unique and unrepeatable. But the implication of what the pope was saying is that morally similar situations could occur elsewhere; and, if so, the same judgments should be made.

It must at once be added, however, that the Mexican situation, though not in principle morally unique, had certain features that made it highly unusual. These help one to see why the question of withdrawing allegiance from the existing government was considered by the pope in the case of Mexico rather than in the case of Russia or of Germany. The first, and probably the most important, of these distinctive features was the fact that there was already a good deal of organised resistance to the government within Mexico.[15] This meant that it was relevant to take account of the traditional theology which laid down 'reasonable hope of success' as one of the criteria for a just war or rebellion. Furthermore, the resistance in Mexico was a source of instability and might even bring about the overthrow of the government. So it would make sense to suggest that there might be a proportion between the existing evil and the proposed remedy; this is another of the traditional criteria to be used in an evaluation of this kind. In other words, the rightness of resistance to the regime would be judged not merely in terms of the extent of its injustices (a purely moral criterion) but also in terms of another criterion which is pragmatic at an immediate level but turns out to be moral as well, because morality has to be judged also in terms of what is likely to happen in practice. This pragmatic criterion is the extent to which resistance to the existing regime is likely to lead to a more stable and effective public order.

Another feature that was significant in the Mexican situation was the fact that its population was largely Catholic and it was seen as in some sense 'a Catholic country', which made it different from Germany and Russia. In medieval times the papacy claimed the right to declare that a people no longer owed allegiance to their ruler; and this right was widely acknowledged. Because Mexico was 'a Catholic country' a statement by the pope about allegiance had to be taken seriously; there could be a *de facto* approximation to the *de jure* situation of medieval times. At least the regime could not afford to assume that any such statement would have no practical effect on their ability to retain power. In these circumstances the statement by Pius

XI could be seen as a warning to the Mexican government. The pope was not saying openly that the people no longer owed allegiance to the government; but that might be implied; and, furthermore, it might be implied that the pope was threatening to make an even more explicit statement unless the harassment of the Church was moderated. If this interpretation is taken, one can see how the pope could regard his statement as being not primarily an incitement to rebellion but rather a warning issued in an effort to promote peace and stability.

In conjunction with the previous two points, one must recall that the pope was dealing here with a left-wing regime—a regime which Pius XI explicitly linked to the communism of Russia (DR 19). The Vatican at this time was still inclined to assume that communism was inimical to all genuine civil authority (e.g. DR 21). This means that the pope would look at a left-wing regime such as Mexico's in quite a different light to the way he would consider a right-wing government. The latter might be seen as unsatisfactory in many respects, but the pope would see it as having a *prima facie* right to exercise legitimate authority. In the case of a regime which he considered to be 'communist' this would be more questionable, since for quite a long time there had been a tendency in Church circles to equate communism with anarchy. So it is unlikely that Pius would have made such a strong statement on the question of resistance if he had been dealing with a right-wing regime.

The unusual bluntness of this part of *Firmissimum* may be largely explained by the combination of the various factors mentioned. One might add that Pius XI was himself a rather forceful character, and never more so than at this particular time. *Firmissimum* was the third of three major encyclicals all on burning political questions and all issued in the space of a fortnight; one might be forgiven for thinking that there was a feeling in the Vatican (or at least in the pope) that it was 'time for a showdown'! But whatever the historical explanation, the fact remains that the pope's statement gave the tradition of papal teaching a quite distinct swing away from what it had been (cf. Coste 200–1). Since the time of Leo XIII (and before) the effect of papal teaching had been to give a notable measure of canonisation to the *status quo*, despite the protests of popes about injustices. That had now changed at least in this one instance. And what is perhaps most significant is that the change was a return to an older tradition, where the possibility of a legitimate rebellion was considered. So the statement of Pius XI cannot easily be dismissed as a temporary aberration.

Almost six years intervened between *Quadragesimo Anno* and *Firmissimum*. But there is a link between the two. The first represents a major challenge to the existing socio-economic order; but it gives little guidance on the political question of how these changes could be brought about. The later encyclical opens up the possibility of disobedience and resistance to civil authorities and even a justified rebellion in certain exceptional circumstances. It would be contrived and historically inaccurate to suggest that the pope intended *Firmissimum* to 'give teeth' to his earlier encyclical. But the radicality of his views on the political issue is of a piece with that of his position on the socio-economic question. In this sense, at least, each of the two encyclicals supports and complements the other.

Conclusion

The experience of the years since the pontificate of Pius XI suggests that it would be unwise of Church leaders today to identify themselves very closely with the views he espoused on socio-economic and political issues. In both of these areas he showed a sympathy for right-wing thinking that went significantly beyond traditional conservatism. This approach is quite out of tune with the main thrust of more recent Catholic social teaching. But if we go behind these historically conditioned opinions we reach a more fundamental level where Pope Pius XI has a lot to offer. In the encyclical *Quadragesimo Anno* he took a 'prophetic' stand on economic questions. In the encyclical *Firmissimum* he took an equally 'prophetic' stand on a political issue. By doing so he showed very clearly that the official Church does not always have to play a conservative role in society. Concern for stability is important; but stability is not the only social value, or even the highest. Justice ranks higher. There may be times when the value of justice calls the Christian community and its leaders to take a risky stand on political, social and economic issues. They may feel called to challenge the basic economic and political structures which are widely assumed to be necessary for the survival of our society—and even for the world as we know it. In taking such a radical stance they may be encouraged by the example of Pope Pius XI, who, while staying within the tradition of Catholic social teaching, nevertheless gave that tradition a distinctly 'prophetic' emphasis.

SUMMARY

In 1931, forty years after the first social encyclical, Pius XI issued *Quadragesimo Anno*. Among its contributions to Catholic social teaching were its use of the term 'social justice' and its articulation of the principle of subsidiarity. This encyclical challenged the capitalist model of society much more strongly and more specifically than Leo's encyclical had done. Though he spoke out against the existing type of capitalism, the pope wanted to retain a good deal of free enterprise. He favoured a corporatist-vocational model of society.

This encyclical convinced many Catholics that the Church has a 'blueprint' for the ideal society and that this requires major socio-political changes in the structures of society. So it could no longer be assumed that the Church was, in the final analysis, a conservative force. The later encyclical of Pius XI, *Firmissimum*, issued in 1938, represented a break with the political theology of Leo XIII on the vital question of loyalty to an unjust regime; it suggested that, in an extreme situation, resistance and rebellion could be justified.

These encyclicals of Pius XI were issued at a time when the Vatican was leaning more to the right than to the left. But, more important than this political orientation, is the fact that they helped the Church to have a clearer understanding of the radical and prophetic role it is called to play in society.

Questions for review:

1. How had the economic situation of the world changed between the time of Leo and the time of *Quadragesimo Anno*?
2. What is the principle of subsidiarity?
3. What is meant by a vocational or corporatist ordering of society?
4. In what way did Pius XI depart from Leo's teaching about resistance to oppression?

Questions for reflection:

1. Does the Church have an ideal of how society should be organised?
2. Is the principle of subsidiarity valid today?

Issue for further study:

How has the Lateran Treaty affected the way in which the Catholic Church exists in, and relates to, the world?

5

The Contribution of Pius XII

When Pius XII became pope in 1939 he took charge of a Church that was highly centralised not merely administratively but also in the sphere of theology and spirituality. His style as pope fostered this centralisation. He produced an almost endless stream of addresses and documents in which he gave a 'teaching' on a very wide range of issues. Social, economic, and political questions were among the many topics on which he made pronouncements. But in his teaching he tended to concentrate more on political issues than on strictly economic ones. The reason for this was the situation in which he found himself—and perhaps also his own character and interests.

In the first section of this chapter I shall examine the teaching of Pius XII on the traditional issues of the social justice agenda which he had inherited from Leo XIII and Pius XI. In the second section I shall take up an issue that came to the fore only during the pontificate of Pius XII—the question of the Church's attitude to colonialism and decolonisation.

SECTION I: ANTI-COMMUNISM

The Preoccupations of Pius XII

During most of the papacy of Pius XII the world was so dominated by political issues that socio-economic questions seemed less pressing and were given less prominence. The first few years of his time as pope were overshadowed by World War II. In that war the political issues of German and Japanese nationalism were so much to the fore that underlying international economic issues tended to be overlooked. The war also had the effect of overshadowing socio-economic tensions within the various countries involved. It provided governments with a justification for an exceptionally high degree of control of economic, social, cultural, and political life. Some of this governmental control had the effect of ensuring that tensions between the richer and poorer classes found little means of expression. Freedom of speech and of organisation were severely restricted; and there was harsh treatment of anybody thought to be 'subversive'. Some of the government interventions in the economic sphere were designed to lessen the causes of social tension, by curbing exploitation—for instance by rationing the supply of scarce commodities and by controlling prices and profits. The effect of all this in the non-communist world was to bring about a notable shift from a 'free enterprise' model of society towards a bureaucratic model; and this was done in a climate that damped down social tensions. By the end of the war Western society had changed considerably. But most of the changes had happened—or appeared to have happened—as a result of extrinsic political factors rather than through a 'normal' development of the socio-economic system.

In the years following the war the dominant issue was once again political rather than overtly economic. Relations between East and West quickly deteriorated into a 'cold war'; and in Asia there was open, but localised, war. No doubt economic and social questions were very much at stake in the East-West struggle. For, after all, the differences between communism and capitalism are primarily concerned with such economic issues as who should own the means of production. But, ironically, these differences had been raised to such an ideological level and had become so politicised that the purely economic and social aspects were less obvious. The struggle between communism and capitalism was now identified with an international political conflict between East and West (D21 55–9).[1]

This situation naturally had a considerable influence on what Pius XII felt the world needed to hear from him. Peace, and the conditions for a lasting peace, were major themes for him during the years of the war (D2; D4; D5; D7; D10). Following the tradition of Benedict XV, he adopted a neutral stance and sought to be seen as a potential mediator. But as the war developed it became increasingly clear that the sympathy of the Vatican lay with the allies. To speak more accurately, one should say that the pope's sympathy lay with the Western allies. For during the war years the communist threat from Russia troubled Pius XII far more than it troubled the Western leaders.

Preference for Democracy

In his teaching, Pius XII showed a clear preference for democracy over other forms of political organisation. This is not surprising, for he could see the effects of German, Russian, and Japanese totalitarianism, as well as Italian fascism, on their own people and on their neighbours. As the war drew towards its close the pope took democracy as his theme in his Christmas message of 1944 (D10). In order to ensure consistency in papal teaching he recalled the statement of Leo XIII that the Church does not condemn any of the various forms of government (D10 par. 9). But he left little doubt that he saw democracy as the system of the future (D10 par. 41), because it is more in conformity with the dignity and liberty of the citizen (D10 par. 6). He even went so far as to say that 'a democratic form of government is considered by many today to be a natural postulate of reason itself', precisely because the modern State is so deeply involved in the lives of people (D10 par. 12)—and because people want a more effective share in shaping their lives and society (D10 par. 8).[2]

Pius XII evidently believed that one of his tasks as pope was to educate people to a deeper understanding of democracy and a greater commitment to it. It is interesting to read the series of addresses which this aristocratic pope gave over a number of years to the nobility of Rome (Savignat II, 1575–1607, paras 3308–74). In speaking to this 'elite' audience the pope interpreted the words 'nobility' and 'elite' in a way that put the emphasis on service (D17 1603), high moral ideals (D21 1605), courtesy and the ability to cross class barriers so as to have a 'compassionate solidarity' with others (D11 1586). He insisted that the nobility should not look to their high birth to give them a privileged place, but should rather give a 'tone' to the life of the area where they live, and should educate people to genuine democracy (D15 1595–6). The attitude of Pius XII towards democracy demonstrates a significant option for the common people, a real trust in them, and a commitment to the principle of participation.

This leaning of Pius towards democracy had what would now be called a geo-political dimension: it identified the pope with 'the West' in the struggle against communism as a world power. In the years immediately after the war this struggle was focused on Europe. But within a few years China, Korea, and other Asian countries came to the fore as the battleground. The United States came to see itself as the policeman of what was called 'the free world'; and the Churches tended to play the role of chaplain. It is hardly surprising therefore that Pius XII was not inclined at this time to make sweeping condemnations of the capitalist order; for it was on this foundation that 'the free world' rested.

In some respects the situation facing Pius XII was more like that which faced Leo XIII than the situation at the time of *Quadragesimo Anno*. There appeared to be only one realistic alternative to capitalism. That was communism—and the pope (like many other Church leaders) saw this as the ultimate abomination in the political order. He even had doubts about whether a communist state would have the fundamental right to command the allegiance of its citizens.[3] The 'third way', represented by fascist-inspired corporatism, had been greatly discredited by World War II (cf. Camp 40). It is true that Spain and Portugal still retained something of this approach. But it no longer seemed a very realistic or attractive option for 'the West' as a whole. On the other hand the capitalist system had survived the economic crisis of the 1930s—though it had done so only by following the policies of Keynes and allowing a good deal of tampering by the State with the market economy. The war itself gave an important boost to the capitalist system—and proved that the system could flourish in much closer partnership with a bureaucratic State than had been envisaged in its earlier ideology. After the war, a crucial part of the Marshall Plan was massive American investment in Europe; this contributed to a quick recovery of capitalism in Europe (and considerable inroads by American companies into the European market). Within a few years of the ending of the war Japan became the new showpiece for the 'free enterprise' system.

The result of all this was that capitalism could again present itself as the system that works, that brings progress. In its new guise it could even claim to have gone most of the way towards solving the traditional 'social problem', namely, the poverty of the working class. This apparent success seemed so obvious that by 1952 Pius XII was inclined to accept that, essentially, the problem had been solved, at least in Western society (D24 791–2;[4] cf. D27 20). Equally and perhaps more important than the effects of the 'free enterprise' system in the social field was the fact that it was seen as the economic face of political democracy; that was what made it particularly difficult for the pope to challenge it in any radical way.

From Corporatism to Capitalism?

One scholar claims that Pius XII changed his emphasis between the mid-nineteen forties and 1950: in the earlier stage he was still issuing 'diatribes against capitalist abuses' while later he came to have 'a growing appreciation of the contribution which capitalism made to general welfare' (Camp 104). This contrast is rather over-stated. It would perhaps be more accurate to say that from the beginning of his pontificate the pope realised that the social situation had changed greatly since his predecessor wrote Quadragesimo Anno. During the war he saw that the future had become unpredictable (D3 198). After the war he felt obliged to give support to 'the West' in the struggle against communism. At no time did he condone capitalist abuses; in fact he spoke out at various times against the subordination of the common good to private greed (e.g. D9 252–3; D16 435–6; D5 16–7). But his tone is rather closer to that of Leo XIII than to that of Pius XI. It is significant that he refers far more frequently to Rerum Novarum than to Quadragesimo Anno. The radio message in which he commemorated the fiftieth anniversary of Leo's encyclical paid surprisingly little attention to Quadragesimo Anno, which of course had its tenth anniversary at the same time (D3).

Like his predecessors, Pius XII was opposed to the underlying philosophy of the capitalist system. He found it unduly individualistic. Though he favoured free enterprise, he did not want personal advancement to be the chief motive for people's actions. He envisaged an organically united society where the service of the common good would be the basic motivation of all the different groupings of which it would be composed (D5 11; D18

1774). For him, as for previous popes, the way to minimise class tensions was to promote the organic unity of society. In outlining how this unity was to be achieved, Pius XII invoked in a rather vague and general way the principles laid down in *Quadragesimo Anno*. The State, he held, requires structures of cooperation (D24 792).[5] But these should not normally be structures of the State itself (D26 1748). Rather, the State should preside over the cooperation and ensure that it takes place, while remaining aloof except where State involvement is obviously needed. It should be particularly careful not to take on a major degree of involvement in the economic sphere, since that is not its field.

When we come to the question of how these general principles are to be put into effect in the concrete, Pius XII was notably less specific than Pius XI. He was perhaps more aware that there is no easy formula which would be the practical solution to the social problem. For instance, he accepts that the mere existence of intermediate organisations is not in itself a solution—for there is no guarantee that these will in fact cooperate unselfishly for the common good (D26 1748).

In one interesting and significant passage of an address given in 1949 he refers explicitly to the professional organisations so favoured by Pius XI. He says they offered a 'concrete and opportune formula'. He defends this formula against the accusation that it was a surrender to fascism—and also against the suggestion that what Pius XI proposed meant a return to medievalism. But then Pius XII goes on to say that this section of *Quadragesimo Anno* must now be seen as an instance of *an opportunity missed*, because it was not seized on at the opportune time (D19 284). This is a good example of how Pius XII preserved a 'doctrinal' consistency with his immediate predecessor while at the same time changing the emphasis and the practical implications to a significant extent. It is clear that, by the time he made this statement in 1949, Pius XII felt that it would be unrealistic and perhaps even counter-productive for the Church to commit itself unreservedly to working for the acceptance of a corporative-type State in most Western countries. For the foreseeable future the most realistic approach for the Church seemed to be to rest content with a tempered version of capitalist society, while working for a further tempering of its more obnoxious features.

Concern for Personal Freedom

Having referred to the 'missed opportunity' to implement the kind of society Pius XI would have wished, Pius XII goes on to address himself to the possibilities and dangers of the current situation. At present, he says, there is an attempt to work towards a very different kind of society: the preference is for nationalisation. So the pope clarifies the Church's attitude to this issue of the nationalisation of the means of production. He recalls the teaching of *Quadragesimo Anno* that some degree of this may be acceptable. But he maintains that the economy is not of its nature an institution of the State; the role of the public authorities is not to replace private rights and initiative but rather to serve them (D19 285). It soon becomes clear that the chief concern of the pope at this stage was not so much the dangers of capitalism but rather the threat of the erosion of free enterprise through excessive nationalisation.

This resistance to nationalisation is an indication of the basic social value that Pius XII felt called to defend, especially in the post-war period. Unlike his predecessor he was not campaigning eagerly for the replacement of the capitalist order by some alternative system. For he believed that the problem was not chiefly the iniquity of one 'system' rather than another. Rather it was that all the massive systems of the modern world tend to swallow up the individual person. The pope wanted to defend individual freedom, rights and responsibilities against any such 'system'. So he rejected the great systems of the right as well as those of the left, believing that both leave the individual at the mercy of the State (D5 5–24). This rejection of systems was not confined to communism and fascism. For he held that slavery of the person could result from the tyranny of private capital as well as from the power of the State (D5 17;[6] cf. D8 252–3). Similarly, he was concerned that the power of trade unions would increase to a point where the freedom of the individual worker would almost be lost (D20 487).

It is interesting to note that Pius XII saw a particular danger arising as a result of war and 'cold war' between East and West. He noted that this kind of situation leads to restrictions of the freedom of the person 'in what is called the free world' (D25 42). Clearly the pope was aware of the dangers of what is now called 'the National Security State' and the ideology on which it is based. Fear of enemies abroad and of 'subversives' within the State creates an atmosphere of suspicion. This gives rise to serious intrusions into the lives of citizens and curtailment or infringement of human rights.

Distribution of Goods

From what has been said so far it is clear that Pius XII was much more concerned about socio-political matters than about strictly economic ones. However, as one might have expected from a pope who gave addresses on such a very wide range of topics, he did have some important things to say on economic questions as well. He did not issue any document or make any statement which as an *intervention* had the same kind of impact as the two great social encyclicals of his predecessors. But he made a most significant contribution to the body of social teaching or '*doctrine*' of the Catholic Church. This contribution has to do mainly with the question of the owner-ship and distribution of property. It came quite early in his pontificate, in the broadcast (D3) he made to commemorate the fiftieth anniversary of *Rerum Novarum*.

At this point we need to advert only briefly to two important points in this address. The first is that economic prosperity is not to be measured purely in material or quantitative terms. Other factors may be more important. For instance, if people are living all the time in uncertainty, the here-and-now possession of goods is not sufficient; so there is need for a certain stability in society (D3 200).[7] Furthermore, and perhaps even more significantly, he insists that there must be an equitable distribution of whatever goods are available. For, no matter how much wealth there may be in a given area, the country cannot be said to be economically prosperous if its people do not have the opportunity to share equitably in its wealth; and, on the other hand, the economy is healthy if there is a just distribution of the available goods, even if there is less to share (D3 200–1). In defining economic prosperity in this way Pius XII was well ahead of the economists and planners of his time. Right into the 1960s it was widely held that the best way for a country to become economically prosperous and 'developed' as quickly as possible was to subordinate equitable distribution to rapid growth of the gross national product. Indeed this view still prevails among many politicians and decision-makers. The 'national cake' is to be enlarged first; later on will be the time to consider a more fair distribution. In recent years this assumption is coming to be questioned fairly widely. The more enlightened economists are adopting a view similar to that outlined in 1941 by Pius XII.

The second major contribution of Pius XII to the socio-economic teaching of the Church concerns private property. Like his predecessors he insisted on the right and value of private ownership. But, in contrast to Leo XIII, he did not hesitate to give the first priority to the general right of all people to the use of the goods of the earth. The right of the individual to a particular item of private property does not negate the more general and fundamental right; rather it is to be a means of actualising the right of all to the use of material goods (D3 198–9).[8] This way of treating the question of private property represents an important development in Catholic social teaching because it is clearer and more explicit than the treatment of private property in *Rerum Novarum* and *Quadragesimo Anno* (RN 19; QA 45–6).

The acceptance of the idea that the right to private ownership is subordinate to the more general right of all to the goods of the Earth provides a solid basis for the social teaching of subsequent popes. It was only many years later that the full importance of the statement of Pius XII could be seen. For his teaching came at the height of a world war when few had time for, or interest in, such matters. So, at the time, this contribution of Pius XII was not very important as an intervention by the pope in an immediate and pressing social problem. Rather its importance lies in the way in which it contributed to the development of the corpus of social teaching. It was left to later popes to draw out the practical implications. The way in which they applied this principle attracted the attention of the world. They played down the sacrosanctness of the right to private property, qualifying it by an insistence on the right of all people to have an equitable share in the goods of the earth. In doing so their position was strengthened by the fact that they could refer back to the teaching of Pius XII.

Conclusion

The most notable feature of the approach of Pius XII to socio-economic issues was his 'realism', that is, his practical accept-ance, especially in the second half of his pontificate, of a capitalistic society. He did not repudiate the call of Pius XI for major restructuring of the social order along lines that would be at least vaguely corporative. But, during the years that Pius XII was pope, this ideal does not seem to have ever appeared to him to be very feasible in practice. So the ideal came to have what one might call an 'eschatological' character—something that was to come about in an indefinite future (D19 284). Indeed Pius XII on one occasion sharply rejected the idea of implementing one of his predecessor's proposals (namely, a degree of co-management) on the grounds that this was one element in an integral scheme and was therefore not to be separated from the whole (D23 1670; cf. D20 487). This means in effect that while giving ritual approval to the proposal for radical reform of existing structures, he was in practice resisting an important step towards a piecemeal implementation of such restructuring.

It would appear that the practical ideal of Pius XII would have been a non-bureaucratic free enterprise economy, with non-centralised agencies to facilitate cooperation between various sectors of the economy. The State would play an unobtrusive 'watchdog' role to ensure that the common good would be served. The pope believed that this ideal was threatened in Western countries not only by overgrown unbridled capitalism but more particularly by socialistic tendencies—especially by nationalisation of the means of production and the introduction of 'the welfare state'. He could only protest and appeal against these tendencies since he was not inclined to encourage any radical political movement which would offer an alternative to the existing capitalist society of the West.

The pope believed in the possibility of gradual and peaceful improvement of the existing system. He held that justice can be promoted not through revolution but through a harmonious evolution (D6 175). In fact he considered that changes of this kind had already taken place, so that capitalism was no longer applied in its full rigour. He believed that the Western economic system had gone a long way towards overcoming poverty. In practice, then, it offered the best hope for the future—not an ideal 'best' but the best available at the time. Consequently, his stance represents a practical option of support for a capitalist order, with the qualification that he disapproved of certain aspects of it. In the socio-economic area, therefore, he effectively (though not 'doctrinally') retreated from the call of Pius XI for a fundamental restructuring of society and even from Leo XIII's outraged protest against the capitalist system.

There is a danger that one might stop at this point and conclude that if 'an option for the poor' meant anything to Pius XII it was largely confined to charitable works rather than the transformation of society. But that would be to overlook the fact that 'the poor' is a term that should be applied not merely to those who have little wealth but also to those who find themselves *powerless*. In other words, there is a political as well as a socio-economic connotation to the word; and this is very relevant when we are considering the views of Pius XII. One of his greatest concerns about modern society was that more and more people were being left practically powerless in the face of massive systems of one kind or another. The kind of deep concern that was aroused in Leo XIII by the plight of the mass of the industrial workers crushed by economic poverty was awakened in Pius XII by the thought of masses of ordinary people deprived of the possibility of taking personal responsibility for many aspects of their daily lives. He spoke out strongly and repeatedly about this powerlessness, just as Leo had spoken out about economic poverty. In this sense he was on the side of the 'poor'. But, again like Leo, he could do little more than protest. He saw what was wrong; and he proposed an ideal in which people would have all the freedoms of a genuine democracy, unencumbered by bureaucracy. But he did not focus attention on any really practical and effective steps that could be taken towards the overcoming of powerlessness and the achievement of real participation and freedom. Had he done so his words would inevitably have been taken by many as a challenge to Western-style democracy—and possibly as an encouragement to its enemies. That was a risk that Pius XII felt he could not afford to take.

SECTION II

FROM COLONIALISM TO INTERNATIONAL DEVELOPMENT

In the years after World War II two major struggles were played out on the world stage: the struggle between East and West and the struggle against colonialism by the peoples of what came to be called the Third World. In the previous section of this chapter I have looked at how the first of these struggles affected the social teaching of Pius XII. In this section I move on to the second issue.

As I noted in an earlier chapter, the moral issue of colonialism was not a topic that had any prominence on the social justice agenda of the Catholic Church in the early part of the twentieth century. Church leaders and theologians in Europe did not seem to realise that the liberation struggles of the colonised peoples would soon come to the centre of the world's stage. The process of decolonisation speeded up enormously in the wake of World War II. Nevertheless, in the late 1940s and the 1950s—and even into the 1960s—the Catholic Church still seemed quite unprepared to address such issues as the morality of a war of liberation; indeed it even seemed *uninterested* in such questions. Pius XII, who gave addresses on almost every conceivable political topic, had very little to say on this issue— though it had become a burning question for millions of Catholics all over the world. It is only within the past generation that the Catholic Church has begun to develop an adequate social teaching on the relationship between the powerful nations of the industrialised world and the weak and poor nations. Despite the fact that he devoted so little attention to this question, Pius XII provided a certain foundation for the teaching of his successors. So I shall look at what he has to say on this topic.

The end of the Colonial Era

Shortly after the end of World War II it became obvious to very many people that the colonial era was indeed drawing to a close. But powerful groups in the European colonial countries refused to acknowledge this change. Their intransigence led to a series of bitter liberation struggles in many parts of the world. In the twenty years between 1945 and 1965 the people of dozens of former colonies in Africa, Asia, the Pacific and the Caribbean gained independence. Pius XII soon recognised that the process of decolonisation was irreversible. Nevertheless, he was quite circumspect about giving support to those engaged in the struggle for independence. This was partly because of his fear that communist governments would come to power in the newly independent nations. In 1945 he made a statement supporting the right of nations great and small to take their destiny into their own hands (D13). The obvious reference was to the European nations but the principle could be taken to apply also to the colonies (cf. Alix 30–1). But at that time the pope preferred not to be too specific. So long as the struggles for liberation in the colonies were still going on he did not openly throw the support of the Church behind them. But as soon as any particular war of liberation was successfully completed, the Vatican was quick to recognise the newly independent nation and to seek an exchange of diplomatic representatives with it.

By the mid-1950s Pius XII was becoming much more explicit: he began to emphasise the right of colonised peoples to their independence (D27 and D29). It is significant that in his statements on this issue he made little reference to the need to respect the established authorities. This may be an indication that the pope considered the 'transitory' authority of the colonial nations had come to an end and they were no longer exercising legitimate power (cf. Alix 37). It may be also that the pope had in mind the teaching of his predecessor Pius XI in 1937 that under certain circumstances rebellion could be justified (see Chapter 4 above). These theological niceties fitted comfortably into the highly pragmatic Vatican policy of the time—a policy which allowed the Church to follow events rather than seeking to lead them by a prophetic challenge to the injustice of colonialism (cf. Alix 38).

Looking back, we may be inclined to think that such a pragmatic approach was entirely opportunistic and compromising. But in fact it was quite compatible with the self-understanding which the Church during this period had of its own nature and role in society. Having laid down general principles about the right of people to self-determination, the pope might in good faith decide that it was not for him to make the political judgment about whether or not the various conditions had been fulfilled in any particular case.

In 1957 Pius XII issued an encyclical, entitled *Fidei Donum*, on the mission of the Church in Africa. One passage reads as follows:

> The Church, which has seen so many nations born and grow up during the past centuries, cannot but give particular heed today to the accession of new peoples to the responsibilities of political freedom. (D31, Hickey 110)

Here we find the pope placing the Church in the position of a wise, experienced and somewhat distanced observer of the international political order. From this high ground he went on at once to warn the colonial powers not to deny 'a just and progressive political freedom' to the peoples who seek it. At the same time he warned those who were seeking independence: they must avoid the dangers of blind nationalism and atheistic materialism.

In this encyclical Pius XII took a highly favourable view of the good effects of the colonial occupation. He suggested that those who were struggling for freedom ought 'to credit Europe with their progress, for without its influence in all fields, they could have been led by a blind nationalism to hurl themselves into chaos and slavery'. He went on to call for a collaboration which would extend to the people of the newly emergent nations 'the true values of Christian civilisation, which have already borne so many good fruits in other continents' (Hickey 111— translation slightly emended).

This sanguine view of the effects of colonialism was, needless to say, shared and propagated by the colonial powers. What is rather more surprising is the extent to which it was more or less accepted by many of the 'elite' in the former colonies themselves. One reason for this was the extent to which the Westernised education system in the colonies had succeeded in undermining the traditional culture and values of the new leaders of these nations. Another reason was the fact that the struggle for independence was focused almost entirely on *political* freedom, with far too little attention paid to *economic* matters.

There was a widespread assumption that once the young nations attained political independence they would become masters of their own economic destiny and could therefore expect before long to 'catch up with' the industrialised countries. This assumption proved disastrously wrong, because it failed to take account of the extent to which the wealthy nations controlled both the world market and the distribution of capital and other resources such as technological 'know-how'.

From the mid-nineteenth to the mid-twentieth century most Western-educated people took it for granted that the countries of the West were more richly endowed by nature (or Providence) than other countries. This view was shared by Pius XII (e.g. D28 and D32). The assumption is, of course, quite unwarranted. The disparity in wealth between, say, Holland and its former colony Indonesia is clearly not due to the bounty of nature but to the history of European colonial and post-colonial history. It is not too much to say that the myth that the West was more blessed by Nature served as a cover-up for the real story of European imperial expansion and exploitation.

It is interesting to note that in the 1940s and 1950s the assumption that the West was better endowed by Nature gradually gave way to another assumption, namely, that the West is more 'advanced' or 'developed' than other parts of the world. This too is based on a myth—the myth that there is just one single path or 'ladder' of development open to all nations and that some are further up the ladder than others. Like the myth that the wealthy nations owe their prosperity to the bounty of Nature, the myth of development served the interests of the West. It led people to assume that because Western countries are wealthy and technologically advanced they are also more civilised. And it gave the impression to the people of the newly emergent nations that they could travel along the Western path to prosperity through 'development'— and could even catch up with the Western countries.

The modern notion of 'development' began to come to the fore in the 1940s. As early as 1941 Pius XII spoke of the right of small states to economic development (D3 16–17); and in 1955 he suggested that one reason for the gap between rich and poor nations was due to the fact that the former had reached a more advanced stage of civilisation and development (D28).

However, this question of 'development' remained rather peripheral for Pius XII; it was only in the time of later popes that it became a central issue. I shall take it up again in later chapters.

SUMMARY

The position of Pius XII was much less radical than that of his predecessor. In his concern about the dangers of communism, Pius XII took a strong stand on the side of Western democracy. During his pontificate the Catholic Church gave strong religious and ideological support to those who opposed communism and socialism at the international, national, and local levels. Pius XII apparently considered that it was no longer realistic to work for a corporatist model of society. He gave tacit support to the capitalist economic model that went hand in hand with the Western political system. He held that the worst excesses of capitalism had already been curbed in the Western world; and he believed that further gradual reforms were possible. While expressing misgivings about certain aspects of the 'free enterprise' approach, he apparently felt that it was the best available option in his time; he saw it as more effective in overcoming poverty and safeguarding human freedom and dignity than the likely alternatives.

His chief concern about the new developments in society related not so much to economic poverty as to the *powerlessness* that arises when people are subjected to bureaucratic structures of any kind. From a 'doctrinal' point of view the main contribution of Pius XII to social teaching was his insistence that the right of private property is subordinate to the general right of all people to the goods of the earth.

Many former colonies gained political independence during the pontificate of Pius XII. He recognised the right of colonised peoples to become independent and to become 'developed'. He tacitly assumed that the Western nations were more 'advanced'. He gave little encouragement to those who were struggling for liberation. But as soon as the struggle was won in any given area he was keen to establish diplomatic relations with the newly independent State.

Questions for review:

1. Why was Pius XII more favourable towards democracy than previous popes?
2. What was the main difference between the social teaching of Pius XI and that of Pius XII?
3. What was the teaching of Pius XII about private property?
4. What was the attitude of Pius XII towards the struggle for freedom in the colonies?

Questions for reflection:

1 Is the Church's commitment to democracy a fundamental part of its social teaching?
2. Why did Catholic social teaching at this time fail to address effectively the issues of the struggle for liberation in the colonies?

Issue for further study:

What was the relationship between Church and State during this period in your own country? Did the Church favour one sector of society?

6

Pope John XXIII—A New Direction?

I t is generally agreed that Pope John made a major contribution to the social teaching of the Catholic Church. My main purpose in this chapter is to identify this contribution and to see how significant it was. There are two sections in the chapter. In the first, I hope to show that in one sense his position was by no means a radical one, nor did it represent any major departure from the direction set by earlier popes, especially by Pius XII. In the second section I shall suggest that, in another sense (and despite what has just been said) Pope John had a major role to play in giving the Catholic Church an entirely new direction in social policy.

SECTION I

A SUPPORTER OF THE *STATUS QUO*?

There was an extraordinary freshness about Pope John XXIII, both in his manner and in his two major encyclicals on social issues—*Mater et Magistra* and *Pacem in Terris*.[1] Those who like to categorise everybody as either a liberal or a conservative have little difficulty in seeing 'good Pope John' as a liberal, in sharp contrast to his predecessor. This is of course an oversimplification but as a journalistic generalisation it contains a good deal of truth, especially in so far as it refers to the *style* of the pope. In his *teaching*, on the other hand, there is much more continuity with Pius XII. The trouble with the labels 'liberal' and 'conservative' is not so much that they are inaccurate as that many people assume that between them they are exhaustive.

The fact is that there is room for at least one other label—'the radical'—which cannot be reduced to either 'liberal' or 'conservative'. The word 'radical' has been given a remarkably wide variety of meanings in history (see Williams 209–11; also Holland and Henriot 37–45). In using it here I take it to mean a readiness to work for a fundamental change in the structures of society. The radical person may be liberal on some issues and conservative on others. In many cases, however, the radical has an outlook which is entirely different to both the liberal and the conservative—one which shows up just how much the other two have in common.

On social issues Pope John was not a radical. On the question of the fundamental re-structuring of society, his approach was not very different from that of Pius XII; and in some ways Pius XI was more radical than either of them. The similarities and the differences between Pius XII and John XXIII can be found in a significant passage near the end of *Pacem in Terris*, written shortly before John died:

> There are, indeed, generous souls who . . . burn with desire to put everything right and are carried away by such an ungovernable zeal that their reform becomes a sort of revolution.
>
> To such people we would suggest that it is in the nature of things for growth to be gradual and that therefore in human institutions no improvement can be looked for which does not proceed step by step and from within. The point was well put by Our predecessor Pius XII: 'Prosperity and justice lie not in completely overthrowing the old order but in well planned progress. Uncontrolled passionate zeal always destroys everything and builds nothing . . . ' (PT 161–2—Waterhouse version adapted).

Pope John's remarks lack the acerbity of his predecessor's. He shows understanding and sympathy for the 'generous souls' who are not satisfied with a step-by-step reform. But, despite this, he in fact reaffirms the gradualist approach of Pius XII. This is no mere verbal acceptance made in the interests of assuring a kind of doctrinal continuity. Pope John really believed that the necessary improvements could come 'step by step and from within', without any radical disruption of the system. He was an optimist (cf. Cronin 242).

Optimism about the World

This optimism of John XXIII has to be teased out, so as to disentangle various elements in it. First of all it represents a new theology of the world. It would perhaps be more accurate to speak of a new spirituality of commitment to the world, a spirituality that contains the seed of a new theology. During the Second Vatican Council this seed sprouted very rapidly indeed. The new spirituality can be detected mostly as a difference of tone. To document it, one would have to note what John omits more than what he says. What comes through is the fact that he is not afraid that commitment to the world and its values will cause people to neglect the highest spiritual values. One significant point in *Mater et Magistra* is the optimistic way in which the pope speaks about human work in general (MM 107) and especially about agricultural work (MM 149). Two years later, in *Pacem in Terris*, the new approach is rather more explicit, especially in the pope's call for a 'synthesis' between scientific and spiritual values (PT 150), an 'interior unity' between religious faith and action in the temporal sphere (PT 152).

One important element in Pope John's conception of the world is his insistence that people have to work together for the common good and that this collaboration is to be facilitated by the civil authorities. On this point there is a clear doctrinal continuity between what he says and the teaching of Leo XIII; but nevertheless there is a difference of tone which has important practical implications. Like his predecessors, John XXIII insists that human authority is derived from God. But, significantly, he immediately adds a text from St John Chrysostom which shows that it is not that a particular ruler is appointed by God but rather that the authority exercised is from God (PT 46). So already in this first paragraph of his teaching on the question, Pope John is distinguishing between authority and the office-holder. In the next paragraph he insists that human authorities are subject to a higher authority (PT 47). He goes on to say that civil authorities can impose an obligation in conscience only in so far as their authority is intrinsically linked to the authority of God (PT 49). If civil authorities make demands contrary to the moral order, or fail to acknowledge human rights, their authority no longer exists and so the citizen is not bound to obey (PT 51, 61).

According to Pope John, the whole purpose of political authority is the promotion of the common good (PT 84). The denial by a government of the right of the individual to an area of personal freedom is branded by Pope John as 'a radical inversion of the order of human society' (PT 104—Campion version). These statements indicate that John was emphasising a very different aspect of authority from that stressed by Leo XIII. The latter was afraid of anarchy, so he insisted that when human authorities make demands on citizens they do so with the authority of God; only reluctantly and minimally did Leo take note of the cases where human authorities forfeited the right to unquestioned obedience. John XXIII, like Pius XII, was more concerned lest individual freedom be stifled by authoritarian rulers or bureaucracies. So he paid more attention to the duty of authorities to fulfil their proper role, namely, the service of the common good. For him, human authority ceases to be real authority when it fails in this regard. Quite clearly this approach leaves much greater scope for the individual to assess whether those in power are in fact exercising a lawful authority; and there is a wider gap where dissent may enter. Pope John is not of course encouraging political dissent, still less any kind of organised resistance. But evidently his conception of human society is that of a community of persons who voluntarily submit to civil authority in order to attain the common good. He does not hold that democracy is the only valid form of government (PT 52) but the values he promotes are those to which democracy at its best is committed and which it should embody.

The general optimism of Pope John about the world finds expression in his teaching about political organisation and authority. He believes people can cooperate successfully not only at the local and national levels but also at the international level (MM 155–65, 170–7; PT 80–145). The whole presupposition of his two great social encyclicals was that people needed only to be encouraged and animated to cooperate more fruitfully. He presumes not merely the ability to cooperate but the fundamental willingness of people and nations to cooperate even at the cost of personal, sectional, or national sacrifice. This presupposition might easily be overlooked. But it is important to note it. For it explains why John XXIII addressed himself mainly to the question, what improvements are needed in economic, social, and political affairs in order that people may live with greater human dignity. He did not concentrate on another question which may be equally or more important: *how* can these changes be brought about, especially where many of those who hold power are reluctant to accept reforms that would curb their power.

Optimism about the Modern World

John XXIII was not just optimistic about the world in general. His optimism and hopefulness were directed specifically to the modern world—meaning the kind of society that had emerged in the Western world as a result of rapid economic growth. Here his tone is notably different from that of Pius XII. He speaks with ringing hope and challenge of this age of the atom and of the conquest of space as 'an era in which the human family has already entered on its new advance toward limitless horizons' (PT 156—Campion version). He asks whether the modern developments in social relationships will entangle people in a maze of restrictions so that human freedom and responsibility will be eliminated; and his answer is a firm 'no' (MM 62).[2] The 'modernisation' of society can, he believes, have more advantages than disadvantages, if it is properly controlled and directed (MM 67).

In a moving passage in *Mater et Magistra* the pope expresses his distress about the plight of poverty-stricken workers of many lands and whole continents. He adds that one of the reasons for this poverty is the fact that these areas are still underdeveloped in terms of modern industrial techniques (MM 68).[3] In a later paragraph he says that usually an under-developed or primitive state of economic development is the fundamental or enduring cause of poverty and hunger (MM 163; cf. MM 154 which refers to primitive and obsolete methods of agriculture). Clearly he has no serious doubts about the need for 'modernisation' and 'development' as the way in which the world must make progress. He is of course aware that this kind of 'development' can create social problems (MM 124–5) and even economic difficulties (MM 154). He also realises that the modern situation offers opportunities for a new kind of elitism. So he warns against abuses of power by the new class of managers of large-scale enterprises—and he makes the important point that such abuses can occur both in private business and in public bodies (MM 104, 118). Furthermore he notes two causes of poverty which are particularly important in this modern world—the arms race (MM 198, 69, 204; PT 109) and the squandering of money by governments on prestige projects (MM 69). But all of this he would see as an argument for control and balance, not a reason for questioning the whole direction of modern 'development'.

Optimism about Capitalism

We have seen that Pope John's optimism is not just about the world but about the modern world, including the processes of 'modernisation' and 'development'. Now it must be added that the optimism extends even further—to the capitalist system which is most conspicuously associated with 'modernisation'. (Of course those nations which rejected capitalism were also dedicated to economic development; but the West, including the Vatican, has tended to assume—and with good reason—that the link between capitalism and 'development' is more natural and more successful.)[4] There are indications that Pope John took a rather optimistic view of what might be expected from capitalist society in the future. Not that he ignored its deficiencies and abuses, or repudiated the condemnations of capitalism by Leo XIII and Pius XI. But he seemed to believe that before too long and without too much trouble the system could be humanised effectively.

In one of the more significant and controversial paragraphs in *Pacem in Terris* the pope drew a distinction between 'false philosophical theories' and the 'historical movements' which are inspired by these theories (PT 159).[5] It is commonly and correctly assumed that Pope John was referring here primarily to those left-wing movements which, historically at least, draw their inspiration from Marx (cf. Utz 136, note 47; Newman 199–201).[6] But the pope would no doubt have also applied the distinction to capitalism: the capitalist ideology or theory remains incompatible with Catholic social teaching; but capitalist society in its actual historical development can be viewed rather more optimistically by Pope John.

Already in his 1959 encyclical *Ad Petri Cathedram* the pope had remarked that class distinctions were less pronounced than before (par. 33; cf. MM 48). He went on to say: 'Anyone who is diligent and capable has the opportunity to rise to higher levels of society' (par. 33). This statement shows the extent to which he accepted one aspect of the free enterprise ideology, namely, the assumption that it gives most people a reasonably equal chance of 'getting on', i.e. of moving upwards in society. The full implication of this belief is that, by and large, the rich and powerful have earned their privileged place in society, while the weak and the poor are in some sense responsible for their 'failure'. Needless to say, the pope did not accept this implication. But his remark suggests that he did not subject the free enterprise ideology to any very thorough and critical examination.

A further indication of a certain naivety is to be found in an important paragraph of *Mater et Magistra* where Pope John insisted on the need for a wider distribution of property of various kinds (MM 115). He maintained that now is a particularly suitable time for countries to adjust their social and economic structures so as to facilitate a wider distribution of ownership—thus overcoming the tendency of capitalism to concentrate wealth in the hands of the few. Why *now*? Because, said Pope John, this is a time when an increasing number of countries are experiencing rapid economic development. This statement suggests that John accepted the common assumption that rapid economic growth offers the easiest way to overcome the problem of the unequal distribution of wealth. That is not surprising; for, on the face of it, this assumption seems almost self-evidently correct. Instead of having to face the difficult task of taking wealth from the rich to re-distribute it to the poor, why not create sufficient new wealth to enable the poor to become reasonably well-off? But, despite its apparent obviousness, this line of thinking can in practice play a part in bringing about the very opposite to what it aims at. This is what in fact has happened in large parts of the world. So it will be useful to look more closely at the process.

How best can rapid economic growth be promoted in a society which follows the 'free enterprise' approach? Both the theorists and the real-life capitalists claim that the only effective way is to allow the entrepreneurs and investors an adequate return for their contribution. What this means in practice is that capitalist investors must be allowed a major share of the new wealth in the form of profits and inducements. The argument is that the 'national cake' must first be enlarged even at the cost of some delay in redistributing the shares of the 'cake'. So a higher priority is given to creation of wealth than to its equitable distribution. Once that pattern is established it becomes exceptionally difficult to change it. There never comes a time which seems right for a more fair distribution. Various 'compelling' objections disguise the fact that those with wealth have the power to retain it. Their power is exercised both politically and through the moulding of opinion in society. Consequently the best hope left to the poorer and less powerful people is that growth will be so great that they will become better off in absolute terms, even though the gap between them and the rich continues to widen. This is what happened in many Western countries during the 1950s and 1960s. But in a world of limited resources it is increasingly unrealistic to expect that all countries can attain such a degree of growth.

The belief that the best way to solve social problems is to speed up economic growth was not confined to Western countries. Almost all Third World countries accepted the view that their best hope of eliminating poverty lay in rapid growth. And in the heyday of communism the leaders of the communist countries imposed almost intolerable sacrifices on their people in order to achieve rapid growth. (More recently, of course, the new non-communist leaders of most of these countries are imposing equally intolerable sacrifices on their people in an effort to achieve growth through switching over their economies to free enterprise!)

There was an important difference between the communist and the capitalist view of economic growth. In the centrally planned economies of the communist countries there was no incompatibility in principle between increased growth and equitable distribution. The governments of these countries failed spectacularly to provide genuine human development for their people—and they failed both in terms of growth and of equitable distribution. Their failure was mainly due to bureaucratic mismanagement, corruption and a pandering to various power elites.

In the capitalist society of the West the relationship between growth and equitable distribution is more complex and is particularly interesting:

— Firstly, capitalism is committed to growth not merely for practical reasons but also ideologically. At a practical level an ever-increasing demand seems to be necessary if the whole system is not to collapse. Hence the need for an ideology of growth; this is promoted in various ways, notably by the advertising industry. The belief is fostered that there is no foreseeable limit either to human needs or to the ability of a free enterprise system to meet these ever-expanding 'needs'.

— Secondly, the growth that actually takes place tends, as we have seen, to concentrate wealth in the hands of a minority rather than leading to a more equitable distribution.

— But, thirdly, another part of the ideology of capitalism masks this lack of equity. It promotes an image of free enterprise where all have a fair opportunity to use their talents profitably. Hard work and initiative are correlated with success and prosperity. The implication is that poor distribution of wealth is to be explained more in terms of the laziness and lack of ability of some rather than of any lack of opportunity imposed by the system (cf. Brookfield 38). Furthermore, the idea is fostered that the new wealth will gradually 'trickle down' from the richer to the poorer sectors of society. These beliefs are illusions. They conceal the fact that the normal tendency of the system is to widen the gap between the rich and the poor. In this way they protect the interests of the wealthy.

Needless to say, Pope John did not set out to promote such dangerous illusions. But they must have had some effect on him. This is shown by his statement (quoted above) that anybody who is diligent and careful can rise to higher levels in society. The fact that the pope uncritically accepted this belief suggests that there was a certain blind spot in his outlook. This becomes more evident when one adverts to the gap between the end he was hoping for and the means he proposed to achieve it. The end-result he wanted was a wider distribution of property (MM 113–14). The means by which he hoped this would come about was a gradual reform of the existing structures and the introduction of controls designed to reverse the tendency of capitalism to concentrate wealth in the hands of a few. But Pope John was unduly optimistic in thinking that this could be brought about fairly easily. He was unrealistic in seeing that time of rapid growth as the best occasion for a relatively painless reversal of this 'normal' pattern. Tampering with the system is never easy—and, ironically, it may be especially difficult when the system is working smoothly as it was at the time *Mater et Magistra* was written.

But surely the pope was correct when he supported his case by noting the progress towards wider ownership made in some economically developed countries (MM 115)? His facts were correct but it is doubtful whether they should have been used as the basis for a generalisation. Undoubtedly the years between 1945 and 1961 saw a considerable growth in prosperity for most workers in Western countries. But this was part of a wider reality—the increased wealth of Western nations as a whole vis-à-vis the Third World. This imbalance was in turn related to the extravagant use by industrialised countries of energy and raw materials, much of which came from poorer countries at a very low price. So whatever improvement occurred within the Western countries has to be seen in the context of an increasingly lop-sided distribution of wealth on the international (or intercontinental) level.

Furthermore, there is a certain ambiguity in the pope's call, at this point in the encyclical, for a wider distribution of ownership of property. What exactly is the end-result that he was looking for here? Which of the following two positions did he hold?

— First position: whatever wealth is available should be distributed more equitably.

— Second position: more people (especially the working class) should become owners of property.

The second of these two positions is compatible with a widening of the gap between rich and poor. It is quite likely that John XXIII did not advert to this possibility. It would seem that he was simply following in the footsteps of Leo XIII by insisting on the importance of more people becoming owners of property (the second position)—and tacitly assuming that this would involve a narrowing of the gap between rich and poor (the first position).

In Western countries since World War II the gap between the richer and the poorer sectors of society has been widening during the very period when more and more ordinary workers were becoming owners of the kind of property mentioned by the pope (e.g. a house and garden). So we have the second position without the first. Did Pope John see this situation as a model for the rest of the world? The answer should be, 'no', because in two earlier paragraphs of the encyclical he had insisted very strongly on the central importance of the first position, namely, the equitable distribution of wealth (MM 73–4). Following Pius XII, he even went so far as to say: 'the economic prosperity of any people is to be measured less by the total *amount* of goods and riches they own than by the extent to which these are *distributed* according to the norms of justice (MM 74).[7]

We must conclude that, in terms of his own principles, Pope John was not entitled to present as a 'success story' those 'nations with developed social and economic systems' where ownership has become more widespread (MM 115—Gibbons version). These Western countries can certainly be cited as proof that in certain circumstances rapid economic growth under a free enterprise system is compatible with, and perhaps even gives rise to, wider ownership of possessions. But they should not be cited as proof that it is possible in practice to reverse the inherent tendency of capitalism towards an inequitable distribution of wealth and power. John XXIII was correct when he said that private ownership had increased in some 'developed' countries. But what he said could leave one with a wrong impression, namely, that if the present free enterprise system of the Western world were extended globally it would bring social justice on a world scale; and that all that is required is a moderate and gradual reform of the system.

The Welfare State

This issue of whether Western countries serve as a model for a humanised version of capitalism is vitally important. It is appropriate to say something here about the Welfare State approach adopted in several Western European countries in the years after World War II; for it is obvious that Pope John's thinking was very influenced by what he had seen happening in these countries in the late 1940s and the 1950s. These countries expanded their social security services in a major effort to cope with the problems of poverty; to pay for these services they raised their taxation levels far higher than before— to levels that would not have been accepted in the USA.

What was the relationship between economic growth and such high levels of 'welfare'? Undoubtedly, the rapid economic growth of those years made it easier for these countries to pay for the welfare services. (And as growth has slowed down in recent years the social services have come under strain through shortage of funds.) But it is important to note that the determination to alleviate poverty through national social welfare programmes came prior to most of the economic growth. It is arguable that the fundamental change in structures and attitudes involved in the Welfare State owes more to the chaos at the end of the war than to the success of a revived capitalism. Workers were determined never again to face the deprivations of the depression years; and the breaking of the moulds that came during and after the war offered the chance to give political expression to this determination. The point is that basic changes in social structures are more likely to be associated with the *failure* of a growth-oriented free enterprise model of society than with its 'success'. This suggests that it is illusory to expect raw capitalism to develop naturally, organically and painlessly into a system characterised by equitable distribution of wealth and effective care for the weaker sectors of society.

It is well to note also the limited aims of the Welfare State approach. It did not set out overtly to bridge the gap in owner-ship between rich and poor by wholesale nationalisation or redistribution of capital goods. In other words it is not to be equated with a full programme of socialism. It presupposed the continuance of a 'free enterprise' economy with its inherent tendency towards imbalance and concentration of wealth. Rather than attempting to overthrow the capitalist system itself, it sought to cope with some of the evil *effects* of the system, namely, the poverty and deprivation which it created in some sectors of society.

In some European countries the Welfare State approach was combined with a limited type of socialism which set out to redistribute ownership through a programme of nationalisation and the imposition of very high levels of taxation on income and profits. But in other countries it was not linked to any serious effort to redistribute ownership. So the Welfare State approach is not necessarily socialistic. In fact its comparative success was due largely to the fact that it was supported not only by moderate socialists but also by people who were quite opposed to socialism. Not that it was universally accepted; there were many champions of a rugged free enterprise philosophy who fought against any build-up of a comprehensive programme of state welfare. But, faced with the ideological struggle between left and right, the majority of voters in Western Europe settled for the Welfare State as a kind of compromise—a way of combining social compassion with the efficiency of the free enterprise system. The Welfare State was seen by many as a way of giving 'a human face' to a society built on a capitalist economy.

In the 1960s this approach appeared to be working well. It seemed to offer a direction which could be taken further in the future, not merely in Europe but in the wider world. So the scenario for the future envisaged by many concerned people—including, most probably, Pope John and at least some of the drafters of *Mater et Magistra*—would have been along the following lines: a healthy ever-expanding economy, primarily free enterprise in character but including some degree of State capitalism, combined with expanding public welfare programmes (supplemented by the welfare programmes of voluntary agencies, especially the Churches) to mitigate the deficiencies and cope with the casualties of such an economic system.

The intervening years have made this scenario increasingly problematical. Firstly, an indefinite period of rapid economic growth can no longer be presumed: there are severe limits to the amount of cheap energy and raw materials that are available to make this possible; and furthermore the inherent problems of a capitalist order (problems of prediction, credibility, cycles, protectionism, etc.) have proved far more intractable than expected. Secondly, it is now quite evident (to all who have eyes to see it) that the 'development' of the West depended on the availability of cheap resources from the Third World; so it cannot be seen as a model which may be repeated all over the world. Thirdly, the Welfare State approach has itself run into serious difficulties in the West: the expansion of the 'national cake' has slowed down at the same time as the demands of the stronger groups in society have increased; the result is that there is less left for the poorer segment of society, which in some Western countries now comprises about a quarter of the population. Finally, government efforts to stimulate the economy are costing the tax-payer a great deal; the heavy tax burden offers a convenient opportunity for opponents of State welfare to mount ideological attacks on the social services as wasteful and as an encouragement to idleness and parasitism. In such an atmosphere it becomes quite unrealistic to hope that something analogous to the Welfare State will emerge at the *international* level, with the rich nations providing adequate help for the poor ones.

The conclusion that emerges from what has been said is that Pope John, like many of his contemporaries, including notable economists and social scientists, showed a rather uncritical optimism about Western-style democratic capitalist society. Most of the scholars and religious leaders of more recent times (including Pope John Paul II) are far more cautious; they are slow to assume that national and international social justice can come about through a gradual and relatively painless reform of the capitalist order of society.

International Development Cooperation

We move on now to look at the contribution of John XXIII to the whole question of international cooperation in economic affairs. As we have seen, Pope John was eager to update the Church's teaching in the whole sphere of social justice. One aspect of this up-dating was the new emphasis which he put on *international* social justice. He devoted a section of *Mater et Magistra* to this topic and began by suggesting that the relationship between the 'developed' and the 'under-developed' countries might well be the most pressing question of the day (MM 157). The pope pointed out that contemporary problems often 'exceed the capacity of individual States' (MM 201). So, even from the point of view of their own self-interest, countries must cooperate in promoting the economic development of all (MM 202).

He put forward some general principles and guidelines on this issue. Looking back at them a generation later we may feel that the ingenuous quality of what he had to say about the whole capitalist order carried over into his treatment of international economic relations. He seemed to accept uncritically the view that was dominant among Western economists of the period. The core of this view was that the problem of the poor countries was 'under-development' and that the solution was rapid economic growth; this was to be achieved by importing both Western capital and Western skills and technology (cf. MM 163–4).

In line with this view, Pope John came out strongly in favour of international loans to promote development; he even felt he had to 'give due praise to this generous activity' (MM 165). He was equally unquestioning in his support for the sending of 'as many youths as possible' from the less developed countries to 'study in the great universities of more developed countries' (MM 165; cf. 183). He did not seriously question the whole model of development that was being exported from the West and imposed on the newly-emergent nations both through the Western education of their planners and through Western investment and aid.

Pope John was not, however, entirely naive in his approach to international economic cooperation. He warned the economically developed countries that they must not seek to dominate poorer countries (MM 171); to do so would be, he said, to impose on them a new and disguised form of colonialism (MM 172). He also insisted that the rich and powerful countries should respect the culture and way of life of the poorer countries—not least because of the high moral quality of their traditional values (MM 170, 176–7).

Two years later, and shortly before he died, Pope John published his other major encyclical, *Pacem in Terris*, which he wanted to leave as a kind of legacy to the Church and the world. On this occasion he addressed himself not only to Christians but also to all people of goodwill. He devoted one important section of the encyclical to the question of the relationship between States. He laid down two fundamental principles:

(1) that 'all states are by nature equal in dignity' (PT 86, 89); and

(2) that each State has the right to play the leading part in its own development (PT 86, 92, 120).

Pope John called for 'active solidarity' (PT 98) between the nations—and especially between the rich and the poor. He insisted that it would be wrong for more advanced states 'to take unjust advantage of their superiority over others' (PT 88). (The phrasing of this paragraph suggests that the drafter of the encyclical accepted the assumption current in the wealthy nations that these countries were superior not only in economic development but even in 'culture and civilisation'.)

According to John XXIII, the urgent need for international cooperation at all levels arises from the fact that

> . . . the interdependence of national economies has grown deeper . . . so that they become, as it were, integral parts of the one world economy. (PT 130)

The effect of this ever-increasing unification of the economies of all the countries of the world is that conferences and international agreements are no longer an adequate means of overcoming economic and political difficulties (PT 134). There is need for some more effective instrument to ensure cooperation and mutual support; and, the pope believed, what is required is some form of 'world government' or 'public authority' (PT 137—two different translations propose these two different phrases; they may mean the same thing but the overtones are very different).

Such a world authority would have to be accepted by common accord rather than imposed by force, since otherwise it could be (or could appear to be) 'an instrument of one-sided interests' (PT 138). The world authority would have to respect the principle of subsidiarity, leaving national governments to exercise their own proper authority and confining its attention to issues that have to do with the common good of all nations (PT 140). (We may note in passing that the encyclical seems to go too far when it claims that a world authority 'is not intended to limit the sphere of action' of national governments [PT 141], for some degree of limitation is implied in the very acceptance of a world authority.) Pope John went on to speak with approval of the United Nations and the Universal Declaration of Human Rights (though he expressed a reservation about some points in the latter). Clearly he saw these as important steps towards the establishment of a governing authority for the whole world (PT 142–5).

More significant than the details of what Pope John had to say about social justice at the international level is the fact that he located this *justice* issue within the context of *'development'*. This meant that his teaching on social justice was weakened by his failure to criticise the naively optimistic and uncritically Western concept of development that was current at the time. On the positive side, however, was the fact that he identified two key qualities of genuine international development, namely, solidarity (PT 98) and subsidiarity (PT 140). Even more important is the fact that Pope John was the first pope to move the topic of International Development Cooperation towards the centre of the social justice agenda. In this way he paved the way for the great encyclical *Populorum Progressio* issued by his successor, Paul VI, a few years later.

Option for the Poor?

Pope John's social encyclicals played a major part in bringing the Catholic Church into a more open relationship with modern society. But was this at the cost of an acceptance of the Western *status quo*, subject only to gradual and relatively minor reforms? Did his openness to existing Western society imply a playing down of the Church's challenge to the world? More specifically, did it involve a failure to make an effective option for the poor? These questions call for a carefully nuanced response.

The first thing to note is that Pope John himself clearly did not see himself as having to choose between an option for the poor and an acceptance of capitalist society. He believed that the latter could be tempered and adapted in such a way as to ensure that the poor really were looked after. His encyclicals appeared at a time when the Western economic model seemed to be working well and to be amenable to the kind of reforms he was looking for. It was not a time when many Church leaders or scholars saw the issue in terms of a clash between capitalism and social justice. To present the issue in terms of such a stark choice is to see it more as it was seen thirty years earlier (at the time of Pius XI's *Quadragesimo Anno*) or as it is seen by a significant number of Church leaders today, a whole generation after the appearance of *Mater et Magistra*.

The scholar Camp maintains that Pope John saw capitalism 'as a positive good' (Camp 159). This is an overstatement. We have to remember that John XXIII consistently adopted the 'spoonful of honey' approach, avoiding condemnations as far as possible, praising what he could, and inviting people to make improvements. The fact that he is less critical than his predecessors in matters of social injustice is no indication that he had abandoned their concern about the exploitation of the poor. Nor does it prove that he had become an enthusiastic convert to the capitalist system.

Nevertheless, John XXIII differed from the popes who went before him in so far as he seems to have approved of the general direction in which the world was moving. Camp is broadly correct in judging that Pope John 'did not want a change of institutions' but instead 'frankly admired what was already being done and wished an expansion of its benefits to more people' (Camp 160). The pope did, however, want *some* changes. He thought gradual reforms could make the world a more just and humane community of people and peoples. But in proposing such gradual reform he was at the same time implicitly giving a considerable measure of endorsement to the existing free enterprise system. From the point of view of their formal teaching the social encyclicals of John XXIII show no very radical departure from the tradition of social teaching of his predecessors. But there are subtle differences in tone and emphasis which give these encyclicals a different effect when seen as interventions by the pope at this particular time. Pope John did not demand a radical reconstruction of society such as Pius XI had proposed. It is significant that the summary of *Quadragesimo Anno* given in *Mater et Magistra* omitted all reference to Pius XI's account of Italian corporatism (QA 91–7). It also preserved a careful vagueness in the way it used such terms as 'vocational groups' and 'intermediate bodies'.[8] So, despite the continuity with the past from a 'doctrinal' point of view, the net effect of the social teaching of Pope John was rather different from that of Pius XI. Its effect was to give a certain approval and legitimation to the Western economic approach, provided this is taken in conjunction with the democratic reformist and socially conscious currents of the thought of that period.

Whether John XXIII's position is considered to be an improvement on that of Pius XI depends of course on the stance of the person making the judgment. A fairly typical evaluation of *Mater et Magistra* is that of John F. Cronin who was assistant director of the Social Action Department of the conference of US bishops. He held that the encyclical was 'realistic, moderate, and progressive' (Cronin in Masse 44). Obviously he saw this as high praise. It is a useful exercise to 'translate' his words into more neutral language:

— In saying that the encyclical was 'realistic' Cronin meant that it did not call in question in any radical way the economic order existing in Western society and dominating most of the world.

— In saying that the encyclical was 'moderate' Cronin meant that the reforms it called for would not seriously disrupt this order either in their extent or by the speed with which they are to be introduced.

— When he said that the encyclical was 'progressive' Cronin meant that it fitted comfortably into the more 'enlightened' and 'liberal' strand of Western thinking (—not the hard economic liberalism of the nineteenth century but the socially conscious liberal thinking of more recent times). Understood in this way, Cronin's words can be applied not only to *Mater et Magistra* but to Pope John's social teaching taken as a whole.

In the light of the clarifications just given, it is now possible to offer a fairly brief answer to the question whether or not the social teaching of John XXIII amounts to a call for an effective option for the poor. He was deeply concerned about the plight of different categories of poor people; and he proposed a variety of measures designed not merely to provide relief but to prevent imbalances in society (MM 124, 150, 154, 157–74, 185; PT 88, 95, 96, 101, 103–7, 121–5). Nevertheless he did not commit the Catholic Church to an option for the poor if one takes that in the very specific sense in which it is frequently used today—namely, a radical challenge to the capitalistic structures of the international economic order, structures that for many years have given an unfair advantage to Western countries and to privileged 'elites' in Third World countries, structures that are now being adopted uncritically in many formerly communist countries whose people hope to share in the prosperity of the West. On the contrary, the effect of Pope John's interventions in social issues was to give a certain sanction and support to these structures, provided they are supplemented and restrained in ways that limit their harmful social effects.

SECTION II

A CHANGE OF DIRECTION

It would be misleading and unjust to stop at this point in the evaluation of the effect of Pope John's encyclicals. For there is a sense in which his teaching made a major contribution towards putting the Church on the side of the poor. More accurately, one might say he removed from the rich and the powerful an exceptionally important weapon which they could use to maintain injustice in society. To explain how he did so it is necessary to look closely at his teaching about 'socialisation'.

Socialisation

Probably the single most important passage in *Mater et Magistra* is the following:

> One of the main features which seem to be characteristic of our time is undoubtedly an increase in the number of social relationships. Day by day people become more inter-dependent and this introduces into their lives various kinds of associations which are generally recognised in contractual or public law . . . . These developments in social life are both a sign and a cause of an increasing degree of State intervention in matters of considerable importance and risk since they have to do with the intimate life of the person (MM 59–60).[9]

The first English translation of this passage followed the Italian version in using the word 'socialisation' where the Latin text speaks of an increase in social relationships.[10] But the more widely used English versions avoid this word very deliberately,[11] either for the purely linguistic reason that it is not used in the Latin text or on the grounds that its omission from the Latin was a significant correction of the original unofficial working text in Italian.[12] It was felt by some that to use the word 'socialisation' in the English translation might give the impression that Pope John had abandoned the papal tradition of being opposed to socialism. In fact some sectors of the media did interpret the encyclical as proposing some version of socialism. Consequently, Church spokespersons were kept busy explaining that as used in the working text 'socialisation' did not really mean the introduction of socialism—and that it didn't even mean what Pius XII meant when he used the word. (For Pius it meant, mostly, nationalisation—see Pius XII D12 68–72 and D23 792). They explained that the word was being used in a technical sense to describe a recent development in Western industrialised society. I would sum up as follows the main elements in modern society which Pope John had in mind when he used the word 'socialisation':

> People are now more closely inserted in a web of relationships where the actions of each individual affect many others. Many aspects of daily living which used to be seen as personal or family matters now have to be organised, or at least regulated, on a larger scale. So the individual and the family have to rely more on large institutions. Some of these are, technically, private institutions—trade unions, for instance, or non-State insurance schemes. But many are new organs of the public authorities—ranging from local councils up to national governments and even international agencies.

The originality of John XXIII lies not so much in his noting this fact of modern life as in his response to it. He held that it would be not merely pointless but positively wrong if the Christian were just to bemoan and resist this development, pining for the simple life of the past (cf. Cronin 44). Of course the pope admitted the dangers it poses—especially the risk of excessive interference with personal responsibilities (MM 62) and an undue degree of bureaucratisation. In this he was taking account of the preoccupations of Pius XII. But Pope John evidently considered the positive aspects of the process to be more important: it promotes the personal welfare of individuals in many ways; and it can also enable people to live, work, and play more as a community (MM 60). So he believed that the process is not inherently destructive of humanity (MM 62). But on the other hand it is not to be seen as automatically beneficial either. In fact it is not a process whose outcome is pre-determined at all (cf. Calvez 8–9). Everything depends on the people involved; it is they who are responsible for the direction it takes (MM 63).[13]

So much for John XXIII's account of 'socialisation'. But what is so significant about his approach? In order to answer this question it is necessary first of all to look closely at the accident of history which makes of resistance to 'socialisation' a policy associated with 'traditional conservatism'. Twentieth-century conservatives in Europe and America see themselves as standing in defence of the *traditional* independence of the individual against the encroachments of society in the form of the State. But how traditional is it for the individual to have a high degree of independence from society? It is not a tradition that goes back very far. It finds its high point in America at about the time the United States came into existence; so it is not surprising that the US constitution enshrines and defends various rights of the individual. But it is well to remember that in many respects the US constitution represented a radical break with tradition. In fact the notion of the independence of the individual as an ancient and 'traditional' value is largely a myth. Traditional societies tend to leave very little room for individual independence; most of a person's behaviour is pre-scribed and enforced by the community (by unwritten custom rather than by written laws and regulations of the modern type). So there is a certain irony in the fact that conservatism has come to be associated with rugged individualism. The more normal type of conservatism would be that which resists individualism in favour of socially determined behaviour!

The important point to note is that the 'socialisation' of which Pope John is speaking is a feature of modern *Western* society, and it can be understood only in the light of Western history. One of the early effects of Western modernisation and urbanisation was to weaken many traditional social relationships and the obligations attached to them. The result was greater independence for individuals. There was a period when the more fortunate and more ruthless of the new generation seemed to have the best of two worlds. On the one hand they had a high degree of freedom from social constraints, allowing them a wide scope for initiative (and at times for opportunism and even exploitation). On the other hand they could still rely on patterns of obedience, respect, and cooperation inherited from the past. The less fortunate people at the bottom of the social ladder had, correspondingly, the worst of two worlds. The decline in social restraints left them open to new forms of oppression. But their efforts to protect themselves were resisted by the rich who justified themselves by invoking a myth they had built around the values of untrammelled freedom and rugged individualism.

In spite of this myth of independence for the individual, the reality was that before long there emerged an obvious need for new and different forms of social institutions and restraints. Society could no longer 'free-wheel' on the traditionally ingrained patterns of cooperation. There was an urgent need for new social systems to look after security, welfare, public health, education, economic development, the environment, etc. And these needs expanded as society became more concentrated in urban areas, less centred on small community units. No wonder then that Pope John felt it was pointless and wrong to resist the expansion of such social institutions. He saw that what was required was that they be intelligently planned and controlled. The aim should be to retain as much as possible of the values of personal freedom while protecting the common welfare. But neither was it any wonder that there should be strong resistance to any new restrictions. Precisely because such restraints are needed to prevent the exploitation of the weak by the strong, they are experienced by the powerful as unwarranted limits to their freedom. And one of the most powerful weapons used to resist these restrictions is the invocation of the myth of the defence of the 'traditional values' of personal initiative and freedom, and old-fashioned rugged independence.

The Newness of Mater et Magistra

Against this background we can understand the position of

John XXIII and the reaction to it. It was a carefully nuanced
position. He preserved a clear continuity with his predecessors
in his teaching about the values that are to be preserved and
the means of doing so. Like them he stressed the principle of
subsidiarity (MM 53, 117, 152). Following them he insisted on
the importance of vocational groupings and similar intermediate
organisations which are not organs of the State itself (MM
65).[14] He maintained that intervention by government or
other public authorities should be limited to those cases where
it is really necessary (MM 117, 152).

On the other hand, John XXIII differed from Pius XI and
Pius XII in his judgment about where *in fact* such State
intervention is required. It is here that the newness of *Mater et
Magistra* becomes very evident. Retaining continuity with
previous social teaching from a 'doctrinal' point of view, it was
startlingly different in its net effect. For in fact it proposed a
programme of action that might well have been borrowed from
the manifesto of a moderate socialist political party! The real
issue then is not whether the *word* 'socialisation' is the correct
translation of the Latin text. Rather the issue is whether the
pope was moving the Catholic Church away from its long-held
suspicion of such 'socialistic' notions as that of the Welfare
State. Those who insisted on a literal translation of the Latin
text of the encyclical were not just removing the word
'socialisation'; they were also trying to rid the encyclical of the
overtones of this word; and these overtones might have
conveyed more accurately what Pope John was referring to.
Conservative Catholics were 'up in arms' when they read a
translation of the encyclical that suggested that 'socialisation'
was not necessarily a bad thing. There was no such hostility to
the phrase 'an increase in social relationships'. But the newness
of *Mater et Magistra* could not be removed by providing this
more literal translation of the Latin text. For the real novelty
comes in the section where Pope John spelled out the practical
implications of the process of 'socialisation'. So it is opportune
to look at some of these implications as presented in the
encyclical.

Pope John developed and extended the teaching of Pius XI
(QA 65), and bypassed the reservations of Pius XII (D19 487),
when he said that in some circumstances employees may be

entitled to a share in the profits of the companies where they work (MM 75–7) and to a say in management both at the level of the individual firm (MM 92–3, 97) and in determining policy at various levels, even on a national scale (MM 97). Again, he said, the State must exercise strict control over managers/directors of large businesses (MM 104). He went on to maintain that an increased amount of State ownership is justified by the needs of the common good in the modern situation (MM 116–7). It must also be recognised, said the pope, that in fact the State and public authorities have taken on a greatly expanded role in coping with social problems (MM 120). Indeed Pope John proposed just such a role for them in dealing with the special difficulties of those working in agriculture (MM 128–41)—and he went into considerable detail in regard to tax assessment (MM 133), credit facilities (MM 134), insurance, (MM 135), social security (MM 136), price support (MM 137) and price regulation (MM 140), and even the directing of industry into rural areas (MM 141). All this was seen as necessary because in modern Western life human interdependence is possible only by going beyond one-to-one relationships and those of the small community; life is lived on a scale that requires the massive apparatus of the State to be actively involved in directing and controlling the economic and social life of the people. Even when a nation keeps this State involvement as low as possible by respecting the principle of subsidiarity (as Pope John asked), still the common good nowadays requires far more State 'interference' than was needed in the past. *Mater et Magistra* gave a mandate for this extra involvement by the State; and the result began to look like an encouragement to 'socialisation' in the popular sense of the word.

Now at last we can see why some conservative Catholics reacted to the encyclical by saying '*Mater si, Magistra no*'; they understood Pope John to be approving of Welfare State policies and they were unwilling to accept this. Their opposition confirms the fact that there really was a distinct change of emphasis in Pope John's social teaching—even when one makes allowance for exaggerations by some commentators of its socialising tendency. It is true, of course, that there was a considerable degree of continuity between what Pope John was saying and the teaching of Pius XII. But there was also quite a lot of discontinuity. After all, conservative Catholics had no objection to the social teaching of Pius XII—even though there are echoes of that teaching in even the most 'advanced' parts of *Mater et Magistra*.[15] Probably the most important effect of the encyclical, seen as an intervention in the continuing debate about social issues, was that it began the process of breaking the long alliance between Roman Catholicism and socially conservative forces.

With the issuing of Pope John's encyclical in 1961 it began to seem credible, for the first time in the modern era, that Catholicism might have more in common with 'the left' than with 'the right'. There is a certain irony in the fact that *Mater et Magistra* should in this sense be more radical than even *Quadragesimo Anno*. For, as I pointed out above, Pope John was no radical. He was looking for moderate and gradual reforms in the capitalist order, while Pius XI was demanding a much more fundamental restructuring of society. But the corporatist ideals of Pius XI were somewhat right-wing, at least in their background and overtones: some strands of corporatism were based on a conservative nostalgia for the guilds of the past; others were drawn from aspects of the fascist model of society. Corporatism was strongly opposed to socialism; and Pius XI rejected even a mitigated form of socialism. Pope John, on the other hand, while continuing to insist on the importance of private initiative (MM 51, 55), private property (MM 109), and intermediate non-State vocational groupings (MM 65), put forward an ensemble of practical proposals that was far more congenial to 'the left' than to 'the right'.

Misuse of Catholic Social Teaching

Perhaps the most important insight of Pope John was his realisation that the Church's traditional defence of private initiative and private property had come to be used in an ideological way. And one of his most important decisions was to put an end to this—even in the face of determined resistance by senior Churchmen within the Vatican itself (cf. Hebblethwaite [1984] 325–40).

Over many years the popes had developed a whole body of social teaching as a vindication of the dignity of the individual against a totalitarian type of collectivism or socialism. But this teaching had become a support for an individualistic type of free enterprise, and for the private interests of individuals or groups over against the public interest. It is important to see how this had come about. There was no time at which the Church's social teaching could seriously be accused of giving sanction to capitalism in the form of ruthless big business. But capitalism has another face, a more attractive one. It is what might be called 'frontier free enterprise', typified in the small-town entrepreneurs who use local resources and their own initiative and skill to meet local needs and provide employment in the area. Different popes wanted to encourage this kind of initiative and to protect it against bureaucracy. And their defence of it could be used as giving a measure of support to capitalism in all its forms.

The idealised image of free enterprise gives a certain respectability to capitalism in its less acceptable forms. Frequently this takes place unconsciously, simply because people have not had the opportunity or education to make the necessary distinctions. But it is not at all uncommon to have a deliberate manipulation, a campaign to justify capitalism in its more unacceptable forms through a glamorisation of the ideal of free enterprise. One feature of this campaign is the reduction of all the various possible options to just two. People are presented with a stark choice between two alternatives: on the one hand is free enterprise with its respect for personal initiative and responsibility; on the other is a massively bureaucratic State socialism which is centralised, inflexible, and inefficient. (The books and television programmes of Milton Friedman provide examples of this kind of over-simplification.)

This background helps one to understand what I mean when I say that the Church's social teaching had come to be used in an ideological way to defend sectional interests. In most cases this was not the result of some sinister plot but an unfortunate accident of history. In the political sphere Catholics were among the strongest opponents of socialism. So it is quite understandable that a lot of emphasis was put on those parts of papal teaching most strongly opposed to socialist tendencies. Meanwhile papal reservations about capitalism were rather underplayed—except for the relatively short period when the corporatist proposals of *Quadragesimo Anno* were taken seriously as providing a workable alternative model of society.

In the social sphere there was a similar process. As the typical social patterns of modern living came more and more to replace the traditional patterns, people could no longer rely on the extended family and the local community as their main support systems for the individual and the family. The anonymity of modern urban-style living did not lend itself easily to the development of new *voluntary* support systems to replace them. So there was a great need for the State or other public authorities to provide the individual and the family with supports in social, cultural, and economic affairs. Without a great increase in public welfare programmes of all kinds—and the taxes to pay for them—only the very wealthy could live a dignified human life in this 'modern' world which had emerged. Up to the time of Pope John, Catholic social teaching had not taken sufficient account of this new situation. Church authorities tended to oppose socialised health care programmes. They were also opposed to giving the State a monopoly in the area of education and culture. Traditional papal teaching was that the State should not intrude itself unduly into the economic sphere; therefore nationalisation of industry or of the economic services such as banking should never go beyond what was proved to be strictly necessary.

The effect of all this was that almost by accident the Church came to be allied with certain sectional interests. It seemed to be more concerned with the defence of the rights of private groups than with the public interest and especially the needs of the poorer classes of society. That was not its intention nor its ideal. The principles proposed in the Church's social teaching were put forward as a defence of people against bureaucracy and totalitarianism. But the way in which they were being applied in practice was now causing the Church to be allied to the opponents of welfare programmes badly needed by the poor. Similarly, the Church's defence of private property—intended to protect the dignity of the person—was now invoked to justify resistance to land reform. There even was opposition to the payment of the high taxes needed to support social welfare programmes for the poor—they were said to be an undue inter-ference in private ownership and a step towards socialism.

The link between sectional interests and Catholic social teaching was further strengthened by the fact that, in most Western countries, dioceses and religious congregations were themselves the 'private' owners of many schools, colleges, hospitals, and other property. They felt themselves threatened by anything that seemed like a move towards nationalisation or a State monopoly of such services. This gave them a certain common interest with the more privileged groups in society. For instance, the medical profession was jealously guarding its privileged position and resisting the expansion of public health schemes designed to help the poor. Catholic social teaching was often invoked to justify this stance. So the Church found itself allied to a conservative group resisting the kind of changes that would make for a more just society.

In the sphere of education the situation was rather similar. There were some Catholic schools designed specifically for the wealthy; so it was not surprising that they should find common cause with other 'elitist' institutions. But more interesting is the situation of the great majority of Church-run schools. These had a policy of catering for poorer families by keeping their school-fees very low. Nevertheless it was often middle-class people (or people with middle-class aspirations) who sent their children to such schools. Consequently these schools were inclined to propagate middle-class values. Those who controlled them were opposed to the type of change in educational structures that would lessen the inequalities in society.

The general image of the Church was therefore that of a socially conservative force giving ideological and 'political' support to those who were opposed to left-wing changes. All this happened despite the fact that the original purpose of most of the educational and medical institutions of the Church was to serve the poor. It even happened when these institutions continued to be at the service of poor people. For they worked *within* the existing system. Originally they had represented a challenge to the current structures of society. But as time went on they became incorporated as parts of the system. In so far as these institutions required a legitimation for their existence this was provided by Catholic social teaching. And so, the social teaching of the Church seemed in practice to be offering support for the *status quo* rather than calling prophetically for structural changes in the interests of the poor.

What has been outlined so far is an unfortunate but almost accidental process by which Catholic social teaching came to justify conservative social stances, as against efforts to minimise the gap between the different sectors of society. But at times this process was taken further by a *deliberate* harnessing of the social teaching of the Church to make it serve a political function. This may have taken place in some of the American campaigns against anything that could be labelled 'communist' or even 'socialist'. But the most obvious and blatant example was the way in which right-wing groups in Latin America sought in the Catholic faith an ideological support for their attitudes. They resisted land reform and a more equal division of wealth, in the name of the sacrosanctness of private property. They also invoked Church teaching about obedience to authority and about non-violence in support of their resistance to the changes demanded by social justice. The social teaching of Pope John was a major step towards the prevention of such an ideological use of Church teaching and towards the recovery of its original purpose.

A Shift to the Left

There are two passages in *Pacem in Terris* which express a key insight of John XXIII:

> One of the fundamental duties of civil authorities . . . is so to co-ordinate and regulate social relations that the exercise of one person's right does not threaten others in the exercise of their own rights . . . (PT 62—Campion version, adapted).
>
> The common good requires that civil authorities maintain a careful balance between coordinating and protecting the rights of the citizens on the one hand, and promoting them, on the other. It should not happen that certain individuals or social groups derive special advantage from the fact that their rights have received preferential protection (PT 65).[16]

There is of course nothing very startling in these as general statements. But the pope seemed to have had in mind actual situations where the entrenched rights of some were the main obstacle to the exercise of the rights of others—especially of the poor. In the modern situation social justice required the recognition of new rights for the people at the lower end of the social scale. But the recognition and promotion of these rights was being hindered, either deliberately or uncritically, by the invocation of Catholic social teaching about the right to private property and the right to personal initiative. This amounted to an ideological use of this teaching, i.e. its use as a cover and legitimation for resistance to the changes needed to promote social justice. So the passages just quoted were intended to prevent such an abuse.

Already in *Mater et Magistra* Pope John had set out to lessen the chances that such things could happen. By means of that encyclical he had publicly and clearly put the weight of the Church on the side of a policy of social reforms in favour of the poor and deprived, both within each country and at the international level. *Mater et Magistra* advocated a considerable degree of control by public authorities over the activity of individuals and groups. It also recommended certain initiatives to be undertaken by the State to help those who are disadvantaged in society. The traditional and philosophical basis for such State control and initiative can be found in this passage: 'Our predecessors have constantly taught that inherent in the right to have private property there lies a social role and responsibility' (MM 119).[17] Leo XIII can certainly be cited as insisting on the importance of property owners using their wealth responsibly (RN 19). Pius XI insisted that 'the right to own private property has been given to people . . . both in order that individuals may be able to provide for their own needs and those of their families, and also that by means of it the goods which the Creator has destined for the whole human race may truly serve this purpose' (QA 45). Pius XII gave priority to the universal purpose of the goods of the earth and saw the institution of private property as a means for the attainment of this purpose (D3 198–9). Quite evidently there is a pattern here: each of these popes in turn lays greater stress than his predecessor on the social obligations attaching to private property. In *Mater et Magistra* John XXIII built on the foundation laid down just twenty years earlier by Pius XII. John's own contribution consisted mainly in drawing the obvious practical conclusions. He saw clearly that quite often private ownership was not in fact serving the purpose for which Pius XII said it had been instituted. So Pope John proposed a variety of measures to ensure that its social function should be attained. By the very fact of owning property a person incurs social responsibilities. John XXIII was not content with *encouraging* property owners to take these responsibilities seriously; he envisaged that they should be *compelled* by law to do so.

As we have seen, Pope John was not looking for a radical restructuring of the present order of Western society. Given that order, he accepted the need for State intervention in social and economic affairs to an extent well beyond what would have been advocated by Catholic leaders in the past. Perhaps even more important was the fact that he eliminated the suspicion of State control and State initiatives which had been a central feature of the Catholic social outlook. In this sense it is not inaccurate to see in *Mater et Magistra* a certain 'opening to the left' (*apertura a sinistra*) in the socio-economic sphere. How closely that was related to an opening towards the left in the political sphere remains open to debate. Certainly, *Pacem in Terris*, issued two years after *Mater et Magistra*, contains a very significant passage (PT 159) which I referred to earlier in this chapter.[18] In it the pope distinguished between false philosophical theories on the one hand and, on the other hand, the historical movements which are inspired by such theories; the latter, says the encyclical, can change profoundly and may contain positive and praiseworthy elements. This statement provided a justification for a significant change of attitude by the Vatican in the political field. It was an irenic gesture directed mainly towards left-wing movements at the national and international level. It left the door open for practical political cooperation between the Catholic Church and communist governments and parties. But it is important not to focus attention on the political question to an extent that plays down the significance of the move towards the left that had already taken place on social and economic matters in *Mater et Magistra*. Perhaps the most accurate way to sum up the effect of that encyclical, and of Pope John's social teaching in general, would be to call it not so much an opening to the left as a decisive move away from the right.

This helps one to understand why *Mater et Magistra* contains detailed directives on such specific matters as the two kinds of insurance needed by farmers (MM 135). The pope scarcely imagined that his proposals were so original and compelling that governments would immediately adopt them! Rather it must be presumed that John was speaking not to governments or political parties or civil servants as such but to those to whom the encyclical was officially addressed, namely, 'the . . . bishops, clergy and faithful of the Catholic world' (MM title). The pope felt the need to go into specific details because the approach he was advocating was quite different from the prevailing interpretation of Catholic social teaching, especially as regards its practical applications. One may show, as Bolté does quite effectively (Bolté I, 245–6), that there is considerable continuity between Pope John's teaching and that of his predecessors. One can conclude quite correctly that he was within a developing tradition. But this continuity applies at the level of 'doctrine' and general principles. In the application of the principles and in the practical implications for the stance of the Christian on social questions, the *discontinuity* is more obvious. It would be wrong to exaggerate this discontinuity, to speak as though Pope John were advocating socialism. But it must be said that *Mater et Magistra* stands as a turning-point in Catholic social teaching.

The extent to which the encyclical was a turning-point has emerged more clearly in recent years. It stands at the source of two important developments whose full implications could hardly have been foreseen at the time. The first of these is in the area of theory, though it has many practical effects. *Mater et Magistra* opened up cracks in what had been a rather monolithic body of social teaching. It raised doubts about attitudes that had not been questioned previously—for instance an attitude of suspicion about State intervention and a conviction that it ought to be kept to a minimum. Before long there was considerable questioning of many other parts of the traditional Catholic social approach and teaching. Furthermore, the encyclical was controversial and was subject to a variety of interpretations. This gave rise to fragmentation at the practical level: there was no longer a clear, universally accepted Catholic 'line' on many socio-economic issues. It was not long before the very concept of a 'social doctrine' was called into question (e.g. Chenu). This is an issue to which I shall return in a later chapter.

The second development was that *the encyclical began the process by which the Catholic Church got new allies and new opponents.* This was perhaps the most important effect of the encyclical—at least for those who recognise that social teaching arises from, and relates back to, social praxis. The speed at which this development occurred varied from place to place and even from continent to continent. Latin America is the region where one can see most clearly what was involved. The 'option for the poor' which the Church began to make in many parts of that continent towards the end of the 1960s could never have taken place unless key leaders in the Church had determined that they would no longer allow the institutional Church to be an ally of the rich and powerful. Their refusal to provide a legitimation for the privileges of the 'elite' was a major factor in enabling the Church to opt for solidarity with the poor and oppressed. The Church of course had always seen itself as having a message for all of humanity and every sector of society. But many Latin American Church leaders became convinced that they must at times give a specific answer to the question: 'Whose side are you on?' In regard to basic issues of social justice they felt that they could not plead neutrality. So they committed the Church to making what came to be called 'a preferential, but not exclusive, option for the poor'. The fact that they made such an option was largely due to John XXIII and especially to the social teaching of *Mater et Magistra.*

SUMMARY

Pope John was optimistic about the world, particularly about the modern world. His two major social encyclicals showed that he was even optimistic about Western capitalist society and did not seek a complete change of the system. He felt it had already been humanised to some degree through various reforms, and that it could become more humane in the future through much more intervention by the State to protect the interests of the poor. So he moved Catholic teaching away from its traditional opposition to the 'Welfare State' approach. At the international level he also favoured a similar approach, with some kind of world government to oversee the process; and he gave a high priority to the issues of international development and social justice at the international level.

In spite of Pope John's 'moderate' position, his encyclical *Mater et Magistra* changed the whole direction of Catholic social teaching. Though he still insisted on the principle of subsidiarity, his proposals for a lot of State intervention amounted to approval of the Welfare State—or at least it gave the impression of doing so. In both economic and political affairs Pope John favoured a certain 'opening to the left'. This meant that left-wing and social democratic people began to see the Church as a possible ally while right-wing and conservative sectors of society could no longer presume that the Church would give them religious backing. Pope John's distancing of the Church from right-wing forces was quite deliberate. He realised that the Church's over-emphasis on the right to private property and its suspicion of State intervention had allowed Catholic social teaching to become an ideological weapon used by the wealthy and the powerful to resist social change. By breaking decisively with this trend he laid the foundations for 'an option for the poor' by later Church leaders; and he gained for the Church new allies and new enemies.

Questions for review:

1. What was Pope John's attitude to the modern world and to Western capitalism?
2. What is meant by 'the Welfare State' and what was Pope John's position in relation to it?
3. How did Pope John change the direction of Catholic social teaching?
4. Why did he do so?
5. What were the effects?

Questions for reflection:

1. Does it make sense to you to distinguish between a 'liberal' and a 'radical'? If so, can you pick out examples of each approach among political leaders and among Church leaders?
2. Is it possible to have the different countries of the world linked together in an arrangement analogous to 'the Welfare State'? If so, how could it come about? If not, what alternative ways are there of promoting international justice?

Issue for further study:

Examine the different shades of meaning of the word 'liberal' from the last century up to today. Is there a close link between an economic liberal and being liberal on moral issues?

7

Vatican II: Another Agenda

This study of Vatican social teaching is concerned mainly
with the teaching of the popes. On what grounds should it
include a study of any documents issued by the Second
Vatican Council? Firstly, these are official Vatican documents.
Secondly, it would be a mistake to make too sharp a contrast
between papal teaching and the teaching of the Council. It is
true that the documents of Vatican II represent much more
than the views of John XXIII and Paul VI, the two popes who
presided over the Council. Indeed there is little doubt that
they contain things that these popes would not have said had
there never been a Council. But these two popes played a
major part in the genesis of the Council documents. Indeed
Paul VI helped to formulate the Council statements; and he
signed them, promulgated them, and set up the procedures
required to implement them. The documents of the Council
represent not merely the consensus of the bishops from all over
the world but also the consensus of these bishops with the
Vatican, above all with the pope. There can be no doubt of the
entire commitment of Pope Paul to the teaching of Vatican II.
It is evident, then, that it would be a serious mistake to study
papal teaching without making a close examination of the
teaching of Vatican II.[1]

The Liberal Agenda

Just nine days after Vatican II began, the Council Fathers issued
a short but significant 'Message to Humanity'. In it they noted
two issues of special urgency which they saw facing them—
peace and social justice.[2] However, before long the bishops and
their 'experts' became engrossed in other issues. So there was
an interval of more than three years before the Council issued

any formal teaching on these two topics which they had singled out in their first message. It is true, of course, that during that interval, work was going ahead on successive drafts of the document which eventually became *Gaudium et Spes*, the Pastoral Constitution on the Church in the Modern World. But until quite near the end of the Council there was considerable doubt as to whether this document would be issued at all. And when it did eventually come, the parts of it dealing with peace and social justice were comparatively short; and in places they showed signs of having been drafted with undue haste.

What happened? Why were these 'urgent issues' left so late in the Council? The standard answer is that the participants in Vatican II had first to work through certain urgent 'internal' theological and pastoral issues such as the sources of faith, the nature of the Church itself, the style of public worship, the nature of the ministry, and the pattern of the Church's authority structure. Only then could they deal satisfactorily with the 'external' issues of the Church's relationship with the world, notably in regard to questions about peace and social justice. This answer is correct as far as it goes but it is not a complete answer. What has to be added is that at an early stage of the Council, 'the liberal agenda' came to dominate both the discussions and the documents of the Council. Among the items on that agenda were: the use of the vernacular in the liturgy, the collegiality of bishops, the renewal of religious life, the role of the Bible in revelation, the Church's openness to other Christian Churches and to other faiths, and the issue of religious freedom. The main drama of the Council was the struggle between conservatives and liberals on these issues, with the liberals being identified as the 'progressive' group. This polarisation applied also in the area of the theology of marriage and sexuality; so it affected one of the major topics dealt with in the second and more practical part of *Gaudium et Spes*. However, the bishops and theologians of Vatican II did not split along conservative versus liberal lines in regard to the issues of social justice and peace. For instance, one of the champions of the conservative line, Cardinal Ottaviani, spoke out strongly in favour of what was called a 'progressive' stance in regard to war and peace.[3] On the other hand some of the more 'progressive' bishops took a much more cautious stance when it came to speaking out against the holding of nuclear weapons. This indicates that the usual categories of 'liberal' and 'conservative' did not apply very well to the views of the bishops and theologians on some socio-political issues. In regard to matters of peace and social justice the issue is to what extent the Church is prepared to take a radical or prophetic stance that challenges the current values of society. A desire that the Church should take up a prophetic posture is compatible with either conservative or liberal tendencies—though the radical-conservative combination has quite a different character from the radical-liberal one. Perhaps the most significant thing from our point of view is that at the Council the struggle between liberals and conservatives on internal Church matters tended to obscure the other issue, namely, the extent to which the Church should mount a radical or prophetic challenge to the world on socio-political questions.

But why did 'the liberal agenda' take over in the Council? Because, by and large, it represented the concerns and priorities of the Northern European theologians—and through them of the majority of European and North American bishops—as against those of the Roman establishment. It is important to note that on the whole the bishops from the Third World (indigenous and expatriate), though they were very numerous,[4] were not very involved or very significant in the polarisation between liberals and conservatives. As Vatican II progressed, there came to be a growing realisation that the Church is not just Western and Eastern but also Asian, Latin American, and African—and therefore that the Council documents would have to take serious account of the Third World. But a fully elaborated Third World theology did not emerge at the Council to challenge the liberal and conservative approaches, both of which were quite Western in their concerns. However, at least some of the major questions that were of interest for the Third World came to be given a rather higher priority than in the past. The drafters of *Gaudium et Spes* tried to take account of these questions. The final result was not altogether satisfactory; a number of the paragraphs of the document read as though statements about the situation in 'developing countries' had been 'patched in' to passages drafted originally with the Western world in mind.[5] Some of the drafting committees included people from the Third World—and it is doubtful whether a fuller representation would have led to any great improvement in the text.[6] What was missing was a coherent Third World theology and a body of 'experts' to articulate such a theology. In the absence of these it is not surprising to find that even Third World problems were looked at to some extent from a First World perspective. This is very evident in the treatment of 'development' and in the chapter on culture (GS 53–62, 64–5).[7] Nevertheless, *Gaudium et Spes* represents a considerable advance on earlier Church documents—even those of John XXIII—in so far as it begins to recognise more clearly that Third World countries have their own history, traditions, and social structures, as well as their own problems; and that none of these are to be treated as though they were no more than adjuncts to those of the West (e.g. GS 69.2, 71, 86).

The Contribution of Gaudium et Spes

What contribution does *Gaudium et Spes* make to the Church's social teaching? Before we look at the more significant points in its *content* it is well to note that the importance of this document lies not only in what it says but also in the *process* that produced it. *Gaudium et Spes* expresses the consensus that emerged after three years of private and public dialogue, debate, and even controversy. It crowns a three-year process of thorough and intense exploration by experts in the various matters it deals with, as well as a process of education of the bishops and of the millions of people who followed the progress of the Council. So, even where it merely repeats the teaching of Pope John or earlier popes, it does so with a greatly increased degree of authority and credibility.[8]

Gaudium et Spes repeats important themes from the two social encyclicals of John XXIII.[9] In general it tends to temper the extraordinary optimism of Pope John's documents. It does so, not by toning down his Christian hope and his high ideals, but by adopting a more dialectical approach: the ideal is contrasted with reality—a reality marred by social evil (e.g. GS 63.3 which notes that economic progress can lead to contempt for the poor).

Another important contribution of Vatican II to socio-political questions is the attempt to offer a solid theological basis for its practical directives. Among the more successful instances of this are the Council's statements on religious liberty (*Dignitatis Humanae*), on peace (especially GS 78), on human work (GS 33-9, 67), on the nature of human authority and the need for it (GS 74), and on the relationship of the Church to the world (GS 40-4). Rather less successful efforts in this direction are the Council statements on 'development' (GS 25-32, 63-72, 85-90) and on culture (GS 53-62). In presenting a theology of these different realities a positive effort was made to ensure that a Scriptural basis was given as well as a more philosophical component. In some cases there is quite a good integration of the two (e.g. GS 78 on peace; GS 34, 37, 39, 57 on work). Elsewhere the integration is not so good (GS 57, 72). In those passages of *Gaudium et Spes* which are more philosophical in tone the drafters distance themselves somewhat from the neo-scholastic approach of earlier documents: the text incorporates what is best in the natural law tradition and integrates it with a more existential idiom.

Pope John's determination to issue an encyclical on peace before he died led him to up-stage the Council document on this question. Nevertheless, those who were drafting *Gaudium et Spes* succeeded in making one major contribution on this subject. The document proposes a conception of peace which provides a philosophical-theological basis for its more practical statements (which follow in the same general direction as Pope John). According to *Gaudium et Spes*, peace is not merely an absence of war. It is an ordering of society; but real peace is built not just on any order but on one which is to be brought into existence by the thirst of people for an ever more perfect justice (GS 78.1). There are three important points here:

— First, peace does not just happen. Though in one sense it is a God-given gift to society,[10] still it has to be brought about by human commitment and effort.

— Secondly, it is not attained once for all but has to be constantly defended[11] renewed[12] and brought nearer to the ideal.

— Thirdly, and most importantly, peace is firmly linked to justice; and it is the passionate desire ('thirst') for justice that motivates people to work for peace.

The justice of which the document speaks is not simply the putting right of 'political' grievances. It extends to the whole *economic* order. That is why this chapter goes on to treat of international cooperation in the economic field (GS 83–7). In this way the Council Fathers reacted against the tendency, common among statesmen in the more 'developed' countries, to think that a more peaceful world can be brought about without too much tampering with the present inequitable economic world order. The Council document helps to make it clear that there are not two distinct international questions, one about peace and one about economics. The two are the same question.

This firm determination to present the problems of the so-called 'less developed countries' in terms of justice marks a subtle but significant development in the social teaching of the Church. It is not entirely original; for Pius XII and John XXIII had both spoken of these problems in terms of the principle that the goods of the world are destined for the people of the world; and the latter had said that it is a matter of justice that the goods of the Earth be better distributed (Pius XII D3 200–1; MM 74, 161).[13] As I pointed out in the previous chapter, Pope John moved the topic of International Development Cooperation towards the centre of the social justice agenda. *Gaudium et Spes* carried this a stage further.

For anybody concerned with the theme of the Church's 'option for the poor' the following passage will be seen as one of the most significant statements of the Vatican Council:

> God destined the earth and all that it contains for the use all people and all peoples . . . Furthermore, the right to have a share of earthly goods sufficient for oneself and one's family belongs to everyone.
>
>   . . . If a person is in extreme necessity, that person has the right to take from the riches of others what he or she really needs. Since there are so many people in this world weighed down by hunger, this sacred Council urges all, both individuals and governments, to remember the saying of the Fathers: 'Feed those who are dying of hunger, because if you have not fed them you have killed them.' According to their ability, let all individuals and governments undertake a genuine sharing of their goods . . . (GS 69—Abbot translation, emended).

The train of thought in this passage is exceptionally interesting. The words 'and all peoples' were deliberately added into the first sentence after some discussion, precisely in order to indicate that the Council had in mind the problem of poor countries, not just poor individuals[14] By going on to speak within the same passage of the person in extreme necessity the document seems to be suggesting that to be in such extreme need is the plight not just of occasional isolated and desperate individuals but of whole peoples. This impression is confirmed by the fact that the very next sentence speaks of so many people in the world weighed down by hunger.

In strict logic one might have expected that the document would go on to conclude that the masses of hungry people have the right to take what they need from the rich peoples of the world. Instead, however, the Council Fathers make an earnest appeal to individuals and governments to share what they have with the poor. Why this rather weak conclusion? Could it be that the hungry masses are not considered by the Council Fathers to be in 'extreme necessity'? That is most unlikely, since there would then have been no point in referring to the person in extreme necessity. Or could it be that the drafters of the document were drawing back from the obvious conclusion of their statements, namely, that these poor people have the right to take what they need? That is not to be assumed, because there is a more likely explanation. It is that the readers are being allowed to draw the conclusion for themselves precisely because it is so obvious. If the passage is understood in this way then the exhortation to the rich to share what they have must be seen as a combination of a timely warning and a moral threat. It means: if you do not share willingly, then the poorer peoples will in any case take what they need—and they will be justified in doing so. In this way the Council document succeeds in taking a very strong stance on the issue of international social justice, without lapsing into fruitless condemnations. The difficulty of course is that not everybody will see or accept the full implications of what the Council is saying. But it is doubtful whether harsh words of condemnation would be any more effective than the nuanced approach adopted in the document, in bringing about the fundamental changes that are called for.

A Change of International Economic Structures

Gaudium et Spes insisted that there is need for profound changes in the way international trade is carried out (GS 85.2). It called for the establishment of 'a truly universal economic order' (GS 85.3)—a phrase that seems to anticipate the 'New International Economic Order' ('NIEO') which was called for, some years later, at the United Nations. *Gaudium et Spes* recognised that a major source of injustice in international trade is the inequality in power between trading partners; to compensate for this the document called for the setting up of institutions to promote and regulate international trade (GS 86.6).[15] This is precisely the kind of thing that the NIEO requires—namely, a major expansion and strengthening of international bodies to regulate the supply and price of Third World products. Such agencies could protect the producers from the exploitation that results from over-production and erratic supply. If such international agencies really had effective power, and if they were not dominated by the wealthy nations, this in itself would constitute a fundamental change in the existing economic order. If they were gradually extended to cover the whole range of goods and services exchanged in international trade, then the cooperating nations would in effect have built up, piecemeal, the basic economic elements of a world government.

The fundamental principle of such an authority, as envisaged by *Gaudium et Spes* (GS 26.1), would be the common good of all rather than the capitalistic 'law' of supply and demand. To seek to form a community of nations devoted to the common good is a very ambitious undertaking. In recent times we have seen the painful struggle of the nations of the European Community to become a genuine community of nations while respecting the uniqueness of each and the principle of subsidiarity. We see the kind of mechanisms that are required to link the economies of different countries; and we have some idea of the juridical framework and binding commitments that are needed in the social, political and cultural fields to ensure that the 'laws' of capitalist economics are tempered by a concern for such moral values as the welfare of the weak, the young, the old, the vulnerable, and those on the periphery. This gives an indication of what would be required if the nations of the world were to make a serious effort to establish a global economic order devoted to the good of all. So the full implications of the changes proposed in the Council document are quite radical—possibly more so than the Council Fathers themselves fully realised.

Gaudium et Spes said explicitly that there is need not merely for a conversion in the mentality and attitudes of people but also for 'many reforms' in socio-economic life itself—that is, in its structures (GS 63.5).[16] But the document did not go into much detail in specifying what these reforms should be.[17] In one very carefully phrased passage the Council said that 'in many situations there is urgent need for a reassessment of economic and social structures' (GS 86.7 my translation). The choice of the word 'reassessment' is noteworthy. Some of the modern language translations speak here of reforming or recasting the structures.[18] But this is to miss the nuance of the Latin version. By choosing the word 'reassessment' the Council Fathers refused to assume glibly that the solution to all social problems was the overthrowing of existing structures. But what is significant is that they did not flinch from calling for a reassessment; they did not start with the presumption that any fundamental restructuring is unnecessary; nor did they rule it out on the grounds that it might be a threat to stability. They did, however, add that there is need for caution lest some of the priceless heritage of non-Western cultures be lost by the hasty imposition of 'technical solutions . . . especially ones that offer people material advantages while being inimical to the spiritual character of the human person' (GS 86.7 my translation).

It is not sufficient, however, to say *what* changes are called for. Two further questions need to be answered:
1. Why should such changes be made?
2. Is it permissible to use violent means in the struggle for social justice?
I hope to suggest answers to each of these questions in turn.

The Reasons for Change

The first thing that must be said is that *Gaudium et Spes* is not entirely clear in the answers it gives to the question why changes are needed. Is it simply to ensure that no significant group of people will be left totally impoverished i.e. in *absolute* poverty? Or are changes called for also in order to tackle the problem of *relative* poverty i.e. to ensure a more even distribution of the goods of the earth, even in situations where the poorer groups are not in extreme necessity? The Council Fathers seemed to assume that the way to overcome both of these kinds of poverty was by the promotion of 'development'; towards the end of this chapter I shall spell out what they understood by 'development'.

As noted above, the Council document suggests that whole nations may be living in a state of extreme necessity—and it points out that this imposes on rich people and the governments of the wealthier countries a serious and pressing moral obligation to make the changes required to meet their needs (GS 69.1). But, clearly, social justice involves something more than the overcoming of such extreme necessity. If the basic principle is that the goods of the earth are destined for all people of the earth, this calls for equity in their distribution. But what does equity mean in practice? It can hardly be some utopian attempt to divide the goods of the earth in exactly equal shares. That would be quite unrealistic, even as an ideal. Indeed various popes over the previous seventy years had insisted that it is of the nature of human society that its people have a diversity of wealth and status; and Vatican II certainly did not explicitly repudiate this teaching. But it undoubtedly went much further in the direction of equality than did the papal teaching of fifty years earlier:

> Excessive economic and social inequalities within the one human family, between individuals or between peoples, give rise to scandal, and are contrary to social justice, to equity, and to the dignity of the human person, as well as to peace within society and at the international level (GS 29.3 my translation).

However, the Council gave very little by way of guidelines that could enable one to decide at what point the inequalities can be considered so great as to be inequitable or unjust.

There is one text that could be significant in this regard. It is the passage in which the Council declares that in certain circumstances it may be right to expropriate and divide up the *latifundia* i.e. those large estates which are so common in the Third World, especially in parts of Latin America. What would justify the confiscation of such properties? Is it the mere fact that such huge estates exist in areas where there are so many poor, powerless, and exploited people? The Council does not say so, at least not explicitly. It seems rather to suggest that the key point is precisely the failure by the owners of these estates to make proper use of the land (GS 71.6).[19] Presumably the argument would be that the owner who fails to use the land productively is failing to ensure that the goods of the earth are used for the benefit of all—and this justifies expropriation. The implication of this line of argument would be that if owners of such enormous estates use the land productively then it would be wrong to confiscate their lands. But whatever about the strict logic of the argument, the text seems to recognise that there is a very close connection in practice between the possession of huge land-holdings and the blatant exploitation of the local population. This exploitation is at least a contributory factor, if not the primary basis for the call for expropriation. In theory the exploitation could be remedied in other ways than by confiscation of the land; but in practice the two are almost inextricably linked. The Council document remains rather vague about the precise basis for expropriation. This may well have been deliberate. For many of the bishops would have been reluctant to make any statement that seemed to restrict unduly the right to private property.[20]

However, in the Council document the traditional emphasis by the Church on the rights of private property owners had to be balanced against the equally traditional protest of the Church against leaving workers in a totally powerless and vulnerable position, with no property of their own to provide them with a minimum of security. What seems to be original in this statement on expropriation is the willingness of the bishops to accept that in very many actual cases the balance tips in favour of the poor and powerless: in the concrete, the right to private property has to yield to the cry of the poor—and therefore expropriation becomes justifiable. The Council Fathers would not have made the statement at all unless they believed it had a fairly widespread application. In his commentary on this section of *Gaudium et Spes*, L. J. Lebret (who himself played an important role in helping to draft the text) raises important questions about the basis on which compensation ought to be calculated in the case of expropriation of land. This issue arises especially, as Lebret notes, in cases where the market value of the land has greatly increased because of such extrinsic factors as the decision to utilise it for housing or for some public purpose (Lebret in de Riedmatten *et al*, 228-9). The Council document itself refrains from entering into such detailed questions and is therefore able to retain a certain vagueness about the fundamental moral principles that lie behind its call for social change.

Obligation to Help the Poor

An important light is thrown on the attitude of the Council Fathers by a late addition which they made to one passage in *Gaudium et Spes*. The text is the one in which we are reminded that the Fathers and Doctors of the Church taught that people are 'obliged to come to the relief of the poor *and to do so not merely* out of their superfluous goods' (GS 69.1 Abbott translation). The italicised words were added at a fairly late stage in the drafting of the document;[21] and evidently this involved a major change in the meaning of the statement. It also involved a correction of Leo XIII's statement in *Rerum Novarum* that people are obliged to give to the poor out of what remains over when they have provided for their own needs and for what is appropriate to their station in life (RN 19). Pius XI had repeated this teaching in *Quadragesimo Anno* but had added that the use of superfluous wealth to provide work for others is an excellent act of liberality, particularly appropriate to our time (QA 50-1). A closer look at the effects of the teaching of these two popes will help to show why a different line was taken at Vatican II.

Pope Leo XIII said that one is obliged to give to the poor out of one's '*superflua*'. This gave rise to a rather distasteful type of casuistry—an attempt to measure what amount of wealth is appropriate to the status of different classes of people, the remainder of the person's income being seen as 'superfluous'. This kind of casuistry allowed the rich to calculate that they had no obligation to give to the poor until the normal status symbols of wealthy people had been acquired (R. Miller 91). The basic intention of Pope Leo's statement thus became perverted and even contradicted: instead of imposing a heavy obligation on the rich to help the poor, it offered a kind of justification for turning a deaf ear to the cry of the poor, on the grounds that one has to live up to one's social standing. No wonder then that Vatican II decided to assert a much more urgent obligation to help the poor. The Council was able to do so by appealing to an even more ancient and honourable tradition than that invoked in *Rerum Novarum*. Pope Leo had referred to St Thomas Aquinas in support of his position; the Council document by contrast refers to Basil, Lactantius, Augustine, Gregory the Great, Bonaventure, and Albert the Great (GS 69.1).

Pius XI introduced a certain modification into the position of his predecessor by trying to take account of the modern economic situation. This is one where wealth cannot be divided simply into that which is used up on consumer goods and that which is hoarded; a third category has to be added, namely, wealth that is invested productively. Given this situation, Pius XI was correct in saying that productive investment can help others by giving employment. But his way of expressing it had a certain air of unreality: it could give the impression that such investment is an act of generosity, whereas in fact it is generally motivated by self-interest.[22] Vatican II, like Pius XI, was in favour of investment.[23] Nevertheless, *Gaudium et Spes* does not refer at this point to what had been said by Pius XI. One may surmise that this was because the drafters of the document did not wish to give the impression that the Council Fathers saw capitalist investors as great benefactors of humanity.

When compared with the teaching of Leo XIII and Pius XI, the text of *Gaudium et Spes* represents a notable change of emphasis. There is a shift away from the undue stress which had been laid on the rights of property owners. These rights have been relativised by the Council document, not merely in principle—as Pius XII had already done (D3 199)—but in the practical applications of the principle to the world of the time.

The Process of Change: Violent and Non-violent

We now go on to seek an answer to the second question posed earlier, namely, whether it is permissible to use violence in struggling for social justice. The key issue here is, who are to be the agents of change—those at the top of society or those at the bottom? If change is to come primarily from the top then the issue of violence scarcely arises, since whatever changes come will only be ones acceptable to those who hold power. But if those at the bottom of society are the main agents of change, then the issue arises whether, or to what extent, they can use force in their struggle.

Vatican II seems to presume that the required action will have to be taken by the rich and powerful. It directs a strong appeal to them to make changes—both for altruistic or moral reasons (GS 69.1; 85.1) and also in their own self-interest, since injustices give rise to discord and war (GS 83). The Council does not have anything very inspiring to say specifically to those who are poor and powerless. Indeed it seems to speak more *about* the poor than directly *to* them. Its strongest statement is the one in which it affirms the right of those in extreme need to take what is necessary (GS 69.1) and to this statement a cautious footnote was appended pointing out that in applying this principle all the moral conditions must be fulfilled. The Council did not really address itself to the question of what could be accepted as a legitimate way of 'taking what is necessary'. Indeed it failed to provide any practical guidelines about the use of force by those engaged, on one side or the other, in the 'liberation struggles' taking place in many parts of the world.

At Vatican II the debate about violence and war was dominated by the East-West struggle rather than the North-South issue. A major question was whether modern atomic, bacteriological, and chemical weapons had caused the traditional just war teaching to be no longer applicable to actual situations. The Council forcefully condemned total war (GS 80.4) but refused to rule out entirely the possibility of a justified war of defence (GS 79.4).[24] But unfortunately the text of *Gaudium et Spes* did not deal specifically with the question of war in the form in which it arises for much of the Third World, namely, whether or in what circumstances a 'war of liberation' might be justified. This omission by the Council reflects the lacuna in theological thinking at that time.

Typical of the state of the theological reflection and interest of this period is a book entitled *International Morality* by the

French theologian de Soras. The author gives a fairly extensive treatment of issues relating to the morality of war between States. But he devotes only a minimum of space to wars of liberation by oppressed peoples. Even more significant is the fact that what he does have to say about such wars is not concerned with whether or in what circumstances a people may be entitled to resist colonial or neo-colonial oppression; rather he considers the question from the point of view of the colonial power. He asks such questions as whether it is permissible to engage in psychological warfare against revolutionary forces (de Soras 87, 95). Undoubtedly this was an urgent issue for French Christians facing the Algerian uprising; but for Christians of the Third World there were far more urgent moral issues, which the book makes no effort to deal with.

It is interesting to note that at one stage in the preparation of drafts for the Council document a text was proposed recognising the legitimacy of active resistance to oppression, parallel to the legitimacy of a just war between States. But in the debate many bishops intervened to say that this was too hasty an answer to a very delicate question. To nuance the text adequately would require much work, so it was decided to drop the statement entirely.[25] However, the fact that the Council omitted the proposed statement does not imply that it rejected the view that it is possible to have a legitimate rebellion or 'war of liberation' (cf. Dubarle in de Riedmatten, 581–2). It is better to see it as an indication that the Third World agenda was not given a very high priority at Vatican II. The failure of the Council to take the time and trouble needed to clarify the issue left something of a gap in the teaching of the Council in relation to war and the use of violence. We may note in passing that the World Council of Churches was paying much more attention around this time to Third World issues (cf. Dorr [1991] 70–1).

High on the agenda for the Third World comes the question of non-violent resistance to oppressive governments. Did the Council have anything to say that would be of help to a people who are the victims of colonial or racialist governments, or of a neo-colonial system operating through repressive governments controlled by privileged minorities? In the course of a fine general statement about peace the Council Fathers expressed

their admiration for those who renounce the use of violence to
vindicate their rights, relying instead on the kinds of defence
that are available to those who do not have power (GS 78.5).[26]
But when it came to saying something more specific on the
question of non-violence, the Council addressed itself to an
issue that was mainly of interest for the First World: it spoke of
conscientious objection and in a carefully worded passage gave
it guarded support (GS 79.3).[27] *Gaudium et Spes* did not
examine the kind of issue about non-violence that would be of
particular relevance and urgency in the Third World. The
major question there would be, what does it mean in practice
to make use of 'the kinds of defence that are available to those
who do not have power' (GS 78.5)? Does such a defence
include the use of political strikes, civil disobedience, mass
marches (even when such marches are prohibited by the government), sabotage of government property, and so on? The Council
did not give an answer; nor did it give any clear guidelines that
would enable people suffering gross oppression to work out an
answer.

A treatment of such questions, in order to be really helpful,
would have to be placed within a wider context. This context
is the right of a people to resist an oppressive government. The
Council document did not offer any clear teaching on this
issue. But it took one important step towards it by giving a
clear account of the nature and limits of human authority (GS
74). Towards the end of this account the conclusion emerges
that people are entitled to defend their own rights and those of
their fellow citizens against the abuses of a tyrannical regime.
There are, however, two provisos: (1) the limits laid down by
the natural law and the Gospel must be observed; and (2)
people should not refuse to obey in those matters objectively
required by the common good (GS 74.5). Each of these two
conditions raises more questions than it solves. There is considerable doubt about what are the limits laid down by natural law
and the Gospel—especially on the question of violent resistance,
or even of any kind of resistance prohibited by law. And the
difficulty about the second proviso is that it is so vague as to be
practically meaningless. At first sight it seems quite specific: it
appears to be saying that people should resist only on the
particular points where there is an abuse of rights by those in

authority. But could it not be that the common good would best be served by an attitude of total non-cooperation with an extremely oppressive government? This is what took place during most successful wars of liberation. Such action seems to be compatible with the *Gaudium et Spes* statement, for the text adopts the common good as the criterion. But at that point the meaning of the passage has become so all-embracing that it has little or no content!

Some Inadequacies

There is not much point in combing the text of *Gaudium et Spes* for guidelines about liberation struggles, violent or non-violent, when in fact the Council was working to a different agenda, set mainly by the First World. As the previous paragraphs should have made clear, one problem about such an agenda is that it does not give a sufficiently high priority to the burning issues of the Third World. But a further problem is that when Third World issues are given consideration they are looked at mainly from the perspective of the First World. To bring out this point we may note some serious deficiencies in the manner in which the notions of authority and poverty are treated in *Gaudium et Spes*.

Let us look first at the question of authority. At a fairly early stage in the Council document there is a deeply moving passage about the human life of Jesus Christ. It contains one statement which would be unremarkable to a person living in a well-run Western democracy but might pose problems for somebody living under an oppressive Third World government: 'Jesus Christ . . . willingly obeyed the laws of his country (GS 32.2 my translation). This statement seems to foster a spirituality of unquestioning obedience to civil authorities that may be quite inappropriate for millions of Christians who are victims of injustice. But these millions seem to have had few bishops or theologians to speak out on their behalf at the Vatican Council. Did nobody think of questioning the accuracy of the statement that Christ willingly obeyed the laws of his country, or at least seek to clarify which set of laws was in question? Was there anybody there to point out some of the important things about Christ that the passage fails to say—for instance, his challenge to the religious authorities of his time; and his judicial murder through an alliance between local religious leaders and the colonial power? To Christians in the Third World, such facts about Jesus Christ could be just as relevant as his obedience.

The treatment by Vatican II of the question of poverty is also deficient; one reason for this is that the perspective is not that of the masses of the world's poor. In the original 'Message to Humanity' from the Council Fathers in the early days of Vatican II there is deep compassion for the poor but no clear indication of solidarity with them. For instance the Fathers say they 'want to fix a steady gaze' on the poor; it is as though they are looking at the poor from outside (*Nuntius* 823).[28] The Council document on the renewal of the religious life, when treating of the vow of poverty makes only passing reference to the poor (*Perfectae Caritatis*, par. 13). This contrasts very sharply with the follow-up Apostolic Exhortation entitled *Evangelica Testificatio*, issued in 1971, in which members of religious communities are exhorted to hear 'the cry of the poor' and to see the links between that cry and social injustice (par. 17–18). All this indicates that it was only in the few years after the Council that the new spirituality of the poor came to the fore.

Perhaps one reason why Vatican II was unable to propose any very rich spirituality of poverty is that, during the years of the Council, bishops and theologians were still in the process of disengaging from an older spirituality. As we saw in a previous chapter, some popes had in the past espoused a rather 'escapist' spirituality, where poverty was to be endured in the hope of future reward; and this view had been widely accepted by Christians. The new 'worldly' theology associated with the Council—and especially with *Gaudium et Spes*—found little place for such an approach. But changes in spirituality—being changes in the heart as much as in the head—come about more slowly than changes in theology. It was too soon to expect a new spirituality of poverty to be available to replace the earlier escapist one. Indeed one could hardly expect the Council theologians from affluent Europe and North America to forge such a spirituality. So, even in this the most radical of the Council documents, poverty was considered mainly from a practical point of view. It was seen as an urgent problem, a problem to be overcome mainly by 'development' (GS 65–71,

85–8). At one point in the document Christians are exhorted to have their whole lives 'permeated with the spirit of the beatitudes, especially with the spirit of poverty' (GS 72.1 my translation).[29] But the point was not developed. Indeed, the manner in which the document emphasised full human development left little opening for an integration of a spirit of poverty as a major element in the spirituality it was proposing or presupposing.

Within a decade it became evident that a notable lacuna had been left in Christian spirituality. If a fatalistic spirituality of poverty is to be replaced, there is need for something powerful to take its place. It is not enough to be concerned *for* the poor; one must discover what it means to be *with* the poor. Only then can one experience what it is like to be humanly weak and powerless, but still to be powerful in the awareness that God is on one's side. Out of such an experience can come a spirituality that is not passive and escapist but active and 'worldly'—though nevertheless open to the transcendent. This will be a spirituality which does not allow itself to be used ideologically by people at either end of the political spectrum: by extreme conservatives, opposed to social change and social justice; or by those revolutionaries whose vision is narrowly materialistic. *Gaudium et Spes* does not propose a fully rounded spirituality of this kind. It was drafted and approved at a period when the leaders of the Catholic Church were so concerned with offering a positive theology of the world that they were as yet unable to discern sufficiently which aspects of the world ought to be challenged. One might say that the document is so taken up with the liberal agenda that it does not deal adequately with the radical agenda.

A *Starting-point*

Despite its shortcomings *Gaudium et Spes* must be judged to be a major achievement. This judgment applies not merely to the document in general but also to its contribution in the area of social justice. For it offers a theology and spirituality of the world which provide a solid foundation for a Christian approach to the question of poverty—an approach which can avoid lapsing into escapism on the one hand or secularism on the other. In the face of issues of social justice, the liberal agenda can lead on naturally to a more radical one. The liberal seeks to be open to the world, accepts the pluralism of modern society, seeks dialogue with those who have a different outlook—all with the aim of making the world a more human place in which to live. One danger facing the liberal is that openness may come to mean that one stands for nothing in particular. Related to this is the danger that service of the world may come to mean simply conforming to the existing situation, accepting the dominant values of society. The radical approach offers a corrective for this. It seeks to be of service to the world precisely by challenging some of its dominant values. The world to which the radical is committed is not the present world but the future—or the present in so far as it is open to a very different and better future. It is not the world of the rich and the powerful—or, more accurately, not the world as structured to favour this privileged group. It is primarily the world of the dominated, the oppressed, the poor—a world in need of liberation.

In regard to the role of the Church in society, *Gaudium et Spes* offers many instances of what I have been calling the liberal agenda. It seeks to make Christians aware that, living in a pluralist world, they must try to understand and engage in dialogue with people of other outlooks—and this applies even in the case of atheists (GS 21).[30] This theme of understanding and dialogue is very evident in the second last paragraph of the document which points out the need for dialogue within the Church itself, with other Christians, with people of other religious traditions, with humanists, and even with those who oppose and persecute the Church (GS 92).[31] The basic principle that is being applied is respect for others, a respect that allows them their freedom; and that is what the word 'liberal' means. All this is quite central to Christianity. Nevertheless it is not the only thing that is central to Christianity. There is a danger that having discovered the principle of liberty (or having restored it to its central place) Christians might stop there. If that were to happen the Church would have become liberal but would have ceased to be prophetic. It would be an exaggeration to suggest that this is what happened during the course of the Vatican Council—especially in the drafting of *Gaudium et Spes*.

But it does not seem unfair to say that on certain matters related to justice, poverty, and 'development', the liberal dimension of this document is stronger than its prophetic dimension.

Nevertheless, *Gaudium et Spes* provides a solid basis for the step from the liberal to the radical or prophetic agenda. It does so especially in the chapter in which the role of the Church in the modern world is treated formally and explicitly (GS 40-5). There the Council Fathers see the role of the Church as making the human family more truly human (GS 40.3). Among the ways in which this is to be done are the proclamation and the fostering of human rights (GS 41.3), the establishing and building up of the human community, and the initiation of action for the service of all—especially of the poor (GS 42.2).[32]

It was precisely in its commitment to freedom—to the liberal agenda in the best sense—that the Council took what may well be its most important step towards the adoption of a prophetic role on matters of social justice. There is one section of *Gaudium et Spes* which treats of 'The Political Community and the Church'. In it there is a paragraph which can be seen as a new charter or mandate for the relationship between the Church and political authorities (GS 76). A key passage states:

> The Church . . . does not rest its hopes on privileges offered to it by civil authorities; indeed it will even give up the exercise of certain legitimately acquired rights in situations where it has been established that their use calls in question the sincerity of its witness or where new circumstances require a different arrangement (GS 76.5 my translation).[33]

The relinquishing of privilege in order to retain freedom of witness, of judgment and of action is central to the liberal outlook. But it is precisely because the Church in Latin America took seriously this liberal principle that it gained the freedom to adopt a *prophetic* role. So long as Church authorities sought patronage, protection and privileges from the State they remained dependent on those who held power in civil society. This dependence inhibited the Church from offering an effective challenge to oppressive governments and unjust social and economic structures. It even allowed the rich and powerful to 'use' the Church by giving an aura of religious legitimation to the existing structures of society and a certain approval to those who held power. The passage just quoted from *Gaudium et Spes* was accepted by much of the Church in Latin America as an invitation to adopt a very different posture—to disengage from the embrace of the privileged elites and to challenge structural injustice. In this sense it was *Gaudium et Spes* that provided the foundation on which was built, three years later at Medellín, the Latin American Church's formal commitment to taking 'an option for the poor'.

The Model of Development

Before finishing this account of the teaching of Vatican II on social justice it is necessary to look more closely at the notion of development which the Council Fathers had in mind when they called for change in the way society was organised. For the whole idea of development was coming to have a major impact at this time both in secular society and in the Church.

As I pointed out in the previous chapter, Pope John, in *Mater et Magistra*, had come out strongly in favour of development; he wanted the wealthy countries to assist the poor ones to overcome poverty by becoming 'developed'. But in his encyclicals the notion of development was largely taken for granted. In *Gaudium et Spes*, on the other hand, the notion of development is much more central; it functions as an organising principle for the whole treatment of socio-economic problems.

A careful examination of the various prescriptions of *Gaudium et Spes* enables one to compile a list of some fundamental values which its authors saw as central to authentic development:

— A more equitable distribution of resources, including land (GS 71, 78.1).
— A better sharing of the fruits of economic activity between the nations (GS 69.1, 70, 85–7) and within each country e.g. between the farmers and the rest of the community (GS 66).
— The right of workers to share in management and in the whole process of economic planning (GS 65, 68.1–2).
— The right of workers to establish trade unions and, as a last resort, to go on strike in defence of their just rights (GS 68.2–3).
— The use of improved methods of production (GS 66.1, 87.1).

— The importance of investing resources to promote development (GS 65.3).

— The need to ensure that workers can live with dignity and have the opportunity to develop their talents, even in their work (GS 67).

— The protection of workers against unemployment (GS 67.2) and against the effects of the automation, relocation and migration which may arise from economic development (GS 66.2–3).

— The importance of taking account of the needs of future generations (GS 70).

— The adoption of more equitable terms of trade between the wealthy nations and the poorer ones (GS 85.2) and the establishment of organisations to regulate this trade (GS 86.6).

In the 1950s and 1960s, economists, planners and politicians spoke of development almost exclusively in economic terms. By and large, they accepted the view of Rostow that there were certain fixed stages of development which every country had to go through; and that if the poorer countries could achieve a certain level of investment then their economies could 'take off' and follow the pattern of Western countries. The Council Fathers were challenging this conception of development. They had in mind a notion of balanced development—one where economic values are not the only consideration but where these are linked to other fundamental human values such as freedom, dignity and participation. They were concerned not just about material welfare but also about the requirements of 'intellectual, moral, spiritual and religious life'; furthermore they saw development as being at the service of all people, all groups and every race (GS 64). So the process of development should not be controlled by a minority of people or nations; the largest possible number of nations and people should have a share in its direction (GS 65.1–2).

The Council document provided important elements for an overall theology of development to underpin the above practical points:

— It offered a theology of work, seeing it as a way in which humans share in the divine work of creation and the redemptive work of Christ (GS 67.2).

— It provided a theology of the community of humankind (GS 33–9).

— It suggested that Christians working for justice and the welfare of humanity should observe the right order of values, in faithfulness to Christ and his gospel, and have their lives permeated with the spirit of the beatitudes, especially the spirit of poverty (GS 72).

The authors of *Gaudium et Spes* believed that the main way to overcome global poverty was to ensure that economic development would be made available to all (GS 65, 69, 70, 71, 85–7). But they were aware of the dangers. The hasty imposition of 'technical solutions' could bring people 'material advantages while being inimical to the spiritual character of the human person' (GS 86.7 my translation). A too impetuous and ruthless imposition of 'development' could undermine such traditional 'worthy customs' as communal modes of owner-ship (GS 69.2). In this way some of the priceless heritage of non-Western cultures could be lost (cf. GS 56.2).

However, I think the experts and bishops who took part in the Council gravely underestimated these dangers. They failed to take sufficient account of two important limitations of the concept of 'development' which they were using. Firstly, the kind of development which had been so successful in bringing prosperity to Western countries could not be applied all over the world. The ecological cost would be so high that the Earth's resources could not sustain it. Furthermore, 'development' in the West was at least partly dependent on 'under-development' in other parts of the world—for instance, through the availability of low-cost primary products from the Third World; so-called development of this kind obviously cannot be extended to all parts of the world (cf. Dorr [1984] 63–6).

The second limitation of the concept of 'development' used at Vatican II was that this notion was itself a product of Western thinking. Those who drafted *Gaudium et Spes* were no doubt aware of this, but they were themselves too Western in their approach. They underestimated the degree to which the extension of 'development' to other continents would itself be a form of cultural imperialism. I am not saying that non-Western cultures must remain static; for they too are open to change and development—and they can even borrow elements of that development from Western thinking and practice (cf. Dorr [1990] 168–9 and Dorr [1991] 129–34). But the Council Fathers and experts assumed too easily that the basic elements of *Western* 'development' and its underpinning values are trans-cultural. In recommending it so enthusiastically they were unwittingly encouraging an imposition of a product of Western culture which could undermine other cultures.

At the heart of the Western model of 'development' is a certain individualism and competitiveness (—a point that is illustrated by the dramatic failure of communism to bring about effective development). These are 'values' (or disvalues) that are utterly alien to many non-Western cultures—and profoundly destructive of them. Western 'development' also presupposes a certain work-ethic that is quite hostile to the understanding of work, leisure and life that lies at the heart of many non-Western cultures. Equally profound differences are to be found in different cultures on a whole range of issues—for instance,

— how various peoples determine the highest priorities in life,

— what they understand to be the purpose of life,

— how people see time (e.g. the extent to which they accept the notion that 'time is money' and the importance they give to keeping to time in the Western sense),

— a people's notion of what gives one person a higher status than others,

— the relative importance people give to the promotion of inter-personal and communal relations, rather than simply 'getting the job done',

— what people consider to be 'enough' of various goods,

— what people see as the fundamental conditions for living a fulfilled human life.

When we speak of different cultures we are referring to fundamental differences of this kind.

The Council Fathers wanted to preserve all that was best in non-Western cultures even while they encouraged the extension of Western 'development' to them. They did not appreciate the extent to which these two aims were incompatible. This failure is related to the way Vatican II treated the question of culture.

Culture

There is a whole chapter of *Gaudium et Spes* devoted to 'The Proper Development of Culture' (GS 53–62). This in itself is a major achievement, as is the fact that the Council clearly accepted the fact of cultural pluralism. *Gaudium et Spes* rejected the very notion of a division of humanity into 'civilised' and 'uncivilised' peoples. It also pointed out that the Church has used the resources of different cultures not merely in preaching the message of Christ but also in understanding it (theology) and celebrating it (liturgy); so the Church is not tied to any one culture (GS 58.2–3). One of the more significant interventions during the Council came from Cardinal Lercaro who said that the Church must be willing to be culturally poor— that is, to have the courage to renounce, if necessary, the cultural riches of its past in order to open itself to other cultures (cf. Tucci in Vorgrimmler V, 267).

Those who drafted *Gaudium et Spes* became almost lyrical when they spoke about 'a new age of human history' (GS 54) and 'the birth of a new humanism' (GS 55). They saw this 'new humanism' as a more universal form of culture which they believed to be emerging in our time through the interaction of different cultures, the sharing of their riches and the conscious building up of a better world where people take responsibility for each other and for the future (GS 54–5).

It is precisely at this point that the Council's treatment of culture was inadequate. It failed to distinguish between the *ideal* unification which it was describing and the *actual* unification which is taking place in the world today. The nations of the earth are becoming increasingly part of one global market; but what is being created is a world where the wealthy nations and classes exploit the others. Again, the world is being linked together ever more closely through the communications media such as television and the great news agencies; but this unity is one where the cultures and even the languages of the less powerful peoples are being swamped by those of the rich and powerful.

The Council Fathers were concerned about the cultural development of vulnerable groups (GS 60.3), but this does not seem to have tempered their enthusiasm for unification. In this part of the document they adverted only very cursorily to the possibility of the traditional wisdom of a whole people being lost (GS 56.2). One effect of their failure to take sufficient account of Western cultural domination was that they themselves were unduly Western in their approach (e.g. they assumed that shorter working hours and more leisure are almost universal—GS 61.3).

Why did *Gaudium et Spes* fail to take sufficient account of the reality of cultural domination? Mainly because its treatment of culture was left to stand alone, without being integrated with related topics. The strength of the Council's treatment of the issue of international peace lay in the fact that it was very closely linked to its treatment of economics. Culture should have been linked to both of these. If that had been done the Council could have produced a very realistic treatment of the topic. But what we have instead is a somewhat abstract account of culture. The chapter on culture failed to take sufficient account of the economic and political underpinning of a people's culture, and of the enormous impact today on the cultures of 'the South' of the political-economic dominance of 'the North'. And the relegation of culture to a separate chapter meant that the treatment of economics failed to take sufficient account not only of the cultural *effects* of economic problems but also of their cultural *causes*.

Despite these inadequacies the Council document made an important contribution to the Church's teaching on the nature of human development. One its most significant passages is the following:

> . . . progress begins and develops primarily through the efforts and endowments of the people themselves. Hence, instead of depending solely on outside help, a people should rely chiefly on the full unfolding of their own resources and the cultivation of their own qualities and tradition (GS 86.2— Abbott version emended).

This indicates that the authors of the document, while still insisting on the importance of foreign aid, were far from accepting a simplistic view of how the problems of poorer countries could be overcome. Development, they realised, is not something that can be brought from outside but is a drawing out of the resources of the people themselves.

Gaudium et Spes also insisted on the importance of 'psycho-logical and material adjustments' that must be made by 'the developed nations' (GS 86.3) in order to meet their obligations to help the rest of the world. This may be taken to include what is called 'adjustment aid' which would make it easier for industries in 'the North' to face increased competition from 'the South'. But economic adjustment of this kind is not sufficient. More important is a change of mentality: the governments and the people of 'the North' must be prepared to accept 'the South' on terms of equality and partnership. Vatican II, taken as a whole, was an important move towards such an adjustment by the Catholic Church of the West.

I have been suggesting that the authors of *Gaudium et Spes* did not always succeed in practice in avoiding the mistaken attitudes which they rejected in principle. But the Council document provided a good basis for the deeper understanding of human development which came just a couple of years later in Pope Paul's great social encyclical *Populorum Progressio*.

SUMMARY

The Second Vatican Council showed considerable concern about the problem of poverty on a global scale. However, the main leaders in the Council were from the Western world; and they felt it essential to deal with their own 'liberal' agenda before addressing the question of the role of the Church in relation to world poverty. When they did get round to discussing the latter issue, they made an important contribution in *Gaudium et Spes*. This document is somewhat more realistic than the encyclicals of Pope John. It presents justice as central both to the issue of poverty and to that of peace. It calls for a change in the international economic structures; it stresses the right of the poor to their share of the Earth's goods—and insists that this imposes on the rich an obligation which is more than that of giving alms from their superfluous goods. It warns the rich that the poor are entitled to take what they need in order to live. It accepts that some huge land-holdings might have to be expropriated and given to the poor. It presents a balanced concept of development. It commits the Church to a relinquishment of its privileges where that is required to make its witness sincere and effective. Such willingness to renounce the patronage of the State sets the Church free to take a prophetic stand against those who hold power; so it was a major step in the progress of the Church towards making an option for the poor.

On the other hand there are some less satisfactory aspects to the document. It offers little by way of a spirituality of poverty. It does not address the moral issues relating to wars of liberation. Above all, it assumes that the main solution to the problem of poverty lies in following the Western model of economic development. It does not take sufficient account of the extent to which this would involve an imposition of Western culture on other peoples. The treatment of culture in the document does not take sufficient account of the links between culture and economics.

Questions for review:

1. Why was the issue of world poverty not fully addressed until very late in the Council?
2. In what ways did *Gaudium et Spes* add to the Church's social teaching?
3. Did the Council authorise poor people or peoples to fight for justice and to take what they needed to live a human life?

Questions for reflection:

1. To what extent can Western-style development really solve the problems of poverty in the poorer countries?
2. In what sense or to what extent does the Church have a privileged position in your country, and what are the effects?

Issue for further study:

Who were the spokespersons for the non-Western Churches at Vatican II? What were their main concerns? What contribution did they make? What did they overlook?

8

Paul VI on the Progress of Peoples

As we have seen, three major documents on social questions were issued by the Catholic Church's highest authorities at two-year intervals in the 1960s—*Mater et Magistra* in 1961, *Pacem in Terris* in 1963, and *Gaudium et Spes* in 1965. One might have expected Pope Paul VI to pause for a while before writing another social encyclical. That he did not do so is an indication of the rapid changes that were taking place at this time in the theology of justice and poverty—and also a sign of the pope's sense of urgency about these issues.

Barely sixteen months after the publication of the Council document he issued *Populorum Progressio* ('On the Development of Peoples'), a major encyclical in terms both of its length and its importance. The teaching in this document was original in two respects. Firstly, it offered a fresh approach to the understanding of 'development'. Secondly, in its approach to social justice it shifted the focus from the national to the international scene. I propose to consider each of these points in turn.

An original approach to Development

During the 1950s, the new idea of economic development brought about an enormous change in the thinking of government leaders and their advisers—and this affected the views of industrialists, trade unionists, agriculturalists, and 'ordinary people'. Essentially this change was the widespread acceptance of the belief that each individual country, and the world as a whole, can 'grow' out of poverty. Prior to this time justice was primarily a matter of ensuring the proper distribution of *existing* wealth and resources. Now it could be seen in terms of the production of *increased* resources which would be used to overcome poverty and to ensure that those who had little could catch up with those who had more.

In the previous two chapters I pointed out how this notion of development was adopted by Pope John and how a corrected version of it was given a central place by Vatican II. *Populorum Progressio* also gave a central place to the concept of development—but its approach was sharply different to that of previous Church documents. The difference was a conceptual one. The encyclical was radically new, not so much in its account of the specific details of what development involves, as in the way it seeks to *define* development. At the heart of *Populorum Progressio* lies a notion of integral development which Paul VI took from Père Lebret, the Dominican scholar and activist who died some time before the encyclical appeared.[1]

To explain the newness of the approach to development of *Populorum Progressio* let me give an analogy. Two people asked to describe their ideal house may respond in two different ways:

— One may say: 'My ideal house would be smaller than my present house; it would have better insulation; it would have solar panels on the roof instead of roof tiles, etc.'.

— The other person may say: 'My ideal house is one where a family can work, eat, sleep, and relax, with a maximum of ease at a minimum cost to themselves, to the community, and to the environment; etc.'.

The person giving the first answer starts from a known existing reality (the present house) and lists the *differences* between it and the ideal. The second answer begins by laying down certain general *criteria* or standards which the ideal house must live up to.

In regard to human development, the first of these approaches was adopted by the Fathers of Vatican II in *Gaudium et Spes* (The Church in the Modern World). Their starting point and term of reference was the kind of economic development to which governments all over the world were committed. They set out to correct and expand this conception, to produce a more integral and balanced conception of human development. In doing so, they made an important contribution to the Church's body of social teaching. But anybody who starts, as they did, from the current concept of 'development' used by economists and planners, is in danger of ending up with a notion of development that is quite inadequate. One great danger is that of assuming, consciously or unconsciously, that *economic* development is the solid core of any authentic human development. Those who start with this explicit or implicit assumption quickly find themselves trapped into an awkward conceptual framework. They find that they have to engage in a kind of trade-off between the solid economic core of development and the 'soft' elements which surround it. By the 'soft' elements I mean those that are not strictly economic—for instance, respect for culture, for the environment, for human rights, for the sense of community, and for the quality of human life. The solid economic core seems to be in competition with the surrounding 'soft' elements. Too much insistence on the 'soft' elements may put so many restraints on economic growth that the economy remains stagnant and so there is no 'development' at all.

In sharp contrast to this whole approach, Paul VI in *Populorum Progressio* adopted the kind of approach used in the second of the answers given above to the question, what is an ideal house. He did not take the current conception of economic development as a starting point and then modify it. Instead, he laid down certain basic standards by which we can measure to what extent any changes brought about in society deserve to be called authentic human development. In other words, what *Populorum Progressio* gives is a framework or anticipation of the 'shape' of genuine human development. In technical terms what it offers is a 'heuristic' notion of development.

In his account of authentic development the pope quotes from Lebret and follows his humanistic approach (PP 14). He insists that what is in question is the development 'of each person and of the whole person' (PP 14). He starts from the obligation of each person to attain self-fulfilment (PP 15–16). But development is not a purely self-centred affair. Each of us is part of a community and a civilisation which has its own history. So we are bound together in solidarity. Just as each of us has benefited from the efforts of others in the community and of those who have gone before us, so each of us has to take account of the welfare of others in the community and of those who will come after us (PP 16–17).

Populorum Progressio does not give a privileged place to the economic dimension of human development, any more than to the cultural, psychological, political, ecological, or religious dimensions. Rather it challenges Christians to take full account of the non-economic elements—for instance, to recognise the value of different cultures and of basic human rights. With this approach one is less tempted to take facile short-cuts—to say, for instance, that in the name of development we must sacrifice the environment or give up some treasured cultural tradition or some fundamental human right.

A heuristic concept of development is of course of no help unless its structures can be filled in so as to give it some concrete content. Pope Paul was no doubt aware of this when, following the inspiration of Lebret, he spoke of 'a development which is, for each and all, the transition from less human conditions to those which are more human' (PP 20). He then went on to indicate who are those who live in less human conditions. They are people weighed down by material or moral poverty or oppressed by bad social structures created by the abuse of wealth or power, by exploitation of workers or by unjust business deals. A move to more human conditions would include an escape from destitution, the elimination of social evils, the widening of knowledge and the attainment of culture (PP 21).

The encyclical goes on to include four other important items in his list of what is 'more human'. They are, greater respect for the dignity of others, an orientation towards a spirit of poverty, cooperation for the common good and a will for peace. By including these items here the pope ensures that personal self-fulfilment is not set in sharp contrast to the welfare of others. This links up with his emphasis towards the end of the encyclical on willing self-sacrifice in the interests of peace and unity (PP 79).

A dilemma arises for those who measure development only in material terms: the development of one individual or nation appears to be at the expense of others. By widening the concept of development to include spiritual values the pope succeeds in avoiding this dilemma. He provides a basis for integrating personal development with community development and recon-ciling national development with global development. His inclusion of self-sacrifice in the definition of development challenges in two ways the assumption of Western economists and development planners that people are motivated mainly by self-interest. Firstly, the pope believes that a human being can be fulfilled personally by a willingness to cooperate with others, even when this imposes a personal cost on the individual;

therefore self-interest is not opposed to concern for others. Secondly, and equally significantly, the pope sees frugality not as a limitation to personal development but as a positive element within it. This means that development can be reconciled with ecological restraint. It also opens the way to reconciling genuine human development with a relinquishment by the wealthy of waste and excess in order to allow the poor a fair share of the resources of the earth. In this emphasis on a simple life-style *Populorum Progressio* was well ahead of its time.

Having laid down some practical standards for defining genuine human development, the pope uses them to evaluate and correct the changes and so-called development taking place in the modern world. He criticises liberal capitalism (PP 26, 58), technocracy (PP 34), a materialistic and atheistic philosophy (PP 39), lack of respect for a people's cultural heritage (PP 40, 72) and racism (PP 63–4).

Can the notion of 'development' be rescued?

The heuristic approach adopted by Pope Paul to defining the concept of development offers the possibility of finding a middle way between two radically opposed schools of thought:

— On the one hand there are those who are broadly in favour of the plans for economic development adopted by practically all modern governments. They may not agree with every detail but on the whole they believe that the only effective way to overcome poverty is through increased economic growth.

— On the other hand there is a large and growing number of people who are profoundly suspicious of all such development plans. Some of these are people who are influenced by the 'small is beautiful' philosophy of Schumacher and by recent radical ecologists. Others are committed Christians who lived in Latin America and witnessed the appalling damage that has been done to people, to traditional cultures, and to the environment, in the name of 'development'. Already in the late 1960s many Church people in Latin America saw that the word 'development' was being used as a cover for exploitation and the creation of dependency. So they challenged 'development' and demanded 'liberation' instead. The ecological and liberationist trends converge in Ivan Illich and his followers (see, for instance, Hoinacki and Sachs). For them the whole notion of development is to be rejected and the very word 'development' is dangerous and unchristian.

The advantage of the heuristic notion of development put forward in *Populorum Progressio* is that, in principle, it is in no way tainted with the conception of economic development which is so widely and uncritically accepted in our world today. Those who adopt the pope's definition cannot be said to condone the exploitation of people and the Earth which has been carried out under the guise of so-called 'development'. For what it involves is an understanding of development that is not borrowed from Western economics but one whose only content comes from such guidelines as 'the flourishing of every person, of all people, and of all peoples'. In this way the encyclical represents a serious effort by the pope to 'rescue' the word 'development'.

The danger, of course, is that those who accept this very general notion may quickly, and perhaps unconsciously, allow it to become tainted with the ideological overtones of meaning which the word 'development' carries in everyday speech. This danger is very real—and Pope Paul himself was by no means immune to it. But at least this approach offers the possibility of a dialogue between those who belong to the two schools of thought outlined above, instead of the situation of mutual incomprehension which prevails today.

International Social Justice

At the beginning of this chapter I noted two distinctive features of *Populorum Progressio*: its original approach to 'development' and its shift of focus from the national to the international scene in matters of social justice. Having looked at the first of these points I now move on to the second. It can be said that *Populorum Progressio* does at the global level what Leo XIII's *Rerum Novarum* did at the level of the nation (Chenu 75). Its concern is primarily with the relationship between rich and poor *nations* rather than rich and poor individuals or classes. This is made clear in the very first section where the pope states baldly: 'Today the principal fact we must all recognise is that the social question has become worldwide' (PP 3).

In saying this Pope Paul was simply taking account of the rapid changes in the world situation which had taken place since the end of World War II. The struggle against colonialism had already reached a peak in the 1950s. Dozens of new nations were affirming their existence by joining the United Nations. The new prominence of agencies concerned with international trade and finance (e.g. GATT, UNCTAD, the IMF and the World Bank) showed clearly that justice was no longer something to be worked out within any given country but was first of all an international matter—even an inter-continental one. Above all it concerned relations between the industrialised nations and the former colonies in what had come to be called the Third World (which is now more commonly called 'the South').

Interest in the Causes of Poverty

Pope Paul does not rush in with solutions to the problem of poverty at the international level without taking the trouble to seek its basic causes. This is one respect in which *Populorum Progressio* represents a notable advance on earlier Church documents. It analyses the global situation and sets out to explain why there is such an imbalance between rich and poor countries. Among the causes of poverty and injustice mentioned in the encyclical are: the evil effects left as a legacy by colonialism in the past, the present neo-colonial situation which has largely replaced the older form of colonialism, and the imbalance of power between nations—an imbalance which gives rise to injustices in trade relations between them (PP 7–9, 52, 56–8).

It may be argued that the encyclical's analysis of the after-effects of colonialism does not go far enough and that its judgments are rather too lenient. For instance the pope seems to suggest that the evils brought by the colonial powers can be balanced against the good they did (PP 7). He does not take full account of the extent to which the colonial powers shattered not only the political and economic structures of the colonised peoples, but also the social, cultural, and religious framework which gave order and meaning to their lives.[2] He seems also to overestimate the extent to which Western science, technology, and culture have been of real and lasting benefit to most of 'the South'. For what has to be considered is not the wonderful advantages that *might* have been derived through the interaction of Western learning with the cultures of these other countries, but rather the *actual* effects of the imposition of Western-type schooling in the so-called 'developing countries'.[3]

In one paragraph, however, the pope does note the way in which past colonial history has left an enduring bad effect on the economy of many poor countries by leaving them dependent on a single export crop that is subject to price fluctuations (PP 7; cf. PP 57). For all its caution the encyclical succeeds in ways like this in challenging the view widely held in the West—that the former colonies have in the long run benefited from their colonial history through being brought into the mainstream of modern civilisation.

Pope Paul is equally cautious but firm in the way in which he speaks of neo-colonialism. He refers to it more as a suspicion or possibility than as a fact. He leaves it to the readers to judge whether there is justification for such suspicion of 'political pressure and economic domination, aimed at maintaining or acquiring control for a few' (PP 52). The pope adverts in different places to the two features characteristic of a neo-colonial situation: economic domination at the international level, and both political and economic domination at the national level. At the national level, he refers to regimes where a small privileged elite hold a monopoly of wealth and power (PP 9). And his treatment of the international issue is perhaps the most trenchant part of the whole encyclical: he challenges the present system of international trading relations (PP 57–60), pointing out that they are such that 'poor nations become poorer while the rich ones become still richer' (PP 57). It is clear then that the pope does not simply assume that poverty and underdevelopment arise from purely natural causes or the laziness of the people living in the poorer parts of the world.[4]

There is a pressing urgency in the way in which Pope Paul calls for change (PP 29). If injustices are to be overcome peacefully there must, he says, be 'bold transformations in which the present order of things will be entirely renewed or rebuilt'(PP 32).[5] What he is calling for is evidently a change in the structures. That is shown not merely by the words he uses here but also by the kind of changes he proposes throughout the encyclical and the basic principle which inspires them. This principle is that 'the rule of free trade, taken by itself, is no longer able to govern international relations'; and therefore 'the fundamental principle of liberalism, as the rule for commercial exchange' is called in question (PP 58). The basic reason for this is that international trade is unjust at present because there is a gross inequality between the trading partners. So what is called 'free trade' must be severely restricted (PP 59). Competition should not be entirely eliminated (PP 61); but the same kind of support system which is now given *within* wealthy countries to the weaker sectors of the economy should be introduced on a *global* scale, between rich and poor countries (PP 60–1).

This proposal for a planned approach on a world scale, aimed at the protection of the weak and the stabilisation of markets, is very close to the demands made a few years later for a 'New International Economic Order' (NIEO). This NIEO, sought by the so-called developing countries in the North-South dialogue, seeks the same goals and proposes the same means as are outlined in the encyclical. As Barbara Ward remarked: 'Many of the ideas of this New Order have such firm roots in *Populorum Progressio* that the Encyclical might almost have been its founding document' (Ward 202).

Comparison with Quadragesimo Anno

In his study of the notion of Catholic 'social doctrine', Chenu discerns a general pattern: the early social encyclicals tend to be 'moralistic' in tone, while the more recent ones recognise that a change of attitudes is not sufficient—there must be reform of the *structures*. So he holds that Paul VI, while still retaining elements of 'moralism', is looking for structural change in society (Chenu 72).

There is a good deal of truth in this view; but the pattern is rather more complex than Chenu suggests. If one compares Leo XIII's *Rerum Novarum* with Pius XI's *Quadragesimo Anno* one finds that while the former is primarily moralistic in tone the latter calls for *both* attitudinal and structural change. Each of these encyclicals focuses the reader's attention mainly on the economic situation within the typical industrialised country of the West. The two major social encyclicals of Pope John in the early 1960s represent a shift towards an outlook that is more international or global. The solutions put forward by John XXIII for these global problems tend once again to be rather 'moralistic' in tone, although he recognises the need for new institutions or structures. In Pope Paul's *Populorum Progressio*, by contrast, there is a much clearer analysis of the problems of the world economic order—and a recognition that they arise largely as a result of the way the existing structures work. Nevertheless, Paul VI remains convinced that attitudinal change is of major importance; and he does not oppose this to structural change.[6] What emerges from the comparison, then, is a fairly close parallel between *Quadragesimo Anno* and *Populorum Progressio*, with each of them calling for changes both in attitudes and in structures. In particular there is a similarity in the outspoken rejection in each of the two encyclicals of the liberalism that underlies capitalism. Pope Paul himself recalls the strictures of Pius XI:

> . . . the baseless theory has emerged which considers material gain the key motive for economic progress, competition as the supreme law of economics, and private ownership of the means of production as an absolute right that has no limits . . . This unchecked liberalism led to dictatorship rightly denounced by Pius XI as producing 'the international imperialism of money'. One cannot condemn such abuses too strongly, because . . . the economy should be at the service of people. (PP 26)

Despite the similarities, there are also significant differences in approach between the two popes. In the first place, as already noted, the international economic order is the principal focus of concern for Paul VI, whereas for Pius XI the individual nation was still central. Secondly, Pope Paul, while making proposals for major changes in the economic system, does not give the same impression as Pius XI of having a ready-made alternative to the present capitalist system. This is partly a difference in style: Pope Paul is more concerned to shun anything that would smack of triumphalism. But the difference is also one of theology: Paul VI is far more reluctant than his predecessor to imply that there is a specific 'Catholic answer' to social and economic problems.

One of the more interesting things that is revealed by a close study of the two encyclicals is that neither of them is quite what it seems. At first sight *Quadragesimo Anno* appears to reject capitalism outright and to propose a corporatist alternative; but what its author actually wanted was a free enterprise system which would be more or less equivalent to capitalism without its abuses and without its ideology. On the other hand Paul VI's condemnations of capitalism are more subdued; but the changes he proposes in the international order would impose such limitations on international capitalism that if they were properly implemented they would transform it entirely.

Does this mean that Pope Paul in *Populorum Progressio* is really rejecting capitalism outright? The reply must be: it depends on what one means by 'capitalism'. Paul VI, like Pius XI before him, condemns the injustices perpetrated by unchecked capitalistic trading (PP 56–9). Like Pius he insists that a just economic order cannot be built on the principles and ideology of liberalistic capitalism (PP 26). He proposes instead the guiding principles of *solidarity* of rich and poor (PP 48–9, 76–7), and of *dialogue*, (PP 54, 73) leading to *planning* on a global scale (PP 50–2, 60–1, 64, 78). But he does not favour a totally planned international economic order in which there would be no room for competition and free enterprise—a kind of world socialism. He says explicitly that 'the competitive market' should not be abolished entirely in international trading but that it should be kept within the limits of what is just (PP 61).

Pope Paul carefully refrains from going into specific detail about how the international economic order should operate. But it is reasonably clear that he would want to apply on a *global* level the same kind of guidelines as he lays down for national development:

> It pertains to the public authorities to choose, and even to impose, the objectives to be pursued, the ends to be achieved, and the means by which these are to be achieved; and it is for them to stimulate all the forces required for this common activity. But they should see to it that private initiative and intermediate institutions are involved in this undertaking. In this way they will avoid an absolute community of goods and the danger of arbitrary planning which, by denying liberty would prevent the exercise of the fundamental rights of the human person. (PP 33 translation emended)

This is a remarkably traditional statement, defending the values with which Catholic social teaching had all along been concerned. But the point I wish to emphasise here is the role that is assigned to 'the public authorities' in ensuring that society is organised in this way. If these guidelines were applied on an international scale there would be need for some kind of world authority to play this role. So one can see why Pope Paul favours a move in this direction (PP 78).[7] Until such a world government can emerge, the role of 'public authority' at the global level can be played, at least to some extent, by international agencies, with a concerted plan agreed to by the different nations, and by a collaboration on a worldwide scale resulting in a common fund to help all, especially the poorer nations (PP 50–5).

One reason why Paul VI stresses the need to move towards a world authority is that he sees the close link that exists between the economic order and the political order. A good deal of the encyclical is concerned with the disparity in *power* between the rich and the poor (PP 9, 58–60). The crucial question is not simply who are the owners of wealth and resources but what individuals or groups or nations have the power to impose their will on others. It is the power of the rich which enables them to become still richer by forcing the weak to make trading agreements that are unjust (PP 59—at this point the pope goes on to recall the teaching of *Rerum Novarum* and adds: 'What was true of the just wage for the individual is also true of international contracts . . . '). Conversely, the deprivation of power, of opportunity to determine one's conditions of living and working, is itself a kind of poverty (cf. PP 9). Individuals and peoples are entitled to become 'the agents of their own destiny' and to assume responsibility for their world (PP 65).

This is one of the central points in Pope Paul's conception of human development—that individuals and peoples should be enabled to have the prime responsibility for their own development (PP 77; cf. PP 35, 70). In the light of this understanding it is only natural that the encyclical should address itself to the issue of power. But when the question of power is raised, one is led to ask a rather awkward question: who has the power to bring about the kind of changes the encyclical proposes? From this a further question arises: are those who have this power likely to exercise it, or is the encyclical just another instance of wishful thinking?

Could a Revolution be Justified?

Quite obviously the pope himself cannot enforce a new international order. He can appeal to statesmen and stateswomen (PP 84), to scholars (PP 85), to all people of good will (PP 83)—and especially to Christians and other believers (PP 82). Above all he can appeal to the members of his own Church, especially the laity, to bring about the basic change in mentality and structures that are called for (PP 81). In addition to a moral appeal made in the name of justice he can offer strong arguments based on the self-interest of those who could bring about the changes required. He does this by noting that what is at stake is not merely the life of poor nations and civil peace in the developing countries but also world peace (PP 55; cf. PP 76, 86). He argues that the rich themselves will be the first to benefit as a result of sharing their superfluous wealth with the needy. And here his argument is based on a threefold threat facing those who fail to respond to the needs of the poor:

— they place their own highest values in jeopardy by yielding to greed;

— they call down on themselves the judgment of God;

— they also call on themselves the wrath of the poor (PP 49). This is a very interesting juxtaposition: there are the moral and religious arguments one might expect, but the third point is a clear warning to the rich that the oppressed may take it into their own hands to bring about change through violent action.

What is the teaching of the pope about such violent action by the poor and oppressed? It is mainly pragmatic rather than moral in character. His attention is not focused principally on whether or not such violence would be justified but on the fact that it is in everybody's interest not to allow such a desperate situation to develop. He warns the complacent of the risks they run:

> When whole populations destitute of necessities live in a state of subjection barring them from all initiative and responsibility, and from all opportunity to advance culturally and to share in social and political life, people are easily led to have recourse to violence as a means to right these wrongs to human dignity. (PP 30)

At once the pope goes on to point out that a revolutionary uprising produces new injustices, imbalances, and disasters (PP 31). So he argues that to fight the present evils in this way only produces greater misery. Of course this does not mean that such evil is to be endured without any resistance. The whole tenor of the pope's teaching is that the situation is to be changed. In the very next sentence he does not hesitate to use militant language: injustices are to be fought against and overcome (PP 32). What Pope Paul is opposed to is not radical change itself but violent revolution as a means of bringing it about.

Even his rejection of revolution is not absolute. The pope inserts a qualifying parenthesis into the passage where he argues against a violent insurrection:

> . . . a revolutionary uprising—unless there is question of flagrant and long-standing tyranny which would violate the fundamental rights of the human person and inflict grave injury on the common good of the State—produces new injustices . . . and provokes people to further destructive outrage. (PP 31 my translation)

The syntax of this sentence is very contorted. The parenthesis is clearly meant to suggest that in certain extreme situations a revolution might be justified. But it does not say this explicitly. For the sentence does not set out to express a formal moral judgment; instead it points out a *fact*—that revolution leads to further injustices. We must assume that the element of vagueness in the passage is deliberate. Indeed there is considerable subtlety in the way the whole sentence is phrased, a subtlety which enables the pope to achieve a number of purposes at the same time:

— Firstly, and most obviously, the main thrust is to show that violent rebellion is a futile way to seek to overcome injustice, because it tends to bring about the very evils that it sets out to overcome. This already constitutes a strong moral argument against insurrection—as the final sentence of the paragraph points out: 'A present evil should not be fought against at the cost of greater misery' (PP 31).[8]

— Secondly, in this passage Paul VI begins to face up to the question of the possibility of a justified revolution, a question that had been shelved by Vatican II. Apparently he recognised that, in spite of the very strong arguments against revolution, it would be flying in the face of a strong Catholic tradition to rule it out entirely. His parenthesis enabled him to take account of this tradition.

— Thirdly, even in this brief parenthesis, the pope succeeds in specifying the kind of conditions in which a revolution might be justified: he speaks of flagrant and long-standing violations of human rights and grave injury to the common good of the State. His language here combines a traditional Catholic element (the common good) with a usage more familiar to the modern secular world (violations of human rights).

— Fourthly, while taking account of the possibility that a revolution *might* be justified, the pope very carefully refrains from saying explicitly that it *would* be justified in such circumstances. Had he done so, it could be construed as an invitation to repressed peoples or groups to begin to measure the extent to which their oppressors are violating fundamental rights and injuring the common good; and in some cases this could almost amount to an incitement to revolution. This thought must have weighed heavily on Pope Paul and on those who helped to draft the text of the encyclical. Their solution to the difficulty was the parenthesis quoted above—a statement which is nuanced to the point of being rather tortuous.

The statement as it stands does not encourage people to use violent means to overcome injustices, even in extreme circumstances. Nevertheless, if the passage was to have any relevance, it had to indicate that the pope was taking some stance or making some judgment, however carefully nuanced, in relation to the possibility of revolution being morally justified. Simply by adverting to violent insurrection and refraining from condemning it absolutely, the encyclical *implies* that there may well be situations in our world today where revolution might be permissible. This point was not lost either on those who looked to the Church for support in maintaining an unjust *status quo*, or on those who wished to enlist the Church on their side in their struggle for liberation.[9] So, despite its brevity and careful phrasing, this passage had, and still has, considerable importance. It serves to clarify the official stance of the Church on an issue which is quite central to the meaning of the notion of an 'option for the poor'.

I am not at all suggesting that 'option for the poor' necessarily means approval for violent resistance to oppression. However, such an option could involve refusal to make a blanket condemnation of *all* violent resistance; and that is what we find in *Populorum Progressio*. It is clear that, faced with the same ultimate choice as that which faced Leo XIII, Pope Paul refused to take the same position as Leo. As I pointed out in Chapter 2 above, Leo XIII had said that, in the last resort, Christians must endure injustices rather than rebel. Paul VI implies that this is not so.

Although the difference between the position of the two popes arises in relation to an extreme situation which may arise only very rarely, nevertheless the effect extends much more widely. For the question has to be asked whether the Church is only bluffing when it claims to be on the side of the oppressed. What happens when the bluff is called? Where does the Church stand when flagrant injustice mounts to a point where violent resistance is the *only* realistic means of bringing about change—as seemed to be the case in the struggles of the people of Nicaragua against the Samosa tyranny and the people of Zimbabwe against the Ian Smith regime?

When there is a struggle against injustice, the Church cannot with any authenticity claim to be totally neutral and uninvolved, on the grounds that it is 'above politics'. So what stance ought it to take? Obviously it may not automatically take the side of the 'law and order' of the established power. May it, then, condone—at least tacitly—the violent resistance of the 'freedom fighters'? The stance taken in such situations is a test for the credibility of the Church's claim to be committed to social justice. If Church authorities balk at this test under the guise of standing for non-violence and the rule of law, then one must conclude that social stability has been given a higher priority than social justice. What is at stake is a major issue involving the definition by Church authorities of the nature and values of the Church. Is commitment to justice in the world so central to the mission of the Church that it may not be compromised without denying or damaging the identity and meaning of the Church?

As we shall see later, this question was formally answered in a document issued by the Synod of bishops four years after

Pope Paul issued his encyclical. And there can be little doubt that what the pope said in this passage contributed significantly to the strong stand taken by the Synod on the indispensability of justice in the Christian message.

We must, of course, remember that even in extreme situations Church authorities are not usually faced with just a straight choice between two alternatives, namely, that of condemning revolutionary action or of supporting it. People on either side often wish to restrict the choices in this way; but in fact a whole range of options is open to Church leaders in these circumstances. For instance it may be that a strategic silence is the best service that they can give: the common good and the credibility of the Church itself may best be served by diligent efforts to promote peace without any explicit public judgments on whether or not the 'freedom fighters' are justified in taking up arms.

In fact it does not at all follow that when Church leaders make an option for the poor and oppressed they must therefore give unqualified support to those who rebel even against intolerable injustice. A more urgent need may be for them to speak out against atrocities committed by the forces on either side; for it can easily happen in a struggle of this kind that, from the point of view of the means employed, *both* sides are wrong. However, the crucial point to be noted here is that a blanket condemnation of *all* violent resistance to a grossly unjust regime could only be interpreted as tacit support for the *status quo*. It is precisely this kind of unqualified condemnation which Pope Paul refuses to give in *Populorum Progressio*. This refusal represents a very important option by the official Church for the cause of the poor and the oppressed.

Models of Change

As we have seen, Pope Paul calls for radical changes in the structures of society. But he believes that violent revolution is not the way to bring them about. What then are the alternatives? The encyclical makes helpful suggestions about various means that could be used. For instance it proposes the following measures:

— a world fund to relieve the destitute (PP 51);

— more foreign aid in the form of money, goods, and skilled people (PP 48–9);

— limits on international competitive trading, so as to restore some equality between the trading partners (PP 61);

— a concerted international plan to promote development (PP 50);

— and moves towards the establishment of an effective world authority (PP 78).

However, these are all instrumental means, whereas the issue I wish to raise here is different: if violence is unacceptable, what does Paul VI consider to be a morally acceptable way of inspiring or compelling individuals, groups, and nations to make use of the appropriate instrumental means?

A first step towards answering this question is to find out what model of change the pope has in mind. Two very different models might be used; and it is also possible that elements from both could be combined. On the one hand there is the confrontation model. In this, the principal means for bringing about change is pressure or threat. It is presumed that those who have wealth or power will yield it up only reluctantly and in the face of some pressure that they dare not ignore. On the other hand there is a consensus model which lies at the opposite pole from the confrontational approach. Here change is envisaged as coming about by the willing agreement of all parties; and the agreement is based on rational argument, emotional appeal, and moral pressure from the various partners in the dialogue. The presupposition in this case is that all the parties have sufficient goodwill and commitment to justice to move them to make concessions; they are prepared to sacrifice immediate self-interest in order to bring about long-term harmony and promote the common welfare of all.

There are many indications in *Populorum Progressio* that what Paul VI had mostly in mind was the consensus model of social change. This is quite evident where he expresses the hope that 'a more deeply felt need for collaboration and a heightened sense of unity will finally triumph over misunderstandings and selfishness' (PP 64). It underlies his commitment to a 'dialogue between those who contribute wealth and those who benefit from it' (PP 54). Its justification is his conviction that the world, despite all its failures, is in fact moving towards greater brotherhood/sisterhood and an increase in humanity (PP 79).

At times, however, the pope warns the powerful and even seems to be threatening them to some extent. For instance, he speaks of the danger that the wrath of the poor may be provoked by the greed of the rich (PP 49). Again he points out that people may be tempted to seek solutions to problems of injustice through violence (PP 30). He also notes that lack of cooperation between rich and poor nations is a threat to the peace of the whole world (PP 55). These remarks show that Pope Paul was prepared to strengthen his case for dialogue and collaboration by reminding the rich and powerful that if they do not make concessions willingly they may eventually be forced to do so—and may in fact lose their wealth and power entirely. But all of this can be understood as part of the rational argumentation involved in using the consensus model. There is very little indication in the encyclical that Paul VI favoured a confrontational approach in the effort to overcome injustice and oppression.

Those who see the need (at times, at least) for a confrontation model for social change encourage the poor and oppressed to *demand* their rights—and to organise themselves in such a way that this demand must be heard. Such a demand (and the organisation that underpins its) can take place at two levels—within any given country, and at the international level of relationships between rich and poor countries. Conspicuously absent from *Populorum Progressio* is any direct and explicit proposal by the pope to the poorer groups or classes within each country that they should mobilise themselves politically and engage in strong, though nonviolent, action in pursuit of justice. Perhaps this was not to be expected in any case, since the main subject of the encyclical is poverty at the global rather than the national level.

What then about confrontation at the international level? What does the pope have to say to the poorer nations? Does he encourage a confrontational approach? Undoubtedly he supports the concept of regional cooperation among the poorer countries (PP 64). But this cooperation is to facilitate planning, investment, distribution, and trade; there is no suggestion that it is for the purpose of *confronting* the rich countries more effectively. Pope Paul's attitude is summed up in this statement: 'The younger or weaker nations ask to assume their active part in the construction of a better world . . . This is a legitimate appeal; everyone should hear and respond to it' (PP 65). Their asking is an appeal rather than a demand. They ought to be heard; but if they are not listened to, the pope makes no suggestion about what they might do about it.

Agents of Change

Having considered the question of the model of change being used by Pope Paul, the next step in finding out how change may be brought about is to ask, who are to be the major agents of change. This has to be answered at different levels. In the first place the encyclical has as a central theme the idea that every person and all peoples are entitled to be the shapers of their own destiny (e.g. PP 15, 20, 65, 70). This is one of the most important contributions of *Populorum Progressio* to the understanding of development: it is not possible to develop people; development is something people have to do for themselves (PP 15, 25, 27). It is for this reason that the encyclical stresses the importance of basic education and literacy. These are seen as the key which enables people to assume responsibility for themselves, their lives, and their world: 'To be able to read and write, and to get training for a profession, is to regain confidence in oneself . . .' (PP 35).

To say that every person and all peoples are called to be agents of change and directors of their own development, though very important, is not enough. For the question arises whether some are called to play a more central role than others. The encyclical seems to give the crucial role to those who hold the top positions in society; so the kind of change envisaged by the pope is mainly 'from the top down'. Those who are considered to have the most important role in bringing about change are nearly all people or institutions that exercise considerable influence in society as it is at present. At the international level the pope stresses the role of the rich countries and their leaders (PP 44, 48, 49, 84), as well as international agencies such as FAO and the UN (PP 46, 78, 83). Within wealthy states he puts the emphasis on the roles of statesmen and states-women, journalists, educators and learned people (PP 83, 84, 85). As regards the poorer countries, special mention is made of those 'elite' who are studying in the 'more advanced countries' (PP 68). Another group who get special mention are the 'experts' and development workers who go from the rich countries to help in the development of the poor ones (PP 71–4).

What role is assigned to the Church in transforming the structures of society? The pope asserts that 'the Church has never failed to foster the human progress of the nations' (PP 12). But in the past, he implies, this was done mainly through 'local and individual undertakings', and these 'are no longer enough' (PP 13). In the new situation, where concerted action on a global scale is required, the role of the Church is to offer 'a global vision of the human person and human affairs' (PP 13). It is in this context that the pope proposes a conception of integral human development, a development of the whole person and of all persons and peoples (PP 14–21). In addition to this, Church leaders—and especially the pope himself—can make appeals, offer arguments, and issue warnings, of the kind noted above. Laity also have a role to play: without waiting passively for directives they should 'infuse a Christian spirit into the mentality, customs, laws and structures of the community in which they live'; and they should commit themselves to bringing about the basic reforms that are indispensable (PP 81). Special reference is made to the role of Catholics in 'the more favoured nations' in bringing into being 'an international morality based on justice and equity' (PP 81). Here again it appears that the more important agents of change are those who already have wealth, power, or influence.

There is a close connection between the model of change one is using and the kind of agents to whom one assigns a major role in transforming the structures of society. Since Pope Paul envisages change as coming mainly through consensus, it is understandable that he gives special importance to those who now hold economic and political power; for they can easily block the crucial decisions that need to be made. Similarly, another very important group are those who mould the opinions of society—the educators, journalists, and in general those who are well educated and privileged.

In sharp contrast to this approach is the view of those who believe that some degree of confrontation will probably be required in order to bring about radical change in society. For them, the major agents of social change are more likely to be the people at or near the bottom of society. But if the poor are to exercise real power they have to become aware of the possibilities open to them; and they need to harness their anger and become organised. In this task they can be greatly facilitated by Church leaders and others who are prepared to forgo their privileged positions and make a real option for, and with, the poor. There is no indication that Pope Paul was thinking along these lines when he wrote *Populorum Progressio*. Such ideas belong to a later stage of Catholic social thought.

Literacy Programmes

The consensus approach and the confrontational one are not entirely incompatible. They begin to converge once stress is laid on literacy and education for the poor. But this will happen only if the education offered enables people to become aware of their dignity and rights, an education that facilitates them in taking responsibility for changing society. What is the position of the encyclical on this issue? It contains a short but glowing statement on the importance of fundamental education and literacy:

> ' . . . basic education is the primary object of any plan of development . . . and . . . literacy is . . . "a privileged instrument of economic progress and of development" ' (PP 35).[10]

In these words there may well be an echo of the views of the great Brazilian educator, Paulo Freire.[11] But if so, there is also a significant omission: unlike Freire, the pope does not clearly and explicitly link literacy and basic education with the awakening of a critical and combative political consciousness. The passage from *Populorum Progressio* which I have just quoted could give the impression that the way in which otherwise marginal people are enabled to take control of their lives is simply by learning to read and write, since literacy opens up for them the possibility of being trained for a meaningful type of work in society (PP 35). But there are certain kinds of literacy programmes which aim only to insert the participants into an unjust and oppressive society; and in this case the literacy training is for the purpose of domesticating people rather than giving them real responsibility. For instance, when the Brazilian military government found that Freire's literacy programme was awakening people to demand their rights, they replaced it with one that seemed to be politically neutral. This meant in fact that the alternative programme provided an implicit endorsement of the *status quo*.

The encyclical does not bring out in any very explicit way the fact that certain political options underlie any adult education programme, or indeed any kind of education. This omission weakens what it has to say. But it does not deprive it of all value. For it is quite true that in modern society literacy has generally become a *sine qua non* for anybody who wants to exercise real responsibility.

The fact that the encyclical does not make a clear link between basic education and the heightening of political aware-ness is quite significant. It lends support to the view that the pope thought changes in society should be brought about mainly by those 'at the top'. It leaves one with the impression that he was not particularly anxious to encourage any great groundswell of pressure for change 'from below'— that is, from the masses of the poor and oppressed. In so far as the encyclical adverts at all to any such movement this seems to be thought of as a threat, leading to the danger of violence and perhaps revolution (PP 30, 49). The pope certainly does not present it as a potentially positive force, which can be harnessed and become a powerful lever for bringing about non-violent change, something which the Church might therefore encourage and become involved in.

This can be understood in the light of the pope's commitment to a consensus approach. Consensus can be valued so highly that one fears to risk it by encouraging confrontation. So long as the positive value of confrontation is overlooked, it is almost inevitable that there will be a failure to take sufficient account of the role which the poor and oppressed can play as agents of change for the better. In *Populorum Progressio* there is no indication that the poor are seen as specially called by God to transform society. That was a theological insight that had not yet come into prominence.

As noted earlier, *Populorum Progressio* does not offer any strong encouragement to the poor and oppressed to organise themselves politically. Perhaps one reason for this is that the pope, like many other Christians, was a little slow to acknowledge—and perhaps even to recognise—that confrontation may at times be compatible with Christian faith, and even demanded by it. It is not uncommon to associate confrontation with angry disagreement, leading on quite easily to violence. That is undoubtedly what happens in many cases, and it is always a risk. But it may be a risk that is worth taking. For, properly handled, confrontation may provide a firm basis for a healthy consensus; the powerful ones may need to be shaken out of their complacency. Furthermore, the act of confronting those in power may give to those who feel powerless a sense of their own dignity and their rights, as well as a belief in their ability to bring about change, with or without the willing cooperation of those whom they are confronting.

The conclusion which emerges from this examination of *Populorum Progressio* is that it contributes very significantly towards committing the official Church to a realistic option for the poor. But the contribution of the encyclical is less than it might have been because the pope has shied away from confrontation. Being on the side of the poor in their cry for justice must surely involve encouraging them to find effective ways of ensuring that their voice is really heard. The encyclical lays so much stress on the value of collaboration of rich and poor, and on the duty of those 'at the top' to initiate such co-operation, that it does not pay sufficient attention to what can and should be done by the poor themselves.

However, it would be a mistake to make too much of this point. For even though the pope did not explicitly encourage the poor to take the initiative, still the overall effect of the encyclical would be to inspire them to do so. By pointing out the injustices of the world and the obligation of the rich and powerful to remedy them, Paul VI was necessarily making the poor more aware of their rights and in some sense encouraging them to seek these rights actively. The pope may not have set out to stir up the poor and to provoke strife; but there is no doubt that, in certain situations, his words could have that effect.

SUMMARY

In its approach to development Populorum Progressio no longer starts from the Western model of economic growth. It seeks to integrate all the dimensions of personal development and also to reconcile personal development with the welfare of other people and peoples. This concept of development should be acceptable even to those who believe that the present style of development is widening the gap between rich and poor, is an imposition of Western values, and is destroying the earth. But the danger remains that one who starts with this ideal notion of development may easily slip back into accepting aspects of the Western model of development.

This encyclical recognises the massive problem of poverty at the global level, and offers some analysis of its root causes. It calls for 'bold transformations' of the structures of the international economic order. Some element of free enterprise would be retained but the present structures of international capitalism would be replaced or at least restrained by a good deal of planning at a global level under the aegis of some kind of world authority.

Paul VI envisaged structural changes coming about through negotiation and consensus rather than through violent revolution. The encyclical comes out strongly against violence, though it implies that in certain extreme circumstances rebellion might be justified. Pope Paul was opposed not merely to violence but to a confrontational approach. He envisaged change as coming 'from the top down'. He did not see the poor as the ones called to play a key role in bringing about change. He did not encourage them to organise themselves politically and demand social change.

Questions for review:

1. How did Pope Paul's understanding of development differ from that of earlier Church documents?
2. What kind of changes did *Populorum Progressio* propose in the international order?
3. What was the teaching of the encyclical about revolution?
4. How did the pope envisage changes coming about?

Questions for reflection:

1. Do the benefits of Western-style development outweigh the disadvantages? Are there realistic alternatives?
2. What do you see as the most effective ways of working to bring justice to the world?

Issues for further study:

1. An ecological approach to development; include 'the Gaia hypothesis' of Lovelock and others; and the critiques by Thomas Berry and Ivan Illich of the Western approach to development.
2. Paulo Freire's approach to empowering the poor. (Read Freire)

9

Medellín and Octogesima Adveniens

One part of the world where the teaching of Vatican II on the role of the Church in the modern world was taken very seriously was Latin America. Many Church leaders and committed Christians in that area also took to heart and applied to their own situation what Paul VI said in *Populorum Progressio*. This was part of an extraordinary change that was taking place there during the late 1960s. It was something that affected every level of Church life, from the grassroots communities to the bishops and the leaders of religious orders. Of course many people, and even whole areas, remained largely untouched by the new approach. But the movement for change was sufficiently widespread and influential to find expression in various local conventions of Church leaders—and eventually to become the dominant force at a major gathering of Church leaders from all over Latin America. This meeting took place at Medellín in Colombia in 1968. In the first section of this chapter I shall consider fairly briefly the documents that were issued by the Medellín Conference. This will lead on to the second section where I shall examine at more length the teaching of the apostolic letter *Octogesima Adveniens*, a document that may be understood at least partly as a response by Pope Paul to all that Medellín came to stand for.

SECTION I

THE DOCUMENTS OF MEDELLIN

It is not my purpose here to study the changes that were taking place in the Latin American Church, in terms of their causes and their effects. But it is necessary to devote some pages to a study of the documents in which the new approach was given classical expression; for otherwise we would be ignoring an event which had a profound influence on Pope Paul VI during the latter half of his pontificate. This event was the second general conference of Latin American bishops which took place in August 1968 at Medellín. For some time before that meeting it had been clear that it would be a most important one. This was recognised by Pope Paul who travelled to South America to address the gathering. But it is doubtful whether anybody could have guessed beforehand the extent to which Medellín was to be a turning point in the life of the Latin American Church—and indeed of the Catholic Church as a whole. The documents that were issued by the conference have an extraordinary freshness, clarity, and power. They became the charter for those who were working for a radical renewal of the Church in Latin America. But their influence did not stop there. Medellín gave inspiration to committed Christians all over the world. The Vatican itself was deeply affected by Medellín and its aftermath. The major documents concerned with social justice issued by Rome in the following decade have to be understood as being at least partly a reaction to all that is represented by Medellín—a reaction that is at times welcoming and at other times worried.

There are a number of topics that are particularly important in the Medellín documents from our point of view. These can be summed up under four main headings: (1) Structural Injustice; (2) A Poor Church; (3) Conscientisation; (4) The Struggle for Liberation. I shall examine each in turn:

(1) *Structural Injustice*: Time and time again the Medellín documents speak of the Latin American situation as being marked by structural injustice (e.g. 1.2; 2.16; 10.2; 15.1 [pp. 33, 53, 126, 182]). These unjust structures uphold and foster dependency and poverty. This is carried to a point where 'in many instances Latin America finds itself faced with a situation of injustice that can be called institutionalised violence' (2.16 [p. 53]). Poverty, then, is not just something that happens; it is caused largely by human action of a kind that does violence to great masses of people. And this is not just particular actions but a

pattern of behaviour that has over many years created a situation of 'internal colonialism' and 'external neo-colonialism' (2.2–.9 [pp. 46–9]).

(2) A Poor Church: Church leaders hear the 'deafening cry' for liberation (14.2 [p. 172]) that rises from the millions of poor people who are the victims of this situation. What is their response? In the Medellín document on the poverty of the Church a distinction is made between different meanings of poverty:

— Material poverty is seen as an evil, caused mainly by injustice.
— Spiritual poverty is described as 'the attitude of opening up to God'.
— Poverty as a commitment is a way in which 'one assumes voluntarily and lovingly the condition of the needy of this world in order to bear witness to the evil which it represents and to spiritual liberty . . . ' after Christ's example (14.4 [pp. 173–4]).

The bishops then outline the role they see for 'a poor Church'. A Church that is poor denounces material poverty caused by injustice and sin; it preaches and lives spiritual poverty; and it is itself bound to material poverty as a commitment (14.5 [p. 174]). The Latin American bishops then go on to recognise that their obligation to evangelise the poor should lead them to redistribute resources and personnel within the Church itself, so as to give effective preference to the poorest and most needy sectors (14.9 [p. 175]). This preference is one important element in what has come to be called the 'option for the poor'. But such an option cannot be confined to what happens within the organisation of the Church. Another aspect, equally or more important, is the stance of the Church vis-à-vis society. In the Medellín document the bishops accept that they have a duty of being in solidarity with those who are poor. This solidarity is made concrete through criticism of injustice and oppression. But criticism from the outside is inadequate. The bishops say that solidarity with the poor 'means that we make ours their problems and their struggles' (14.10 [p. 176]). It is against this conception of solidarity with the poor and commitment to their struggle against injustice that one must locate the 'conscientising' role of the Church.

(3) Conscientisation: The Medellín document on peace points out that people become responsible for injustice by remaining passive, by failing to take courageous and effective action, for fear of the sacrifice and personal risk involved in doing so. So the document favours a process for inspiring and organising 'the ordinary people'.[1] It says that justice and therefore peace, can prevail 'by means of a dynamic action of awakening (*concientización*) and organisation of "the ordinary people" who can then put pressure on public officials—for these are often unable to implement social projects without the support of the people' (2.18 [p. 54] my translation; see also 2.7; 7.19; 10.2; 16.2 [pp. 48, 103, 126, 194]). This statement is especially important because it recognises the need to stimulate action for justice from the grassroots. What is envisaged is a political campaign: an education of the masses of poor people to under-stand the causes of their poverty and a process of facilitating them to work for improvement by putting pressure on the authorities in order to attain social justice. In the last line of the passage just quoted, the writers tactfully imply that this pressure is a service to the authorities, enabling them to put into practice their plans for reform. The document does not mention the fact that if there had been no pressure from below the people in authority would often be quite happy to allow such reforms to remain empty promises!

This account of what is involved in 'conscientisation' helps one to appreciate the significance of the undertaking made by the Latin American bishops at Medellín to commit the Church 'without counting the cost' to the basic education of illiterate and marginal people (4.16 [p. 76]). The bishops were well aware of what they were taking on, and of the possible cost. Their statement makes it clear that the type of basic education they have in mind is one that is not limited to teaching these people merely to read and write; rather it aims at enabling them to become the conscious agents of their own integral development (4.16 [p. 76]). The commitment is undertaken in the knowledge that this kind of basic education will increase the recognition by oppressed people of the fact that they are oppressed, with a consequent increase in tension and a risk to peace (2.7 [pp. 47–8]). It is significant that it is in the document on peace that there is insistence on the awakening of the masses

to political consciousness. This indicates that Medellín is committed to the view that there can be no genuine peace that is
not based on social justice. So it may happen that an apparent
peace, built on oppression, has to be put at risk in the effort to
attain true peace and liberty.

(4) *Struggle for Liberation*: Already in the 1960s many social
scientists in Latin America had concluded that the word
'development' was being used as a cover for exploitation and
the creation of dependency. The 'Alliance for Progress' between
the US and Latin America was to have ensured the 'development' of the latter during the first development decade, the
1960s. But the economic development that took place in
countries like Brazil did not solve the problems of poverty;
instead the gap between rich and poor became even wider. So
the radical social scientists of Latin America challenged the
whole notion of 'development' and demanded 'liberation'
instead. For them, 'development' became a bad word—a word
that could not be rescued. Most of the key Church leaders at
Medellín accepted this viewpoint. This helps to explain their
emphasis on liberation.

The word 'development' conjures up the image of a nation
harnessing natural forces more effectively and becoming more
organised and scientific in agriculture and industry. The word
'liberation' on the other hand suggests shaking off an oppression
imposed by other people. This oppression might be the obvious
political and economic control exercised by the colonial powers
in the past; it might be the dependency and poverty created in
'the South' by an unjust international economic order and
maintained by the wealthy nations of 'the North'; it might be
the domination of a rich and powerful minority within the
country; or it might be a combination of at least two of these
elements.

The word 'liberation' is used quite frequently in the documents of Medellín (1.3–4; 4.2, 4.9; 5.15; 8.6; 10.2, 10.9, 10.13;
14.2, 14.7 [pp. 33–4, 70, 73, 87, 110, 126, 128, 130, 172, 174]). It
does not evoke the cautious and even fearful reaction produced
in some Church leaders by the word. In these documents 'liberation' has a very positive connotation and it is closely linked
to 'humanisation' (10.2, 10.9, 10.13 [pp. 126, 128, 130]). The
bishops leave one in no doubt that they want to help the poor

and oppressed to attain liberation. But what does it mean in practice for them to be in solidarity with the victims of injustice and to support them in a struggle for liberty? How far should Church leaders go? Are they to give approval to revolutionary movements using violent means to overthrow unjust structures and oppressive regimes? The Medellín document on peace addresses itself to this question, making use of the statement on this topic in paragraph 31 of *Populorum Progressio*. I have already quoted (p. 192 above) the text of this statement by Pope Paul. There I noted that it contains two elements. The main one is that a revolution is an unacceptable remedy for injustice because it gives rise to worse evils. The second point is the parenthesis in which the pope indicates that there might be certain rare exceptions to this general guideline.

The Medellín document quotes from both parts of Pope Paul's statement—but it does so in reverse order, putting first the point that revolutionary insurrection can sometimes be legitimate, and then the point that it generally gives rise to new injustices (2.19 [pp. 54–5]).[2] The document then goes on to state the judgment of the Medellín conference on the situation in Latin America:

> If we consider then, the totality of the circumstances of our countries, and if we take into account the Christian preference for peace, the enormous difficulty of a civil war, the logic of violence, the atrocities it engenders, the risk of provoking foreign intervention, illegitimate as it may be, the difficulty of building a regime of justice and freedom while participating in a process of violence, we earnestly desire that the dynamism of the awakened and organised community be put to the service of justice and peace. (2.19 [p. 55]).[3]

Nobody could claim that this powerful statement of Medellín distorts the meaning of the passage in *Populorum Progressio* to which it refers. Yet there are important nuances to be noted. It is already a significant difference that what was a parenthesis for Pope Paul has now been moved to a more central position. This means that the words are given an added weight. They become the basis for a detailed and careful evaluation of the Latin American situation. There is an obvious comprehensiveness and balance in the passage just quoted. It shows that the bishops at Medellín have carefully weighed up the case for and against violent revolution. On balance, because of the convergence of all the factors listed, they suggest that Christians should commit themselves to peace rather than violence. The implication must be that if there were to be a change in some of the key circumstances, then the balance might well tip in the other direction.

Indeed, even in regard to the situation depicted in the document, there is a certain reserve in the way in which the bishops express their moral evaluation. What they present is not so much a firm and explicit moral judgment that revolution would be wrong but rather an exhortation—'we earnestly desire . . . '. Once again this is not really contrary to what the pope had said in his encyclical. But it seems to push his words a little further, and to draw out implications which he had perhaps deliberately left vague. Confronted with the starkness of poverty and the harshness of oppression in Latin America, and the urgency of the pressure to take a stand on one side or the other, the bishops at Medellín felt they could not take refuge in vagueness. Perhaps more than anything else it is the clarity with which they present the options facing the Church that is most significant in the Medellín documents. They sharpen the issues related to social justice and option for the poor and thereby pose a serious challenge to the whole Church.

SECTION II

OCTOGESIMA ADVENIENS: A SHIFT TO POLITICS

Less than three years after the Medellín conference, and only four years after *Populorum Progressio*, Pope Paul issued another major document on social issues. This was *Octogesima Adveniens*, published in May 1971 to commemorate the eightieth anniversary of Leo XIII's *Rerum Novarum*. Although this apostolic letter of the pope contains several references to *Populorum Progressio*, nevertheless it has a distinctly different tone and perspective. This difference may be partly expressed by saying that in this new social document 'development' no longer plays such a central role as it did in the earlier one.

When 'development' is taken as the overall integrating concept for the treatment of social issues there is a tendency to see difficulties such as poverty, apathy, and poor distribution of resources as problems which have *not yet* been solved. The half-hidden assumption here is that in general the world is 'developing', but that in some areas or spheres this process is still at an early stage—and that is why the problems remain as yet unsolved. *Octogesima Adveniens* disengages itself to a considerable extent from this almost mythological conception of development, by questioning the notion of 'progress' as 'an omnipresent ideology' (OA 41).[4]

When one speaks of development the emphasis tends to be mainly on economic issues; and this applies even when the word 'development' is used in the very broad and rich sense which Pope Paul gives it in *Populorum Progressio*. On the other hand, when the word 'liberation' is used it indicates a perspective in which political action is central.

Once one adverts to the fact that the gap between rich and poor areas is not due simply to the fact that the latter have not yet become developed, then it becomes more evident how deceptive can be the image that likens the poor to those at the bottom of a ladder which all can climb. The sad truth is that some nations or groups are poor not just because they have so far failed to climb the ladder but because they have been prevented by others from doing so—or have even been thrown down the ladder! When poverty is seen in this perspective the solution that comes to mind might be described more properly as 'liberation' rather than 'development '.

As I have already pointed out, the Medellín document, issued in 1968, used the word 'liberation' freely and in a positive sense. Ever since that time the more radical committed Christians in Latin America have been inclined to reject utterly the very notion of 'development'. On the other hand, in Africa and other parts of 'the South', Church people were much slower in waking up to the inadequacies of 'development'. They generally saw 'development' as a good thing. As time went on they became more critical of an unbalanced form of development which widened the gap between the rich and the poor. But they still did not reject the word 'development' out of hand. This was the viewpoint adopted by Paul VI, even in *Octogesima Adveniens* where the focus on development is much less than in *Populorum Progressio*.

Octogesima Adveniens does not follow Medellín in more or less replacing 'development' by 'liberation'; it uses the word 'liberation' only rarely and in contexts that do not suggest that it is seen as an alternative to 'development' (e.g. OA 28, 45). This is scarcely an accident. Presumably the pope was reluctant to use the word 'liberation' on the grounds that it might be taken to mean violent revolution. Nevertheless, the tone and content of this apostolic letter indicate that Pope Paul was concerned about the kind of issues for which 'liberation' is proposed as the solution. Indeed, one of the more significant features of *Octogesima Adveniens* is that the major issues with which it deals are not purely economic ones. The focus has shifted from economics to politics.

In the few years after *Populorum Progressio* was issued it began to dawn on more and more people—inside and outside the Church—that underlying most economic difficulties are political problems. This became especially evident in Latin America and led, as I have said, to a cry for 'liberation' rather than 'development'. The problems were political; for even the choice of a particular model of development is itself a political rather than an economic decision. The Latin American bishops and their experts at Medellín were aware of this; so the Medellín documents were notably political in their perspective. No doubt this encouraged Pope Paul to shift his focus of interest to the underlying political questions. Indeed *Octogesima Adveniens* can be seen as a nuanced response by the pope to Medellín—a somewhat qualified approval of at least some aspects of its approach.

A well-known expert on Catholic social teaching, Philip Land, holds that Pope Paul is 'in notable contrast to papal tradition' when he recognises 'that most social problems are at bottom political problems' (Land, 394). This statement is true in one sense but it requires some qualification. Many of the proposals made in earlier social documents of the popes refer to the political sphere. In fact most of the remedies proposed for socio-economic problems by various popes are obviously political—ranging from the espousal by Pius XI of a corporative type of system within the State, to Pope Paul's insistence in *Populorum Progressio* on the need for new international institutions leading towards a world government. However, it is one thing to propose political solutions to economic and social problems but quite a different thing to recognise clearly that designing and bringing into effect such solutions brings one into the sphere of political activity. The novelty of *Octogesima Adveniens* lies largely in the extent to which it consciously addresses itself to some of the political problems involved in choosing and implementing an equitable order in society.

At one point in the document the change of perspective is made quite explicit: the pope says, 'the need is felt to pass from economics to politics' (OA 46). In order to bring out the full significance of the passage it is well to quote also some important sentences from the preceding and following paragraphs. This will help to show the kind of issues that come to the fore when the focus shifts from economics to politics. It will be noted that certain key words or phrases are prominent—'liberation', 'model of society', 'structures', and 'share in . . . decision-making':

> People today long to be freed from need and dependence. But this liberation starts with the interior freedom that people must find again with regard to their goods and their powers . . . Nowadays many are questioning the existing model of society. The ambition of many nations . . . blocks the setting up of structures which would put some limits on the drive for advancement, in order to ensure greater justice . . .
>
> Is it not here that there appears a radical limitation to economics? Economic activity is necessary and, if it is at the service of people, it can be 'a source of brotherhood/sisterhood and a sign of Providence' . . . . Though it is often a field of confrontation and domination, it can give rise to dialogue and foster cooperation. Yet it runs the risk of unduly absorbing human energies and limiting people's freedom. This is why the need is felt to pass from economics to politics. It is true that in the term 'politics' many confusions are possible and must be clarified, but each person feels that in the social and economic field, both national and international, the ultimate decision rests with political power . . . .
>
> The passing to the political dimension also expresses a demand made by people today for a greater share in the exercise of authority and in consultation for decision-making.
>
> (OA 45–7—translation emended)

It is from this political perspective that Pope Paul calls for a revision of the relationships between nations in the economic sphere and questions the models of growth that operate within the rich nations (OA 42). He then goes on to express concern about the growing and uncontrolled power of multinational corporations (OA 44); these too create economic problems that have to be controlled by political action. In an earlier paragraph he had spoken of the power exercised by the mass media and the need for political control to prevent abuses of this power (OA 20).

But how is political control to be exercised in practice over economic activity? *Octogesima Adveniens* calls for the devising of new forms of democracy, of a type that will not merely make it possible for all to be informed and to express themselves, but will also involve everybody in a shared responsibility (OA 47). Pope Paul sees himself as going beyond John XXIII in this regard: the latter called for a sharing of responsibility in economic life, especially within each company or business; but Paul VI extends the demand to the social and political sphere (OA 47). However, he does not have much to say here about the means by which this can come about. He adverts rather briefly to the role that should be played by trade unions (OA 14) and by the media (OA 20); and he makes some general but very important remarks about the role of 'cultural and religious groupings' (OA 25)—of which of course the Church is the one that most concerns him.

Basis and Guidelines for Political Action

As we have seen, it is made quite clear in *Octogesima Adveniens* that economic questions have to be subsumed within the wider sphere of the political. But that has to be balanced against another very important point, namely, that politics is not an ultimate either. Political activity has to be based on an adequate concept or model of society and this in turn derives from an integral conception of what the human vocation is, and an understanding of the wide variety of ways in which that vocation is realised in society.[5] The component elements in this concept of society are convictions about the nature, the origin, and the purpose of the human person and of society. It is not for the

State or political parties to impose their views on these matters. If they did so it would lead to a dictatorship over the human spirit. It is the role of cultural and religious groupings to promote such convictions—and in doing so they are obliged to respect human freedom and not compel people to accept their views.

Pope Paul suggests that neither Marxist ideology nor liberal ideology are compatible with the Christian understanding of the human person (OA 26). He goes on to point out the inadequacies of social ideologies in general, noting especially the danger that an ideology can become 'a new idol'—an ultimate justification for action and even for violence. Ideologies, he holds, tend to have a totalitarian character and can impose slavery on people in the name of liberation (OA 27–8).

The pope develops this point further by examining in some depth the relationship between socialist or Marxist-inspired movements and Marxist ideology. He begins by recalling the very important distinction made by Pope John XXIII in 1963 between false philosophies and the historical movements that have sprung from such philosophies (OA 30; PT 159). What follows might be described as a commentary by Paul VI on Pope John's statement in so far as it refers to Marxism. Pope Paul notes certain distinctions that have been made between four different meanings or levels of Marxism (OA 33). The most attenuated of these versions of Marxism is one which would see it merely as a scientific method of analysing society. But the pope makes it clear that he finds even this limited Marxism quite unacceptable. He sees it as offering a false objectivity and an unjustified certainty, based on a selective and biased interpretation of the facts. In the next paragraph Pope Paul goes on to say that it would be 'illusory and dangerous' to forget that the various aspects of Marxism are intimately linked and radically bound together. In particular he notes two dangers:

— that of accepting a Marxist type of analysis of society without adverting to how this is related to ideology:

— that of becoming involved in class struggle and the Marxist interpretation of it, without adverting to the totalitarian and violent kind of society to which this activity gradually leads (OA 34).

It is clear then that for Paul VI, Marxism as such—at least in any of the versions or aspects he describes—is not compatible with a Christian approach. Furthermore, he is very hesitant in the way in which he even speaks about socialist movements. He recognises in a vague and general way the possibility that Christians might in some circumstances be entitled to play a part within such movements (OA 31).[6] But he notes that the various forms of the socialist movement drew their inspiration in the past (and still do so in many cases today) from an ideology that is, he says, incompatible with the Christian faith. He stresses the danger that Christians may idealise socialism and be misled in their practical activity by purely abstract and theoretical distinctions between the ideal of a just society, the historical movements that propose to bring about such a society, and the ideology that still influences these movements (OA 31).

All this seems to indicate that for Pope Paul the distinction made by his predecessor between movements and philosophies, though valid in theory, ought not to be used as a basis for a rapprochement between Catholicism and socialism—or at least only with extreme caution. Perhaps the pope felt that such caution was the appropriate response from Rome at a time when many Catholics all over the world—and not least in Italy, and even in Rome itself—were attracted by the prospect of 'an opening to the left'. (At around this time Rome got its first communist mayor—despite the best efforts of many senior Roman Church figures.)

However, it would be a distortion of *Octogesima Adveniens* to interpret it as an endorsement of Western capitalism. For the pope made a serious effort to balance his misgivings about socialism by making a strong criticism of the liberal ideology (OA 35, 26).

A Pluralist and Inductive Approach

In spite of the reservations of the pope about a move to the left, *Octogesima Adveniens* still leaves plenty of space for it. This comes not from any enthusiasm of Pope Paul for socialism but rather from the basic approach which he adopts in this document. He takes the view that in the face of 'widely varying situations' it is difficult for him 'to utter a unified message and to put forward a solution which has universal validity'; and he even adds that it is not his ambition to do so (OA 4).[7] This leaves room for a wide measure of pluralism in relation to options about political activity.

It would appear that there are in fact two different but interacting reasons why a certain pluralism of options is accepted in the document. On the one hand there is the personal discernment that each individual Christian has to make, with the likelihood that not everybody will come to the same conclusion (OA 49–50).[8] On the other hand there is also the much more objective diversity of situations arising from differences of region, of culture and of socio-political systems (OA 3, 4). It is this latter which is of particular concern here since it raises the possibility that Christians in Latin America might be entitled and even obliged to collaborate far more closely with left-wing movements than would be appropriate in Europe or North America. Even the very paragraph in which the pope issues his warnings about socialism also contains references to 'different continents and cultures', to the variety of circumstances that need to be taken into account, and to the need for careful discernment and judgment (OA 31). The effect is that, in spite of a certain similarity between Pope Paul's reservations about socialism and the judgments of Pius XI forty years earlier (QA 113–26), there is a very great difference between the two.

Philip Land describes the position outlined in *Octogesima Adveniens* as a dramatic departure from the approach of previous papal documents (Land 394). He sees it as the relinquishment by Rome of the practice of 'handing down solutions to specific questions'. Chenu, too, believes that at this point the pope has made a truly radical change of approach. Formerly there was a deductive method by which a universally valid 'social doctrine' was applied to changing circumstances. But now there is an inductive method in which the different situations are themselves the primary location from which theology springs, through a discernment of 'the signs of the times' (Chenu 80). It is doubtful whether Pope Paul himself would have wished to make such a very sharp distinction between what he said here and the approach adopted in earlier papal teaching. But undoubtedly there is a notable difference of emphasis in his approach; and this has implications both for the role of the pope as a moral teacher and for the nature of theological method:

— As a moral teacher the pope cannot hope to be familiar with situations all over the world; so he must respect the discernment done at local or regional level.

— As regards theological method: Paul VI is far more willing than earlier popes to adopt an inductive approach; this means accepting that if one is to discover universal principles about social morality one must start from the variety of cultural and geographical situations in which moral issues arise.

A discernment of 'the signs of the times' at the regional level is precisely what the Medellín conference set out to offer—and what its documents claim to represent. So one must conclude that *Octogesima Adveniens* really offers very solid support to the Medellín conclusions—not so much because the pope agrees with the details of the evaluation as because he recognises the right and duty to make the kind of moral evaluation which the Latin American bishops undertook there. The caution and misgivings of *Octogesima Adveniens* are to be understood against this background. They ought not to be seen as a rejection of anything in the Medellín conclusions. But they constitute a salutary warning against *generalising* the Medellín outlook and attitudes without going through the same kind of process. In each area the Church must make its own assessment of the social, economic, cultural, political, and religious situation in order to discern what needs to be done. In this evaluation the points made in *Octogesima Adveniens* about the dangers both of socialism and of liberalism ought to be given due weight; they may help local Church people to take a more detached and objective view of their situation.

Given the general approach adopted in this document there are strict limits to the kind of direction it can give. It must of necessity restrict itself to examining general trends (OA 8–21) and promoting general values such as participation in decision-making (OA 47), education to a sense of solidarity with others (OA 23), and preferential respect for the poor (OA 23). Even within these limits, however, it could have been rather more specific in addressing itself to some of the more political issues not dealt with in *Populorum Progressio*.

A central issue that the pope had left hanging in his earlier document is how the poor and powerless can in fact be facilitated in taking responsibility for their lives. In *Octogesima*

Adveniens he made a very important contribution on this topic by emphasising that the Gospel calls for a 'preferential respect' for the poor; and by going on to insist that 'even equality before the law can serve as an alibi for flagrant discrimination, continued exploitation and actual contempt (OA 23). But there is a certain incompleteness in the remedy he proposes for the problem. He calls for 'a renewed education in solidarity' (OA 23). This is certainly needed; but is it enough? It does not seem to take sufficient account of the fact that in some situations those who hold power have no interest in yielding it to the poor. Indeed, as the pope himself was aware, the temptation to resort to violent revolution arises in those areas where those in power remain unaware of, or insensitive to, the injustices of the present situation and are determined to prolong it (OA 3).

Trade Unions and Politics

Octogesima Adveniens does not move to any significant extent beyond the consensus model of social change adopted in *Populorum Progressio*. It does not go as far as Medellín in calling for a conscientisation of the masses. In contrast to the Latin American bishops the pope does not appear to be in favour of encouraging the poorer people of society to demand change (Medellín 2.18 [p. 54]). It is not so much that this is directly ruled out; it is simply not mentioned as a major way in which injustices are to be overcome.

There is one passage in *Octogesima Adveniens* which is quite significant in this connection; it is where the pope speaks about the role of trade unions. Having defined the scope of their activity he notes the danger that they may abuse their power. One such misuse is in the economic sphere: they may demand more than society can afford—and the demand may be enforced by calling a strike, or threatening to do so. The second misuse of power is much more important from our present point of view: 'Here and there the temptation can arise . . . to desire to obtain in this way demands of a directly political nature' (OA 14). What is notable here is the pope's insistence that unions should not be involved in matters that are 'directly political'. Apparently Paul VI wanted trade unions to confine their representation of workers to specific economic issues and, presumably, other 'local' grievances. The implication is that unions would be 'trespassing' on the territory of political parties if they were to concern themselves with issues that can be labelled 'directly political'.

It is very difficult to draw a clear line between matters that are 'directly political' and the more limited issues that are only indirectly political or not political at all. Obviously the pope himself was well aware of this, since a central point in *Octogesima Adveniens* was, as we have seen, the need to 'pass from economics to politics' (OA 46). Nevertheless Pope Paul finds himself forced at this point to rely on a distinction between economics and politics. It is not difficult to guess why. Trade unions represent workers over against employers. If the unions were to become concerned with issues that are 'directly political' this could lead to a sharp political polarisation of society along class lines. The weapons used by both sides would be mainly economic ones—strikes and lockouts. The end result could be an overt class war. This would go against the whole thrust of Church social teaching since the time of Leo XIII. Pope Paul, like his predecessors, had an ideal of fruitful dialogue and collaboration between all groups in society, particularly across class barriers. So he did not wish to have a political division which reflected and reinforced the existing economic and social divisions of society. And certainly he did not want the strike weapon, which was designed to rectify specific economic abuses (mainly local ones), to be employed as a political weapon against governments. Consequently he insisted that it is an abuse to call a strike for any 'directly political' purpose. That means he had to maintain the existence of a sphere that is 'directly political' and had to define the role of unions as not concerned with that sphere of activity.

In fact the pope's account of the role of trade unions is quite vague. The only point at which it becomes rather specific is when it refers to 'lawful collaboration in the economic advance of society' (OA 14). The pope does not spell out any role that trade unions might play in ensuring that workers have adequate participation in decision-making in a given factory or in a particular industry. To do so would show up just how difficult it is to delineate an area that is directly political; for participation at this level is a political matter in one sense, though not yet political in the fullest sense. The problem becomes much greater when there is an expansion of the traditional role of trade unions so that they come to be accepted as one of 'the social partners' in society, with an acknowledged voice in determining the wider pattern of the economic and social life of the nation; for it is clear that such a role is 'directly political'.

Pope Paul strongly advocates the need for 'a greater sharing in responsibility and decision-making' both 'in economic life' and in 'the social and political sphere (OA 47). It is easy for him to make such general proposals for new structures to promote participation in industry and society. But the difficulty for the pope arises when it comes to moving from this desirable end to the means that might bring it about in practice. It is not easy to overcome the traditional Church suspicions of trade unions of a certain type, suspicions that have their basis in the history of the trade union movement in continental Europe. Furthermore, the pope was aware of the strength of class divisions in our world and was reluctant to approve of anything that might exacerbate them further. No wonder then that Pope Paul's treatment of trade unions and of the strike weapon is so limited and cautious. All the indications are that he would be quite reluctant to approve of a general strike designed to put pressure on an unjust regime and perhaps even to bring about its downfall. This would be the clearest instance of the use of an economic weapon in a matter that is 'directly political'.

One can certainly sympathise with the pope's wish to preserve some kind of distinction between economic affairs and political affairs. For it may be of real benefit to society if political divisions do not follow exactly the economic and social divisions in the country and if economic grievances and tensions can be prevented from taking on an overtly political form. However, the main benefits that come from this approach have to do with the *stability* of society. Stability is a very good thing in a society which is reasonably just. On the other hand stability may not be a good thing in a country that is highly stratified socially and economically, a society built on flagrant social injustice. In this situation radical change may be a higher priority than stability. And for this to take place it may be necessary for economic and social divisions to be reflected in politics. In practice this means that in such situations of blatant injustice it is far more difficult for trade unions to avoid playing a political role.

Take a situation where the economic difficulties of workers are due mainly to the grossly unjust structures of the society: if unions are really to promote justice for workers then they must become involved in wider political issues. To claim that, even in such circumstances, trade unions ought not to concern themselves with matters that are 'directly political' would be to condemn them to impotence and futility. Furthermore, to say that the strike-weapon should not be used even in such situations for 'directly political' purposes would be to deprive the poor of the most effective means they have of changing society in a not-too-violent way. It is true that in theory, even in a very unjust society, political grievances could be left to political parties. But in practice a repressive regime will seldom tolerate such overtly political opposition. It is not so easy for a repressive government to eliminate or control the activity of trade unions and their use of strikes in a quasi-political way.

It would seem then that Pope Paul, while acknowledging that it was not possible for him 'to utter a unified message' of 'universal validity' (OA 4), did not take this limitation suf-ficiently seriously in what he said about trade unions and strikes. He was still inclined to generalise from an experience that is too limited, too European.

The significance of this goes beyond the particular issue of the role of trade unions. It throws light on why *Octogesima Adveniens*, for all the important advances it made, still did not face up fully to the major issue left hanging in *Populorum Progressio*—the question of confrontation. The pope has now, in this second document, acknowledged that social and economic progress require political action. But his ideal of politics is a very high one—perhaps so high as to be unrealistic, except in certain situations. It is one in which there is room for political debate and even, presumably, a measure of political confrontation. But this political activity is to remain in some sense partitioned off from other spheres of life by being chan-nelled through political parties (or perhaps by other analogous types of formal political action). Such a version of democracy has worked reasonably well in most of Western society since the end of World War II. It seems to offer Europe a greater measure of stability than it had in the 1930s when political activity was less insulated from other spheres of life. So one can see why Pope Paul should favour it.

Unfortunately, the presuppositions for such a model of political activity are not always present everywhere in the world. Formal political activity is frequently restricted in places where the gap between rich and poor is very wide; for the rich soon find that they have to exert oppressive political power in order to retain their privileged position; and the poor, if they have sufficient spirit left to resist at all, will do so with little regard for the niceties of the political rules. In such circumstances it is no longer realistic to think that political struggles can be confined to a limited sphere where 'the political game' is played out within an agreed understanding in which political activity is differentiated from economic activity. For there no longer exists the fundamental social consensus which provides the underpinning for a contained measure of disagreement and struggle in the narrowly political sphere. To take account of such situations the Church's social teaching would have to face up to the question of a much more radical kind of confrontation in society than that which takes place between the political parties in a democratic state. *Octogesima Adveniens* does not seem to address itself to situations of that kind.

In my examination of *Populorum Progressio* I noted that Pope Paul seemed in danger of overlooking the positive value of confrontation. In general the same must be said of his position as given in *Octogesima Adveniens*: he sets such a high value on consensus that he does not take sufficient account of the fact that genuine dialogue presupposes a degree of equality between the partners; and this equality may be achievable only through a confrontation in which the rich and powerful are compelled to yield some of what they have to the poor. There is, however, one short cryptic statement in *Octogesima Adveniens* which indicates that the pope was aware of this. In saying that relationships based on force do not lead to a true and lasting kind of justice he adds the following qualification: ' . . . even if at certain times the alternation of positions can often make it possible to find easier conditions for dialogue.' (OA 43).[9] This obscure remark could be taken to mean that some confrontation may at times be helpful. But the statement is so vague that it cannot be taken as representing a significant departure from the pope's commitment to a consensus model of political action—particularly in view of the fact that he does not distinguish here between force and confrontation.

Nevertheless there is a sense in which *Octogesima Adveniens* goes much further than previous papal teaching on the question of confrontation as on other issues. It does so not primarily because of what it says directly on the question but because of the basic methodological principle that it lays down. This is that solutions to social problems have to be worked out in the light of local cultures and socio-political systems (OA 3–4). This leaves an opening for a more positive appreciation of the role of confrontation of the rich by the poor.

The relatively painless consensus model, which worked fairly well in Europe in the time of Pope Paul's papacy, does not have to be taken as the model for the whole world. 'For everything there is a season . . . a time to break down and a time to build up . . . a time to embrace, and a time to refrain from embracing . . . ' (Ecclesiastes 3:1–5).

SUMMARY

At Medellín in 1968 the Latin American bishops took the single most decisive step towards an 'option for the poor'. While pointing out the massive structural injustice in society in their part of the world, they committed themselves and the Latin American Church to giving 'effective preference to the poorest and most needy sectors of society'. They accepted the obligation to be in solidarity with the poor and marginalised. Most important of all, they came out in favour of a process of 'conscientisation' of the poor, the masses of ordinary people; this process involves educating the poor to an awareness of the basic causes of the marginalisation they experience, and helping them to organise themselves to overcome injustice and achieve liberation. They recalled Paul VI's statement that in extreme circumstances a revolutionary uprising might be justified; but they proposed that in the Latin American situation the Christian community should commit itself to using peaceful means in working for justice.

Three years later, in *Octogesima Adveniens*, Pope Paul offered what may be taken as his response to Medellín. It is a remarkable document which integrated a good deal of what the Latin American bishops had said and showed some sympathy for the kind of liberation which they envisaged. Above all, it recognised that economic problems call for political solutions. In this context the pope expressed his misgivings about Marxism, and he also strongly criticised the liberal capitalist ideology. He stressed the importance of people being allowed to participate in the decision-making that shapes society. Another important point in this document was the acceptance by the pope of the need for an inductive approach to social problems—and his admission that this would result in a certain pluralism; in different parts of the world different approaches might be adopted. In this document the pope noted that the Gospel calls for a preferential respect for the poor. But he was reluctant to acknowledge that the search for justice may at times call for a measure of confrontation. He did not want trade unions to become involved in issues that are 'directly political'. He still retained his hope that change could come about through consensus.

Questions for review:

1. What are the key elements in an option by the Church for the poor?
2. What is the link between liberation and conscientisation?
3. What reservations did Paul VI have about the Marxist ideology?
4. In what way was Pope Paul's approach more inductive and pluralist than that of earlier popes?

Questions for reflection:

1. Are there significant differences between development and liberation?
2. What are the advantages and disadvantages of trade unions engaging in overt political activities? Are there circumstances in which they would be morally obliged to do so?

Issue for further study:

How the perspective of an option for the poor affects the assessment of the so-called 'discovery' of America. (Read Boff and Elizondo.)

10

Two Synods and Pope Paul's Response

A few months after Pope Paul issued *Octogesima Adveniens* the question of social justice came to the fore once again in Rome. The occasion was the Synod of Bishops which took place there in 1971. At the Synod, Church leaders from Latin America had the opportunity to engage in formal dialogue on the theme of justice with bishops from the universal Church and with members of the Vatican Curia. The Synod marked a major step in the effort of the Catholic Church to come to terms with the issue of justice in the modern world. In the first part of this chapter I shall examine the document which it issued. The Synod document opened up deep controversy on the question of justice and liberation. These topics came up again for discussion three years later at the next Synod of Bishops in Rome. A year later (in 1975) Pope Paul issued a major document entitled *Evangelii Nuntiandi* ('Evangelisation in the Modern World'), making use of the materials of the 1974 Synod and giving his own response to the issues which arose there. The second part of this chapter will be devoted to an examination of the pope's teaching in *Evangelii Nuntiandi*.

SECTION I

'JUSTICE IN THE WORLD' (SYNOD 1971)

Late in 1971 the Synod of Bishops, having met in Rome, issued a document entitled 'Justice in the World'. Though relatively brief, it is one of the most important statements on social justice ever issued by Rome. The document is important not only for its content but also because of its sources.

The Synod brought together bishops from Churches all over the world, leaders encouraged by the renewal initiated at Vatican II, people who were ready now to take bold steps in the area of the relationship between Church and world. The Latin American bishops and their advisers, who were working hard at that time to implement the directives of Medellín, were a particular source of inspiration at this Synod. The actual text owed very much to a few key people working in or with the Pontifical Commission for Justice and Peace. This Commission had been established by Paul VI in 1967, and by 1971 it was at the height of its power. It had become the focus in Rome for fresh approaches and deep commitment on social justice questions.[1]

The document 'Justice in the World' has 'a quality of concreteness and realism' (O'Brien and Shannon's introduction to the document) which is reminiscent of the Medellín documents. Its overall plan is also clearly influenced by the approach adopted at Medellín. A genuine attempt is made to begin from the real situation in the world, in order to discern there 'the signs of the times',[2] the specific ways in which God is speaking to today's world and calling people to respond.

Structural Injustice and Misdevelopment

One of the more significant points in the text is the emphasis on structural injustice. The document does not oppose personal conversion to structural reform, nor does it merely juxtapose the two. Instead it indicates how the former is conditioned by the latter, for it speaks of 'the objective obstacles which social structures place in the way of conversion of hearts' (JW 16). Many bishops at the Synod spoke out strongly about structural injustice at the international level. The document reflects their views. It does not hesitate to say that the conditions left by the colonial domination of the past may evolve into 'a new form of colonialism in which the developing nations will be the victims of the interplay of international economic forces' (JW 16). This outspoken linking of past imperialism with present structural injustices in the international economic order is much stronger than the position adopted by Paul VI about colonialism and neo-colonialism in *Populorum Progressio* (PP 7, 52, 57).

In the very same sentence the Synod document insists that this danger can be avoided only by 'liberation'. So the word 'liberation' is used in a positive sense, in a way that seems to be a definite advance on the usage of Paul VI in *Octogesima Adveniens*. However, there is a significant difference between the way the word is used here and its use at Medellín. 'Justice in the World' speaks of attaining 'liberation through development', a usage that does not appear in the Medellín documents. These latter frequently speak of liberation without any mention of development, and occasionally put the words 'liberation' and 'development' side by side. But the more nuanced usage of the Synod document does not mean that it is less daring than Medellín. Rather it had to take account of a variety of different situations. In Latin America the word 'development' was irretrievably associated with a model of economic growth that widened the gap between rich and poor. However, as I pointed earlier (p. 212 above), in other parts of 'the South'—especially in the newly independent countries of Africa—'development' was still a positive word. Leaders, including Church leaders, still believed that the way to overcome poverty was through development. The Synod phrase 'liberation through development' represents an attempt to take account of these different situations and outlooks.

It is to be noted, however, that the authors of the document were well aware of the myths and illusions associated with the concept of development. They insisted on the need to get rid of 'those myths and false convictions which have up to now gone with a thought-pattern subject to a kind of deterministic and automatic notion of progress.' (JW 16). One of the most succinct and striking parts of the document is where the bishops point out that the hope has been in vain that poverty would be overcome through development:

> In the last twenty-five years a hope has spread through the human race that economic growth would bring about such a quantity of goods that it would be possible to feed the hungry at least with the crumbs falling from the table, but this has proved a vain hope in underdeveloped areas and in pockets of poverty in wealthier areas . . . (JW 10)

The document goes on to list several interrelated reasons for this failure:

— rapid population growth;

— rural stagnation;

— lack of land reform;

— massive migration to the cities;

— high technology industry that does not give sufficient employment.

On a first reading, the paragraph could give the impression that a variety of unfortunate circumstances (population growth, migration, etc.) have undermined what would otherwise have been a healthy form of development. But the overall tone indicates support for the view that things have gone wrong not so much in spite of 'development' but more because of it. The paragraph concludes with a deeply moving sentence—very Latin American in style—which confirms this impression:

> These stifling oppressions constantly give rise to great numbers of 'marginal' persons, ill-fed, inhumanly housed, illiterate and deprived of political power as well as of the suitable means of acquiring responsibility and moral dignity. (JW 10)

Taken as a whole, the paragraph amounts to a very radical criticism of the 'development' process that has actually taken place (as distinct from some ideal development which might have occurred). It is not simply that this so-called development has failed to meet the needs of the poor. It is that it has actually increased the numbers of the poor, by creating a whole category of marginal people. In fact, then, the document makes a far more trenchant criticism of 'development' than appears at first sight.

In the next paragraph the Synod puts forward an even more serious criticism of the kind of 'development' that has taken place: the environmental costs of the benefits are so heavy that it is simply not possible for all parts of the world to have the kind of 'development' that has occurred in the wealthy countries:

> Furthermore, such is the demand for resources and energy by the richer nations, whether capitalist or socialist, and such are the effects of dumping by them in the atmosphere and the sea, that irreparable damage would be done to the essential elements of life on earth, such as air and water, if

their high rates of consumption and pollution, which are constantly on the increase, were extended to the whole of humankind. (JW 11)

This passage, if taken seriously, would on its own completely demolish the myth of development on which rich and poor countries had lived for a generation. Both the wealthy and the deprived had assumed that what had been achieved by some could soon be achieved by others, and eventually by all. The relative poverty of some nations compared with others could be endured by them so long as people thought it was temporary. And the use of the term 'developing countries' to describe what were really very poor countries (sometimes growing still more poor) helped to ease the consciences of the well-off in the face of the absolute and abject poverty of millions of people.

To recognise that what had been called 'development' is available only to a limited number of countries is in effect to accept that it is not true development at all, but rather a kind of exploitation. This is a less obvious type of exploitation than one finds in colonialism or in failure to pay proper prices for Third World products. For what is being directly exploited in this case is not other people but the resources of the earth.

In recent years it has become evident that exploitation of the earth's resources also involves an indirect exploitation of other people or peoples. For those countries which were first to get into 'development' have taken far more than their fair share of the available benefits, leaving much less for others. Until quite recently it was assumed that new technologies, inventions, and discoveries could ensure that shortage of energy or raw materials would not limit growth, and that toxic wastes could be dumped and dispersed in the sea or the air. Today however, as the Synod document points out, it is clear that there are severe limits to this destructive type of growth; and this changes the situation entirely. Now that it is recognised that those at the end of the queue for development cannot take as much from the earth as those who came early, it becomes formally unjust and exploitative for the 'developed countries' to refuse to share more fairly the benefits they have received from what was the common heritage of all.

The fact that the Synod document takes so seriously this issue of the limits to growth, shows that in speaking of 'liberation through development' the bishops do not imagine that poverty in the world is to be overcome simply by rapid economic growth. What poor countries and poor groups need is a type of development that is not modelled on that of the richer countries and regions. Indeed a major element in the real development of the poor is that the rich should be stopped from imposing misdevelopment on the world. The notion of 'liberation through development' needs then to be complemented by that of 'development through liberation'. Although the Synod document does not use this latter phrase, its teaching about justice amounts to more or less the same thing, though the language is more nuanced and polite.

The Core of the Problem

According to 'Justice in the World' there is one central issue which lies at the heart of the structural injustices of today's world: lack of participation by people in determining their own destiny. The new industrial and technological order 'favours the concentration of wealth, power and decision-making in the hands of a small public or private group' (JW 9). The kind of positive action required to reverse this inherent tendency of the system is not being taken; and the result is marginalisation of masses of people (JW 9–10). To be in a marginal situation is not simply to be economically deprived but, perhaps more basically, to be deprived of the political power to change one's situation.[3]

The Synod document says: 'We see in the world a set of injustices which constitute the nucleus of today's problems'; to solve them concerned people, including Church leaders, must 'take on new functions and new duties' (JW 20).[4] The required action is to be 'directed above all at those people and nations which because of various forms of oppression and because of the present character of our society are silent, indeed voiceless victims of injustice' (JW 20). This statement implies a definite option in favour of the powerless, the oppressed, the victims of structural injustice. It goes a step beyond what Paul VI had said in *Octogesima Adveniens* about the need to move from

economics to politics (OA 46). For it applies this principle to
the action of the Church itself in a way that is reminiscent of
the commitment undertaken by the Latin American bishops at
Medellín (e.g. Medellín 2.7 and 4.16 [pp. 47–8, 76]).

Unfortunately, the document seems to lose its thrust for a
while at this point. Instead of spelling out at once what such
an option for the voiceless would mean, the following paragraphs
go into examples, giving lists of various victims of injustice—
migrants, refugees, those persecuted for their faith, people
whose rights are restricted, etc. (JW 20–6). No doubt this ensures
that the statement does not become too abstract; but it is no
longer clear how the various injustices listed spring from a
common root, apart from the general tendency of people to
victimise the weak. Furthermore, no effort is made at this stage
to clarify what is meant by saying that action is to be directed
at the victims of injustice. The phrase is ambiguous at best.
Does it imply simply working *for* such people, or is it supposed
to mean real solidarity *with* them?

There is also a certain lack of clarity in the way the Synod
categorises those who are victims of injustice. In the passage
quoted above it refers to 'people and nations'. In general the
Synod pays a good deal of attention to poor nations, and gives
a penetrating account of their plight. But who is being referred
to when the document speaks of the 'people' (as distinct from
the 'nations') that are victims of injustice? The document does
not say explicitly that these are the members of the poorer
classes, oppressed by the upper classes. Like the popes, the
Synod bishops were reluctant to highlight the class structure of
society. Instead they listed a variety of categories of victimised
people, ranging from migrants to political prisoners, to orphans
(JW 20–6); and they also referred to regional imbalances (JW
18). What they had to say is undoubtedly true; but it seems to
distract attention from the crucial point made earlier in the
document itself, that the present pattern of society and its
model of development is itself creating a mass of people who
are economically and politically 'marginal'—in effect a whole
class of people who are poor and powerless.

The document encourages the poor nations to take their
future into their own hands through 'a certain responsible nationalism' and by forming 'new political groupings' (JW 17). But it

does not have anything quite so strong and clear to say to the marginal people *within* any given society. Instead, it offers two short and rather platitudinous paragraphs under the heading *The Need for Dialogue* (JW 27–8). These contain vague remarks about the need for mediation. But it is not made clear what this means, who is to do it, or at what level (local, national, or international) it is to take place. Once again the issue of confrontation, especially between the rich and the poor classes in society, seems to be evaded. That impression is strengthened by the fact that in a later paragraph the issue of how a Christian should act is posed in over-simplified terms; the choice offered is between conflict on the one hand and love, right, and non-violence on the other hand (JW 39; cf. JW 71 which lays great stress on cooperation). This presentation does not pay sufficient attention to the importance of a non-violent kind of confrontation, one that aims ultimately at establishing more equal conditions for dialogue.

There is, however, one section of 'Justice in the World' which goes some distance in the direction which Medellín took when it called for conscientisation. The heading is *Educating to Justice*. There the Synod document speaks of awakening a critical sense and making consciences aware of the actual situation (of injustice) as a step in the process of transforming the world, enabling people to take in hand their own destiny, and bringing about communities that are truly human (JW 51–2). But it is not made clear who are to be the subjects of such education. Is it the rich, or the poor, or both? If it is the rich, then the assumption remains that change is to come mainly from the top. If it is the poor, then the question of some measure of confrontation has to be faced. If it is rich and poor alike, then the danger is that a crucial point may be glossed over—namely, that Church leaders who seek to promote change in society, can hardly escape the need to make a certain option. They can assume that those at the top of society are the key agents of change; or they can acknowledge that the poor are more likely to bring about the kind of changes that justice requires. Of course, Church leaders will feel called to avoid exacerbating divisions in society; and they must also avoid identifying the Church too closely with the interests of any particular group or class. So they will wish to work with all sectors of society. Nevertheless, on certain issues a choice, or a series of choices, must be made; and people soon sense where the Church leaders stand in practice—especially in countries where there is gross injustice and oppression.

That the Synod bishops wanted to show special concern for the poor, and even to affirm their special role in bringing about a just society, is not in doubt. That is made clear once again in the final paragraph of the document which says, 'the Church calls on all, *especially the poor, the oppressed and the afflicted*, to cooperate with God to bring about liberation from every sin and to build a world which will reach the fullness of creation . . . ' (JW 77 —emphasis added). The doubt that remains concerns the *means* by which all this is to take place. It would appear that the Synod, like Pope Paul himself, hesitated to offer open encouragement to the poorer classes of society to challenge existing structures by demanding change and organising themselves in support of their demands.

Justice within the Church

The area where the Synod of Bishops seems to take most seriously the option for the poor is in the organisation of the Church itself. 'Justice in the World' is strikingly new and encouraging in the way in which it commits its authors to practise justice within the Church. That commitment is given expression in these words:

> While the Church is bound to give witness to justice, she recognises that anyone who ventures to speak to people about justice must first be just in their eyes. Hence we must undertake an examination of the modes of acting and of the possessions and life style found within the Church herself. (JW 40)

In the following paragraphs the document goes on to mention various ways in which the rights of people within the Church have to be respected. These include respect for economic rights (wages), juridical rights, and the right to share responsibility and participate in decision-making; the document makes special mention of the rights of women (lay and religious) and of the laity in general (JW 41–6). This support for the rights of the more vulnerable and voiceless groups in the Church itself gives real weight to the Synod in speaking out against the marginalisation of people in civil society.

In the next two paragraphs the bishops address themselves to the question of the image of the Church in the world: 'If . . . the Church appears to be among the rich and the powerful of this world its credibility is diminished' (JW 47). This leads the bishops to say that the possessions, privileges, and lifestyle of the Church and of its ministers and members must be looked at; they must be judged not simply in terms of efficiency but to see whether they hinder the Church in its proclamation and witness of the Gospel to the poor (JW 47–8). This section of the Synod document undoubtedly owes much to the new emphasis of the Latin American Church. Even the crisp simple style in which it is written conveys the same sense of quiet commitment as one finds in the documents of Medellín.

Theological Aspects

Only a relatively small part of 'Justice in the World' treats of strictly theological issues. Nevertheless the theological contribution of the document is one of its most important aspects. A real attempt is made to sketch out a scriptural theology which links poverty with justice: God is the liberator of the oppressed and Christ proclaims the intervention of God's justice on behalf of the needy (JW 30–1).

The authors of the document emphasise that there is a very close connection between our relationship to God and our relationship to our neighbour (JW 34). They want to repudiate the dualism which would see Christianity as essentially 'spiritual' and other-worldly, so that issues of justice in this world would be of secondary or peripheral importance to it. So they insist that the 'present situation of the world, seen in the light of faith, calls us back to the very essence of the Christian message'; and they maintain that the mission of preaching the Gospel now calls Christians to dedicate themselves to human liberation even in this world (JW 35). For, 'the Gospel message . . . contains a . . . demand for justice in the world, and so the Church, though it does not claim to be the only agency responsible for justice in the world, sees itself as having 'a proper and specific role, which is its task of giving witness before the world to the demand contained in the Gospel message, a demand for love and justice' (JW 36).

The passage in which this theology is best summed up comes quite near the beginning of the document. It is the most quoted part of 'Justice in the World', a statement that has made this document famous and controversial:

> Action on behalf of justice and participation in the transformation of the world fully appear to us as a constitutive dimension of the preaching of the Gospel, or, in other words, of the Church's mission for the redemption of the human race and its liberation from every oppressive situation (JW 6).

Despite the importance of this passage I have held over any reference to it until my examination of the document is almost finished. The reason is that the full significance of the statement and its controversial character emerged clearly only after the Synod was over. So a discussion of the passage leads one quickly to the debate at the next Synod, in 1974, and to Pope Paul's Apostolic Exhortation *Evangelii Nuntiandi* which came as a follow-up to that Synod.

It appears that the passage just quoted was not considered unusually new or daring when it was presented in draft form to the Synod. Perhaps it was accepted rather too easily because the time available was short; and because the bishops and the Vatican officials wanted to avoid the kind of divisive debate and polarisation which had characterised the Synod during its earlier stages while the priestly ministry was on the agenda.[5]

But soon after the Synod the passage became very controversial—and most of the debate focused on the word 'constitutive'. By saying that 'action on behalf of justice and participation in the transformation of the world' is a constitutive dimension or element (*ratio constitutiva*) of the preaching of the Gospel, the Synod was ensuring that justice work could never be dismissed as being merely incidental to the task of the Church; it would have to be given a central place.

Ever since the document was issued, this passage—and this word 'constitutive'—have been cited on innumerable occasions to show that the Church officially rejects the view that action to bring about a more just society takes second place to more 'spiritual' or 'religious' matters (cf. O'Brien and Shannon, 385— their introduction to the Synod document). In fact the statement has become a kind of manifesto for those who are working for political liberation against oppressive regimes or structures and who want to invoke the Church's support for such activity.

For this very reason the statement came under attack from those Church leaders and theologians who saw the evangelising mission of the Church as primarily 'spiritual'. Their tactic was to replace the word 'constitutive' by the word 'integral'. This latter word refers to something that is not absolutely essential to the life of the Church but pertains rather to its fullness. Those who rejected the word 'constitutive' argued that this word should be used only of something that can never be absent without the Church failing to be itself; whereas, they claimed, the Church, without ceasing to be Church, may at times find itself so restricted by political authorities that it is totally prevented from undertaking 'action on behalf of justice'.

This argument about the use of words was the focus for a more fundamental disagreement about how the Church ought to respond when faced with major injustice in society. Should it take an overtly political stand like some of the more 'prophetic' leaders of the Latin American Church? Should Church leaders distance the Church from unjust regimes and then encourage active resistance by those who are oppressed? Should Church workers even help to organise such resistance? Or, on the other hand, should this kind of activity be seen as an excessive politicisation of the Church? In certain influential Church circles there was real distress about the new trends that were emerging, especially in Latin America. It was feared that the new liberation theology was emptying the Christian faith of its deepest transcendent meaning and reducing it to a religious legitimation for revolutionary activity. Those who resisted the use of the word 'constitutive' generally wanted to dissociate the Church from liberation struggles of a political kind.

It may be added that many of those who were worried about liberation theology and the politicisation of the Church were people who also wished to minimise the importance of Synods of Bishops. They emphasised the fact that a Synod has a merely consultative role. Its function is to advise the pope; and the pope remains free to accept or reject what is said by a Synod. The campaign of these people to replace the word 'constitutive' with the word 'integral' had a further purpose over and above the immediate issue: by implication it brought out the point that the Synod document was not fully authoritative or binding but could be superseded by a statement of the pope. So the dispute about this one word became a focus and symbol for different views about the exercise of authority in the Church— about the extent to which the power of the Roman curia should be limited by a Synod of bishops. This in turn related to a dispute about how much autonomy should be left to Church authorities in a region (e.g. Latin America) and how much control should be exercised by the Church's central administration in Rome.

Our concern here is only peripherally with these questions of Church authority. What is mainly of interest to us is that the controversy about the word 'constitutive' brought to the fore two closely related theological issues that arise in relation to the Church's action to promote justice:

— What is the nature of human salvation, and how is it related to political, economic, and cultural liberation?

— What should be the role of the Church in working to further these forms of liberation?

Even those who accepted without reservation the teaching of the Synod document on these issues would have to admit that there was need for a much deeper and more extensive treatment of both questions. Clearly then there was a very good reason for choosing the topic 'evangelisation' as the subject for discussion at the following Synod, that of 1974. This choice of topic offered an ideal opportunity for the bishops to deal with these two questions.

SECTION II

EVANGELII NUNTIANDI

The Synod of 1974 was an exciting event with a disappointing ending. Some of the excitement in the discussions came from the contributions made by participants from Africa. What they had to say, and their style of saying it, helped the Synod to take more seriously the whole question of the Church and non-Western cultures. It became clear that other parts of 'the South' besides Latin America had challenges to issue, and a contribution to make, to the wider Church. In the short term this helped to ensure that political and economic liberation were not the only important topics discussed; the agenda was broadened considerably. In the long term the way was paved for a wider and more integral conception of human liberation, one that gives a central role not just to economics and politics but also to culture.

The ending of the 1974 Synod was disappointing because the participants failed to agree on the text of the major document which they had hoped to issue. Two draft texts were put forward and there was a failure to work out a compromise acceptable to both sides (cf. Land [1979] 393). The result was that both texts were handed over to the pope along with the other synodal materials, in the expectation that he would issue a document on evangelisation, making use of this material.

Procedurally, this was a major victory for those who wished to play down the importance of Synods in the life of the Church. This was especially so since it established a precedent and set a pattern for subsequent Synods. It gave the pope a completely free hand to pick and choose from the materials presented to him, and also to add new material. It was also used in support of the argument that Synods were a rather ineffective invention, an innovation that could be divisive and that needed the strong hand of the pope and the Vatican Curia to draw some fruit from them. On the other hand, however, this handing over of the Synod material to the pope ensured that more time was available for a deeper and more nuanced treatment of the issues raised at the Synod.

After an interval of just over a year Pope Paul issued an Apostolic Exhortation *Evangelii Nuntiandi* (called in English 'Evangelisation in the Modern World'), as his response to the request of the Synod for a document based on the fruits of its work.[6] It is an exceptionally valuable document, one that explores in depth several vital theological and pastoral issues that had arisen since the time of Vatican II. Needless to say, it builds on the teaching of the Vatican Council, but it does not hesitate to deal with new questions and to offer fresh insights about old questions. One of the most important features of the document is the broad sweep of the vision of evangelisation which it offers. Precisely because of this comprehensive character of the Apostolic Letter, it contains a lot of material that is not of direct concern to us here. It should be noted then that I shall confine my attention to the points directly relevant to our subject, omitting other valuable aspects of the document.

Good News of the Kingdom

Perhaps the best way to begin is to see how the pope deals in *Evangelii Nuntiandi* with the controversial theological question raised by the document of the 1971 Synod when it said that action on behalf of justice is a *constitutive* dimension of preaching the Gospel. Paul VI does not say overtly that he is taking sides in this controversy. But there can be little doubt that what he says in this new document provides a thorough vindication for the statement of the Synod. To see how he does so we need to look at what the document has to say about three key concepts—Kingdom, evangelisation and liberation. I shall look at each in turn, the first two briefly and the third more extensively.

What *Evangelii Nuntiandi* has to say about the Kingdom, though brief, is vitally important. The central point is summed up in one short passage:

> As the one who proclaims the Gospel, Christ announces above all a kingdom, which is the Kingdom of God; he attributes so much importance to this Kingdom that by comparison with it everything else becomes the 'other things that shall be added unto you'. Therefore the Kingdom of God must be treated as an absolute, to which everything else must be referred (EN 8).

If Christ's primary concern was the Kingdom, then even the Church must not be seen as an end in itself. Rather it is a community of believers gathered 'in the name of Jesus so that they may together seek the Kingdom, build it up and implement it in their own lives' (EN 13).[7] Building the Kingdom is not confined to what might be called 'churchy' activities, or even to actions that are religious or 'spiritual' in the usual sense of these terms. It also requires very secular activity such as working to overcome oppressive or inhuman structures in society. It follows, then, that by refusing to make the Church itself the ultimate term of reference and insisting instead on the Kingdom as the only absolute value of the Christian, Pope Paul has taken a major step towards justifying the claim that action for justice is a constitutive aspect of the work of evangelisation.

A second important contribution in this regard is made by the pope in the way he clarifies the nature of evangelisation and the means by which it takes place. Some key lines are the following:

> The proclamation [of the Gospel] must take place above all by witness . . . a witness which requires presence, a sharing of life, and solidarity; in the carrying out of evangelisation this witness is an essential part, and often the first one . . .
>
> However, even the most perfect witness will be of no avail in the end unless there is a clear unambiguous proclamation of the Lord Jesus, to throw light on and justify the witness . . . and to reveal explicitly its true meaning. (EN 21–2; cf. EN 41–2)

This position represents a notable theological advance on what had been said at Vatican II. There, priority had been given to verbal preaching, while witness was relegated to a secondary place. Pope Paul, by contrast, insisted that words and witness are both of fundamental importance—each in a different way. Witness without words may remain ambiguous or opaque; words without witness lack credibility. By refusing to put Christian witness in a secondary place Paul VI was rejecting an older theology which would tend to see worldly activity as just a preparation for the Gospel ('pre-evangelisation') or at best an indirect evangelisation;[8] and such an older theology could not easily show how action for justice is a constitutive element in evangelisation in the proper sense.

However, it is not enough to show that Christian living is as important as verbal preaching. A further step is required: one must show why a privileged place should be given to action for justice, over and above many other kinds of secular work. To do this we must go on to look in some detail at the third important word in *Evangelii Nuntiandi*—the word 'liberation'.

Salvation and Liberation

'Development', rather than 'liberation' was the key word in the Vatican Council's document *Gaudium et Spes* and in Pope Paul's 1967 encyclical *Populorum Progressio*. Medellín gave sanction to the alternative word 'liberation' in the Latin American Church. Pope Paul in writing *Octogesima Adveniens* in 1971 was very cautious in his use of the word 'liberation'. But at the Synod of Bishops in Rome later that same year the word was coming to be accepted as one that could be relevant for the universal Church. Three years later at the Synod of 1974 there was a lot of talk about 'liberation'. After that Synod Pope Paul apparently decided that there was no longer any point in shying away from the word. It would be better to provide a thorough theological analysis of the concept of liberation. In this way he could take what was of value in the word while correcting inadequate or mistaken ideas about its meaning or implications. This is what *Evangelii Nuntiandi* set out to do; and that is why the notion of liberation was given a very central role in the document.

One of the more valuable aspects of the treatment of the theme of liberation in the document is the way in which it is rooted in the Gospel. After a few introductory paragraphs explaining the occasion and purpose of the document the pope plunges at once into an account of the liberating mission of Christ. He says that the two words which provide the key to understanding the evangelisation of Christ are 'Kingdom' and 'Salvation' (EN 10). Christ came to bring the Good News of the Kingdom of God, that 'good news to the poor' which was promised in the book of Isaiah (EN 6). The content of this Good News is summarised by the pope in a striking passage:

> As the main point and the very centre of his Good News, Christ proclaims salvation; this is the great gift of God which is liberation from everything that oppresses people, particularly liberation from sin and the Evil One, together with the joy experienced when one knows God and is known by God, when one sees God and entrusts oneself to God. (EN 9)

The most important thing to note here is that the word liberation is given real theological respectability. But this is done in a very nuanced way that is typical of Pope Paul. Aware that many people took the word 'liberation' to be almost equivalent to 'revolution', the pope set out to extricate it from this very restricted meaning. *Evangelii Nuntiandi* speaks of being liberated 'from everything that oppresses people, particularly from sin and the Evil One'. This clearly presses the meaning of the word far beyond political and economic liberation. Furthermore, the word liberation is used in the document in a way that does not allow it to replace the word salvation, or even to be seen as entirely equivalent to it. Instead it is given a more limited role; it becomes one of the everyday words (such as 'gift' and 'joy') that are used to explain the meaning of the more fundamental biblical and theological word 'salvation'.

Evangelii Nuntiandi makes a notable contribution to the development of a coherent and comprehensible use of theological language by helping to locate the word 'liberation' within a network of other theological concepts. This is a step towards the emergence of a scientific theological vocabulary in which the various concepts are defined in terms of their relationship to each other (cf. Lonergan [1958] and [1972]). But the development of theological language was scarcely the primary purpose of the pope in this pastorally oriented document. He was more concerned to communicate an overall vision of evangelisation, one that transcends any division such as 'religious versus secular' or 'spiritual versus temporal'. The reader of the passage quoted above is offered such a global vision; and it is one in which action for justice can be clearly seen to be a constitutive dimension of evangelisation.

Evangelisation literally means bringing good news. The passage quoted above says that the Good News of Jesus involves liberation from everything that oppresses people; and economic and political oppression are among the more obvious of such things. So liberation from these forms of oppression (and from cultural oppression which, though perhaps less obvious, is equally evil) is part of the core of the Good News of Jesus—and therefore of evangelisation; provided of course that, as the passage suggests, it comes as the gift of God. It is part of the subtlety of the passage that this proviso has to be added, although the pope's statement does not put it in the form of a strict condition.

The passage does not entitle one to claim that any and every overcoming of political oppression is automatically a part of that 'salvation' which is the core of Christ's Good News. For 'salvation' is presented as something that is the gift of God. So if it were the case that a particular form of political liberation were contrary to God's will, then it would not be part of 'salvation'. On the other hand, one is not entitled to argue that any particular event of political liberation is not part of the gift of salvation merely on the grounds that it was brought about by human activity; for human action and divine gift are by no means mutually exclusive.

To sum up: the pope here offers an integral vision to those who are engaged in what the Synod of 1971 called 'action on behalf of justice and participation in the transformation of the world'. It is a vision that enables them to situate their activity within the total creative-redemptive pattern by which God in Christ brings salvation to the world; their action and their struggles contribute to the saving work of God, God's gift of salvation. In this sense their activity is part of the Good News, part of evangelisation. It is not of course the whole reality of evangelisation. As noted above, the pope insists that a verbal proclamation is also essential. Indeed one of the strengths of the concept of evangelisation as presented in this document is the insistence that it is a complex reality comprising many elements, no one of which on its own should be taken to be the total reality (EN 17; cf. McGregor 63).

The integral vision of human salvation presented in *Evangelii Nuntiandi* includes, as one would expect, a good deal of synthesising and balancing of various aspects. Like most theologians, the drafter of the document finds it impossible to satisfy those who ask for a simple, either/or answer to the question, 'Is salvation found in this life or in the next?' To this question the answer of the document is that it has its beginning in this life but is fulfilled in eternity (EN 27). But what is particularly valuable in the document is that it offers terms in which the relationship between the present and the future can be explored more fruitfully. It speaks of 'a hereafter' which is 'both in continuity and in discontinuity with the present situation' and of 'a hidden dimension' of this world, an aspect that will one day be revealed (EN 28).[9]

By using this kind of language the document is able to avoid that naive dualism which would equate salvation with spiritual welfare as distinct from merely temporal or material welfare. The contrast offered instead is between on the one hand a purely 'immanent' salvation (including both material and spiritual elements) and on the other hand 'a transcendent and eschatological salvation' (EN 27). It must be noted at once that this is not a simple contrast between an immanent and a transcendent salvation. Rather the contrast is between one that is *merely* immanent and one that is both immanent and transcendent— that is, a salvation which relates to earthly 'desires, hopes, affairs, and struggles' but which also 'exceeds all these limits' (EN 27).

Concern about Misunderstandings

A significant part of the teaching of *Evangelii Nuntiandi* hinges on this vital distinction between a conception of salvation that limits it to this world and one that includes worldly affairs but also transcends them. It provides Pope Paul with a solid basis for using the word liberation quite freely and, at the same time, correcting what he considers to be false or inadequate ways of understanding the word itself and also the core of the Christian message. The main worries expressed by him in regard to incorrect ideas about liberation are to be found in paragraphs 31–38 of the document. His reservations can be grouped under the following five headings: Reductionism, Politicisation, Inherent Limitations, Violence, and Attitudinal Change. As I examine each in turn I shall add some comments on the pope's treatment of these different issues.

(1) Reductionism: The first and main concern of Pope Paul is that the liberation heralded by Christ and promoted by the Church might be reduced to a much more limited version of liberation, through a failure to take account of the deepest dimensions of what it means to be human. Speaking of the liberation that is proclaimed and promoted by evangelising activity he insists that:

> It cannot be limited to any restricted sphere whether it be economic, political, social, or cultural. It must rather take account of the totality of the human person in all its aspects and elements, including the openness of the human person to what is absolute, even to the Absolute that is God. (EN 33)

There appear to be two slightly different emphases in the way in which the reservations of the pope are expressed. The first is found in the passage just quoted. It is the concern that every aspect of the human person be taken seriously, including that of a religious openness to God. A somewhat different expression is found in the very next paragraph. There the pope says that the Church re-affirms the primacy of its spiritual function (EN 34). This statement goes a step further than the previous one: it suggests that the religious aspect is not only indispensable but is also the *primary* concern of the Church. However, this can best be understood as an insistence that the religious dimension of the human person is what is deepest in humanity and is therefore of particular concern to the Church. There are no solid grounds in *Evangelii Nuntiandi* for claiming that social and political concerns are of secondary importance for the Church.[10]

(2) *Politicisation:* Closely related to the danger of reductionism, and following on from it, is the concern of the pope about an excessive politicisation of the role of the Church. If a narrowing down of the Christian concept of liberation were to take place, then the Church's function would also be reduced. The Church would lose its deepest meaning and its activities would be confined to the purely political or social order. That would deprive the liberating message of the Church of its distinctive character. As a result, the message would be liable to be distorted by ideological groups and political parties using it for their own purposes (EN 32).

The central point here seems to be that what the Church has to offer is not a specific political or social programme but rather an integral vision of what it means to be human—what the pope calls an anthropology, which includes a theology of redemption (EN 33, 31). If the more transcendent aspects of this vision are ignored, then Christians precisely as Christians will have nothing specific to add to what political movements have to offer.[11] In that case the main value of the Church would be simply its ability to animate and mobilise people for social and political action through the invocation of powerful religious symbols and the arousing of religious fervour. It is a great boost for the morale of any political movement if its followers are assured that their political beliefs are endorsed by the Church and by God. Pope Paul wanted to ensure that the Church's commitment to liberation could not be interpreted as support for Marxist ideology. He seemed less preoccupied by the danger that Christianity could be harnessed in support of a right-wing political ideology of 'National Security'.

(3) *Inherent Limitations*: 'The Church sees the links between human liberation and salvation in Jesus Christ, but does not consider the two to be identical' (EN 35). This is an important statement which is supported by a variety of reasons in the remainder of the paragraph. One valuable point emerges: the achievement of (earthly) liberation and prosperity are not in themselves sufficient to constitute the coming of the Kingdom, for all temporal and political liberation contains within it the seed of failure. This is a point that has been developed more fully in recent theology, especially Third World theology (e.g. EATWOT 129). The achievement of political liberation in a particular area may truly be seen as a salvific event, as the Exodus was for the Jewish people. Nevertheless this does not mean that salvation has been definitively attained in this liberation. Various inadequacies are there from the beginning; and they tend to grow and to create a widening gap between the ideal salvation that is being reached for and the very limited degree of liberation that has been achieved.

Unfortunately, this important point made by the pope tends to become somewhat obscured because in the passage it is confused with another, slightly different, point. This second point is that even people who invoke the Bible in support of their actions may in fact be operating on the basis of a notion of liberation that is not fully Christian; indeed some interpretations of the word 'liberation' are simply incompatible with the Christian view of the human person and of history. No doubt this warning of the pope was needed; but coming here it tends to distract attention from a major theological issue—namely, how the gift of divine salvation is embodied in human history, and in what sense any particular achievement of justice may be called salvific in the proper Christian sense.

(4) *Violence*: Pope Paul was concerned lest there be any confusion between the Christian conception of liberation and the kind of political liberation sought by revolutionaries. He saw the danger that a certain kind of liberation theology, based

largely on the Old Testament, could be invoked to justify violent rebellion against unjust regimes. Of all the objections raised against the word 'liberation', this was the most obvious one. It led many rich and powerful groups, including people with power in the mass media to put considerable pressure on the pope to come out strongly against liberation theology; and this pressure came also from many conservative Church leaders.

Pope Paul, as we have seen, responded not by rejecting the word 'liberation' but by clarifying the Christian meaning of the word and then correcting wrong interpretations. Obviously he felt the need to dissociate the Church unequivocally from violence. He devotes one short paragraph of *Evangelii Nuntiandi* to this question (EN 37). What he says is very close to what he had already said in *Populorum Progressio*: violence is uncontrollable; it provokes further violence and gives rise to new forms of oppression, more serious than before. He adds that sudden or violent structural changes are illusory and of their very nature ineffective; and furthermore, violence is contrary to the Christian spirit. All these points are made in support of his initial stark statement that the Church cannot accept violence—especially armed violence—or the death of anybody as the way to liberation.[12]

The tone of this whole passage is rather more pacifist than that of the corresponding passage in *Populorum Progressio*. In this statement, by contrast to the earlier one, there is no reference to exceptional situations in which violence might be justified; nor is there any footnote reference to the earlier statement. Should one draw the conclusion that Pope Paul had changed his mind in the intervening eight years? It would seem to be more accurate to see this as a change of emphasis rather than a change of mind. The pope was no doubt aware that any mention of exceptional circumstances justifying violent action could be used by revolutionary groups to provide a justification for armed resistance. Perhaps he was not quite happy with the way Medellín had treated his earlier statement, giving rather more prominence to the exceptional situations than he had. It would appear that on this occasion he decided it was inappropriate to mention such exceptional situations.

Presumably this decision reflects the pope's assessment of the world situation at the time of writing the document. And indeed in the world of 1975 there did not seem to be any obvious situation where all the various factors required to justify violent rebellion were clearly present. Had the document been written three or four years later, when the struggles in Nicaragua and Zimbabwe had come to a head, it is doubtful whether the pope could have omitted all reference to exceptional situations in which violence might conceivably be justified. The point I am making here is that the passage in *Evangelii Nuntiandi* was not really intended to be a comprehensive theological statement covering all eventualities; rather it should be understood as a strong pastoral-inspirational exhortation, urging Christians to choose the way of peace. For it is quite unlikely that Pope Paul intended to commit the Church unconditionally to a pacifist position. Furthermore, he would not have wished his words to give any comfort or support to unjust regimes; elsewhere in the document he spoke out strongly against structural injustice (e.g. EN 30).

(5) *Attitudinal Change*: Pope Paul was concerned that a particular notion of liberation could give the impression that a change of structures alone is sufficient to bring about human liberation. So, like his predecessors, he insists that there is need for attitudinal change as well as reform of the structures of society. He speaks of the need for 'a conversion of the hearts and minds of those who live under these systems and of those who have control of the systems' (EN 36).

This warning was no doubt justified, for left-wing reformers have at times been guilty of 'dreaming of systems so perfect that no one will need to be good', as T.S. Eliot says. But insistence on the importance of conversion can sometimes be used as a way of playing down the importance of structural change or of suggesting that those who insist constantly on the latter are perhaps a little unbalanced or extremist in their approach. There may be some element of that attitude in this paragraph of the document; certainly the relationship between structural and attitudinal change is not treated very helpfully here. However, another section of the document offers an exceptionally valuable treatment of this topic, and it is to this question that I now turn.

Structures and Culture

The topic of structures is dealt with in paragraphs 18–20, where Pope Paul explores in some depth what the task of the Church in the world really is. These paragraphs provide some of the most memorable and enlightening passages in the whole document—or indeed in any of the papal writings considered in this study. We begin with the following two statements:

> For the Church, to evangelise is to bring the Good News into all the strata of the human race so that by its power it may permeate the depths of humanity and make it new . . . (EN 18)
>
> The various strata of the human race are to be transformed. This means something more than the Church preaching the Gospel in ever-expanding geographical areas or to ever-increasing numbers. It also means affecting the standards by which people make judgments, their prevailing values, their interests and thought-patterns, the things that move them to action, and their models of human living; in so far as any or all of these are inconsistent with the Word of God and the plan of salvation they are to be in some sense turned upside down by the power of the Gospel. (EN 19)

Having outlined the task of the Church in this comprehensive way the pope then sums up his teaching by saying:

> It is necessary to evangelise, and to permeate with the Gospel, human culture and cultures. This has to be done, not superficially, as though one were adding a decoration or applying a coat of paint, but in depth—reaching into and out from the core and the roots of life . . . The Gospel and the process of evangelisation can penetrate all cultures while being neither subordinate to any of them nor the monopoly of any. (EN 20)

The pope is here taking the word culture in a broad and rich sense. It refers to the shared understanding and attitudes of any group of people who together live in their own particular 'world'. Some of these meanings and values are common to many cultures; while others differ from culture to culture (e.g. the status given to old people, to women, to handicapped people, to twins; the value set on cattle, on gold, on cats, on brevity, on burial sites . . .). These shared attitudes and values might be called structures or patterns of thinking and feeling. They become embodied in traditions and in this way they are passed on from one generation to the next. The pope is saying that the Gospel does not belong solely to any one such culture and is not embodied exclusively in any one set of traditions. Rather, it is compatible with all. Nevertheless, this does not mean that it fits comfortably into the different cultures. Quite the contrary: it poses a challenge to every culture and it calls for basic transformations in the traditions, the thought-patterns, and the value systems of each culture.

The most helpful aspect of this whole account is the way in which it bridges the gap which is usually presumed to exist between attitudinal change and structural change. It is commonly assumed that changing one's attitudes is a matter of personal morality; and this is generally what people have in mind when they speak of 'conversion'. Structural changes, on the other hand, are thought of as belonging to the political order, extrinsic to the person as such, and not a matter of personal morality in the usual sense. This dichotomy is challenged by the pope's statements quoted above. They suggest that perhaps the most important structures in our world are our patterns of thinking and feeling and valuing. These are deeply personal; yet in many respects they transcend the individual. They are social realities which are often our unexamined presuppositions. They are 'within' the person without being private. They are a crucial part of the 'strata' of the human race that are to be evangelised and transformed.

It is against this background that the pope says that the aim of evangelisation is to bring about an *interior* change (EN 18). To make sure that this is not taken to refer to a purely private and individualistic conversion he adds at once that, in evangelising, the Church is 'seeking to convert the individual and collective conscience of people, as well as their activities, their lives, and their whole environment' (EN 18). To change the collective conscience of a people is to change their value system; and this is linked to changes in the social, political, and economic structures of their society.

People can be oppressed by structures of the mind—by distorted value-systems and patterns of action, by misguided expectations, and by inherited prejudices and insensitivities. Indeed this kind of imposition is especially serious because it makes a person less human in ways that he or she may be quite unaware of. So there is need for liberation from this oppression of the human spirit. In fact the question may be asked whether there can be any lasting value in a liberation from political oppression which is not linked to this more intimate liberation. When Marxists like Mao Tse Tung insisted on the importance of a 'cultural revolution' they had in mind such a transformation of the structures of human thinking and feeling. For Pope Paul, as for them, such a change is essential because 'even the best structures and the most wisely planned systems soon become dehumanised if the inhuman tendencies of people's hearts are not healed' (EN 36).

Political and Economic Structures

This account of the need for the transformation of culture and cultures deepens our understanding of the nature of human liberation and is perhaps the most valuable part of *Evangelii Nuntiandi*. But the document does not provide an equally detailed and careful treatment of the other more visible kinds of oppressive structures. It would have been particularly helpful if it had given an indication of how economic and political structures relate to cultures. The pope could have shown that oppressive political and economic systems in today's world reflect and express those cultural distortions that are typical of Western society—e.g. excessive competitiveness, consumerism, cultural arrogance, restlessness, and an exploitative attitude towards nature. Conversely, it could be shown how these cultural evils are fostered and intensified by the present social, economic, and political structures. Such an analysis would provide the basis for a treatment of human liberation that would be at once profound and comprehensive. But unfortunately there seems to be a certain imbalance and incompleteness in this regard in *Evangelii Nuntiandi*. Having taken the major step of showing the need for the transformation of cultures, the pope did not go on to draw out the implications as regards changing structures in the economic, social, and political spheres.

Why is it that Pope Paul seems reluctant in this document to examine in any depth the role of the Church in promoting liberation in these more public aspects of human living? Perhaps he felt that his treatment of these questions in earlier documents was sufficient and that what was needed now was an analysis of the underlying cultural issue. Probably also he was reluctant to say anything at this time that could contribute to a further heightening of the polarisation between rich and poor, powerful and powerless, especially in the Latin American Church. He may have felt it would be less divisive to emphasise the cultural issue; for many of the same cultural distortions may be common to rich and poor in a particular area. (Pope Paul does not go into the interesting question of what might be called 'the culture of the poor'—a set of thought-patterns and values that contrast sharply at times with those of the rich and powerful; a study of this difference between rich and poor would be essential for a proper understanding of why the Bible presents the poor as privileged and more open to God.)

Whatever the reason for the incompleteness in the treatment of the question of liberation, the effect is that the account of the role of the Church remains rather abstract. It does not spell out in any very concrete way the commitment of the Church to the overcoming of the many forms of injustice in society. When the pope devotes a paragraph to poverty, marginalisation, neo-colonialism, and the struggle for liberation, he does it in the context of a reminder that these were the concern of many bishops at the Synod. He agrees with the bishops in saying that the Church has the duty of proclaiming the liberation of the myriads of the poor and oppressed, as well as helping this liberation come to birth, and witnessing and working to ensure that it comes to completion. Then the pope adds curtly: 'All this is in no way foreign to evangelisation' (EN 30). It would be quite incorrect to suggest that he was half-hearted in his acceptance of these points or reluctant to see such activity as part of evangelisation. But it is as though he were using these points as a launching-pad for something else, which is his main concern; and that is that the Church must affect the strata of humanity at a deeper level, a level which lies behind the political, social, and economic order.

The Poor

The fact that *Evangelii Nuntiandi* does not have much to say about the economic and political structures of society means that it does not emphasise the particular importance of the poor and oppressed to the Church in its task of evangelisation. An early paragraph, dealing with Christ the evangeliser, mentions that he was sent to bring Good News to the poor (EN 6). One might therefore have expected that this theme would be given some prominence in the treatment of the evangelising role of the Church. There might have been special emphasis on the place of the poor in the chapter entitled 'The Beneficiaries of Evangelisation', or the one called 'The Methods of Evangelisation'. Furthermore, when the document deals with the question of 'basic communities' it does not pay any particular attention to what many of those who advocate them consider to be a central feature of such groups—the fact that they are normally communities of poor people (EN 58). It would appear that the pope, when dealing with the nature of evangelisation, was reluctant to single out the poor and marginalised as a distinct social class; perhaps he feared that to do so would weaken or compromise his stress on universality and unity, two values which should characterise the preaching of the Gospel.

Despite these elements of incompleteness in the way in which *Evangelii Nuntiandi* treats the issue of liberation and the role of the Church in promoting it, it must be emphasised once again that the document makes a very significant contribution towards a better understanding of this whole question. In fact an interesting contrast can be seen in this regard between this document and the first of the great social encyclicals, issued in 1891 by Leo XIII. *Rerum Novarum* was particularly important, perhaps not so much because of its content as because it represented a decisive intervention by the pope on behalf of the poor. *Evangelii Nuntiandi*, on the other hand, is important in relation to the poor for precisely the opposite reason. It does not give the impression of being a major protest against the plight of the poor, comparable to Leo's encyclical or to Pope Paul's own *Populorum Progressio*. In fact if anything it seems to be urging caution and moderation in the face of the eagerness of the liberation theologians to promote a decisive 'option for the poor' by the Church. But some of the *content* of the document is exceptionally important in enabling Christians to know how the deepest roots of poverty and oppression can be overcome. What the pope says here about the transformation of culture and cultures is central to the question of liberation and the task of the Church in witnessing to and fostering it. Cultural oppression is just as important as economic and political oppression. Liberation calls not only for the transformation of society structures in the sphere of economics and politics but also for radical changes in the patterns and structures that mould the way groups of people think and feel and evaluate.

SUMMARY

The document 'Justice in the World', issued by the 1971 Synod of Bishops, made a major contribution to the development of the social teaching of the Church. It spoke out strongly against structural injustice and against the mis-development that is doing so much damage to the poor and to the environment. It questioned the myths of 'development'—and especially the assumption that the Western type of economic development could be applied all over the world. The central failure, it maintained, is the lack of participation by people in making the decisions that affect their lives. But the document was reluctant to highlight the class divisions in society. One of the most important sections of the document is where it says that a Church which presumes to speak to the world about justice must itself practise justice in its own life and structures. It held that action on behalf of justice is 'a constitutive dimension' of the preaching of the Gospel. This phrase became a rallying-cry for many engaged in the struggle for justice but it was played down by those who feared the Church would become too politicised.

In 1975 Pope Paul issued the document *Evangelii Nuntiandi*, as his response to the Synod of 1974. In it he noted that the Church is there to promote the Kingdom or Reign of God, and that its 'good news' is brought both by witness and by words. He wholeheartedly accepted the word 'liberation' and clarified its theological meaning, especially by relating it to the liberating work and word of Christ and by situating it within an integral vision of human life and salvation. This document emphasised the cultural aspects of liberation—the need for a change in the structures of thought as well as in economic and political structures. But this was not balanced by an equally detailed treatment of oppressive political and economic structures, and a strong emphasis on the special role of the poor and oppressed. In this respect the document reflects the caution of an ageing pope somewhat fearful of liberation movements and liberation theology.

Questions for review:

1. What does the Synod document have to say about justice in the Church?
2. What is meant by saying that action on behalf of justice is a constitutive dimension of the preaching of the Gospel?
3. Explain the ways in which *Evangelii Nuntiandi* goes further than previous Vatican documents on the issue of liberation.

Questions for reflection:

1. Compare the strengths and weaknesses of spiritualities in which commitment to justice is central with those of ones where there is less emphasis on justice; which are more truly Christian?
2. To what extent is justice in the Church an urgent issue for Christians today?

Issue for further study:

Two visions of the Church as seen in the history of the Synods in Rome in 1971 and 1974.

11

John Paul II: An Integral Humanism

Ten years after the Medellín meeting of 1968 another General Conference of the Latin American bishops was to have taken place. This was postponed when Pope Paul VI died in mid-1978; and the death a few weeks later of his successor, John Paul I, caused a further delay in the meeting. However, the new pope, John Paul II, quickly agreed that the conference should go ahead in Puebla, Mexico, in January of 1979—and he announced that he would himself travel to Mexico and address the meeting.

Commentators and journalists revealed, and sometimes exaggerated, the tensions behind the scenes in the preparation for Puebla (cf. articles by Lernoux, Sandoval and Sobrino in Eagleson and Sharper). There can be little doubt that a determined effort was made by some Church leaders to ensure that both the style and the outcome of Puebla would be quite different to those of Medellín. The preparatory document circulated to participants before the meeting was heavily criticised by the more 'progressive' elements in the Church in Latin America.

The main body of Brazilian bishops, who had played a key role in implementing the Medellín programme, were obviously dissatisfied with this document. But they were also concerned about the serious polarisation that was taking place in the Latin American Church. So the Brazilian episcopal conference issued a document of its own, as a contribution towards the preparation for Puebla (Bishops of Brazil, *Documento*). In content and style it followed the pattern set by Medellín. But it also attempted to cater for the reservations of those who were afraid that the Church was becoming too political, too identified with the cause of the poor in a sense that turned it against others.[1] From a strategic point of view the most significant thing in this Brazilian document was its suggestion that Pope Paul VI's *Evangelii Nuntiandi* should be the point of reference or model as regards style and approach.[2] This offered a middle ground where most of the Latin American bishops could meet. It is not surprising, then, that the final document of Puebla relies heavily on *Evangelii Nuntiandi*; and in doing so it takes a lead from John Paul II, who in his address to the conference, quoted from the document a good deal—especially, as we shall see, on the controversial issue of liberation.

The major issue facing the Puebla Conference was not really whether it would say something strikingly new and radical. Rather it was whether it would re-affirm the basic thrust of Medellín or whether it would allow the commitments of Medellín to die the death of a thousand qualifications. The most likely way in which the inspiration and direction of Medellín could be clouded at Puebla would be by a combination of conservative statements on the more obviously theological issues and, on the pastoral issues, an emphasis on secularisation and culture rather than on economic and political matters.

The final document that emerged from Puebla was one that could give a good deal of satisfaction to those who wanted to re-affirm the direction set by Medellín. Undoubtedly there were some compromises and disappointments; and the Puebla document is much more uneven than the documents of Medellín. There are sections in which the older style of theology is dominant. In general these are the more doctrinal parts. Perhaps the more socially committed bishops decided that their best strategy would be to concentrate on pastoral matters, leaving the 'high theology' to their opponents. Whatever the reasons, the outcome is that, as Sobrino remarks, 'we are faced with the irony that the Christology and, in particular, the ecclesiology underlying the pastoral documents are more inspiring than the doctrinal presentations of Christ and the Church in themselves' (Sobrino 300). Despite all this, the Puebla document as a whole re-affirms the direction set by Medellín in regard to the crucial pastoral issues. At first sight this may seem to be a rather minor achievement. But in fact it was of major importance. For it is one thing to propose a programme of engagement in the struggle for justice, as Medellín did; but it is a far more difficult thing to re-affirm commitment to that programme more than a decade later, when the full cost has become apparent—and that is what Puebla did.

Option for the Poor

Since the focus of this study is Vatican teaching I shall examine the Puebla document only in that context. The main achievement of Puebla, unlike that of Medellín, was not the document produced at the Conference. The Medellín documents had a profound effect on the life of the Church, not merely in Latin America but far beyond it; and they evoked a significant response both from Paul VI and from the Synod of Bishops in Rome. The Puebla document could hardly have had the same kind of effect. In fact its main significance is that it shows that, despite political and ecclesiastical pressures, the Church leaders were not prepared to compromise on the central elements of the policies adopted at Medellín.

There is, however, one section of the Puebla document that is important in its own right. This is the chapter entitled 'A Preferential Option for the Poor' (Puebla 1134–65). The most notable thing in it is its title. For here the conference is adopting this controversial phrase which has become a powerful summary and symbol of the new approach. The use of this term in recent years has evoked strong opposition both inside and outside the Church. Critics maintain that the Church would be abandoning its universal mission if it were to make such an option: it would no longer be preaching the Gospel to all people equally. Some of the more hostile critics go further: they see an 'option for the poor' as more or less equivalent to a Marxist 'class option', implying that the Church is taking sides in a 'class struggle'. On the other hand those who favour the term insist that that is not what they mean by it.[3] They believe that the concept has a firm foundation in the Bible, which, they say, shows that God has a preferential care for the poor and oppressed (e.g. Gutiérrez, 287–306; Tamez; Ferraro 92–5). For those in favour of the term, its main value is that it expresses succinctly and uncompromisingly the practical implication for the Church of committing itself firmly to the promotion of social justice. The presence of the term in the Puebla document is perhaps the clearest indication of the commitment of the conference on this issue.

The Puebla document does not attempt to give a systematic account of what the phrase 'option for the poor' does and does not mean. But in a very practical way it indicates what is involved:

> With renewed hope . . . we are going to take up once again the position of . . . Medellín, which adopted a clear and prophetic option expressing preference for, and solidarity with, the poor . . . . We affirm the need for conversion on the part of the whole Church to a preferential option for the poor, an option aimed at their integral liberation.
>
> This option, demanded by the scandalous reality of economic imbalances in Latin America, should lead us to establish a dignified, fraternal way of life together as human beings and to construct a just and free society.
>
> We will make every effort to understand and denounce the mechanisms that generate this poverty. (Puebla 1134, 1154, 1160)[4]

The document makes it clear that what is required is a change in the *structures* of society—but it adds that this must be accompanied by a change in people's 'personal and collective outlook', a change that 'disposes us to undergo conversion' (Puebla 1155). A very brief response is given to the objection that an 'option for the poor' would mean an abandonment by the Church of an evangelisation of the rich: ' . . . the witness of a poor Church can evangelise the rich whose hearts are attached to wealth, thus converting and freeing them from this bondage and their own egotism' (Puebla 1156).[5]

The Pope and Puebla

What contribution did Pope John Paul II make to the Puebla Conference and its document? Endless words were written about the position he adopted in his address to the conference itself and in his other Mexican addresses. Intense efforts were made by journalists and theologians in both the 'conservative' and 'progressive' camps to convince the public that the pope was on their side—that he had condemned liberation theology out of hand or that he had come down in favour of what the liberation theologians stood for. Very little of this material is of any value. Even apart from the special pleading that marks such writing there is the further fact that if one really wishes to understand the outlook of John Paul II the Mexican addresses are by no means the best sources to study. This is not to say that the pope did not express himself clearly or would not stand over what he said; for in fact he contributed significantly to what was said by the Puebla Conference. But in many respects the Mexican agenda was already set for the pope. He was not in a position to decide his own terms of reference, so his choices were somewhat limited. He was coming into a highly polarised situation; so it was more or less inevitable that his addresses—especially his talk to the Puebla Conference itself—would contain a good deal of, 'on the one hand . . . and on the other'. His opening address to the conference represents a careful balancing exercise in which he warns against dangerous tendencies in regard to the theology of Christ and the Church, while at the same time encouraging the Latin American Church not to back down on the commitments made at Medellín (cf. Filochowski 18).

In the first major section of his address the pope spoke out strongly against those who 'purport to depict Jesus as a political activist, as a fighter against Roman domination and the authorities, and even as someone involved in the class struggle' (I, 4). He insisted that Jesus 'unequivocally rejects recourse to violence' and 'opens his message of conversion to all' (I, 4). He went on to speak out against a conception of the building of the Kingdom 'merely by structural change and socio-political involvement' without taking sufficient account of the role of the Church (I, 8). Having issued these warnings the pope was then in a position to take a strong stand on social and political issues. In the third section of his address he spoke of human dignity and of human rights and their violation. Towards the end of this section he went on to speak of the need for 'a correct Christian conception of liberation' (III, 6). The most striking thing about this passage is that it relies almost entirely on *Evangelii Nuntiandi*; Pope Paul's document is quoted from or referred to no less than six times. John Paul ends this section with the remark: 'As you see, the whole set of observations on the theme of liberation that were made by *Evangelii Nuntiandi* retain their full validity.' Evidently he had decided that this was not the opportune time to make any major new statement on the subject; he offered instead the teaching of his predecessor as a middle ground where bishops of different outlook could come to a measure of agreement.

One of the more interesting sentences in the Puebla address occurs where the pope paraphrases the controversial passage of the 1971 Synod—the one in which the bishops had said that they saw action on behalf of justice as 'a constitutive dimension of the preaching of the Gospel'. In his address the pope said: 'the Church has learned that an indispensable part of its evangelising mission is made up of works on behalf of justice and human promotion' (III, 2). It will be noted that the disputed word 'constitutive' has been replaced—not, however, with the word 'integral' as its opponents had wanted, but with the word 'indispensable'. In the pope's paraphrase the central meaning of the Synod statement has not been lost; but a certain verbal concession is made to the opponents and at the same time the whole idea is presented more clearly and simply. This sentence might be taken as a typical example of what the pope was doing throughout his Mexican visit—trying to bridge the gap between different viewpoints but without compromising on the central issues.

In regard to the question of 'option for the poor' the pope adopted the same approach. In his address at Puebla he did not use the term. But he found another way of expressing the same idea: he said that the Church 'is prompted by an authentically evangelical commitment which, like that of Christ, is primarily a commitment to those most in need' (III, 3).[6] On other occasions in Mexico the pope expressed this idea in different words:

— In a sermon at Guadalupe, he said Medellín was a call of hope showing 'preferential yet not exclusive love for the poor' (AAS 71, 174).[7]

— In an address in the Santa Cecilia district of Guadaljara, he said: 'I feel solidarity with you because, being poor, you are entitled to my particular concern. I tell you the reason at once: the Pope loves you because you are God's favourites' (AAS 220; cf. address in Monterrey AAS 243).

Two of the pope's addresses to Mexican audiences are notable for their outspoken character on justice issues. Speaking in the industrial city of Monterrey he insisted that,

> the Latin American peoples rightly demand that there should be returned to them their rightful responsibility over the goods that nature has bestowed on them . . . . Bold and renewing innovations are necessary in order to overcome the serious injustices inherited from the past . . . (AAS 242)

His remarks to poor Mexican Indians at Cuilapan were even more explicit. To them he presented himself as one who 'wishes to be your voice, the voice of those who cannot speak or who are silenced'. Then he insisted on the need for 'bold changes, which are deeply innovatory' to be carried out 'without waiting any longer'. Since he was speaking to very poor peasants he went straight to what for them would be the crucial change: he pointed out that there is 'a social mortgage on all private property' so that 'if the common good requires it, there should be no hesitation even at expropriation, carried out in due form' (AAS 209). Turning then to the 'leaders of the peoples' and 'powerful classes', he insisted: 'It is not just, it is not human, it is not Christian to continue with certain situations that are clearly unjust.' He added: 'It is clear that those who must collaborate most in this, are those who are in a position to do most' (AAS 210). This address shows how keenly the pope was aware of the need for social, political, and economic changes. But it also suggests that he was still convinced that the best way for him to promote such changes was to state the need bluntly and to appeal to the consciences of those who hold wealth and power.

The addresses of John Paul II, both in Puebla itself and in other places in Mexico, were of major importance for the Puebla Conference. This is obvious from the fact that his words are quoted very many times in the document issued by the conference. Quotations from his addresses were used as the basis for reaching consensus on divisive issues, notably the questions of liberation, 'option for the poor', and the Church's attitude towards ideologies (Puebla 489, 1141, 538, 551–2). The Puebla document is a written proof that the pope succeeded in achieving the main purpose of his visit—to contribute to the unity of the Latin American bishops and to help them find a direction in which they could go forward together.

Social Doctrine

Towards the end of his opening address to the Puebla Conference, Pope John Paul spoke about the 'social doctrine' of
the Church, using this term four times within the space of a
few minutes (III, 7). This usage caused some surprise and
unfavourable comment (Chenu 26; Hebblethwaite [1982]
85–98). Did it signal a return to an approach that had been
abandoned? The phrase 'social doctrine' as used in the generation
prior to Vatican II had suggested a corpus of unchanging
teaching on social issues. One of the more trenchant critics of
the term is Chenu who associates it with an outlook that is no
longer acceptable—one that is deductivist and abstract, insensitive to historical and geographical variations, and particularly
inappropriate in the Third World since it imposes Western
categories unrelated to local circumstances (Chenu 88–9).
Chenu attributes considerable significance to what might have
appeared to be minor changes in terminology in the drafting of
Gaudium et Spes during Vatican II: the phrases 'the social
teaching of the Gospel' and 'the Christian doctrine about
society' were deliberately substituted for the term 'social
doctrine' (Chenu 87–8).[8] For him the gradual abandonment of
the older term coincided with a new flexible and inductive
approach; and this process reached its culmination in the
document *Octogesima Adveniens*, issued by Pope Paul in 1971.
Chenu seems quite shocked that John Paul II, in his address at
Puebla, should have reintroduced the term and insisted on the
importance of the Church's 'social doctrine' (Chenu 13).[9]

However, one can interpret the pope's use of the term
'social doctrine' in a more sympathetic light than is done by
his critics. John Paul was by no means trying to re–impose on
the Latin American Church a body of 'social doctrine' that
was to be seen as universal and timeless. He was well aware
that the social teaching of the Church had undergone considerable development since the time of Leo XIII. (This became
much more evident two and a half years later when he issued
the encyclical *Laborem Exercens*; as we shall see, this document
combines real continuity with the past with a good deal that is
quite new and unusual in Church teaching.) When John Paul
uses the term 'social doctrine' he normally understands it in a

rather generic sense (cf. Heckel 23). It seems clear that what he wanted to do was to 'rescue' the term. On the one hand he wanted to rescue it in the sense of bringing it back into use as a theologically respectable term. But in order to do this he had, on the other hand, to rescue it in another sense—to remove the connotations of an unchanging dogmatism. One way in which he does this is by using it as just one term that is interchangeable with a variety of other phrases that refer to the teaching that the Church has developed over the years on social issues, e.g. 'social morals' or 'social thought of the Church'.

Furthermore, as Heckel (21) points out, John Paul's use of the term 'social doctrine' is *'discreet* and *relatively rare'*. In the first year of his pontificate he used the term mainly in the context of the Church in Latin America and in Poland. In each case there was a particular reason for doing so. Right-wing governments in South America and left-wing governments in Eastern Europe would like to restrict the activity of the Church to a private, so-called 'religious' domain. When the pope found himself in confrontation on social issues with such regimes, the use of the term 'social doctrine' gave him a certain advantage; the word 'doctrine' suggests that what is at stake is something on which the Church will not yield to pressures from an authoritarian government since it is fundamental to the nature of the Church; the overtones of something unchanging and timeless strengthen this impression; and the word 'doctrine' is a suitable one to use when the confrontation is with the 'doctrines' of national security or of a rigid Marxism.

In Latin America, the use by the pope of the term 'social doctrine' has a further purpose. It represents his rejection of the view of some extreme exponents of 'liberation' that the Church must at this time identify itself fully with the forces of the left. In the years after Medellín, Latin American Christians found themselves increasingly squeezed between ideologies of the right and of the left, each anxious to legitimise itself by enlisting Christian faith in support of its position. One way of escaping this dilemma was to hold that Christianity offered a 'third way', neither of the left nor of the right. For some people, this 'third way' was to be embodied in the Latin American version of Christian democracy. However, as a realistic political alternative this option became less and less credible during the 1970s. The result was that a number of influential Latin American Christian thinkers strongly rejected the notion of a 'third way'—and became highly sceptical about the notion of a 'Catholic social doctrine' on which it relied so heavily. Some of them said openly that committed Christians could no longer afford the luxury of standing on the side-lines; they ought to throw in their lot with the forces of the left, while working *within* these movements to promote Christian values.

By reinstating the term 'social doctrine' the pope was undoubtedly putting a large question mark over this line of argument. When he used the term in this context he was not trying to impose on his opponents an immutable body of social dogma. His aim was rather to encourage them not to submit themselves and the Church entirely and unconditionally to an ideology of the left. He wanted them to continue to believe that the Church has a distinctive contribution to make in working out solutions to social injustices; and to do so it should maintain a certain distance from all ideologies and all sectional interests.

This is not to say that the pope was himself endorsing the notion of the 'third way' in a strictly political sense. But he would be seen as giving some encouragement to those Church leaders who felt that the best course of action was for the Church to distance itself clearly from ideologies of both the right and the left. This was in fact the stance adopted at the Puebla Conference. The Puebla documents contain strong condemnations of three different ideologies—capitalist liberalism, Marxist collectivism, and 'the so-called doctrine of national security'. Quoting the pope's address, the text goes on to state that the Church chooses to maintain its freedom with regard to the opposing systems. It opts 'solely for the human being' and 'does not need to have recourse to ideological systems'. It finds its inspiration in the tenets of an authentic Christian anthropology (Puebla 542–53). This position was very much what the pope would have wanted; and the 'authentic Christian anthropology' from which it derives its inspiration is the basis for—and is indeed more or less equivalent to—Catholic 'social doctrine' in Pope John Paul's sense of the term.

In speaking of this 'authentic Christian anthropology' the Puebla text adds the significant words: 'Christians must commit themselves to the elaboration of historical projects that meet the needs of a given moment and a given culture' (Puebla 553). By inserting this statement the drafters of the text ensured that there would be no abandonment of the principle laid down by Paul VI in *Octogesima Adveniens*, that the solutions to social problems have to be discerned in each particular time, place, and culture. To accept the term 'social doctrine', as Puebla did following John Paul II (Puebla 539), does not mean accepting just one universal and timeless model of how society is to be organised (cf. Puebla, 472–6).[10]

The insistence of Puebla that Christians must commit themselves to particular 'historical projects' is especially significant because it comes soon after quotations from the pope's opening address to the conference. The crucial quotation is to the effect that the Church opts 'solely for the human being' (Puebla 551—quoting John Paul's opening address III, 3). It would be tempting to conclude from the pope's statement that Christians can somehow opt 'directly' for the human person, without getting involved in awkward political choices. The Puebla statement makes it clear that the pope is not to be understood in this way. Rather the normal way in which Christians, like other people, opt for the human person is through making difficult practical choices between alternative political systems. The Christian cannot remain outside history and therefore cannot normally be 'above' the actual politics of each particular time and place. Puebla is here adding an important point to what the pope had said. It is not exactly a corrective, since there is no reason to think that the pope would disagree with the point. But it was not the point that the pope chose to make at that time, for his concern was to insist that Christians do not have to limit themselves to the unacceptable ideologies of left or right that are proposed to them. This is one case in which Puebla made a significant contribution to the dialogue in the Church about how Christians can best work for justice. It ensured that the pope's statement would not be misunderstood or mis-used.

Integral Humanism

A few weeks after his return from Mexico to Rome the pope issued his first encyclical, entitled *Redemptor Hominis*, 'The

Redeemer of Humankind'. This was followed within two years by his second encyclical, *Dives in Misericordia*, 'Rich in Mercy'. These documents gave him the opportunity to outline a good deal of his vision on his own terms, without the restriction of having to relate it to the demands of a particular local situation. *Redemptor Hominis* is a document of considerable importance, both in its own right and because it provides a background against which one can understand various other statements made by the pope. In this first encyclical he ranges over a very wide area, but there is a unifying thread running through it all. The unifying vision of the pope may perhaps be summed up in two phrases from the encyclical: 'in Christ and through Christ, human persons have acquired full awareness of their dignity' (RH 11; cf. RH 10); and, 'all routes for the Church are directed towards the human person' (RH 14 title). These phrases indicate that, while the encyclical is concerned above all with the mystery of Christ and the activity of the Church, these concerns in no way take the author into a 'spiritual' or 'religious' world unrelated to everyday living. Quite the contrary: the pope's concern is directed precisely towards the human person, human society, and the world we live in. He sets out to show that these 'secular' realities are the very things on which Christ and the Church throw light, the things about which they give hope:

> The human person in the full truth of his or her existence and personal being and also of their community and social being—in the sphere of their own family, in the sphere of society . . . . and in the sphere of the whole of humankind—this person is the primary route that the Church must travel in fulfilling her mission: *the human person is the primary and fundamental way for the Church*, the way traced out by Christ himself . . . (RH 14)

The encyclical helps one to realise that whenever the pope makes statements emphasising the primacy of the spiritual—as he did at Puebla (III, 4) and in his address to the United Nations (para. 4), as well as in the encyclical itself (RH 11)—he is not reverting to an old-fashioned dualist theology that would justify an 'escape' by Christians from social and political involvement. What he envisages is just the opposite: it is an integral humanism embracing all dimensions of life, including the economic, the political, the cultural, and the religious. Within this humanistic vision, 'the spiritual' means for him those dimensions and aspects of human life that are deepest (cf. Baum [1979] 57). The Christian is called to explore whatever is found to be deepest in human experience, and to be particularly concerned about such matters.

It is on the basis of such an approach that John Paul can say:

> . . . the Church considers this concern for human beings, for their humanity, for the future of the human race on earth and therefore also for the direction of the totality of development and progress—to be inextricably linked to the Church's own mission and an essential element of it (RH 15)

This statement is a vindication of the position adopted by the bishops at the Synod of 1971. By using the word 'essential', the pope is really accepting what the Synod bishops intended when they used the controversial phrase 'constitutive dimension'. As we saw in the previous chapter, Paul VI in *Evangelii Nuntiandi* provided a certain theological basis for the Synod statement. In *Redemptor Hominis* John Paul carries this a step further. In fact he deepens it considerably because he grounds all action for justice and human progress in a rich integral humanism. It is a humanism that is Christological; and this not in a super-ficial sense in which Christ is seen as adding something on to humanity or merely rescuing the human race from sin. It is more profound than that: for the pope, it is in Christ that we learn what it really means to be human.

The humanism of John Paul II is very comprehensive. He includes the economic and political dimensions; but, like Vatican II and Paul VI, he lays special stress on the cultural dimension. What is significant about his statements on culture is that there is no hint of dualism or escapism in them. One does not have any sense that he is stressing culture because it is easier and safer for a Church leader to talk about culture than about the more delicate and dangerous issues of economics and politics. If he speaks out strongly about culture—as indeed he does in Mexico (AAS 71, 206, 208), and in his address to UNESCO (735–52)—this is because he sees people being injured and exploited in this area of culture as much as in the economic and political spheres. The cultural rights of people can be trampled on just as tragically as can their other rights. It is all part of the same process of marginalisation and impoverishment against which the Church is bound to protest.

Development and Misdevelopment

Against the background of his integral humanism one can understand better the very fundamental misgivings expressed by John Paul about the present state of society. People, he says, now live 'increasingly in fear', afraid of a radical self-destruction (RH 15; cf. DM 11). The ordinary person lives under the constant threat of atomic warfare; and people also live under the threat of a ruthless oppression and subjugation that can deprive them of their freedom without even having to resort to military means (DM 11). The fundamental reason for all this is that we have adopted a type of 'development' that has got out of control, that is no longer serving humanity as any genuine development ought to. What has been termed 'progress' now has to be called in question. Does it really make us more human? Of course it does, says the pope, in some respects. But, he asks, 'is the human person as such developing and progressing or, on the other hand, regressing and being degraded in humanity?' (RH 15).[11] Clearly the pope's own answer to that question is that in many respects modern 'development' is destroying humanity rather than promoting real progress.

First of all, the world economy is not solving the problems of starvation and malnutrition; in fact we have in the present international world order the parable of the rich person and Lazarus writ large (RH 16). The institutions on which the world economic order rests—the systems that control production, trade, and finance—have proved incapable, says the pope, of 'remedying the unjust social situations inherited from the past or of dealing with the urgent challenges and ethical demands of the present' (RH 16).

Secondly, modern so-called development is doing harm not only to the poorer peoples but also to those who live in the better-off countries—the very people who might have been expected to benefit most from it. The 'fever of inflation and the plague of unemployment' affect them at the economic and social level; while at the cultural and psychological level there is in them a sense of alienation (RH 15). People can easily be manipulated by political and economic means and also by the communications media. In fact we are running the risk of being enslaved by the very products we have made (RH 16). Furthermore, the massive social injustice that now exists in the world is giving rise to remorse and guilt in those who live in wealth and plenty (DM 11).

There is another major failure of modern development, one that affects the whole world, rich and poor alike. The world economy today depends on activities and systems that are 'depleting the earth's resources of raw materials and energy at an ever-increasing rate and putting intolerable pressures on the geo-physical environment' (RH 16). Here the pope is adverting to environmental issues—the poisoning of air, water, and land— and to the risk that we will exhaust the resources of energy and raw materials on which the whole modern type of production is based.

The pope's view is that the cumulative effect of all these major inadequacies of modern development is the continual expansion of zones of grinding poverty, accompanied by anguish, frustration, and bitterness. This is aggravated by the fact that the extravagance and wastefulness of the people of the privileged classes and nations take place before the eyes of the poor. To make matters worse, the poorer nations are being offered armaments to serve nationalistic, imperialistic, or neo-colonial purposes, rather than being given the food and cultural aid that could be of real benefit to them. The arms race squanders resources that could have been used to overcome poverty (RH 16).

These very strong criticisms of the modern process of 'development' are in marked contrast to the optimism displayed by John XXIII and Vatican II. It is clear that John Paul II wants a very radical restructuring of our world order. And he is well aware that this will be no easy task:

> There is need for brave and creative initiatives . . . The task is not impossible . . . The only way forward is transformation of the structures of economic life. But this road is so difficult that it requires a real conversion of mind, will, and heart. The task calls for the strong commitment of

individuals and peoples who are both free and in solidarity with each other. (RH 16)

The pope is here taking it for granted that moral conversion is no substitute for structural reform of society. But at the same time he is insisting that such structural changes cannot be expected to take place without the free cooperation of morally committed people.

By what means can a more genuinely human type of development be brought about? The pope is not very specific as regards details but his general proposal is clear. Economic progress must be *planned*. The plan or programme must be one that takes account of each person and of all people, one that is universal and is based on the solidarity of all. It must above all ensure that economic growth does not damage society through becoming the highest value; economic growth must rather be at the service of people (RH 16). This proposal for a planned global economy follows in the line of Paul VI's *Populorum Progressio*, but makes it somewhat more explicit (cf. Cosmao *Le Redempteur* 24–5).

The pope goes on to write movingly about human rights. He insists that peace comes down to a respect for the rights of people. The real test of whether or not justice is present in a given situation is whether human rights are respected there (RH 17). The pope refers here to the United Nations' Declaration of Human Rights. A few months later, in his address to the United Nations, he called this document 'a milestone on the long and difficult path of the human race . . . the path of the moral progress of humanity' (AAS 71 1147–8 [para. 7]). In this same address he invoked what he called 'the humanistic criterion' as the proper standard for evaluating various systems:

> . . . the fundamental criterion for comparing social, economic and political systems . . . must be . . . *the humanistic criterion*, namely the measure in which each system is really capable of reducing, restraining and eliminating as far as possible the various forms of exploitation of man and of ensuring for him, through work, not only the just distribution of the indispensable material goods, but also a participation, in keeping with his dignity, in the whole process of production and in the social life that grows up around that process. (1156 [para. 17])

The humanistic vision which pervades *Redemptor Hominis* and underlies the pope's addresses is filled out and rounded off by some deeply moving passages in *Dives in Misericordia*. There he notes how easily and often it happens that human actions 'undertaken in the name of justice' can in practice 'deviate from justice itself' by becoming distorted through spite, hatred, and cruelty (DM 12). He strongly resists the idea that justice and mercy are opposed to each other. Mercy and forgiveness, he maintains, do not 'cancel out the obligations of justice'; rather, mercy, when understood properly, is seen to be 'the most profound source of justice' (DM 14). Furthermore, mercy is not to be seen as something that leaves a distance between the benefactor and the recipient and creates a relationship that is one-sided. On the contrary, mercy includes the reciprocity of justice. Indeed, it even deepens this mutuality because it brings about an encounter between people that is not confined to external goods but is focused directly on the value of the persons involved; it enables them to meet in reciprocal tenderness and sensitivity (DM 14).

This teaching of Pope John Paul about mercy and forgiveness can go a long way towards allaying the fears and reservations experienced by some religious people in relation to an 'option for the poor'. The misgivings of such people arise when they see how this phrase is invoked by certain angry or over-enthusiastic activists to justify a strident, combative attitude towards all authorities, towards ordinary 'respectable' people, and even at times towards anybody that ventures to disagree with them! The pope's insistence on the importance of mercy as well as justice does not by any means result in a 'watering down' of the commitment of the Church to an 'option for the poor'. But it does invite us to think about the kind of world we would like to bring about through such an option; and also to reflect about what would be the most effective and human strategy for bringing such a world into existence. If gentleness and human sensitivity are to characterise the world we are working for, then they must also be present in the manner in which we seek to attain it.

The Brazil Addresses

Of the various 'pastoral visits' made by John Paul II to different parts of the world, by far the most significant, from the point of view of an 'option for the poor', was his first trip to Brazil. It lasted twelve days—from 30 June to 11 July 1980. During that time he gave very many addresses, several of which made valuable contributions to the Church's social teaching. But perhaps more important than the content of his talks was the overall impression the pope gave, which was that of being broadly in solidarity with the main body of Brazilian bishops in their commitment to putting the Church on the side of the poor and oppressed.

John Paul was well aware that the government would have liked to use his visit to convey the impression that the Brazilian bishops were being admonished for their outspoken criticism of the regime. So he made his position clear from the start. On the first day of his visit he addressed the president of Brazil. Having outlined his humanistic vision (para. 4, AAS 72, 831–2), he went on at once to state that the Church advocates 'reforms that aim at a more just society' (paras. 5 and 6, AAS 832–3); and he insisted on the importance of respect for human rights. That same day, in an address to the diplomatic corps, he took up this theme again. He made an obvious reference to the 'doctrine of National Security' when he said that, while each country has the duty of preserving its internal peace and security, it must 'earn' this peace by ensuring the common good of everybody and by respecting human rights. He went on to insist that the Church 'will constantly endeavour to recall concern for "the poor", for those who are under-privileged in some way' (AAS 835). In a very subtle way the pope took issue with another aspect of the National Security ideology when he spoke to Brazilian cultural leaders the following day at Rio de Janeiro. Stressing the importance of culture in the process of humanisation, he went on to insist that culture must not be imposed on people; there must be respect for their freedom (paras. 1 and 2, AAS 72, 848–9). This challenges the view of those right-wing Latin American ideologues who see culture, and indeed religion, as an integral and vital part of the system that is to be imposed on all, in the interests of the security of the State.

Two of the major addresses given by the pope in Brazil were the talk he gave at Rio (AAS 72, 858–73) to 150 members of CELAM (the Latin American Conference of Bishops) and his speech at Fortaleza to the bishops of Brazil (AAS 944–60). There are a number of similarities between the two talks. In each case there is generous approval for the general direction taken by the bishops, combined with some expressions of the need to avoid certain dangers. The tone of his CELAM speech is distinctly warmer than that of his opening address at Puebla eighteen months previously. He makes it quite clear that he has given wholehearted approval to the Puebla document, after some modifications had been made to parts of the text in the interests of 'accuracy' (III, 1, AAS 867).[12] Referring to Puebla he says, 'you rightly called for a preferential option for the poor, not an exclusive nor excluding one' (III, 7, AAS 868). In speaking to the Brazilian bishops he complimented them very warmly on their commitment in matters of poverty; he says it gives him joy to see their witness to poverty and simplicity and their insertion in the midst of their people (para. 6, AAS 868). A little later he clarified his understanding of the meaning of the term 'option for the poor':

> You know that the preferential option for the poor, forcefully proclaimed at Puebla, is not an invitation to exclusivism, and would not justify a bishop's refusal to proclaim the Word of conversion and salvation to this or that group of persons on the pretext that they are not poor . . . because it is his duty to proclaim the *whole* Gospel to *all* people, that *everyone* should be 'poor in spirit'. But it is a call to a special solidarity with the humble and the weak, with those who are suffering and weeping, who are humiliated and left on the fringes of life and society, in order to help them to realise ever more fully their own dignity as human persons and children of God. (para. 6.9 AAS 956)

In various addresses—to CELAM (II, 8, AAS 72, 865), to the Brazilian bishops (para. 6.9, AAS 957), to the shanty-dwellers of Vidigal (para. 5, AAS 856), and to the workers of São Paulo (para. 4, AAS 890–1)—the pope insisted that the Church is completely opposed to class struggle. The aim of the Church is not to exacerbate divisions in society but to heal them; so it refuses to condone violence or to identify itself with the interests and ideology of any one group or class. In his CELAM address he ruled out not merely the Marxist concept of class warfare but also the use of a Marxist analysis; but in doing so he carefully made use of the Puebla text on this question, without adding to it (III, 8, AAS 870). While stressing the need for effective structural reforms, he also maintained in several addresses that these must be introduced prudently and peacefully, and therefore in a gradual and progressive way (e.g. to São Paulo workers, para. 4, AAS 890; to diplomatic corps, AAS 835; at Vidigal, para. 5, AAS 857; to the president, para. 5, AAS 832).

In his address to workers in the industrial city of São Paulo, Pope John Paul spoke very strongly and movingly about the plight of the urban poor, and the need to transform the city into a more human place. He referred to overcrowding and the frustration to which it gives rise. He also spoke about the pollution of the environment—a topic that was particularly relevant and urgent in view of the scandalous conditions in that city (para. 8, AAS 894–5). Just before he delivered this address, the pope had listened to a trade union activist speak in public of the economic and political repression of workers in Brazil (cf. Kirby 363). Part of the pope's response to this cry was a firm insistence on the right of workers to form trade unions (para. 7, AAS 893). This, of course, is a right which had been affirmed by the Church as far back as the time of Leo XIII. But for John Paul to reaffirm it publicly in an address to workers in São Paulo, where in the previous months workers had been harassed, arrested, and even shot for trying to exercise that right, was a clear challenge to the government. It also represented firm support for Cardinal Arns who had helped the workers of São Paulo during the strikes in which they claimed their rights.

In Recife, the city where Helder Camara was Archbishop, the pope spoke in an equally challenging way on the question of the ownership and use of land:

> . . . the land is a gift of God, a gift that God gives to all human beings, men and women . . . It is not lawful, therefore, . . . to use that gift in such a way that its benefits accrue to only a few, leaving the others, the vast majority, excluded . . . (para. 4, AAS 926 [my translation])

Once again, the *content* of the pope's statement was by no means startlingly new; it was the *context* that made all the difference. He was speaking to exploited rural workers, people who were being impoverished through the loss of their title to the land they had considered their own, or people who were being deprived of work or of a living wage. In this situation the pope's address was a forceful protest against current abuses. It was also a strong vindication of the stand taken by Helder Camara, whom the pope pointedly called 'brother of the poor and my brother' (AAS 924).

The Poor and the 'Poor in Spirit'

The most striking witness by the pope to his concern for the poor and marginalised in Brazilian society was his visit to the favela or shanty-town of Vidigal, outside Rio de Janeiro. He told the people that what he had to say to them was also addressed to all those in Brazil who live in similar conditions (para. 1, AAS 72, 853). And what he offered them was a reflection on the text, 'Blessed are the poor in spirit'. The commentary of the pope on this text is of particular importance for this study of 'option for the poor'. So I propose to look closely at this address and to relate it to two other talks given by the pope in similar situations and on the same theme; the other two talks are one given five days later in the favela of Alagados, near Salvador da Bahia in Brazil, and one given several months later to the shanty-dwellers of the Tondo area outside Manila in the Philippines.

In the first of these addresses the pope notes that the Church in Brazil wishes to be the Church of the poor; so he proposes to clarify what is meant by 'the poor in spirit' and to see who are these people. He says they are those who are open to God, ready to receive God's gifts, aware that they have received everything from God (para. 2, AAS 853). The 'poor in spirit' are merciful and generous. For to be 'poor in spirit' means to be open to others—to God and one's neighbours. Those who are not poor in spirit are closed to God and to other people; they are merciless (para. 3, AAS 854). Wealthy people are 'poor in spirit', says the pope, when they constantly give themselves and serve others in proportion to their riches (para. 4, AAS 854).

This last statement, taken on its own, could be used to justify a highly spiritualised notion of poverty of spirit that would have no connection with the presence or absence of wealth or with its use or abuse. The rich could then patronise the poor, for instance by giving them alms while leaving intact the structures in society that leave the poor trapped in poverty. But the pope makes his statement here in a context where he is trying very hard to show the inadequacy of such an approach; he wants to make clear that being open to God ('poor in spirit') is intimately linked to working for structural change in society. He does this by pointing out that the first beatitude, while addressed by the Church today to everybody, has in fact something different to say to each of three different categories of people:

— To those who live in want, it says that they are very close to God and that they must maintain their human dignity and their openness to others.

— To those who are somewhat better off it says: ' . . . do not close yourself off in yourselves. Think of those who are more poor . . . share with them . . . in a systematic way . . . '

— To those who are very wealthy, the Church of the poor says: 'Do you not feel remorse of conscience because of your riches and abundance? . . . If you have a lot . . . you must give a lot. And you must think about how to give—how to organise socio-economic life . . . in such a way that it will tend to bring about equality between people, rather than putting a yawning gap between them' (para. 4, AAS 855–6 [my translation]).

There are two very important points to note in the pope's teaching here. First, being 'poor in spirit', though it is understood by him in a religious sense, is nevertheless firmly linked to social justice because it means being open not only to God but also to other people. Secondly, if one belongs to the very wealthy group in society, then being open to others is not simply a matter of giving alms, however generously; it means transforming the unjust structures of society.

In the next section of his address the pope develops this point more explicitly when he makes a direct appeal on behalf of the Church of the poor to those who make the decisions that affect society and the world:

Do all you can, especially you who have decision-making powers, you on whom the situation of the world depends, do everything to make the life of every person in your country more human, more worthy of the human person.

Do all you can to ensure the disappearance, at least gradually, of that yawning gap which divides the few 'excessively rich' from the great masses of the poor, the people who live in grinding poverty. (para. 5, AAS 857 [my translation])

This eloquent appeal is addressed to the powerful, the decision-makers. It is up to them to change the structures of society (cf. address to São Paulo workers, para. 4, AAS 890: 'This is especially the duty of those who hold power, whether economic or political, in society'). Though the task is urgent, the pope recognises that it may take time to bring about the necessary radical changes; so he asks that these decision-makers ensure that the wide gap between rich and poor disappears 'at least gradually'.

What then does the pope have to say about economic poverty? On this point the main thrust of the Vidigal address may be summed up as follows:

(i) Poverty is largely the result of injustice, structural injustice; therefore there is urgent need for a transformation of the structures that sustain it.

(ii) The main responsibility for bringing about these radical changes falls on the rich and powerful, since it is they who are in a position to make the decisions that really matter, they on whom the future depends.

Without playing down the importance of the first of these two points (namely, the need for structural change) I want here to look particularly at the second point. According to this address the crucial agents of change are to be those who hold wealth and power in society. What are the implications of this for the poor, and for a Church that seeks to be the Church of the poor? If change is to be brought about mainly by the rich, what then does the pope, in the name of the Church, have to say to the poor?

At Vidigal the pope tells the poor:

— that they are close to God;

— that they must 'do everything that is lawful to ensure for themselves and their families all that is required for life and upkeep';

— that they must maintain their human dignity and continue to have that magnanimity, openness of heart, and availability to others that characterise the 'poor in spirit' (para. 4, AAS 72, 855 [my translation]).

The first and third points here offer some spiritual consolation to the poor; but from a practical point of view the crucial point is the second one. What does it mean to tell the poor to do everything that is lawful to support themselves? Does it, in effect, mean telling them *not* to do anything *unlawful?* Certainly, there is no indication here that the pope is encouraging the poor to organise themselves politically in order to bring about change. It must be admitted that anybody relying on this Vidigal address for guidelines about how to inspire the poor would find a notable gap at this point.

Pope John Paul may have sensed this, or even been advised about it by some of the Brazilian bishops. But, whatever the reason, he added some very important points to what he had to say to the poor, when he spoke a few days later to the shanty-dwellers at Favela dos Alagados, near Salvador da Bahia. In this address he notes that the poor are actively involved in shaping their own destiny and lives. Then he says:

> God grant that there may be many of us to offer you unselfish cooperation in order that you may free yourselves from everything that in a certain way enslaves you, but with full respect for what you are and for your right to be the prime authors of your human advancement. (*L'Oss. Rom.*, 9 July 1981, p.1, para. 2)

The important thing here is the pope's stress on the fact that the poor themselves are to be the main agents in bringing about their human development. Others are to see themselves not as making the changes in society needed by the poor, but simply as *cooperating* with the poor—with full respect for the right of the poor to take primary responsibility for their own lives. And in a humble and touching way the pope indicates that he himself would like to be one of those who cooperate with the poor.

John Paul goes even further. He encourages the poor to struggle to overcome their poverty:

> You must struggle for life, do everything to improve the conditions in which you live; to do so is a sacred duty because it is also the will of God. Do not say that it is God's will that you remain in a condition of poverty, disease, unhealthy housing, that is contrary in many ways to your dignity as human persons. Do not say, 'It is God who wills it.' (para. 3 [translation emended])

In this passage the pope is addressing himself to the sense of apathy which helps to keep the poor in a state of poverty. He is aware that this apathy is given a religious legitimation—poverty is accepted as being the will of God. John Paul challenges this assumption, insisting that what God wants is not that the poor stay poor but that they struggle to escape it. He goes on to note that strong action is required not only by the poor themselves but also by others; but he insists that the prime movers have to be the victims of poverty themselves (para. 3).

It is quite significant that the pope, when speaking to the poor should encourage them to *struggle*. He does not, of course, say they should engage in a class struggle; his phrase is 'struggle for life'. And he clarifies what he has in mind by giving some examples:

> To wish to overcome the poor conditions, to help one another to find—together—better times, not to wait for everything from outside, but to begin to do all that is possible, to try to educate oneself in order to have greater possibilities of improvement: these are some important steps along your way. (para. 3)

There is a very notable difference in emphasis between what the pope had to say to the poor in this address and what he had said at Vidigal. It is as though he had become convinced (perhaps during the Brazilian trip itself) that it is not enough to encourage the rich, the powerful decision-makers, to initiate and bring about social change. The Church must also encourage the poor to see themselves as the primary agents of change. This new approach was reiterated and carried a little further by Pope John Paul in his address to the shanty-dwellers of Tondo in the Philippines early the next year. The topic chosen by the pope for his address there was the same as that at Vidigal—the beatitude, 'Blessed are the poor in spirit'. Much of what he had to say was an echo of the earlier talk. But when he speaks to the poor on this occasion about what the beatitude says to them he includes the fact that 'their inviolable human rights must be preserved and protected' (Tondo, Philippines para. 5). This is not, of course, the first time the pope had spoken of the rights of the poor. But here he is speaking directly *to* the poor, assuring them that the beatitudes tell them of their rights.

A little later the pope said:

> I encourage you, the people of Tondo, and all the People of

God in the Philippines, to exercise your individual and corporate responsibility for increasing catechetical instruction as you endeavour to implement fully the social teachings of the Church. (para. 6)

This is a very subtle passage. Three points may be noted. First, the pope is encouraging the poor themselves to work for social justice—and this is carefully expressed as the implementing of the social teaching of the Church (so a professedly Catholic regime cannot easily object to this!). Secondly, though addressed specifically to the poor people of Tondo, it is also directed to all the Christians in the Philippines; so there is nothing exclusive in this encouragement to the poor. Thirdly, the pope seems to be encouraging a continuance of the process of consciousness-raising; but this is expressed in the term 'catechetical instruction' which is both wider in scope and less radical in tone than the word 'conscientisation'; and as a traditional Church phrase it is not open to objection by the Filipino government.

In what it has to say to the poor, the Tondo speech is closer to the second of the Brazilian shanty-town addresses than to the one at Vidigal. John Paul tells them that, 'they themselves can achieve much if they pool their skills and talents, and especially their determination to be the artisans of their own progress and development' (para. 5). Like the address at Alagados, this goes notably further than the vague words of consolation offered at Vidigal. It is an encouragement to the poor to organise themselves, to take charge of their own destiny; they do not have to wait for the rich, 'the decision-makers', to initiate social change, for they themselves can become decision-makers. The pope tells the poor of Tondo and Alagados that they find 'strength in human solidarity' (Tondo para. 5; cf. Alagados, Brazil para. 2). One may speculate that some of what the pope said later in his encyclical *Laborem Exercens* came out of what he experienced, and reflected on, in the shanty-towns of Brazil and the Philippines. Certainly, the new and more active encouragement to the poor, and the reference to their 'solidarity' with each other, are an anticipation of an important theme of the new social encyclical.

SUMMARY

In January 1979 John Paul II went to Mexico and faced there his first big challenge in the area of social justice. He played a key role in the Conference of Latin American Bishops at Puebla. The big issue was whether or not the conference would reaffirm the basic thrust of Medellín. In spite of a lot of opposition, it eventually did so. The more radical bishops at Puebla had to make some compromises on 'doctrinal' topics; but there was no drawing back from the options taken at Medellín. The final document of Puebla has one section entitled, 'A Preferential Option for the Poor'. The Puebla document as a whole is a consensus statement in which Paul VI's *Evangelii Nuntiandi* and the Mexican addresses of John Paul II provided the basis for agreement on the more divisive questions, above all the issue of whether the Church should commit itself to justice, liberation and the poor.

The pope encouraged the Latin American Church to continue to take a strong prophetic stance on questions of injustice; but he also noted the danger of seeing Christ as a political revolutionary. His strong statements about poverty and oppression showed his special concern for the poor. But it was only in the following year, during his visit to Brazil, that he openly approved and used the controversial phrase, 'a preferential but not exclusive option for the poor'. The pope used the term 'social doctrine', not in the sense of a timeless blueprint for society but as a body of beliefs and values that can and should be respected in a variety of different societies.

In his first two encyclicals and his address to the United Nations, John Paul put forward his own vision of what it means to be human, of the place of Christ in this, and of the mission of the Church. It is a vision of integral humanism in which the spiritual is not opposed to the material, in which social justice is of major importance, and in which mercy is essential—but not as a substitute for justice. For the pope, respect for human rights is the test of whether a society is truly just. He challenged and criticised in a very radical way the current model of 'development'—seeing it as a cause of injustice, poverty, alienation, destruction of traditional cultures, and ecological disaster.

In Brazil and Mexico the pope addressed himself to the issue of the role of the poor in bringing about change in society. He indicated that they are to be the main agents of their own advancement, struggling together to improve their conditions.

Questions for review:

1. Was Puebla a step forward or a step backward from Medellín?
2. Outline the gradual development in the pope's teaching about the poor over the course of his visits to Latin America in 1979 and 1980.
3. Examine different understandings of the phrase 'social doctrine'.
4. What does it mean to say that John Paul in his first two encyclicals put forward a vision of integral humanism?

Question for reflection:

What have the Vatican and the Latin American Church learned from each other? What do they still have to learn from each other?

Issue for further study:

The emergence of Third World theology as something much wider than a liberation theology rooted in Latin America. (Read EATWOT, Ellis and Maduro.)

12

An Encyclical on Work and Solidarity

To commemorate the ninetieth anniversary of Leo XIII's *Rerum Novarum*, Pope John Paul prepared the encyclical *Laborem Exercens*, called in English, 'On Human Work' or (in America) 'On Human Labor'. It was to have been issued on 15 May 1981 but its publication was delayed by four months as a result of the attempt on the pope's life. It is a document of major importance, a worthy successor to the encyclical it commemorates, and to the other great social encyclicals. I shall make some general remarks about the approach and contribution of this new encyclical; then I shall examine three major themes of the encyclical which are especially relevant to the issue of 'option for the poor'. These are, the concept of the indirect employer, the issue of women and work, and the idea of solidarity.

Social Teaching

Laborem Exercens represents a new *style* of social teaching. What John Paul offers us here is a painstaking and profound reflection on the nature of human work and the organisation of economic life. This is more than 'teaching' in the usual ecclesiastical sense of propounding truths. It is far more like teaching in the ordinary sense of the word, namely, explaining and helping people to understand why things are the way they are—and how they might be changed. In adopting this approach the pope goes a long way towards resolving the doubts that had arisen in relation to the very notion of a 'social teaching' of the Church. His approach is 'radical' in the literal sense: it goes to the root of the issues, rather than simply repeating or adapting traditional formulas.

John Paul believes that there are some general truths and values that underlie the particular teachings on social issues put forward by the Church over the years. Two of these underlying truths stand out in the encyclical. The first is that, 'the basis for determining the value of human work is not primarily the kind of work being done but the fact that the one who is doing it is a person' (LE 6). Therefore human labour may not be treated simply as a tool in the process of production and an item to be sold to those who control the means of production (LE 7, 8). A second key point is that 'capital' is simply an instrument which is to be at the service of the human person, the worker. There is no opposition *in principle* between capital and labour, because what we call 'capital' is really the cumulative result of labour (LE 12). The *present* opposition between capital and labour is the result of a wrong direction taken by Western society in the last century (LE 13).

By using these key points the pope is able to bring out why the Church insisted on certain things in its social teaching in the past (e.g. LE 12, 14, 15, 16). He can rightly claim that his reflections are 'in organic connection with the whole tradition' of the Church's social teaching and activity (LE 2). This organic unity can be seen despite the fact that the pope does not strive for a purely verbal coherence between what he is saying and what was said by his predecessors. In fact the continuity with the past is more clear because it is not forced; the pope resists the temptation to repeat *verbatim* the social teaching of earlier documents. It is remarkable that *Laborem Exercens*, which was issued to commemorate the ninetieth anniversary of *Rerum Novarum*, does not have a single footnote reference to that encyclical; and the references to the other social encyclicals are sparse.

Organic unity allows for notable differences in details and in priorities between the social teaching of earlier encyclicals and that of *Laborem Exercens*. It is clear that the attitude of John Paul towards socialism is significantly different from that of his predecessors. The earlier social encyclicals had critical things to say both about capitalism and about socialism; but they almost invariably showed a preference for the Western ideal of 'free enterprise'. Pope John Paul is more even-handed in his approach. There is great objectivity—indeed an almost ruthless honesty—in the way in which his philosophical and historical analysis shows up the weaknesses of the socio-economic models of society of both East and West (e.g. LE 7, 8, 11, 14).

Gregory Baum has put forward a strong case for saying that in *Laborem Exercens*, John Paul is advocating a modified version of socialism (Baum [1981] 4; Baum [1982] 55–6 and 80–6). That case is more difficult to sustain in the light of the third social encyclical, *Centesimus Annus*, issued by Pope John Paul ten years later. But it is certainly clear that the pope is very trenchant in his criticism of capitalism. *Laborem Exercens* contributes notably to a process which has been accurately described in these words by a left-wing writer: 'The Catholic Church is consciously, though slowly and deliberately, disassociating itself from capitalism and its institutions as presently structured' (Marzani 27).

Pope John Paul's reservations about the capitalist order are at least as serious as those of Pius XI in *Quadragesimo Anno*. The overall impression given by his approach is that he does not see it as part of his task to favour one of the existing systems over another, but rather to show where the different systems have gone wrong in relation to the values that ought to be promoted by an adequate socio-economic order (e.g. LE 8, 13–9). He does not do this in a moralising way but by reference to the structural inadequacies of each system, understood in the light of their historical development. The presupposition of *Laborem Exercens* is that there may be a variety of quite different ways in which a structurally just society could take shape. The social teaching of the Church, according to this view, provides some basic principles by which any given society could be evaluated; but it does not opt for any particular socio-economic order as the correct one (see LE 11, 13, 14).[1]

The Indirect Employer

Moving on from these rather general reflections on the contribution of *Laborem Exercens*, we can now look more closely at one of the more striking and effective elements in the teaching of the encyclical—the concept of 'the indirect employer'. The importance of this term lies in the fact that it acts as a bridge, leading the reader from an understanding of injustice in terms of a one-to-one relationship (which is easily grasped) to an understanding of structural injustice (a concept that many people find difficult to comprehend).

If an employer refuses to pay a worker a living wage, that would seem at first sight to be an obvious case of one-to-one injustice. But what if the situation is such that it is economically impossible for the employer to pay a just wage? Many employers are trapped in an economic system that does not enable them to pay their workers properly; if they did so, their products would be priced out of the market. The encyclical notes how this kind of situation arises particularly in the poor countries of 'the South':

> The gap between most of the richest countries and the poorest ones . . . is increasing more and more, to the detriment, obviously, of the poor countries. Evidently this must have an effect on local labour policy and on the worker's situation in the economically disadvantaged societies. Finding themselves in a system thus conditioned, direct employers fix working conditions below the objective requirements of the workers . . . (LE 17)

The poor countries are not the only places where conditions hinder or prevent the payment of an objectively just wage. There are sectors of the economy in practically all countries where this happens. It is most likely to arise in any situation where workers do not have an opportunity to become highly organised e.g. where there are migrant workers, or part-time women workers doing menial work, or in that rapidly growing sector called 'the black economy', where governmental and trade union controls are evaded.

The workers in these situations are undoubtedly the victims of injustice. But the person who is employing them may not be to blame for the evil, or may be only partly to blame. Who else may be held responsible for the injustice? To answer that question the pope introduces a distinction between what he calls the 'direct' employer (who is the employer in the usual sense of the word) and the 'indirect' employer. The latter term he explains as follows:

> . . . we must understand as the indirect employer many different factors, other than the direct employer, that exercise

> a determining influence on the shaping both of the work contract and, consequently, of just or unjust relationships in the field of human labour. (LE 16)

The encyclical goes on to mention some of these determining factors—but only in rather general terms. The State is mentioned, and later on there is reference to those ministries or public departments within the State which make decisions affecting workers or the rights of workers (LE 17). The pope also mentions 'various social institutions' set up for the purpose of safeguarding workers' rights (LE 17). These would presumably include trade unions, farmers' organisations, and even employers' associations. Voluntary agencies concerned with justice in the economic and social sphere could also be covered, as well as some political parties.

However, the pope insists that his idea of the indirect employer is not adequately understood if it is limited to agencies within any particular State. Account must also be taken of the 'links between individual States' which, he says, 'create mutual dependence'; and this dependence 'can easily become an occasion for various forms of exploitation or injustice and as a result influence the labour policy of individual States; and finally it can influence the individual worker' (LE 17). The pope goes on to spell out what this involves: the policy and practices of the highly industrialised countries and of transnational corporations cause the *national* income of poor countries to remain low; and this is directly related to the unjust wages paid by employers to *individual* workers in these countries—because in the poorer parts of the world there is simply not enough money to enable workers to get a just wage (LE 17).[2]

To illustrate the kind of situation the pope is referring to, one might cite the international beef trade, or the sugar industry. Farming agencies in Western countries put pressure on their governments to protect their interests by restricting the entry of beef from Botswana or Argentina. Similarly, the entry of cane sugar from the Caribbean is limited because of pressures from both industrial and farming agencies. What the pope is saying, in effect, is that among the 'indirect employers' of the cattle herders and sugar-cane cutters of such poor nations are Western farmers, factory owners and workers in the beef and sugar industries. These use their protective associations and trade unions to lobby for the restrictive policies which are partly responsible for the unjust wages paid to workers in 'the South'. By using the phrase 'the indirect employer' the pope has found a vivid way of expressing the reality of that responsibility—and the fact that it may not be shirked on the plea that such matters are the concern of governments or international bodies.

If the concept of 'the indirect employer' is taken seriously it provides the basis for an answer to the objection that the pope is unrealistic in this encyclical. It is all too easy to accept that it is utopian of the pope to suggest that disabled people have a right to employment (LE 22). Again, it is easy to assume that when he speaks (LE 19) about the right of workers to a vacation, or the right of the old and the sick to social welfare benefits, he could scarcely be taking account of the reality of the Third World. But what he says about 'the indirect employer' is a clear challenge to all of us to create a world in which such apparently unrealistic ideas can in fact be realised universally.

It is *not* unrealistic to envisage employment for most handicapped people, or a family wage and vacation for Third World workers, or adequate maternity leave for all mothers. All of these things are attainable if a sufficient number of people are prepared to pay the price. One part of the price is indicated— but tactfully understated—by the pope when he says, 'these changes . . . will very probably involve a reduction or a less rapid increase in material well-being for the more developed countries' (LE 1). There must, of course, be other things as well—notably a coordinated series of plans and education programmes aimed at bringing about a truly just international order (LE 1, 17, 18). But the crucial factor remains the willingness of people to submit to the sacrifices required by such programmes and their readiness to change their life-style accordingly.

To sum up this section we may say that the introduction of the term 'the indirect employer' helps one to have a better understanding of what an 'option for the poor' implies and of *why* such an option should be made. *What* it implies is a dedicated and consistent effort to disentangle oneself from the unjust structures, practices, and traditions that help to keep the poor in poverty; and a serious commitment to building alternatives that will be just and truly human. The reason why it should be done is that we cannot evade responsibility for the injustices that mark our world. Almost everybody has some degree of complicity in these injustices—the well-off who protect their own interests at the cost of the poor, and the poor themselves who often remain sunk in apathy.

Poverty and Impoverishment

The teaching of *Laborem Exercens* about 'the indirect employer' helps to bring home to people an important fact about poverty in today's world—the fact that it is generally not just an unfortunate reality, attributable to the lack of the bounty of nature, or even to laziness; it is more likely to be the result of injustice. This point has been stressed by Third World theologians, who distinguish between poverty and impoverishment (e.g. EATWOT 127–33). Poverty is a state or condition which may be the result of misfortune—something that just *happens* to people. But the word 'impoverishment', as used by these theologians, connotes a deliberate action. To impoverish nations or people is to inflict poverty on them. Studies have helped to bring out the fact that the mis-development and poverty of the Third World are due less to nature than to human intervention; they are largely the result of unjust actions in the past and present—mainly the actions of people in the wealthier countries (though now, increasingly, a small group of collaborators in the poorer countries must also be held responsible) (e.g. Stavrianos, Elliot). One must conclude that a crucial element in an 'option for the poor' is a commitment to ensure that one is not guilty of complicity in the impoverishment of vulnerable individuals, or groups, or countries.

This distinction between poverty and impoverishment, together with the related notion of 'the indirect employer', throws some light on a controversy that has arisen between theologians on the subject of an 'option for the poor'. Ostensibly, the controversy is about the scriptural meaning of the word 'poor'. But this seems to be a case where the general attitude of the scholars affects the way in which they interpret the Scriptures. For instance, in an article about 'the Church of the poor', the Scripture scholar Martin Tripole claims that Moltmann and some Latin American theologians have understood the word 'poverty' too narrowly; he claims that the meaning of the term should be extended to cover those who, while being materially rich, are spiritually 'poor', in the sense of being open to the life of the Kingdom:

> While quantity of money and possessions is never totally to be ignored in this discussion, the more fundamental question is *how one makes use of them.* Thus, if one who has abundance of money and possessions is nevertheless totally oriented to God for meaning and security in his life and uses his wealth in the service of God and mankind, he does not in effect fall under the category of 'the rich' as described in the Synoptic Gospels . . .
> Jesus was not really partisan to the poor in the way that society tends to use that term today. (Tripole 652)

This author is not slow to draw conclusions about what the Church should be doing today:

> The ecclesiological significance of this broader perception of 'poverty' is of enormous importance, for it allows us to overcome an overly confined perception of where the efforts of the Church need to be directed today. I am not saying that Jesus was not on the side of the poor. I am saying he was also on the side of those among the materially rich who were nevertheless numbered among those who were 'poor in spirit'; and that the efforts of the Church must be directed toward those as well. (Tripole 654)

Tripole believes that he has provided a basis which would justify the Church in establishing 'a political theology of influence at the higher levels of our society' rather than one that calls for working 'against those in the upper levels of society on behalf of those materially deprived' (Tripole, 654).

There are obvious differences between Tripole's scriptural position and the outline of biblical teaching which I have given in the introduction to this book and elsewhere (Dorr [1984] 87–100). This study of Vatican teaching is not the place to examine the validity of Tripole's understanding of the biblical teaching. But it is important to comment on his conclusion about what the Church ought to be doing today.

Whatever one may say about poverty in the time of Jesus, the crucial point is that in *today's* world poverty is largely the result of injustice, of impoverishment. The concept of 'the indirect employer' as propounded in *Laborem Exercens* can help one to locate that injustice and see what needs to be done to eliminate it.

To be a Christian today is to be called to work for justice in society; and an elementary (though difficult) part of this is to stop being unjust, to disentangle oneself from unjust structures for which one is partly responsible. It is true, of course, that wealthy people may become open to God, today as in the past. But, as the pope pointed out in his address in the Brazilian shanty-town of Vidigal, such openness involves a call to dismantle unjust structures. The situation of many rich people and of practically all rich nations today may be compared to that of the wealthy tax-collector Zaccaeus (*Luke* 19:1–10). His turning to Jesus involved a call to make recompense for the injustice he had practised in the past. Today, too, the call to openness to God is at the same time a call to moral conversion, to renunciation of the fruits of injustice—and no exegesis of Scripture should be allowed to obscure this basic reality. For this reason 'a political theology of influence at the higher levels of society' should not replace a preferential option for the poor.

To introduce a sharp distinction between material poverty and poverty of spirit is to invite a good deal of confusion into the discussion about the appropriate stance for the Church and the Christian in the face of poverty in the world today. We have been looking at the views of a writer who maintains that a wealthy person may be spiritually poor, in the sense of being open to God. Other people use the same kind of language but with an exactly opposite meaning; they say that the rich are spiritually poor in the sense that they are lacking in spiritual riches i.e. they are selfish, lonely, alienated from God and from other people. Some Church people use this kind of language to justify the work they are doing. They see themselves as helping the spiritually poor when they educate the children of the rich or provide medical services for the wealthy. This, they argue, is just as important for the Church as service of those who are materially poor. The effect of this use of language is to deprive the notion of an 'option for the poor' of any effective meaning, since everybody can be seen as poor in some respect.

The main problem here is a rather misleading use of language, which may or may not be deliberate. Perhaps it will be helpful at this point if I try to describe the situation of rich and poor in our world in a way that avoids a dualist opposition between material and spiritual poverty. In doing so I shall rely largely on the kind of integral humanist vision that is expounded so well by Pope John Paul in his first two encyclicals, and on the concept of 'the indirect employer' found in *Laborem Exercens*, as well as on the list of the qualities of poor people given by the pope in his addresses in the shanty-towns of Brazil and the Philippines. Such a description might take this form:

In general the people at the bottom of society are being impoverished by the way in which our world is structured. This impoverishment is both material and spiritual (if one must use these unduly polarised terms): the poor are deprived of adequate food and housing; they are not allowed to participate in decision-making that affects them; they are despised because of their language, or accent, or customs; they are deprived of education and of the leisure and opportunity to cultivate the things of the spirit. Nevertheless, their humanity resists this multiple oppression; and to a surprising degree many of the poorest people succeed in finding ways of being deeply human and Christian—in spite of all the handicaps imposed on them.

On the other hand, the interests of the rich and powerful are served by the way in which our world is structured. The system offers them advantages of many kinds, both material and in the area of 'higher' or 'spiritual' values (e.g. education, leisure for reflection and prayer, access to works of art). In today's world (especially), great wealth and power are very often linked to injustice—either in the way they are acquired or in the refusal to share them with others. So very many rich and powerful people must be held responsible in some degree for failing to change the unjust order of society. Because they fail to do so they may become corrupted to a greater or lesser extent—perhaps mainly through their selective and semi-deliberate blindness to social injustices. Furthermore, the present system has now become so distorted and misdirected—and so much out of human control—that it has become a major cause of alienation; it creates a sense of isolation and of threat even in those who are benefiting from it in economic and political terms. This combination of blindness and alienation in the 'privileged' ones of our society entitles one to say that they may be spiritually corrupted or at risk.

On the basis of this kind of description of the present situation of rich and poor, one may come to a better understanding of what is involved in an 'option for the poor'. It implies a commitment to trying to change the unjust structures of society. This includes giving encouragement and hope to those who are being impoverished, while challenging the complacency of those who are responsible for this impoverishment, or are guilty of complicity in it.

How can this best be done? The answer will vary according to the situation, but some general points may be noted. Clearly there is a need for many people to work directly with the poor—not just *for* the poor but in a way that involves sharing their experiences in some degree. Of course the rich and powerful should not be entirely neglected or ignored. However, the crucial question is, what should committed Church people be saying to the rich, by their words and actions? There are people who believe they can move the rich towards greater social awareness by working closely with and for them—for instance, by providing expensive high-class education for their children. More recently an increasing number of committed Church people have come to the conclusion that this approach is not sufficiently effective. So they choose to challenge the rich by transferring their energies to working with the poor.

Does an 'option for the poor' mean an option *against* the rich and powerful? By no means—at least not in John Paul's view. As we shall see in a later section, the pope is firmly opposed to class struggle; so he does not advocate the rejection of rich *people*. However, an option for the poor does mean the rejection of an evil system and of bad *structures* in society. The Church has always insisted that people make an 'option against sin'. Correctly understood, an 'option for the poor' is simply one aspect of an 'option against sin'. For in recent years theologians and Church leaders have come to realise more clearly that an option against sin must include an option against what is called 'social sin' and 'structural' injustice. One aspect of social sin is the way in which injustice has become embodied in our world through an unequal distribution of wealth and power. If we opt to resist injustice we must be opposed to the process of impoverishment and the systems that promote poverty.

Women and Work

The foregoing reflections flowed from an examination of the concept of the 'indirect employer', which was the first of the three main points in *Laborem Exercens* that are especially important from the point of view of an 'option for the poor'. The second of these points is the issue of women and work. What the pope has to say on this question is important because it represents a serious attempt to update the Church's teaching and even to change it in a significant way.

The first thing to note is that the pope addresses three slightly different issues in three successive sub-paragraphs (all in LE 19). In the first of these he speaks about the *family*; in the second he speaks about *mothers*; in the third he speaks about *women*. It is very important to differentiate these three, for otherwise we miss the originality—and the subtlety—of what he is saying.

The pope insists that any adult who has to support a family should receive an adequate income either directly from the employer or through a subsidy from society. He says it should not be necessary for both spouses to be employed outside the home. Most Catholics reading these statements would presume that John Paul is simply repeating the views of his predecessors: that in speaking of 'the head of a family' he presupposes that this is a man; and that in saying that 'the other spouse' should not have to go out to work he presupposes that this spouse is a woman. This presumption is strengthened by the use of sexist language in the English translation, so that the head of the family is referred to as 'he'. Nevertheless, a close reading of the text shows that it is very carefully worded. In referring to the one who has to support a family the Latin text speaks of a person (*homo*) rather than a man (—the Italian text is *persona adulta*); and the word 'spouse' seems to have been deliberately chosen instead of the word 'wife'. It is at least possible that the passage was phrased in this way so that it could also cover the case where the one who goes out to work is a woman and 'the other spouse' is a man.

The pope goes on at once to speak of mothers. He insists that society should recognise that the mother who cares lovingly for children in the home is doing real and valuable work. He suggests that society should make it possible for a mother to take care of her children without penalising her or discriminating against her for doing so. A mother should not be forced to abandon these tasks in order to take up paid work outside the home. In a significant parenthesis he adds that this should be possible 'without inhibiting her freedom'. The parenthesis is vitally important because it represents a major turn-about in Catholic social teaching. If he had omitted it, the pope would have been reinforcing the traditional position. But its insertion means that what the pope is saying is quite close to what is being said by a major section of the women's movement: a woman should have the economic freedom to devote time to her young children if she chooses to do so.

In the third sub-paragraph the pope notes the fact that 'in many societies women work in nearly every sector of life'. He maintains that society and work should be organised in such a way that 'women do not have to pay for their advancement by abandoning what is specific to them and at the expense of the family'. This is an interesting statement which can be interpreted in two very different ways:

— It may be taken as a reaffirmation of traditional ideas about 'the woman's role' as wife and mother.

— It may, on the other hand, be understood as a quite radical proposal which would be welcomed by many in the women's movement, namely, that women should not be forced to fit into an economic system which grew up catering mainly for the needs of men. For example, the pope may be seen as criticising what happens nowadays in many of the professions: if a woman takes a break in her career to spend time with her young children it is often almost impossible for her to 'catch up' again with men or single women who have devoted those crucial years to their career. Such a high degree of specialisation may not be good for the profession—and it amounts to discrimination against women who choose to give priority for some time to their children.

Laborem Exercens does not repeat the traditional teaching that a woman's place is in the home. Neither does it 'reduce' the role of the woman to that of being a mother. In fact it seems that the wording of this section is very carefully chosen to avoid the accusation that it is doing so. However, the passage does not overtly challenge the older view of the nature and role of women. The pope does not clearly dissociate himself from the tendency of Church leaders in the past to identify women primarily in terms of their role as mothers. In fact one has to read the text very carefully indeed to realise that it amounts to a remarkable break with the traditional view.

Why should the pope play down this change of direction on such an important issue? Why should he leave himself open to the accusation that he is perpetuating the traditional abstract ideal and the consequent unrealism about the exploitation of women in practice? I can suggest two reasons why he might have done so:

— Firstly, he may still have been clinging to the older ideal of 'the mother in the home' precisely as an ideal, even while admitting that it is seldom realised in the modern world; and he may well have believed that this ideal would be further eroded by a strong and clear statement from the pope acknowledging the right of women to work outside the home.

— Secondly, like each pope who went before him, on taking up his role as the main current standard-bearer of the long tradition of Catholic social teaching, he probably found that this very tradition imposed on him a very strong pressure to emphasise its continuity; so it may have seemed more prudent not to emphasise such an untraditional point as the equal right of women to work outside the home.

We cannot be sure of the exact reason why the pope was so circumspect in the way he formulated his teaching on this crucial issue. But there can be little doubt about its effect: the media and the ordinary readers of the encyclical did not recognise in it any significant departure from the traditional Church view about the place of women. Quite the contrary; it was widely reported as a reaffirmation of the older view and this led many commentators to react against the encyclical. This means that if the passage of the encyclical under consideration here amounts to a very notable change in the teaching on this topic (as I believe it does) then there has been a major failure to communicate this change. And I am not aware of any later statement of the pope where he sets out to clarify the point. There is not much point in adopting a more enlightened position if this is not communicated clearly to those who are interested to know the official position of the Church on these questions. In the final chapter of this book I shall return to the issue of the Church's teaching about women.

Solidarity

I move on now to the third key issue in the encyclical, namely, the concept of solidarity. The issue here is one that we were concerned with at the end of the previous chapter—namely, what does the Church have to say to the poor? We saw that, in two of his addresses to shanty-dwellers in Brazil and the Philippines, the pope stressed the importance of the poor taking responsibility for their own destiny. We saw, too, that John Paul noted that the poor exercise the great virtue of solidarity in the way they help each other. In *Laborem Exercens* he elaborates these points more fully. They are also placed against a historical background, namely the struggle of workers in the last century to break out of the degradation that was imposed on them through the industrial revolution (LE 8).

Laborem Exercens offers a trenchant criticism of the two major economic systems of the world of 1981—that of the West and that of the East (e.g. LE 7, 8, 11, 14). It is insistent in calling for a transformation of the present structures, with the aim of ensuring that the person is respected. But what kind of action does the pope envisage to bring about such radical changes? Not a class struggle. In this encyclical, as elsewhere, the pope rejects the idea that the way to achieve social justice is to struggle 'against' others (LE 20). He favours a struggle *for* justice, rather than *against* other people or classes.

However, Pope John Paul is quite prepared to approve of resistance to exploitation. He accepts that in the last century industrial workers had to oppose a 'system of injustice and harm that cried to heaven for vengeance', in order to protect their human rights and dignity (LE 8). There is a certain solemnity—almost a judicial quality—in the way in which the pope states that this reaction of the workers 'was justified from the point of view of social morality' (LE 8). In the remainder of the same paragraph he goes on to examine the need for similar action to secure social justice in *today's* world. He notes that there are various sectors where the old injustices persist, or other forms of injustice are present—injustices that are 'much more extensive' than those of the last century.

The key word used by Pope John Paul in this connection is 'solidarity'. For him the word 'solidarity' seems to play a role analogous to the phrase 'class struggle' in Marxist writings. He uses the word ten times—nine of them in the space of one paragraph (LE 8—nine times, and LE 20). His repeated use of the word when he is referring to the reaction of workers against an unjust and exploitative system, suggests that the 'Solidarity' union of Lech Walesa and his ten million fellow workers was very much in the mind of this Polish pope.

The fact that a pope from Poland spoke so strongly about solidarity at the very time when the Polish trade union 'Solidarity' was so much in the news could give a wrong impression. It might appear that his ideas about worker solidarity were inspired mainly by what was happening in Poland at the time. This would be incorrect—or at least incomplete. In fact, if anything, the position might be the other way round: John Paul's views about solidarity, propounded several years earlier, undoubtedly played some part in creating a climate in Poland favourable to the emergence of the 'Solidarity' trade union—and may well have helped to inspire this choice of name for the movement.

In 1969, when John Paul was still Karol Cardinal Wojtyla, archbishop of Cracow, he published a study entitled *Osoba i Czyn* (The Self and the Act) (Wojtyla 30–56). In it he put forward a philosophical analysis of the concept of solidarity. This provides a very important background for an understanding of what he wrote twelve years later in *Laborem Exercens*.

So it is worthwhile quoting some important passages from this study.

A first passage indicates what the author means by 'solidarity'; and it shows how it relates to participation by people in the building of community:

> The attitude of solidarity is a 'natural' consequence of the fact that a human being exists and acts together with others. Solidarity is also the foundation of a community in which the common good conditions and liberates participation, and participation serves the common good, supports it, and implements it. Solidarity means the continuous readiness to accept and perform that part of a task which is imposed due to the participation as member of a specific community . . . (Wojtyla 47)
>
> The attitude of solidarity respects the limits imposed by the structures and accepts the duties that are assigned to each member of the community. (Wojtyla 48)

The next point is particularly important in our present context. It is that solidarity does not always exclude opposition and confrontation. The following passages throw light on what *Laborem Exercens* has to say about oppressed people asserting their rights—and being entitled to do so:

> The attitude of solidarity, however, does not exclude the attitude of opposition. *Opposition is not a fundamental contradiction of solidarity.* One who expresses opposition does not remove himself from participation in the community, does not withdraw his readiness to act for the common good. (Wojtyla 48)
>
> There are instances . . . when solidarity demands . . . contrariness. In such instances, restricting oneself to the assigned duty only could be tantamount to a lack of solidarity. (Wojtyla 48)
>
> Opposition is also an expression of the vital need for participation in the community of existence, but especially in the community of action. Such opposition has to be viewed as constructive . . . (Wojtyla 49)

The author goes on to make it clear that it is not sufficient to have an opposition which emerges spontaneously, more or less in spite of the existing structure. The structure itself must facilitate the expression of opposition:

> We are concerned with such a structure of community that permits the emergence of opposition based on solidarity. Moreover, the structure must not only *allow the emergence of the opposition, give it the opportunity to express itself, but also must make it possible for the opposition to function for the good of the community* . . . (Wojtyla 49)

The final point to note in this important study by Cardinal Wojtyla before he became pope is his notion of dialogue. For him, dialogue serves the function of ensuring that opposition is not cut off; it ensures that the structures which seek to promote the common good do not become too restrictive. It is especially important in a situation characterised by militancy, since it can help the participants to eliminate purely personal attitudes and preferences, and enable them to agree on what is objectively required. In this way opposition, though it can make it difficult to live and act together, can at the same time contribute to a deepening of human solidarity (Wojtyla 49–50).

In the light of this account of the meaning of solidarity, one can now see how ideal a word it is for the pope's purposes in the encyclical *Laborem Exercens*. The word 'solidarity' is action-oriented. But it does not have the negative connotations of the word 'struggle'. Instead of evoking an image of divisiveness, it suggests that the primary thrust of the workers' activity is towards unity and community. Their unity may often come in and through their confrontation with those who try to maintain unjust structures. However, that is not a necessary part of the order of reality but is due to a perversion of the way things ought to be.

In the paragraph in which the pope examines the concept of 'solidarity' in some depth he never once speaks of the 'struggle' of the workers for justice. Instead he speaks of a 'reaction'—a justified reaction—of the workers to an unjust and exploitative system (LE 8). This nuanced use of language suggests that what he sees taking place is not the struggle of two morally equal groups, the employers and the workers. Rather there is 'a wide-ranging anomaly', a perversion of right order, which calls forth a justified 'reaction'. It is only in a much later paragraph, dealing with the role of trade unions, that the pope speaks of the *struggle* of workers; and then it is only with the qualification noted above, namely, that it is always a struggle for justice, rather than against other people or classes (LE 20).[3]

A further advantage of the choice of the word 'solidarity' is that the confrontational aspect of working for justice does not have to be spelled out. Anybody reading the newspapers in the months prior to the publication of the encyclical would be very well aware that action for justice through workers' solidarity is not all sweetness and gentleness; the story of the Polish 'Solidarity' shows that quite clearly.

In *Laborem Exercens* the pope does not explore the morality of different kinds and levels of confrontation in a variety of different situations. Had he done so, it could have given the wrong impression: it might have been seen as an incitement to workers and others to seek confrontation. In fact there is no indication either in the encyclical or in other writings or addresses that John Paul wanted to provoke confrontation. What he has to say about opposition is only a small part of his teaching on solidarity; and this in turn is just one part of a balanced and comprehensive social teaching. Indeed, there is a sense in which I may appear to have given an inordinate amount of space to this one issue. But it was necessary to go into the question in some detail because what the pope has to say about opposition is a small but crucial part of the whole edifice of his social teaching. Its significance lies above all in the fact that it plugs a gap that had existed in previous papal teaching.

A final advantage in the choice of the word 'solidarity' (and one that was probably quite important for the pope personally) is that the repeated use of this word in a papal encyclical undoubtedly had the effect of giving a certain discreet aura of Vatican approval to the Polish workers' movement—at least in its overall direction. And why not? If the pope could pronounce a judgment that the reaction of nineteenth-century workers to an oppressive system was justified, why should he not imply that the same was true of the activity of the Polish workers of his own time?

Pope John Paul does not claim to have made an exhaustive listing of the kinds of injustice in the present world that call for 'new movements of solidarity of the workers and with the workers' (LE 8). But he goes quite some distance in that direction. He mentions 'various ideological or power systems, and new relationships which have arisen at various levels of society'; these have, he says, 'allowed flagrant injustices to persist or have created new ones' (LE 8). This general statement can be taken to refer, among other things, to power bureaucracies in East and West and to the ability of rich nations to exercise economic power for their own advantage through such agencies as the International Monetary Fund, as well as to the economic abuses of transnational corporations. But the pope's words may apply equally well to structures that give undue or unchallenged power at the local level to politicians or administrators—or even to clergy.

The pope also notes that he has in mind not only indust-rialised countries but also those countries where most workers are engaged in agricultural labour. It can be taken that he is alluding here to the gross injustices associated with land ownership in many countries of the 'South'—and to other abuses in the less industrialised parts of the world. He also makes specific mention of the need for a movement of solidarity among groups of people who may have had a privileged position in the past but now find themselves in a 'proletariat' situation; these would include some categories of the working intelligentsia (LE 8). The point here is an important one: the proletariat is no longer confined to those who work with their hands. No doubt the pope derived some satisfaction from pointing out that old-style Marxist descriptions are no longer adequate to describe the present reality.

The introduction of the concept of solidarity provides a perfect solution to a problem that had arisen for Paul VI and even for John Paul himself in earlier teaching. They could point out and condemn injustices in society at the international or national level. They could appeal to those in authority to put things right. But if that was not enough, as clearly it was not, what then? Should a pope invite the poor and oppressed to take matters into their own hands and put things right? Would not this amount to an incitement to open confrontation? Is it not likely that any such statement would be hailed by revolutionary groups as approval for their cause and their activity? All this would seriously weaken the stance of the Church in favour of nonviolence. It could also lessen the effectiveness of the Church from a purely strategic point of view: the explicit identification of the Church with the political struggle of the oppressed could provoke further repression and persecution by those in power.

The word 'solidarity' offers a way out of this dilemma. As has been noted already, it is not to be identified with an all-out revolutionary struggle. But on the other hand it does not exclude whatever degree of confrontation is necessary and prudent. No a priori theory can enable one to predict the risks that are involved or how far the workers would be entitled to go in pressing for justice. Traditional Catholic principles about violence, war and rebellion could help one in exploring each individual unique situation; but they would not excuse one from the need to make prudent judgments in each case.

By coming out strongly in favour of 'solidarity', Pope John Paul is accepting the need for confrontation. This means he has avoided the false dilemma of having to choose between direct approval for violent action or on the other hand simply issuing warnings about the danger of violence in a way that would look like acquiescence in the *status quo*. The effect is that the stance of the Church in the struggle for justice is strengthened considerably. It seems, then, that the pope's Polish experience has provided the basis for an important new step in the social teaching of the Church.

Dialogue with Marxism?

As I said earlier, the word 'solidarity' seems to play, in the thinking of John Paul, a role analogous to 'class struggle' in Marxist writings. 'Solidarity' is a master image which does not have the overtly aggressive overtones of the phrase 'class struggle'. But how different really is the pope's position from Marxism? Is it mainly a matter of words and a different emphasis, or is there a fundamental incompatibility between the two approaches? I shall not attempt here to answer this question fully; but the following remarks may at least help to open up the topic for further discussion.

Catholic thinkers in the past generally followed the Greek tradition of defining the human person as a thinker. In presenting the human person as fundamentally a *worker*, the pope in *Laborem Exercens* is breaking from this Greek tradition and following in the tradition of Karl Marx. Of course he does not become a Marxist merely by adopting this approach. Nevertheless, it is evident that his understanding of human life and of society have been profoundly affected by some aspects of Marxist philosophy.

However, it must be added at once that the pope takes a much broader view of what is meant by 'work' than is common in the Marxist tradition. In a good deal of Marxist writing there is a tendency to use the word 'work' mainly to refer to industrial labour (Baum [1982] 13)—or at most to manual labour. For John Paul, on the other hand, the meaning of the word 'work' is so comprehensive that *everybody* can be called a worker in some sense (cf. Hennelly [1982] 34). Work, for him, includes such intellectual occupations as study; and it also takes in organisational work such as management, as well as the work of caring for a family. What about the unemployed, the disabled, those who are retired, and children? It would appear that the pope intends his teaching on human work to refer to them also, since they can all in a certain sense be thought of as potential workers. This may sound rather contrived—but only if one is thinking of work in the limited sense of doing a task for which one can be paid. The pope's conception, however, is one of *homo faber*—the human person as a 'maker', one who shares in the making of the world.

One of the most important effects of this broadening of the conception of work and the worker is that the notion of 'the working class' ceases to have the meaning it had in traditional Marxism. Central to Marxist thinking was the view that the interests of the working class were different to those of owners and managers. What happens when the definition of the worker is extended to cover everybody? The idea of a fundamental clash of interest between 'the workers' and others is eliminated. This explains why John Paul can insist that cooperation is fundamental, and that solidarity is more basic than opposition (cf. Schotte 23).

So much for the basic nature of society as it ideally exists. But John Paul is also prepared to look at the actual situation. He is not so foolish as to think that the problem of class struggle is eliminated by re-defining the meaning of the word 'worker'. He recognises that there have been major clashes of interest between employers and their employees. In his view, however, it was not predetermined that things should happen in this way; it did not occur because of any 'law'. Rather it was due to free decisions made by human beings. Initially, the people mainly responsible were the early capitalists; they were determined to maximise their profits—and they did so by exploiting their workers (LE 11). This provoked what the pope calls a justified 'reaction' on the part of the workers (LE 8).

Having begun in this way, the struggle between the classes has, according to the pope, gone on to develop into an ideological and political struggle between capitalism and Marxism (LE 11). John Paul's purpose in *Laborem Exercens* is to unmask the myths and over-simplifications that are part of this struggle. He points out the inadequacy of economic liberalism, the ideology of capitalism. He also rejects the Marxist notion that class struggle is a matter of historical necessity. For him, as we have just seen, it is the result of human decisions[4] and it is something that can be avoided. More fundamentally, the pope rejects the view of those Marxists who maintain that history is totally determined by economic processes and that human freedom is an illusion. He is opposed to Marxism understood as an ideology: he does not accept that it provides a system that has universal applicability, giving one a 'scientific' understanding of reality (cf. Baum [1982] 85); such a notion of Marxism as an exact science is bound up with the belief that history is determined by economic factors which follow rigid 'laws' (cf. Miranda 69–105).

It should be noted, however, that there are thinkers within the Marxist tradition whose views on these issues are quite close to those of John Paul. Their conception of history is not a determinist one; rather it finds a place for human responsibility (cf. McGovern 68–80; and Miranda *passim*). These Marxists agree with the pope in rejecting the kind of doctrinaire approach that would claim to be able to understand the world 'scientifically' by means of a ready-made theory (cf. Baum [1982] 85–6).

Even on the question of class struggle, there is by no means as much difference as might appear at first sight between the views of the pope and those of some of the more 'critical'

Marxists. He would agree with them that class struggle has actually taken place. They could perhaps agree with him that this was not due to some necessity of nature but was a matter of history in which humans played a determining part—a history that might well have developed differently in other circumstances and if different key decisions had been made. These Marxists could even agree that, in the long run, human solidarity is more basic than class struggle. After all, they would say, do we not envisage a classless society in which the divisions between the classes are finally resolved? Is not this, fundamentally, the same goal as the one to which the pope aspires, when he seeks the elimination of class struggle and the effective solidarity of all? As for the crude accusation that Marxism calls for the elimination of the enemies of the working class: their response would be that what is sought is the ultimate elimination of *classes*, but not of the *people* who belong to the upper classes.

Another point on which there is room for clarification is the motivation of the poor in struggling to overcome injustice. Pope John Paul frequently warns against any understanding of an option for the poor which would be an incitement to hatred (e.g. address to CELAM in Haiti in 1983). But does the Marxist conception of class struggle necessarily include a stirring up of the instincts of hatred and revenge? Or has it even done so invariably in practice? These are questions requiring careful answers. Certainly, it is not part of Marxist belief to hold that the poorer classes can be moved to action only by the crudest of motives; and if the ultimate aim is the achievement of a classless society, then there is room for higher ideals than those of 'class interest'.[5]

I am not suggesting that there are no real differences between the views of John Paul and those of 'critical' Marxists. But there is certainly room for dialogue; and such a dialogue may show that some of the differences are due to a different use of language. The dialogue might also lead to a discovery, by people on either side, of points which they had not taken sufficiently seriously. By way of example I mention here a question to which I believe those who propound Catholic social teaching have not given enough attention. The question is: what compromises should one make in working for justice, and at what point should one be quite uncompromising? This question arises for me from reflection on situations where liberation movements, having more or less won a political and military victory over their oppressors, stopped short of dismantling those State structures in which the oppression was embodied; the result was a change of rulers rather than the elimination of injustice. Church leaders frequently call for compromise and reconciliation—and rightly so. But there is need for serious consideration of the need to replace unjust structures as well as unjust rulers; and even to face up to the question of compensating for the imbalances in wealth which have developed over a long period of oppression.

I have said enough to indicate that there is room and need for a good deal of study, reflection, and dialogue on the relationship between the new current in Vatican social teaching and the more liberal and critical strands in the Marxist tradition. Over many years the Church has been in dialogue with the more moderate strands in the tradition of liberal political philosophy. As a result of this dialogue, Church leaders now find a wide measure of agreement with moderate Western political theorists and social scientists about the kind of values they would like to see embodied in society. On the other hand, the Church's dialogue with Marxism has always been inhibited, largely because of the anti-religious bias of communist governments. The tyranny of communism is no longer a major threat, so this may be an appropriate time for dialogue with moderate Marxists about issues of social justice. For it would be extremely naive to equate the collapse of communism in Eastern Europe with a discrediting of all Marxist thinking.

The Role of the Church

One of the most surprising features of *Laborem Exercens* is how little it has to say about the role of the Church in working for justice. Of course, in John Paul's view, the great contribution of the Church lies precisely in the teaching he was proposing in the encyclical—and the long tradition of experience and reflection out of which this teaching came. But the pope says little in this encyclical about the role of the Christian Church in actually implementing the principles and proposals. This is scarcely an accident. Presumably one reason for it is that in this encyclical, as in his first one, John Paul wished to emphasise his 'humanistic' perspective (cf. LE 13). Christians can stand alongside sincere non-Christians in working for the kind of just society envisaged in *Laborem Exercens*.

What Pope John Paul has to say about the action of the Church in the effort to overcome injustice is, though brief, nevertheless powerful. Significantly, it comes towards the end of the paragraph dealing with the need for new movements of solidarity of and with those who are degraded and exploited. He says: 'The Church is firmly committed to this cause, for she considers it her mission, her service, a proof of her fidelity to Christ, so that she can truly be the "Church of the poor".' (LE 8). What more needs to be said? These lines offer a firm commitment to the cause of the poor and the oppressed, together with the fundamental reasons for this engagement. On other occasions the pope elaborated on these points. One has the impression that here he preferred to be short and pungent because that makes it clear that what is now called for is action—decisive action by committed Christians in solidarity with the poor of the world.

If this study of Vatican teaching on 'option for the poor' had been written prior to *Laborem Exercens*, the ending would have had to include a major question-mark about the adequacy of what the Church had to say on this topic. The failure of earlier popes to face up to the question of confrontation was a serious weakness. With the publication of *Laborem Exercens* this weakness has been, at least partially, overcome. The result is a very rounded body of teaching which offers both inspiration and guidance to Christians concerned about issues of social justice.

It is interesting to reflect that the major advance made by Pope John Paul on the issue of organised opposition by 'the poor' to oppressive authorities is closely related to the pope's own experience in Poland. Church leaders in other parts of the world who become fully committed to the promotion of social justice can, like the pope, develop a theology that is rooted in practical experience. Obviously, the theology that emerges in each region will have its own specific flavour. But there will also be common themes—among them the major themes the pope has taken up in *Laborem Exercens* and in his other writings and addresses. For the Polish experience is now echoed in different ways in many parts of the world: great masses of people are left voiceless or marginalised, the victims of an insensitive ruling group; and their only realistic hope lies in learning how to assert their dignity and in organising themselves to claim their basic human rights.

SUMMARY

The encyclical *Laborem Exercens* offers a profound historical and philosophical analysis of the nature of human work and of how society should be organised if workers are to be treated in a way that respects their dignity.

The pope's concept of 'the indirect employer' is helpful in understanding the causes of the poverty and exploitation endured by workers in 'the South' (and by certain categories of workers in 'the North'). We may not be the direct employer who pays these workers unjustly; but we (and the agencies which serve our interests) can be seen as 'indirect' employers in so far as we have some degree of responsibility for their poor pay and conditions. This helps to bring home to us that these injustices cannot be simply dismissed as an unavoidable result of 'the system' for which nobody is really to blame. The poverty of most of those who are poor today is not just a fact of nature but is a result of their impoverishment by human actions in the past and present. So those of us who benefit from this exploitation are challenged to take responsibility for our complicity in the system and called to play our part in changing the structures. We must not evade this call by maintaining that those who are materially wealthy may be spiritually poor, or by making too sharp a distinction between ordinary poverty and 'poverty of spirit'.

The pope insisted on the importance of all families receiving an adequate income either from employers or through a subsidy from society. He spelled out the need for society to be organised in such a way that women will not be penalised if they choose to devote time to caring for their children. But he also recognised the right of women to go out to work.

In this encyclical the pope laid great stress on the *solidarity* of the poor and oppressed. He encouraged them to struggle to overcome the disadvantages imposed on them, emphasising especially the importance of trade unions in the struggle for the protection of workers' rights. But this is a struggle for justice, not a class war. The pope's understanding of solidarity includes an element of opposition or confrontation in the service of the common good; this is an important contribution to Catholic social teaching, which had previously been slow to acknowledge the need for confrontation. The pope also commits the Church to solidarity with the poor and oppressed.

The pope, like Marx, defines the human person as a worker. But for him work is not just physical labour; all people share in the work of creation. The views of some of the more moderate Marxists are fairly close to those of the pope. There is room and need for further dialogue.

Questions for review:

1. What is the difference between the 'direct employer' and the 'indirect employer'?
2. Clarify the meanings given to the phrases 'spiritual poverty' and 'poor in spirit'; how do they relate to economic poverty and powerlessness?
3. Does the pope hold that 'woman's place is in the home'?
4. Why is the concept of solidarity so central to John Paul's teaching?

Questions for reflection:

1. What kind of action by 'ordinary' people in 'the North' would help to improve the working conditions for people in 'the South'?
2. How would you reconcile the right of women to go out to work with the need of young children for a great deal of time and attention?
3. To what extent is it inevitable that society becomes stratified into classes; and what can be done to lessen class tensions?

Issue for further study:

To what extent is John Paul's account of work and society influenced by the work of Marx?

13

Concern and Consolidation

The two terms 'concern' and 'consolidation' in the title of this chapter sum up the main thrust of John Paul's papacy in the period 1981–92. It has been a time when the Vatican has appeared anxious about many aspects of Church life and has made strong efforts to reinforce and consolidate traditional teaching. It is more than a coincidence that 'concern' is also the first word in John Paul's second social encyclical (*Sollicitudo Rei Socialis*, translated into English as 'On Social Concern'), written in late 1987 half-way through this period. And the word 'consolidation' may serve as a one-word summary of his third social encyclical *Centesimus Annus*, issued in 1991 to commemorate the hundredth anniversary of *Rerum Novarum*.

SECTION 1: MANY CONCERNS

In the area of social justice John Paul's concern ranged widely. He continued his custom of making a number of pastoral visits each year to various parts of the world. On many of these occasions he took the opportunity to speak out strongly against injustices of various kinds. But there seems to be a certain change of tone and emphasis between what he was saying up to 1983 and what he said in later years. In the first period he spoke out very strongly on issues of political oppression, challenging governments quite directly. In the later period his statements on political matters seem rather more muted. This may be related to the ongoing concern in Rome about what are seen as the excesses of liberation theologians and to the Vatican's sustained effort to counteract their influence.

Early in 1983 Pope John Paul undertook what was probably the most controversial of his missionary journeys: he travelled

to Central America and Haiti and gave major addresses in El
Salvador, Nicaragua, Guatamala, and Port au Prince. In these
there are clear indications of both aspects of the pope's concern:
his outrage in the face of regimes that were blatantly oppressive;
and his fears that the Church's role might be reduced to that of
working for political and economic liberation—above all if this
liberation were seen in Marxist terms.

What the pope said in El Salvador and Nicaragua brought
out more clearly than ever before his reservations about the
Marxist answer to problems of social injustice; he objected to
what he saw as an 'instrumentalisation' of the Gospel and to
its subjection to an 'ideology' (e.g. in Managua AAS 75, 720–2).
Linked to this is his warning to priests and members of religious
communities not to confuse their role with that of political
organisers. For instance, he said to priests in San Salvador (*L'Oss.
Rom.* 7–8 Oct. 1983, 4), 'Remember that . . . you are not social
directors, political leaders, or officials of a temporal power . . . '[1]

During this same trip, however, the pope made a very outspoken demand in Haiti that things must change; he insisted
on the crying need for justice, and for equitable distribution of
goods, as well as for participation by the people in decision-
making and for freedom in the expression of opinion (Port au
Prince AAS 75, 768–9).

At this time also he spoke to a group of people who were
among the most oppressed in the whole world—the American
Indians of Guatamala. To them he made what is perhaps the
strongest and most specific statement he has ever made on a
burning issue of justice. He assured them that; ' . . . the Church
at this moment knows the marginalisation which you suffer,
the injustices you endure, the serious difficulties you encounter
in defending your lands and your rights.' He encouraged them
to resist these injustices: 'Your brotherly love should express itself
in increasing solidarity. Help one another. Organise associations
for the defence of your rights and the realisation of your own
goals' (AAS 75, 742–3).

The pope told these oppressed people of the attitude of the
Church in the face of the injustices they suffer:

> . . . in fulfilling her task of evangelisation, she seeks to be
> near you and to raise her voice in condemnation when your

dignity as human beings and children of God is violated . . . .
For this reason, here and now, and in solemn form, in the
name of the Church I call on the government to provide an
ever more adequate legislation which will protect you effectively against abuses . . . (AAS 75, 742–3—my translation).

In the same paragraph the pope very significantly demanded
that the process of authentic evangelisation should not be
branded as subversion. In other words, he was vindicating the
right of the Church to speak and act in the interests of justice
even when this is interpreted by authorities such as those in
Guatemala as a political activity, or as subversive of the State
authority.

Both aspects of the pope's concern found expression in his
address to the Council of Latin American Bishops (CELAM)
at Port au Prince on 9 March 1983. In the first section of his
talk he expressed his concern about poverty and injustice: 'A
sincere analysis of the situation shows that at its root one finds
painful injustices, exploitation of some by others, and a serious
lack of equity in the distribution of wealth and the benefits of
culture.' In the third section of the address he warned against
distortions of the Gospel and one-sided or partial interpretations of Puebla: ' . . . it is necessary to spread and . . . to
recover the *wholeness* of the message of Puebla, without deformed
interpretations or deformed reductions, and without unwarranted applications of some parts and the eclipse of others'
(AAS 75, 775–6—my translation).

In more recent years the pope has continued to stress the
importance of social justice. But his talks have not been
perceived as a clarion call in the same way as in his earlier
years as pope. When he visited Southern Africa in 1989 there
was considerable disappointment about the reticence and
caution of his remarks about the struggle for liberation in South
Africa (e.g. AAS 81, 331–4). And the addresses of his second
visit to Brazil seemed more reserved on issues of justice than
those of his earlier visit e.g. his address in the shanty-town of
Vitória (*L'Oss. Rom.* 4 Nov. 1991, 4) and to Amazonian Indians
at Cuiabá (*L'Oss. Rom.* 28 Oct. 1991, 10).

There is, however, one issue of justice on which the pope
has focused particular attention—that of the rights of cultural

and ethnic minorities. On this question he spoke out strongly on numerous occasions e.g. to the Indians and Inuit of Canada in 1984 (AAS 77, 417–22), also in 1984 to Koreans (AAS 76, 985 and 947), in 1985 to Africans in the Cameroons (AAS 78, 52–61), to Amerindian people in Ecuador again in 1985 (AAS 77, 859–69), to the Aborigines of Australia in 1986 (AAS 79, 973–9), in 1991 to Amazonian Indians in Brazil (*L'Oss. Rom.* 28 Oct. 1991, 10), and in 1992 in West Africa (*L'Oss. Rom.* 26 Feb. 1992, 8).

Liberation Theology

From the early 1980s onwards the Vatican began appointing many conservative bishops in Latin America (and in other sensitive areas). This was a clear indication of the concern felt in Rome about what were perceived to be the dangers of liberation theology. In 1984 this concern took a more obvious form when the Vatican Congregation for the Doctrine of the Faith issued its *Instruction on Certain Aspects of the 'Theology of Liberation'*. The document was widely understood to be the work of Cardinal Ratzinger, though there was some insistence on the fact that its contents were approved by the pope. It mounted a strong attack on liberation theology (or at least some versions of it) from several points of view. Among the notable points are:

— its insistence on the priority of personal sin over social sin (IV, 12—5);

— its emphasis on the incompatibility of Marxist theory with Christian faith (VII, 9) and its assumption that the theologies of liberation have adopted Marxist positions which are incompatible with the Christian vision (VIII, 1);

— its accusation that theologies of liberation have radically politicised the faith (IX, 6), have perverted the Christian meaning of 'the poor' by confusing 'the poor' of Scripture with the Marxist proletariat and have then transformed the fight for the rights of the poor into a class struggle (IX, 10), and have rejected with disdain the social doctrine of the Church (X, 4).

There was a very strong reaction to this document, including a comprehensive and sustained attack on it by one of the leading liberation theologians, Juan Luis Segundo. Like other liberation theologians he claimed that what the document put forward was a gross distortion of the main thrust of liberation theology. But he went much further: he argued that the theology with which it was imbued was one which located transcendence outside human history (e.g. Segundo 48, 72, 154); and for him this represented a regression to a pre-Vatican II theology.

The 1984 *Instruction* had included a promise of a further document on the theme of liberation. As a result of the poor reception given to the *Instruction* a consensus soon emerged that it needed to be supplemented if not superseded by another Vatican document. The new '*Instruction on Christian Freedom and Liberation*' was duly issued by the Congregation for the Doctrine of the Faith in 1986. Its teaching was widely seen as representing the views of the pope himself (cf. Hebblethwaite [1987] 85). While stressing the continuity between the two documents, it presented a balanced account of liberation theology without the harsh judgments and warnings of the earlier document.

This second document reaffirmed many of the themes of liberation theology such as the special place of the poor (21), the link between earthly liberation and eschatological hope (60), the Church's 'special option for the poor' (68) and the need for changes in the structures of society (75). It recognised that armed struggle against oppression could be justified in extreme cases as a last resort; but it suggested that in today's world passive resistance would be more effective and morally acceptable (79). It warned against 'the myth of revolution' (78); it stressed the importance of solidarity, subsidiarity (73, 89) and participation (86) and the need for a cultural trans-formation of society (81).

This second *Instruction* could be seen as an acknowledgment by Rome that the main teachings of liberation theology were thoroughly Christian. However, neither it nor its predecessor gave any indication of sympathy for liberation theology as a *project*—or indeed any real understanding of it. They showed no enthusiasm for the notion that theology emerges from reflection on the ongoing struggle for justice and liberation, or for the idea that theology should be worked out with and for ordinary 'grassroots' people (cf. Boff 416). And the Vatican continued its policy of appointing Church leaders who were quite unsympathetic to such an approach.

International Debt

Throughout the 1980s the problem of international debt was becoming ever more serious and urgent, and had been moving ever higher on the social justice agenda (cf. Potter; Dorr [1991] 11–4). In response to this situation the Pontifical Council for Justice and Peace issued in 1986 a document entitled 'At the Service of the Human Community: An Ethical Approach to the International Debt Question'. It explored the problem of debt in some detail, pointing out the burdens imposed on poor nations and especially on the poorer people.

The document was by no means radical in its analysis or its proposals. For instance, it did not condone the idea that debtor nations should repudiate their debts unilaterally or that payment defaults should be allowed to happen (13, 25); it suggested, however, that in the cases of the poorest nations the loans should be converted by the creditors into grants (26). And it did not put forward any serious and sustained criticism of the policies of the International Monetary Fund (IMF), on the grounds that 'it is not up to the Church to judge the economic and financial theories behind their analyses and the remedies proposed' (28).

Proposals put forward in the document were that the international creditors should take immediate action to meet emergency situations (13) and that, as part of a more long-term solution, they should reduce interest rates (19), reschedule debts (25), and eliminate protectionist measures which hinder exports from poorer countries (18). The document went on to suggest that international financial agencies (World Bank, IMF, etc) should have more representatives from developing countries and should allow these countries a greater share in determining their policies (29). The guiding principle of the authors was that people and their needs should be given priority over financial rectitude (e.g. 22, 31).

Pope John Paul has spoken occasionally on the issue of debt, following much the same lines as those of the Council for Justice and Peace; for instance in an address to diplomats in 1991 (*L'Oss.Rom.* 14 Jan. 1991, 3).

A New Social Encyclical

The twentieth anniversary of *Populorum Progressio* was in 1987. To commemorate it John Paul issued his second social encyclical, *Sollicitudo Rei Socialis*, known in English as 'On Social Concern'. It was dated 30 December 1987 but was not actually issued until February 1988. It gave rise to a certain amount of controversy in the United States where it was criticised by neo-conservatives such as Michael Novak for appearing to be as critical of the capitalism of the West as it was of the Marxism of Eastern block countries (cf. Walsh, p. xx). The main contribution of the document lay in its teaching on solidarity; and this was largely ignored not only in the mass media but even in theological and religious reviews.

After some initial observations on the significance of *Populorum Progressio*, the pope goes on to make an extended 'Survey of the Contemporary World' (SRS Chapter 3). It is quite significant that he chooses this approach. It means that his teaching is not abstract and deductive in style but is rooted in a penetrating socio-political and historical analysis of the situation.[2]

In this survey John Paul does not simply give a value-free account of the situation. He does not hesitate to make moral judgments. For instance he complains that the gap between 'the North' and 'the South' has persisted and is often widening. He criticises in a strong and even-handed manner the systems of both 'the West' (liberal capitalism) and 'the East' (Marxism), maintaining that each of them has a tendency towards imperialism and neo-colonialism (SRS 22). And he cries out in protest against the arms trade, the plight of refugees, the horror of terrorism (SRS 24) and the damaging effects of international debt (SRS 19).

Invoking various indicators of genuine human development, the pope has no hesitation in claiming that there has been a failure or delay in fulfilling the hopes of development which were so high when *Populorum Progressio* was written (SRS 12, 20). One reason for this, according to the encyclical, is the political, geo-political and ideological opposition between the East and the West. The pope strongly condemns the way in which the ideological conflict between East and West has widened the gap between 'the North' and 'the South'. He blames both sides for fostering the formation of ideological blocs, for the arms race, for failing to promote genuine inter-dependence and solidarity, and for imposing on other countries two opposed concepts of development, both seriously flawed (SRS 20–5; cf. Coleman 92).

When he uses the terms 'the North' and 'the South' the pope immediately points out that this terminology is 'only indicative, since one cannot ignore the fact that the frontiers of wealth and poverty intersect within the societies themselves' (SRS 14). He shows a preference for a different set of terms, namely, the First World, the Second World, the Third World and the Fourth World. The advantage of this usage is that it brings out the fact that these different worlds are all part of our *one world* (SRS 14). (In a footnote he clarifies that 'the Fourth World' refers especially to 'the bands of great or extreme poverty in countries of medium and high income'.)

Development

The main purpose of this encyclical was to meet the need for 'a fuller and more nuanced concept of development' in continuity with that of *Populorum Progressio* (SRS 4). Like his predecessor, John Paul II understands development to cover all aspects of human life. His emphasis, like that of *Populorum Progressio* (and of Lebret from whom Paul VI borrowed the phrase) is on 'being more' rather than 'having more' (SRS 28; cf. Goulet 134). In the light of this he speaks out not only against the underdevelopment of the poor countries but also against what he calls 'superdevelopment' existing 'side-by-side with the miseries of underdevelopment'; this he explains as 'an *excessive* availability of every kind of material goods for the benefit of certain social groups' linked to a civilisation of 'consumerism' and waste (SRS 28).

Development includes an economic and social component. The encyclical refers to a number of ways in which this can be measured, such as the availability of goods and services, of food and drinking water, good working conditions and life expectancy (SRS 14), as well as proper housing (SRS 17), the extent of unemployment and under-employment (SRS 18) and the burden of international debt (SRS 19).

But the pope insists that development cannot be assessed simply in terms of such economic and social indicators. To limit development to its economic aspect, he says, leads to the subordination of the human person to 'the demands of economic planning and selfish profit' (SRS 33; cf. 28). One must also take account of cultural aspects such as literacy and education, and of political aspects such as respect for human rights and human initiative, the extent of discrimination, exploitation and oppression, and also the degree to which people are allowed to be involved in building their own nation or, on the other hand, deprived of initiative and left dependent on a bureaucracy (SRS 15; cf. 33).

One difficulty about using these indicators of development is that it gives the impression that there is just one pattern of human development which all nations must follow. It is as though there were one 'ladder of progress' on which various countries have reached different heights. But the pope does not make this assumption. In fact he is careful to insist that different groups of people have '*differences of culture* and *value systems* which do not always match the degree of *economic development*' (SRS 14).

The pope sets out to present a theological basis for his teaching on development. He works this out by reflecting first on Old Testament texts such as the Genesis accounts of the relationship of Adam to the earth, to the animals and to God (SRS 29–30); then he goes on to reflect on the role of Christ in human history and human progress—and the role of the Church in promoting this vision of the meaning of life (SRS 31).

Towards the end of the encyclical the pope takes up briefly the topic of liberation. He says

> Recently . . . a new way of confronting the problems of poverty and underdevelopment has spread in some areas of the world, especially in Latin America. This approach makes *liberation* the fundamental category . . . (SRS 46)

He refers to the two Vatican documents on the topic of liberation. He also speaks of the intimate connection between development and liberation and goes on to say that 'the process of *development* and *liberation* takes concrete shape in the exercise of *solidarity*' (SRS 46). In this way he attempts to integrate the theology of development elaborated by Paul VI and himself with what might be called a moderate theology of liberation. This does not really work very well; for the approach and pattern of thought in the encyclical as a whole has little in common with the 'from the ground up' approach of the liberation theologians.

Solidarity

John Paul maintains that genuine development must be understood in terms of solidarity (SRS 33). In fact his notion of solidarity is the very heart of his understanding of development. His treatment of this topic in the encyclical is a notable contribution to moral theology. But, rather than discussing it in abstract philosophical terms, he situates what he has to say in the context of the distinctive contribution of *Populorum Progressio* to our understanding of human development. He sees his treatment of solidarity as an expansion of the brief reference made by Paul VI in *Populorum Progressio* to 'the duty of solidarity' (PP 44, 48).

As I noted above (p. 181), Paul VI's account of development began with self-fulfilment. He then extended it outward by including among the criteria of genuine development an increased concern for others and a desire to cooperate with others for the common good (PP 21). John Paul develops this further, offering his teaching on solidarity as a strong bridge to span the gap that might arise between personal fulfilment and concern for others. What he has to say about it can be summarised schematically as follows:

— Firstly, he spells out the fact of *interdependence*. By this he means that we live within a system which determines how we relate to each other in the economic, cultural, political, and religious spheres (SRS 38). (For instance, the livelihood of coffee-farmers in Brazil or Kenya depends on the markets of North America and Europe; and the television 'soap-operas' of the USA and Australia now influence the values of people in remote parts of Africa and Asia.)

— Secondly, solidarity is a *moral response* to the fact of interdependence. People are now convinced 'of the need for a solidarity which will take up interdependence and transfer it to the moral plane.' (SRS 26). This is a moral call to overcome distrust of others and to collaborate with them instead (SRS 39).

— Thirdly, such *acts* of collaboration spring from the *virtue* of solidarity (SRS 39). As a virtue, solidarity is not just a feeling but 'a firm and persevering determination to commit oneself to the common good' (SRS 38). It is an attitude of commitment to the good of one's neighbour, coupled with a readiness to sacrifice oneself in the service of the other (SRS 38). (I shall return in the next section to the pope's account of solidarity as a virtue.)

— Fourthly, the virtue of solidarity transforms the *inter-personal* relationships of individuals with the people around them. It causes the more powerful people to feel responsible for those who are weak and makes them ready to share what they have with them. It leads those who are weak or poor to reject destruc-tive or passive attitudes. It enables those in an in-between position to respect the interests of others (SRS 39).

— Fifthly, the virtue of solidarity is exercised also by whole *nations* in their relationships with other nations. Nations, like people, are linked in a system which makes them dependent on each other. Within this international system, the powerful and wealthy nations are morally bound to resist the temptation to 'imperialism' and 'hegemony'; they must not dominate, oppress or exploit the others (SRS 39, 39, 39). What the pope proposes here is a community of *peoples*, each with its own unique culture. 'Solidarity' means taking seriously the different value-systems of the various cultures (cf SRS 14), rather than the imposition of a Western model of development on other peoples.

— Sixthly, by transforming the relationships both between individuals and between nations, the virtue of solidarity brings about a radical change in society as a whole. (I shall develop this point below.)

— Seventhly, there is a sense in which one might speak not merely of 'human solidarity' but even of 'ecological solidarity'. The pope does not quite use this phrase, but it seems to sum up what he has in mind. For he speaks of 'a greater realisation of the limits of available resources and of the need to respect the integrity and the cycles of nature' (SRS 26). He insists that we are morally obliged to respect 'the cosmos' i.e. 'the beings which constitute the natural world' (SRS 34). He goes on to expound at some length on the moral obligations imposed on us by our ecological situation (SRS 34). Later, he speaks of 'the urgent need to change the spiritual attitudes which define each individual's relationship with self, with neighbour, with even the remotest human communities, and with nature itself' (SRS 38). This indicates that the moral dimension of genuine human development involves a sense of responsibility for the whole cosmos; such moral responsibility is either a part of the virtue of solidarity itself or else it is a sister virtue that has very much in common with it.

— Finally, there is the matter of what happens if people refuse the challenge to be in solidarity with others—if they respond with disinterest instead of concern, if their attitude is one of 'using' others rather than respecting them. If individuals or groups or nations act in this way they may grow more wealthy but they cannot be said to be truly 'developed', for they are ignoring the crucial *moral* dimension of human development (SRS 9). The pope notes that the lack of solidarity between the nations has 'disastrous consequences' for the weaker ones; but it also has serious 'negative effects even in the rich countries' (SRS 17). These include negative economic effects such as inadequate housing and growing unemployment (SRS 17, 18). Even more serious are the moral and political effects. For instance, failure of the nations to overcome their distrust of each other leads to continued imperialism and a turning away from the path to peace (SRS 39, 22); and the so-called 'developed' nations of East and West become locked into ideological and military opposition (SRS 20), wasting on an arms race the resources needed for development (SRS 22).

Solidarity as a Virtue

As I pointed out when examining the encyclical *Laborem Exercens*, the pope there employed the term 'solidarity' as it is commonly used, to denote the mutual support by which members of an oppressed group strengthen each other to resist injustice. In an earlier work written before he became pope he gave a more philosophical account of solidarity as a virtue. He saw it as an *attitude*, a commitment on the part of those who form a community, to participate in the life of that community in a way that promotes the common good.

In the present encyclical the pope puts forward a more theological analysis of the virtue of solidarity. Firstly, it is an enabling power which gives us the capacity to respect others:

> Solidarity helps us to see the 'other'—whether a person, people or nation—not just as some kind of instrument with a work capacity and physical strength to be exploited at low cost and then discarded when no longer useful, but as our 'neighbour', a 'helper' (cf. Gen. 2:18–20), to be made a sharer, on a par with ourselves, in the banquet of life to which all are equally invited by God. (SRS 39)

In this way the virtue of solidarity enables us to overcome distrust and to collaborate with others (SRS 39). Consequently, the exercise of this virtue is the path to true peace (SRS 39). The pope points out that the achievement of peace requires not only justice but also 'the practice of the virtues which favour togetherness, and which teach us to live in unity, so as to build in unity, by giving and receiving, a new society and a better world' (SRS 39). So solidarity presupposes justice but goes beyond it by including generosity and care for others.

The aspect of generous self-sacrifice is developed more fully by the pope when he goes on to focus attention on the *Christian* character of the virtue of solidarity. He suggests that 'solidarity seeks to go beyond itself, to take on the specifically Christian dimensions of total gratuity, forgiveness, and reconciliation.' John Paul finds the basis for this selfless love in the fact that each person is the living image of God (SRS 40). He goes on to say that, for the Christian, the ultimate inspiration for solidarity comes from a unity that is even deeper than any unity based on natural and human bonds; this is a *communion* which is a reflection of the unity of the three Persons in one God (SRS 40).

Structures of Sin

The pope's account of solidarity is part of his sustained effort in this encyclical to overcome the individualistic viewpoint which marred moral theology in the past; by emphasising solidarity he is saying that virtue is not just a private affair. But just as virtue is not a private matter, neither is sin. So the pope takes up the notion of the social dimension of sin under the title 'structures of sin' (SRS 36).

He tries to strike a balance between two extremes. On the one hand he wants to correct the idea that sin is a purely personal action. So he insists that sin becomes embodied in attitudes, traditions and institutions which endure long after 'the actions and the brief lifespan of an individual' (SRS 36). On the other hand he resists the idea that structural evil is the primary reality—a notion that is linked to the Marxist emphasis on the need for a revolution to overthrow the structures. John Paul insists that structures of sin are 'rooted in personal sin, and thus always linked to the *concrete acts* of individuals who introduce these structures, consolidate them and make them difficult to remove' (SRS 36). In giving primacy to personal, deliberate sin the pope no doubt saw himself as correcting a dangerous tendency of liberation theology.

John Paul also insisted that structures of sin are to be understood not merely in terms of a social analysis (SRS 36) but in theological terms:

> . . . hidden behind certain decisions, apparently inspired only by economics or politics, are real forms of *idolatry*: of money, ideology, class, technology. (SRS 37)

The essence of this idolatry is an absolutising of certain human attitudes—for instance an all-consuming desire for profit and thirst for power at any price (SRS 37). In making this point the pope was repeating one of the favourite themes of the liberation theologians (e.g. Gutiérrez, Segundo 55–65, Galilea 230). However, as Baum notes, his heavy stress on the personal roots of social sin means that he pays less attention than Medellín to its unconscious aspects such as the blindness caused by ideology and the dominant culture (Baum [1989] 113–16).

If the structures of sin are so pervasive and powerful how can we hope to bring about genuine development? At the personal level there must be a conversion in the biblical sense, that is 'a change of behaviour or mentality or mode of existence' (SRS 38). The social dimension of this conversion is the virtue of solidarity. Solidarity brings about a radical change in society because it gives people the ability to oppose diametrically the all-consuming desire for profit and the thirst for power, and the structures of sin which spring from them (SRS 37–8). In this way it provides the foundation of a whole new set of *structures*, which can be called '*the civilisation of love*' (SRS 33). So the crucial importance of solidarity in the pope's theology of development is that for him it is the only effective response to the mis-development and corruption of our world.

Inadequacies

Pope John Paul's account of the virtue of solidarity is a valuable one. He has made a praiseworthy attempt to give solid theological content to a word that is widely used in the world today, a word that describes a feature of modern moral consciousness at its best. There can be no doubt that he has met a real need, since a moral account of human development that is confined to such traditional words as 'charity' and 'justice' can seem at times to lack the flavour of real life.

However, there are some points at which his account of solidarity seems to be insufficiently developed. There is the fact that the treatment of solidarity in this encyclical fails to put any particular emphasis on the special role that God has given to those who are weak and poor in bringing liberation to all. Linked to this is the very cursory treatment in the encyclical of the whole notion of a preferential option by the Church for the poor (SRS 42, 46).[3] These are issues of theology, but they can have very practical implications. For, if the poor are called to be key agents of change, it is unlikely that they can play this role without some confrontation (cf. Baum [1989] 120–1); and if the Church is committed to an option for the poor then it too must face up to the challenge of serious confrontation.

This points to another inadequacy in the encyclical's treatment of solidarity: the model of social change which the pope envisages here seems to be very much a consensus model. As noted in previous chapters, when John Paul spoke to the shanty-dwellers of Brazil and the Philippines and to the American Indians of Guatemala, he encouraged them to take responsibility for their lives, to struggle against injustice and to stand up for their rights; he reaffirmed this approach in *Laborem Exercens*; and it could be linked to the views he expressed in Poland before he became pope.

In the first edition of this book, completed in early 1983, I made much of these facts. I saw them as indications that John Paul was willing to break with the tradition established by his predecessors; that he had come to acknowledge that, at least in some circumstances, progress can come only through con-frontation. But I must admit that the position adopted in *Sollicitudo Rei Socialis* is a backward step in this regard. In this encyclical the pope does not encourage the poor and powerless to see themselves as key agents of change. Nor does he repeat here what he had said before he became pope about the role of opposition as one aspect of solidarity. Quite the contrary; his treatment here is distinctly more reserved in this regard.[4] Perhaps this reserve may be attributed to the pope's determination to distance himself from the stance of the liberation theologians— not so much in terms of their teaching but in respect of their encouragement to the poor to see themselves, and organise themselves, as the key agents in the struggle for liberation.

Closely related to this is a certain blandness and unreality in the encyclical's treatment of the relationship between different groups or classes in society (SRS 39). What is lacking is a social analysis which would take more seriously the causes of the class structure in society and which could then go on to examine ways in which tensions between the different classes can be overcome or lessened.

Another significant point about the treatment of solidarity in *Sollicitudo Rei Socialis* is that it appears to lack an *affective* dimension. This is surprising since the pope's account of solidarity obviously owes a great deal to the strong affective bonds which have linked him so closely to his own people in their history and their struggles. His treatment of solidarity could be enriched significantly by a fuller account of the *experience* of solidarity and the strong *feelings* that are part of it.

By the 'experience' of solidarity I mean the actual sharing of life with a group of people. When one shares the living conditions of a community one can begin to share their sufferings and joys, their fears and their hopes. Out of this lived solidarity grow the bonds of affection that make one feel part of this people and enable them to accept one as truly part of themselves. These bonds of shared life and feelings evoke and nourish a strong sense of responsibility for the whole community and especially for its weaker members. So the virtue of solidarity should not be defined as purely an attitude of the *will* in contrast to 'mere feelings'. The gap between the fact of interdependence and the undertaking of an appropriate moral response is not adequately bridged by academic knowledge or even by prayer. Study and prayer must be situated within the context of some degree of shared life with people and the bonds of affectivity to which such sharing gives rise.

It is interesting to note that with the collapse of communism in the Soviet bloc the issue on which the encyclical became controversial—its equal criticism of East and West—has already been overtaken by history. Much more significant is its treatment of solidarity. Despite the incompleteness or weaknesses in what it has to say on this topic, its teaching adds a significant component to the corpus of Catholic social teaching (cf. SRS 1, 3, 41), one that should endure and be fully integrated into moral theology.

A Document on Ecology

As I pointed out in the previous section, Pope John Paul took some account of the ecological issue in his second social encyclical. But Vatican teaching on this topic lagged a long way behind that of the World Council of Churches and even behind the teaching of various groups of Catholic bishops (e.g. the bishops of the Philippines and the bishops of the Appalachian region of the USA). This gap was further widened in 1989 when the Council of the European Catholic Bishops co-sponsored with the Conference of European Churches a major conference in Basel, out of which came a strongly worded and inspiring statement entitled 'Peace with Justice for the Whole of Creation'. This adopted a very radical stance. It called for a 'complete reversal of the concept of sustained economic growth' (87a) and for a reduction of 50 per cent in the *per capita* energy consumption in industrialised countries (87d). At this time, too, the Vatican was under pressure to join with the World Council of Churches in sponsoring a world convocation on Justice, Peace and the Integrity of Creation, or 'JPIC' as it had come to be called (cf. Dorr [1991] 77–81). No wonder then that the pope felt it was time to give a more comprehensive treatment to the topic of ecology.

This came in his message for the World Day of Peace on January 1st, 1990. In this document the pope insists strongly on the close links between peace, justice and ecology, noting that one of the threats to peace is 'lack of *due respect for nature*, . . . [and] the plundering of natural resources' (1). These in turn are often caused by unjust land distribution and exacerbated by the need of heavily indebted countries to increase their exports in order to service their debts (11).

The document seeks to provide a biblical and theological basis for ecological concern. In God's plan there was 'a fixed relationship' between humankind and the rest of creation.[5] When the first humans deliberately went against this divine plan the result was that the earth was in 'rebellion' against humanity and all of creation became 'subject to futility' (cf. Rom 8:20–21)'. So human sin has repercussions on the rest of creation (3–5).

Perhaps the most significant aspect of the document is its insistence that there is 'an integrity to creation' (7); the universe is 'a "cosmos" endowed with its own integrity, its own internal, dynamic balance' which must be respected (8). Environmental pollution and the reckless exploitation of natural resources show lack of respect for life and are ultimately to the disadvantage of humankind (7).

The document seems to envisage two reasons why we should respect the integrity of creation:

— Firstly, those who fail to do so are rejecting God's plan for creation.

— Secondly, to fail to respect creation is to damage human life.

However, neither of these points provides us with a criterion for deciding what degree of 'interference' with nature would amount to lack of respect for its integrity.

There is an urgent need for some criteria to govern our relationship with the rest of creation. Christians now find themselves pulled in two opposite directions. On the one hand, most governments are committed to an ever greater economic growth, linked to an ever-expanding degree of 'exploitation' of the resources of nature. On the other hand, a growing number of concerned people are calling for a halt to this model of economic growth and even a reversal of it.

Justice for Women

In 1988 the pope issued an important document on the dignity of women. The most significant part of the document is that in which he sets out to show that there is a true equality between women and men. He offers an elaborate analysis of the text in the Bible where the first woman is said to be a helpmate for the first man. He concludes that the wife is 'subject to' the husband only in the same sense as the husband is 'subject to' her; each is called to be at the service of the other (7, 10, 24–5).

This teaching could go a long way to overcome the older Catholic tradition in which wives were expected to obey their husbands without any suggestion that this was to be reciprocated. However, this radical change of direction has gone almost unnoticed. Much more newsworthy is the strong stance taken by the pope against the ordination of women. Feminists and others claim that this amounts to a denial of the equality of women. But the Vatican maintains that what is at issue is not the fundamental equality of women but an unchangeable tradition based on Christ's choice of men as his apostles.

The US Bishops

In recent years the bishops of the USA have made an important contribution to Catholic social teaching by issuing a number of joint pastoral letters on questions of justice and peace. The most significant aspect of their programme has been the process which they have used in preparing these pastorals. They organise many formal and informal consultations on the topics in question. Then they publish a series of drafts of each of their pastoral letters; these drafts are discussed and debated in great depth before the definitive document is issued. This consultative process has been a very effective means of educating both the bishops themselves and the Christian community as a whole.

The first of this series of joint pastoral letters was issued in 1983 under the title, *The Challenge of Peace: God's Promise and Our Response*. The second draft of this document had come out quite firmly against nuclear deterrence. There was a strong reaction against this position within the USA. More significantly, there was also resistance to it from the Vatican— mainly, perhaps, because at this time Pope John Paul II seemed to be suggesting that deterrence could be considered acceptable if it was a step on the way to progressive disarmament. The bishops bowed to the pressure and in the final draft of their pastoral letter they did not condemn the idea of deterrence (cf. Geyer 3).

In 1986 the US bishops issued another joint pastoral, entitled *Economic Justice for All: Pastoral Letter on Catholic Social Teaching and the US Economy.* This too went through several drafts; and the final text put forward a fairly strong critique of American capitalist society. As a result, the document was greeted with some hostility by defenders of the system. On the other hand, quite a number of socially committed Christians felt dissatisfied with the letter because it seemed to be critical of abuses of the system rather than of the whole capitalist model of development.

The theme chosen for the third joint pastoral letter in this series was the role and situation of women. This proved to be an exceptionally difficult topic. One reason for this is that many feminist theologians (and others) are resistant to the very idea that a group of men should attempt to define the place of women (cf. Price 125). Another reason is the disappointment and anger of many Christians about the unwillingness of Rome to make any concession on the question of the ordination of women (and related issues).

The focus of attention in this book is on Vatican teaching rather than on the teaching of any regional grouping of bishops. So I am not concerned here with the detail of the contents of these documents of the US bishops. However, there are two points about these pastoral letters which are of particular interest, from my present point of view. The first is that the Vatican has kept a keen eye on their proposed contents and has not hesitated to subject the US bishops to considerable pressure to ensure that what they say conforms to the current Roman line. This does not fit in well with the teaching of Paul VI in *Octogesima Adveniens* that, given the variety of situations in which the Church finds itself, it cannot propose a detailed unified message of universal validity on social issues (OA 4). It would appear that the Vatican has taken a very restricted interpretation of Pope Paul's words.

The second significant point is that the participative process used in the preparation of these US documents contrasts sharply with the very secretive approach used in the Vatican during the preparation of documents of all kinds, including those on social justice issues. The adoption of a consultative process in the USA has led many Christians to ask why Rome does not use a similar process. So the US bishops have in this way issued a strong challenge to Rome, whether or not they intended to do so.

An Encyclical on Mission

At the end of 1990 Pope John Paul issued an encyclical about missionary activity, entitled *Redemptoris Missio*. It is a document of major importance but only a few points of it are relevant to the issue of justice, poverty and liberation. In general it helps to clarify John Paul's understanding of the mission of the Church, particularly in distinguishing between (1) pastoral ministry to those who already belong to a solidly Christian community, (2) re-evangelisation of peoples who used to be Christian and (3) the 'mission to the nations' (or primary evangelisation).

This encyclical is not, for the most part, written in the discursive, philosophical, dense and diffuse style which is so typical of the pope's other encyclicals; and people who claim to know what goes on inside the Vatican have suggested to me that it was not drafted by the pope himself or his inner circle of advisors but rather by (or under the direction of) the Congregation for the Evangelisation of Peoples.[6] This might help to explain the fact that, while the overall presentation is consistent with what the pope has written and said elsewhere, there are some passages which seem to reflect a less subtle and comprehensive vision, and are somewhat dualistic in tone.

Towards the end of the encyclical there is a passage which reads:

> It is not right to give an incomplete picture of missionary activity as if it consisted principally in helping the poor, contributing to the liberation of the oppressed, promoting human development, or defending human rights. The missionary Church is certainly involved on these fronts but her primary task lies elsewhere: the poor are hungry for God, not just for bread and freedom. (RM 83)

It is unfortunate that, in rejecting an incomplete and inaccurate picture of missionary work, the encyclical seems to make an unduly sharp contrast between the hunger for God and hunger for bread and freedom. When it speaks of 'the Church's primary task', it could give the impression that everything else is only secondary. What is needed is a reaffirmation of the vision of Paul VI's *Evangelii Nuntiandi* and John Paul's *Redemptor Hominis* which see human liberation and development as an essential part of the Church's missionary work.

At an earlier point the encyclical says that in its commitment to dialogue, human promotion (i.e. development) and justice and peace, the Church never loses sight of the priority of transcendent and spiritual realities (RM 19–20). The phrasing here could give the misleading impression that these 'transcendent and spiritual realities' are quite distinct from what is involved in working for human development-liberation and for justice and peace. Whereas in fact one of the most important ways in which committed Christians give priority to transcendent and spiritual values is precisely by their involvement in promoting peace, justice, dialogue and human liberation.

It may be noted in passing that there is one infelicitous phrase in this part of the text. Speaking of non-Christians who live according to Gospel values and are open to the Spirit, the encyclical refers to this as the 'temporal dimension of the Kingdom' (RM 20). It would have been more accurate to acknowledge that such non-Christians may be in touch not just with the *temporal* aspect of the Kingdom or Reign of God but with its transcendent and eschatological aspect as well.

Somewhat later the encyclical speaks of the role of the Church in 'promoting human development by forming consciences'. The point is that the mission of the Church is not 'to work directly on the economic, technical or political level' (RM 58). The message of the Gospel affects these matters only *indirectly*. It brings about human development 'precisely because it leads to conversion of heart and of thinking, fosters the recognition of each person's dignity, encourages solidarity . . . and service of one's neighbour' (RM 59). This way of describing the role of the Church seems somewhat individualistic. It appears to give insufficient weight to what Paul VI had said in

Evangelii Nuntiandi about transforming the culture (EN 18–20). And there is little emphasis here on the role Church people can play in helping to bring about changes in the economic and political structures of the world.

This part of the encyclical taken in isolation could give the impression that there is a playing down of the importance of the Church's 'prophetic' work in challenging injustice in society and helping to build a new world. It might seem that what is envisaged is a slow and careful education of the personal consciences of individual Christians in the hope that if sufficient people are 'converted' then there is the possibility that society will be transformed. But earlier in the encyclical there is an acknowledgment of the importance of a more public activity of the Church, including the promotion of justice and peace, and the advancement of women and protection of the environment (RM 37, 42). There is even the clear statement that: 'The Church is called to bear witness to Christ by taking courageous and prophetic stands in the face of the corruption of political and economic power' (RM 43). Furthermore, the encyclical recalls the pope's declaration in Brazil that the Church all over the world 'wishes to be the Church of the poor'; and it goes on to throw the pope's authority behind the Puebla statement that 'the poor deserve preferential attention' (RM 60).

All in all this mission encyclical gives a rounded and valuable account of the evangelising role of the Church. But the overall vision which permeates the document seems to lack some of the spirit of universality and integral humanism which are typical of John Paul. The vision seems at times to be unduly 'Churchy'. And, as the above instances suggest, there is a tendency at times to define the work of the Church as 'spiritual' in contrast to what is 'temporal' or secular, with a consequent playing down of the centrality of a commitment to justice. It would be going too far to suggest that the encyclical is lacking in consistency; but it does not have the clarity of vision which illuminates most of John Paul's earlier teaching.

SECTION II: THE CENTENARY ENCYCLICAL

Unlike many other encyclicals which came unexpectedly, Pope John Paul's third social encyclical was long-awaited. Various efforts had been made to prepare for it, partly in response to the request of the Pontifical Council for Justice and Peace that the centenary of *Rerum Novarum* be celebrated all over the world by conferences. A number of people had asked or hoped that the encyclical would be preceded by a fuller consultative process than that envisaged by the Council for Justice and Peace; they would have liked to see a public sifting of suggestions from Christians in different parts of the world about the content and style of this centenary document. This expectation had been aroused by the elaborate consultation process used by the bishops of the USA in the preparation of their pastoral letters on peace, on economic justice, and on the situation of women.[7] Furthermore, just about the time that the new encyclical was being drafted, the World Council of Churches was engaged in a complex process of consultation and revision of the draft document for its 1991 General Assembly in Canberra. The pope undoubtedly engaged in some consultation prior to writing the encyclical. But when he published *Centesimus Annus* in May 1991 both its contents and its style indicated that this new encyclical was very much the pope's own document.

The contents of the encyclical caused a good deal of surprise. This was not the wide-ranging document which many had expected on this occasion. Nor was it, as the more ecologically-minded had hoped, a profound critique of the expansionist model of economic development on which most governments rest their hopes. The heart of the document consisted rather of the personal reflections of a man who had played a key role in the transformation of Europe. In this encyclical the pope looked back on his own struggle and that of his people, and he shared the lessons of this experience with his world-wide audience; he also extended his reflections back over a hundred years of European history, and adverted occasionally to the situation of the wider world.

A striking feature of *Centesimus Annus* is the extent to which it re-affirms the teaching of *Rerum Novarum*. The first chapter is devoted to a lengthy examination of Leo's encyclical. But John Paul does not read this hundred-year old document in the manner of an academic historian. Rather his reading is unashamedly selective, because of its pastoral intent. He is concerned above all with the various ways in which its teaching can be seen as still very relevant today. He points out various ways in which it pioneered a new approach and has enduring value:

— Leo insisted that the Church has a *corpus* of 'social doctrine' the teaching of which 'is an essential part of the Christian message' (CA 5).

— *Rerum Novarum* insisted on the dignity of work and of the worker (CA 6).

— It also upheld certain fundamental human rights—the right to own private property (CA 6), the right to form professional associations or trade unions (CA 7), the right to proper working conditions (CA 7) and to a just wage (CA 8), the right to discharge one's religious duties—which John Paul sees as 'a springboard for the principle of the right to religious freedom' (CA 9).

— Over against socialism and liberalism, *Rerum Novarum* defended the principle of solidarity (though Leo did not employ this term but used instead the term 'friendship') (CA 10).

— John Paul sees *Rerum Novarum* as 'an excellent testimony to the continuity within the Church of the so-called "preferential option for the poor"' (CA 11).

— Finally, the pope sums up by noting how these themes which he has highlighted in Leo's encyclical are all situated within a coherent Church teaching which deals with private property, work, the economic process, the role of the State and the nature of the human person (CA 11).

John Paul's re-reading of *Rerum Novarum* in *Centesimus Annus* verges on the anachronistic; he sees in it a depth of insight which the secular historian would never find. At times, too, his praise for Leo's encyclical is almost triumphalist. He does not refer at all to the inadequacies of *Rerum Novarum*, e.g. its overemphasis on the right to private property, its ambivalence on the question of a family wage (see Molony 85–7), or its very limited conception of what a trade union should be. Clearly John Paul's purpose is to nourish the faith of his readers by writing a kind of 'salvation history' of the document, one that emphasises its positive points, that develops points that were not at all clear in the document itself, and that by-passes negative aspects.

The Events of 1989

If we take the concept of salvation history as a key category for understanding the style and tone of *Centesimus Annus* it can throw light not only on the first chapter of the encyclical but also on the following two chapters where the pope examines the 'new things' of today, and particularly the great events of 1989. For salvation history is always written in the light of a particular experience of God's saving power. The Jews wrote their history largely in the light of the Exodus experience. It would seem that in the writing of *Centesimus Annus* the key experience for Pope John Paul II is the collapse of communism in Eastern Europe.

The pope was no detached observer of this process. No less an authority than the former Soviet president, Mikhail Gorbachev, testifies to the major political role played by the pope in the collapse of communism:

> . . . everything that happened in eastern Europe during these last few years would not have been possible without the presence of this pope, without the leading role—the political role—that he was able to play on the world scene. (Gorbachev)

And the pope himself has indicated a qualified acceptance of this assessment (*La Stampa* article). So John Paul's view of the events of the years 1989 and 1990 is that of a committed activist with his own perspective and particular interests. He says openly that his analysis of the events of recent history 'is not meant to pass definitive judgments since this does not fall per se within the Magisterium's specific domain' (CA 3).

Most people who look back on the extraordinary months of late 1989 and early 1990 are left with two dominant images. The first is the dismantling of the Berlin wall and the second is Nelson Mandela walking with extraordinary dignity out of the prison where he had been buried for 27 years. If the Pope had been an African he might well have been inclined to see the second of these events as even more important than the first—

and he might have chosen it as the key development on which to base his reflections on the centenary of *Rerum Novarum*. The result could have been an extremely interesting encyclical. For the pope might then have insisted that the basic split in our world is not between East and West but between North and South; the East and the West would be seen as just two variants of 'the North'; then the collapse of communist economics and ideology in Eastern Europe might be seen as an early stage of the mortal illness of the whole 'Northern' approach to the world.

But John Paul wrote his encyclical out of a Polish experience, not out of an African one. What he offers in much of the encyclical are pastoral reflections (cf. CA 3) arising largely from his own deep involvement in the struggle against an oppressive tyranny. So what he writes has the feel of life. That is its strength. But it also accounts for its limitations.

It has been suggested that in this encyclical the pope's vision is unduly Eurocentric. Perhaps it would be more accurate to suggest that he has a global view, but one that is deeply anchored in a long and exciting Eastern European experience. This is undoubtedly a healthy corrective to the excessive weight given by many of his predecessors to Italian or Western European experience. But it may mean that at times the East European experience unduly colours his interpretation of situations in other parts of the world.

An Acceptance of Capitalism?

Two crucial issues arise in relation to the teaching of this encyclical. The first is whether the pope is accepting capitalism and the second is whether he is rejecting the notion of 'the Welfare State'.

As regards capitalism, John Paul's position is very much in line with the tradition of social teaching laid down by the Church over the previous 100 years: he favours a good deal of free enterprise but is not satisfied with the ideology of liberal capitalism. He distinguishes two meanings of the word 'capitalism' and accepts one of them—though he prefers to use such terms as 'business economy', 'market economy' or 'free economy'(CA 42). He maintains that the free market is 'the most efficient instrument for utilising resources and effectively responding to needs' (CA 34); the mechanisms of the market 'help to utilize resources better . . . promote the exchange of products . . . meet the desires and preferences of another person' (CA 40). He also acknowledges 'the legitimate role of profit as an indication that a business is functioning well' (CA 35).

On the other hand he spells out clearly that there is an unacceptable conception of capitalism—involving an 'absolute predominance of capital' (CA 35), where the economic sector is not controlled by 'a strong juridical framework which places it at the service of human freedom' (CA 42). For the pope the market must be 'appropriately controlled by the forces of society and by the State, so as to guarantee that the basic needs of the whole of society are satisfied' (CA 35). This position is almost exactly what had been demanded by Leo XIII a hundred years earlier.

Despite his acceptance of 'the market economy', John Paul does not back away from the strong stance taken by Paul VI in *Octogesima Adveniens* (CA 42; cf. 4) that the Church has no ready-made universal model for society. Immediately following his acceptance of one meaning of the word 'capitalism', John Paul goes on to insist: 'The Church has no models to present; models that are real and truly effective can only arise within the framework of different historical situations . . . ' (CA 43); and at this point he refers to *Octogesima Adveniens*. We must conclude, then, that in opting for a 'market economy' John Paul is not really giving approval to capitalism as *the* correct system. He is simply laying down certain *minimum conditions* for any acceptable model of society, namely, that the right to own, buy and sell goods, and the right to take other economic initiatives, while they may need to be controlled, must not be entirely abolished. Having asserted the need to respect certain basic rights, the encyclical goes on to insist that the Church 'is not entitled to express preferences for this or that institutional or constitutional solution' (CA 47).

In line with the tradition of his predecessors, and especially of Leo XIII and Pius XI, John Paul concludes that neither liberal capitalism nor communism fulfil the minimum conditions required in order that an economic system should be morally acceptable. The former subordinates people to profit; it gives rise to alienation in workers since it is not concerned whether they grow through their work or are swamped in a maze of destructive, competitive and estranging relationships (CA 41). Communism, on the other hand, turns out to be State capitalism, or what the encyclical (rather oddly) calls 'Real Socialism' (CA 35, 56).[8] This collectivist system actually increases alienation rather than doing away with it (CA 41). In various parts of the encyclical the pope puts forward a philosophical critique of Marxism and Marxist-Leninism (e.g. CA 44–5). He maintains that the deepest cause of the collapse of communism in Eastern Europe was 'the spiritual void brought about by atheism' (CA 24).

The Welfare State

One section of the encyclical caused disappointment, if not dismay, among many committed Catholics who have been concerned about the casualties of the Western capitalist system (e.g. Fitzgerald, 11). It is the part where the pope speaks out strongly against the Welfare State which has, he says, been dubbed 'the Social Assistance State' (CA 48). He maintains that 'the Social Assistance State' has failed to respect the principle of subsidiarity. By intervening directly and unnecessarily it has, he says, given rise to bureaucratic ways of thinking and has deprived people of responsibility and caused a loss of human energies. He goes on to suggest that various categories of people in need, ranging from refugees to drug abusers, can be helped effectively not by the State but only by people close to them who offer them personal care and support (CA 48).

This is undoubtedly a very strong attack on the Western model of State welfare, one that is reminiscent of Catholic social teaching of fifty years ago. Indeed John Paul's concern about the effects of bureaucracy seems to be an echo of the views of Pius XII. No wonder, then, that the encyclical gave rise to some gloating by neo-conservatives who hailed it as an indication that the pope had at last come to his senses and returned Catholic social teaching to its original and true position.

The question has to be faced: has John Paul moved backwards on this aspect of the social question, reinstating a more old-style Catholic approach to social issues, reversing the remarkable advances made by John XXIII, Paul VI and Vatican II?

At first sight it would appear that he has. Some of his remarks about the Welfare State sound quite like the kind of things that were said in the 1980s by Margaret Thatcher and her followers.

However, it is possible to read *Centesimus Annus* in a very different light. There is a strong case for saying that, instead of moving backwards from the Welfare State, John Paul is suggesting that we move onwards towards an approach where the poor are not just objects to be assisted but are subjects in their own right. They are not just to be helped but to be empowered. There is one important passage which lends support to such a reading of the encyclical. Having reaffirmed the Church's 'preferential option for the poor' (CA 57), the pope points out that love for the poor has to be made concrete through the promotion of justice. Justice is not fully attained, he says, so long as the poor are seen as a burden. Then he goes on:

> It is not merely a matter of 'giving from one's surplus', but of helping entire peoples which are presently excluded or marginalised to enter into the sphere of economic and human development. . . . . this . . . requires above all a change of life-styles, of models of production and consumption, and of the established structures of power which today govern societies. Nor is it a matter of eliminating instruments of social organisation which have proved useful, but rather of orienting them according to an adequate notion of the common good . . . (CA 58)

The pope seems to be thinking here mainly of poor nations, but there is no doubt that he would also want his words to apply to poor or marginalised groups within any given country. He wants deprived nations and groups to be allowed and enabled to become self-sufficient economically and so to be no longer a 'burden' to be supported reluctantly by others. So his criticism of what he calls the 'Social Assistance State' is an invitation to committed people to devise ways in which poor people can be empowered economically and in this way get out from under the dead hand of bureaucracy.

The pope himself lived for years at the mercy of the awful Polish communist bureaucracy. So he has had direct experience of how such bureaucracies can smother people, while claiming to be looking after them. And the experience of some groups of marginal people in most Western countries is not so very different from that of Poland. Many of those who are dependent on some kind of unemployment benefit from the State feel themselves disempowered and marginalised by the way in which this 'assistance' is provided.

The real test of a social security system is whether it creates unnecessary *dependency* or whether on the other hand it goes some way towards *empowering* people, making them aware of their own dignity and supporting them in taking initiatives on their own behalf. It may be argued that *Centesimus Annus* does not put forward any practical proposals for how such an empowerment can take place. That is true. But the pope may respond that it is not his task to get into such concrete detail. It is up to committed citizens (both Christians and non-Christians) to find a way forward.

My conclusion is that the pope is not suggesting that Western social security systems be discontinued and that we go back to old-style private 'charity' towards the poor. What he is calling for is that, respecting the principle of subsidiarity, we modify the existing systems so that they become a more humane and empowering way of exercising our solidarity with the victims of our society. It is regrettable that this is not immediately evident to those who read the encyclical superficially. It is even more regrettable that the pope's harsh criticism of the 'Social Assistance State' provides convenient ammunition for those who want to play down their obligation to help the poor, leaving it to be a matter of voluntary and private charity. But, even though there is a danger that the pope's words will be misunderstood or deliberately misinterpreted, nevertheless they are valuable; they stand as a strong and necessary challenge to committed people to go beyond the 'welfare' approach and seek a more radical and effective response to the problems of poverty in today's world.

Anthropocentric

The second half of the encyclical puts forward a philosophical account of the economic and cultural aspects of human society. Much of the writing is very dense and the direction of the argument is not always clear. One interesting and controversial point emerges. It is the extent to which the pope's social philosophy is anthropocentric. Speaking of the goods of the earth, he maintains that, in the past, the primary factor in wealth was 'the natural fruitfulness of the earth' (CA 31). Nowadays, however, human work and human 'know how', skill and technology have become more important (CA 31–2). He does not quite say that these have now become the primary factors, but this seems to be implied.

Many philosophers and scientists share this view. But in recent years an alternative view has gained a good deal of respectability. It suggests that modern scientists have often grossly undervalued the skills and technologies of the past (e.g. the development of seeds, of domestic animals, of ecologically sustainable methods of farming). It maintains that in recent centuries the achievements of modern science and technology have been exaggerated and the Earth has come to be seen as a resource to be exploited. According to this view, the popular glorification of modern technology and scientific achievement has generated an unwarranted optimism; it has led people to the arrogant assumption that new technologies will be found to solve the major problems of development. The only way forward is a recognition that we remain as dependent as ever on the gift of the Earth itself with all its resources of food, water, air, light, energy and raw materials. We must avoid being unduly anthropocentric and learn once more to see ourselves as part of a wider creation, called to live in partnership with the rest of Nature.

The encyclical *Centesimus Annus* shows little sympathy for this 'alternative' and ecological approach to the human situation. Indeed the pope's strong anthropocentric stance is particularly evident when he comes to address the issue of ecology. Having acknowledged that it is a worrying question (CA 37), he nevertheless seems to play it down by suggesting that the destruction of what he calls 'the human environment' is 'more serious' (CA 38).

But behind this obvious difference of approach there is a certain convergence. For the anthropocentrism of John Paul is not absolute. He strongly rejects the notion that we humans are entirely free agents, entitled to shape the world according to our own arbitrary decisions. For the pope, the limits to human freedom come from the 'prior God-given purpose' of the Earth (CA 37). This is quite close to the 'ecological' view which I outlined in the previous paragraph; for the ecologists also hold that humans must respect the order of nature. But there is a significant difference. The pope's corrective for human arrogance is an immediate and explicit reference to the plan of God. The ecologists' approach is more secular. They rely on the earth sciences, on art, and perhaps on nature mysticism to help them discern the order or pattern in nature. If they are believers they may then go on to attribute this pattern to God.

This whole discussion is rather more important than may appear at first sight. For it highlights a point to which I referred above when discussing John Paul's message for the World Day of Peace 1990, which is his main document on the ecological issue. This is the need for some criteria to help people in deciding to what extent they may 'interfere' with nature while still respecting the integrity of creation. Without some guidelines on this question we can hardly begin to decide what would constitute genuine human development. Catholic social teaching still has a long way to go in tackling this issue.

I conclude my commentary on the centenary encyclical by noting an important point made by the pope towards the end of the document. He points out that the social message of the Church will gain credibility not so much from its internal logic and consistency as 'from the witness of actions' (CA 57). In other words he is saying that, in matters of social justice, actions speak louder than words.

SUMMARY

From 1983 onwards Pope John Paul continued to express his concern about injustice in society; he focused particular attention on the right of people to maintain their own culture. The pope has taken up some of the key themes of the liberation theologians. But he and Vatican officials have been greatly concerned about liberation theology, fearing that the Christian faith will be reduced to the service of a Marxist political ideology.

The encyclical *Sollicitudo Rei Socialis* adopts and extends Paul VI's approach to development. At the heart of the encyclical is an elaborate and valuable teaching on the virtue of solidarity; but this does not take much account of the role of confrontation. The encyclical also gives an account of the structures of sin, one which emphasises the priority of personal sin.

The Vatican has been slow in developing its teaching on ecology and the integrity of creation, but it partly made up for this with the Pope's Message for the World Day of Peace in 1990. Catholic Church teaching on justice for women is still underdeveloped.

The consultative process used by the bishops of the USA in preparing joint pastoral letters on social issues is an important contribution to the tradition of Catholic social teaching.

The pope's encyclical on mission is valuable but in some respects it does not reflect the breadth of vision of his earlier encyclicals.

The Centenary encyclical *Centesimus Annus* highlights and reaffirms many of the traditional elements of Catholic social teaching, stressing the continuity of that teaching over the past 100 years. The pope distinguishes two meanings of the word capitalism, rejecting capitalism in so far as it means economic liberalism and accepting it in so far as it means allowing people to take economic initiatives. The encyclical is critical of the Welfare State. But this should not be seen as approval by the pope for the liberal capitalist approach. It can rather be understood as a challenge to people to develop caring societies where the State protects the weaker sectors but does not cripple their initiative or make them dependent on the State. The vision of the pope is anthropocentric, but he tempers this by insisting on the plan of God for the world. This means that there is some convergence between his view and that of those who emphasise the need for humans to respect the integrity of creation.

Questions for review:

1. What aspects of the social justice agenda has John Paul highlighted in his overseas journeys from 1982 onwards?
2. What are the differences between the two Vatican documents on liberation?
3. Why is the notion of solidarity so central to the encyclical *Sollicitudo Rei Socialis*?
4. In what sense does the centenary encyclical accept capitalism and in what sense does it reject it?
5. What is the attitude of the encyclical towards 'the Welfare State'?

Questions for reflection:

1. Why does John Paul's teaching on solidarity in *Sollicitudo Rei Socialis* have a different emphasis from some of his earlier views on the subject?
2. Can you see any acceptable alternative to 'the Welfare State'?
3. How does the practical policy of the Church relate to its official teaching on justice in society and in the Church itself?

Issues for further study:

1. The effect of the collapse of communism in Eastern Europe and central Asia on the countries of 'the South'. The policies of the wealthy nations in GATT negotiations and how they affect the poorer countries.
2. The teaching and action of the World Council of Churches (and its member Churches) on 'Justice, Peace and the Integrity of Creation'. (Read Dorr [1991].)

14

Evaluation

In this concluding chapter I shall try to draw together the threads from the preceding chapters. First of all I shall look at the overall flow of Vatican teaching on social issues, focusing on the elements of continuity and discontinuity in it. This will lead on to an examination of whether, or in what sense, there is a coherent and organic tradition of social teaching in the Catholic Church, stretching over the period of a hundred years. Then I shall outline some of the strengths of Catholic social teaching and some of the areas where it needs further development.

The first Seventy Years

During the period between 1891 and 1961, 'Catholic Social Doctrine' developed into a fairly coherent body of teaching. Two central themes lay at the heart of this teaching:

(1) A particular concern for the poor and powerless, together with a criticism of the systems that leave them vulnerable.

(2) A defence of certain personal rights (above all, the right to private property) against collectivist tendencies.

Throughout these seventy years the popes were consistently critical of both liberal capitalism and socialism. And they put forward certain fundamental principles about human nature and the nature of human society in its economic, political, social, cultural and religious aspects. I have given an account of these principles elsewhere (Dorr [1991] 83–102) so here I shall merely list a few of the more central ones:

— the right of the individual to own property,

— the right of workers to join trade unions,

— the right of the head of a family to be paid a family wage for work done,

— the obligation of mothers to care for their children in the home,

— the duty of the citizen to obey lawful authorities,

— the duty of governments to work for the common good,

— the right of citizens to resist oppression by lawful means,

— the obligation of governments and of the rich and powerful to help the poor,

— the duty of governments and larger agencies to respect the principle of subsidiarity,

— the right of believers to freedom of worship,

— and the right of the Church to carry out its functions and to speak out on issues of public morality.

As we look back on the Catholic social teaching of that period we can see that these principles were so general that they were compatible with a variety of social, economic and political systems. At the time this was not at all so clear. In fact many committed Catholics would have considered that the Church's teaching represented 'a third way' that was neither capitalist nor socialist. The truth is, however, that it was only for a few years after *Quadragesimo Anno* was issued in 1931 that the Vatican was really suggesting such a 'third way', namely the 'corporatist' or vocational system. For the rest of the time the popes did not try to spell out how Catholic social principles should be applied in practice.

Nevertheless, there was a pervasive 'Catholic ethos' which determined the limits of what would be considered a proper implementation of the general principles. For instance, it came to be accepted that governments could and should pay modest old age pensions and that there should be free universal primary education. On the other hand, it was not considered acceptable that there should be a free health service for all, or that the government should have a monopoly of second-level education. This Catholic ethos was a strongly conservative cultural force in society. It was very hostile to anything that smacked of socialism or even social democracy, and of any political movements working for radical social change e.g. re Australia, Hogan *passim*.

In practice, then, the Church gave a certain religious legitimation to the 'free enterprise' model which was dominant in Western society. Its protests against the excesses of capitalism—protests that had reached a peak in the early 1930s—had become muted during the later years of the papacy of Pius XII. The Church still challenged the ideology of liberal capitalism; but its hostility to all forms of socialism was more total, explicit, systematic, and effective. The Church reacted less quickly and strongly against right-wing excesses than against those of the left.

During the late 1920s and early 1930s, the Vatican worked out a rather uneasy *modus vivendi* with fascist leaders in Europe and the pope expressed a certain approval of the fascist-corporatist model of society. Many local Church leaders and lay Catholics followed suit. The accommodation with the fascists in Italy and the Nazis in Germany did not last long. But in Spain, Portugal and much of Latin America the alliance with 'the right' lasted for decades and caused the Church to be perceived as a very right-wing force in society.

The effect of the prevailing Catholic ethos was that the Church became (or continued to be) one of the key agencies opposed to those political movements working for the kind of changes which would have redistributed wealth and power and brought greater equity into society. It remained true that Catholic social teaching was marked by genuine concern for the plight of the poor; and the Church was very deeply and sincerely involved in providing the whole gamut of services needed by the poor. Nevertheless, Catholic teaching, and its associated ethos, had come to represent in practice almost the exact opposite of what is now meant by an 'option for the poor'; it provided support and legitimation for those who resisted the efforts of the poor to gain a fair share of power in society and of its resources.

I have been looking at the elements of continuity in Catholic social teaching and in the Catholic ethos in the period 1891 to 1961. But there was also some discontinuity. As I have noted, there was a period, mainly in the first half of the 1930s, when Vatican teaching seemed to favour a corporatist model of society as an alternative to the capitalist order. What was untypical in this was that it seemed rather more specific than has been customary. Perhaps this impression came not mainly from the content of *Quadragesimo Anno* but from the context: the Italian State was at that very time implementing an elaborately worked out corporatist plan. As time went on, the context changed—and there was a readjustment of emphasis in the interpretation of the papal teaching, with little formal recognition that this was taking place; the teaching of Pius XI simply came to be understood in a less specific way, more typical of the general tradition of 'social doctrine'. In the chapter on Pius XII, I mentioned how he presented his predecessor's view as an ideal that was not realisable until some indefinite future time; this is one of the few occasions when there was an implicit acknowledgment that there was some incompatibility between the teaching of the two popes.

A Change of Direction

A much more significant element of discontinuity came with the teaching of John XXIII. His encyclical *Mater et Magistra* in 1961 shifted the focus of Catholic social teaching by coming out in favour of what amounted to a 'Welfare State' model of society. Furthermore, Pope John no longer gave the right to private property a uniquely privileged place in Catholic social teaching. These modifications quickly led to a significant change in 'the Catholic ethos'. From the time of Pope John, the Catholic Church was no longer the natural ally of the forces in society which were most opposed to structural change.

I have suggested that his two major encyclicals can best be understood not precisely as 'an opening to the left' but more as a decisive move away from the right. Further light may be thrown on the contribution of Pope John by seeing it, not as a change in the main content of Catholic social teaching, but rather as a shift of emphasis from the second to the first of the two main themes in Catholic social teaching—from concern about the right to private ownership to concern about poverty. Pope John and the Church leaders who came after him saw more clearly and insisted more forcefully that the right to private property is not an end in itself; it is simply a means of ensuring that people are not left at the mercy of powerful people or, especially, of an all-powerful State.

This change of emphasis had very profound practical repercussions on the spirituality of Catholics and on the life of the Church. It led to a change in 'the Catholic ethos'. Most Catholics became willing to accept more intervention by the State in economic and social life. Furthermore, a sizeable number of Catholics (including some priests and an occasional bishop) began to *demand* more intervention by the State. They were encouraged by Pope John's 'opening to the left' in the political sphere. With the fervour of new converts they called for a radical restructuring of society of the kind socialism stood for. In support of this stance they could invoke that strand in traditional Catholic social teaching which expressed concern for the poor and which criticised the systems that create poverty and marginalisation.

However, it was not to be expected that the traditional Catholic ethos would be replaced in a short time by such a radical outlook. Many Catholics of the 'new breed' wanted changes of a more modest kind. Others remained largely untouched by the new ideas. They held on to the traditional understanding of Catholic social teaching and continued to be allied with, or supportive of, the conservative forces in society. In many cases the reaction of traditional Catholics was one of real incomprehension in the face of the call for what they saw as socialism if not anarchy. When Church leaders seemed to share some of the new attitudes, the incomprehension of the traditionalists gave way to a sense of betrayal and even a suspicion that left-wing theorists had managed to delude the bishops or even the pope.

The effect of all this was that the old monolithic Catholic ethos began to break up rapidly and was replaced by a new pluralism in Catholic thinking about social, economic and political affairs. This pluralism was welcomed by many not just as an unfortunate fact but as a positive value. Their acceptance of a pluralist approach led them to adopt much of the liberal agenda. These liberal Catholics found support in the widespread assumption that Pope John shared their liberal outlook.

The Vatican Council contributed greatly to the dissolution of the traditional Catholic ethos. It did so mainly by coming out firmly in support of the new 'liberal Catholicism' of the time. Its contribution to 'radical Catholicism' was more limited. But, in declaring the Church's willingness to relinquish privilege and patronage in the interests of its mission, it was adopting a position that was not merely liberal but also radical; for it was distancing the Church from the rich and the powerful.

On the side of the Poor

In Chapter 6 I suggested that Pope John's encyclical *Mater et Magistra* stands as a turning point in Catholic social teaching— the beginning of a process in which the Church came to have new allies and new opponents. This change may turn out to be as profound as that which took place at the time when the Emperor Constantine made Christianity the religion of the Roman Empire. Since that time the Christian Church has generally been part of 'the establishment' in most of the Western world. There were, of course, occasions when governments harassed or persecuted the Church. But almost invariably this was not because Church leaders did not want to be part of the establishment but simply because they had backed the wrong side in political struggles. The crucial point is that it was taken for granted that in normal circumstances the Church should be part of the establishment—and *wanted* to be part of it. Furthermore, when the West became dominant at a global level, the Christian religion was seen as going hand in hand with Western 'civilisation', offering little effective challenge to Western imperialism (again allowing for some few exceptions).

The new Catholic ethos which developed as a result of the work of John XXIII and Vatican II prepared the ground for a truly remarkable shift in the relationship between the Church and the dominant powers in society, a break from the Constantinian conception of the role of the Church. This shift is summed up in the term 'option for the poor'. The first full-fledged commitment to such an option came at Medellín, when Latin American Church leaders pledged themselves to side with the poor in the struggle for justice.

Before long the stance of the Church began to change in other parts of the world where resistance to gross oppression was coming to a head—for instance, in the Philippines, Zimbabwe and South Africa. In these crisis situations the Church as a whole, or key sectors of it, came to be seen—both by defenders of the *status quo* and by those seeking liberation—as one of the most effective opponents of oppressive governments. Far from offering religious legitimation to unjust regimes, it became a powerful 'voice for the voiceless', as Pope John Paul said to the Mexican Indians; and frequently it set out not just to speak on their behalf but to help them to find their own voices.

Though it is mainly on the frontiers of the Western world that the strong prophetic voice of the Church emerged, the repercussions gradually began to be felt nearer the centre. All the Churches—and the Catholic Church especially—are international movements of solidarity. When Christians are persecuted for standing up for justice and human rights in one area, the sense of outrage tends to spread to fellow-Christians elsewhere. This process is speeded up enormously on those occasions when the martyrs of the Third World happen to be citizens of North America or Europe. For instance, the murder of four women missionaries from the USA in El Salvador helped Christians in the West to realise what had been going on in Central America.

It has also become ever clearer that the West can no longer disclaim responsibility for the poverty and exploitation which characterise the Third World. Many Christians in the West have begun to challenge the international economic policies of their own governments in the name of the Gospel. Meanwhile, rising unemployment and other economic difficulties have hit the poorer sections of the population of the Western countries. As a result, large numbers of jobless people have been excluded from the benefits of the Western way of life. Some of the areas where they live have become centres of alienation and, at times, of crime. This has posed a threat to the existing system; and the threat has been met by an increasing tendency in the West to adopt the 'national security' mentality and ideology which had been more typical of the Third World.

For all these reasons many committed Christians and a large number of religious congregations have distanced themselves from 'the establishment' and set out to be with, and on the side of, the poor and the powerless. Furthermore, an increasing number of Church leaders, including the pope, have adopted a prophetic stance and voiced strong protests against the systems which create so much suffering, alienation, and powerlessness.

Facing the Future

Nobody can foretell the outcome of this process. It is possible that most Church leaders will suffer a failure of nerve and will continue to remain establishment figures who occasionally make ineffectual sounds of disquiet. If this happens, then most prophetically-minded Christians will probably become more and more alienated from the Church leadership. On the other hand, it is possible that many Church leaders will take a prophetic stance and will be willing to suffer the consequences. Even if most bishops and other Church leaders take up a challenging position, it is unlikely that they will carry the whole Church membership with them. Some divisions and polarisation are almost inevitable; but their extent will depend on the degree of moral authority the leaders can exert. The position of the pope will be of crucial importance.

It is clear that recent popes have played a key role in setting the direction of Catholic social teaching and giving a lead in social action. They have done so both directly through their own moral authority and charisma, and indirectly through their appointment of bishops and their influence on national hierarchies. Needless to say, some local bishops or hierarchies may still remain quite far to the left or to the right of the pope. But what the pope says and does is usually taken very seriously. (One good example is the key role played by John Paul at the Bishops' meeting in Puebla in 1979.)

The tradition of social teaching in the Catholic Church might be compared to a large ship. For years it was moving forward in one direction, with some relatively minor diversions due largely to the surrounding tides and currents. When Pope John took the helm he began to turn the ship in a different direction. At first there was some pitching and rolling of the ship and some observers thought it was sinking. But eventually the new direction became fairly well established—due to skilful steering and courageous leadership by Paul VI and by John Paul II in the first four years of his papacy. In the decade between 1983 and 1992 a certain doubt has crept in. On the one hand, John Paul played an exceptionally prominent part in the struggle against tyranny in Eastern Europe. But, on the other hand, the pope and the Vatican sent rather mixed messages to Christians struggling for justice in other frontier situations; there was a reaffirmation of the Church's commitment to liberation, to justice, to human rights and to the poor; yet there seemed to be a determined effort to distance the Church from the individuals and the movements that were in the forefront of the struggle for liberation. This caused some confusion. To some it suggested that the Vatican was weakening in its commitment to justice, while others saw it mainly as concern that the Church should not become politicised and should not become tainted with Marxist ideology.

Precisely because of the great weight given to papal teaching there have been many attempts by ideologues to 'harness' this teaching in support of their own political views. The result is that Catholic social teaching has become a battleground on which the ideological struggle between the right and the left is carried out. It is commonly assumed by the ideologues on both sides that John XXIII and Paul VI were moving the Church to the left while John Paul is swinging it back again to the more traditional conservative position. Quade, for instance, claims that Paul VI's *Populorum Progressio* and the documents of the Synods of 1971 and 1974 represent a drift away from the mainstream of Catholic social teaching—a drift that has been sharply corrected by John Paul II (Quade 6–10). To sustain such an argument requires a very selective reading of recent Church documents and statements.

The truth is more complex. Where John Paul has taken a conservative line is primarily in the area of Church discipline; and his actions in this area have had only an indirect impact on social teaching (e.g. action against liberation theologians). In regard to social teaching proper, he has been 'conservative' only in the sense that he has refused to take the kind of stances that more radical Catholics would have liked him to take. For instance, he did not give outright support to the liberation movement in South Africa or to activists in the land agitation movement in Brazil. He has been unwilling to move the Church to the left side of the political spectrum, preferring to hold the moral 'high ground' where he speaks out against oppression in more general terms. Furthermore, he occasionally uses the term 'Catholic social doctrine', a term which seemed to have been abandoned by Paul VI because of its overtones of a timeless, monolithic body of principles. But, as I pointed out in Chapter 11, John Paul's reinstatement of this term is a highly sophisticated one, which effectively purges it of the overtones of dogmatism.

As regards the content of his social teaching there is no real 'backtracking' from the position of Paul VI or John XXIII. Indeed, he has taken much stronger stands against injustice and in defence of human rights than were ever taken by his predecessors. On the two key issues of liberation and 'option for the poor', his teaching has moved forward further than Paul VI rather than backward to an older line.

The refusal of John Paul to move the Church to the left on political issues causes disappointment and even dismay among the people in one ideological camp; and it gives rise to some gloating by those in the opposite camp. This refusal tempts the enthusiasts on *both* sides to claim that the pope has returned Catholic social teaching to a 'traditional' or conservative position. But to make such a claim is to misunderstand both what the pope is trying to do and why he is doing it. He is determined not to get drawn into what he sees as political issues. He was willing to accept the view of Mikhail Gorbachev that he had a major political impact on Eastern Europe; but he was very careful to clarify it in this way:

> 'I do not believe that one can talk about a political role in the strict sense,' replied the Pope, 'because the Pope has as his mission to preach the Gospel. But in the Gospel there is man [*sic*], respect for man, and, therefore, human rights, freedom of conscience and everything that belongs to man. If this has a political significance, then, yes, it applies also to the Pope.' (*La Stampa*)

Obviously there is a very thin line between taking 'a political role in the strict sense' (to use his own words) and taking stances which have 'a political significance'. Critics may disagree with his judgments about particular situations such as those in Lebanon, Poland, Croatia, Nicaragua, Brazil or South Africa. They may have questions about whether the Church can always remain 'above politics'. But it is a gross misunderstanding (or misinterpretation) of the pope's position to assume that he has returned to old-style 'Catholic social doctrine' simply because he adopts a stance on these situations which is different to that of more radical Catholics.

There are 'new right' political theorists who try to use Catholic social teaching as an ideological support not merely for Western democracy but for liberal capitalism. They would like to have John Paul as an ally. But his social teaching, taken as a whole, cannot be used in this way; it is far too critical of 'the West'. So they pick out passages from his statements which, taken out of context, can be used as weapons in their ideological struggle. Some years ago the theorists of the left were engaged in a similar project—making their selections from papal statements to be used as ideological weapons; but in recent years John Paul has given them very little material which can be used in this way! The task facing theologians today is to help people to understand the main direction of Catholic social teaching and to avoid being manipulated by the ideologues of the left or the right.

A Struggle within the Church

It is easy to see why the notion of an option for the poor is divisive in society; but why should it be even more controversial and divisive in the Church itself? One reason is the traditional concern of Church leaders about anything which may cause major disruption in society. A second reason is the tendency of many Church leaders to work out a *modus vivendi* with those who are powerful and wealthy. But there is something more, a point at which the notion of an option for the poor may be perceived by some Church leaders as a threat to *themselves* and not just to the wealthy and powerful in civil society. In the Introduction I suggested that this option can only be understood as an aspect of liberation theology. Those who make such an option are committing themselves not just to helping the poor to resist exploitation and oppression; they also undertake to be an empowering presence with 'ordinary' poor people, helping them to explore and articulate the meaning of the Gospel in their daily lives and struggles. That is a further reason why some Church leaders find it so hard to accept, or even to understand. They experience it, perhaps only half consciously, as a threat to their exclusive authority to interpret the Word of God and the message of Jesus for today.

This helps to explain why there has been very strong resistance from the beginning to the new emphasis on the prophetic role of the Church in society, as this is articulated and lived out by those sympathetic to liberation theology. As I pointed out at the beginning of the book, the issue of an option for the poor has been as divisive as the issue which split the Church at the time of the Reformation. But this time the Roman authorities have been rather more flexible; and the new 'reformers' have not allowed themselves to be pushed out of the Church. There has been an ongoing encounter between the two sides. At its best this has been a dialogue and at its worst it has been a painful conflict. The encounter has taken place in three spheres—the theological, the political and the ecclesiastical.

By and large the liberationists seem to be winning the *theological* debate. In 1975 Pope Paul VI, in the document *Evangelii Nuntiandi*, gave the word 'liberation' a high measure of theological respectability. Pope John Paul II has come more and more to use the language of liberation theology. And the 1986 Vatican document on liberation represented an important 'backing down' by Rome from the hard line adopted only two years previously. However, the movement has not been entirely on one side. The liberation theologians have distanced themselves more and more from Marxism, except in the very broad sense that they still speak of a global imperialism of Western capitalism and they still emphasise the need for a structural analysis of society and for changes at the structural level. One major factor in the growing acceptance of liberation theology has been the convergence between it and feminist theology. This has led to a broadening of both the agenda and the approach of the liberation theologians.

At the *political* level the liberationists won a spectacular early victory. In 1979 the Samosa regime in Nicaragua was overthrown by an alliance of freedom fighters of whom a significant segment were committed Catholics inspired by the theology of liberation. But there was bitter disappointment for those who expected that these 'first fruits' would be followed quickly by others. The alliance between the US government and reactionary forces all over Central America succeeded in holding the line against committed Catholics and others who were struggling for liberation. However, over the following decade, democracy was restored as a result of non-violent struggles in Brazil, Argentina, Chile and in several other parts of the world; and Catholics fired by the ideal of liberation, contributed a great deal to the winning of these victories.

At the *ecclesiastical* level those who favour the liberationist approach have had a more mixed success. Their achievements have been mainly 'on the ground' at the local level. Many thousands of lay leaders, trained and 'formed' in basic communities, have provided a very effective ministry and have helped many Christians to come to a deeper understanding of their faith and to play a far more active and effective part in the life of the Church. There have also been significant efforts in some dioceses to adopt a participative model of planning; where this has succeeded it has led to a real empowerment of lay people. On the other hand, the development of a more collaborative model of Church organisation has been blocked or even reversed in many places as a result of the Vatican policy of appointing bishops who are unsympathetic to such an approach. And Church authorities have often attempted to silence or marginalise theologians who are considered to be liberationist in outlook.

An Organic Tradition?

I have suggested that there was notable continuity in Catholic social teaching over the seventy years between 1891 and 1961; and that since then there has been a shift in emphasis and even, to some extent, in direction. Is there any sense in which we can speak of a consistent tradition of social teaching spanning the whole century? Not in the sense of repeating today the very specific 'principles' which I listed earlier (pp. 352–3) as characteristic of the first seventy years; and not in the sense of having the same 'Catholic ethos' which I described as typical of that period. The 'principles' have been adapted quite significantly, in ways which I have spelled out elsewhere (Dorr [1991] 83–102). And the Catholic ethos has changed enormously both in regard to the attitudes held by typical Catholics and in being far less monolithic than in the past.

It is, however, possible to speak of an organic tradition in a more general sense—a sense that is, nevertheless, authentic. Pope John Paul presents his own teaching on socio-political and economic issues as part of an organic tradition. By this he does not mean a rigid system made up of a body of immutable truths, but rather a pattern of teaching which has been consistent over the years, while allowing for development and even, perhaps, changes of emphasis. In this view the coherence or consistent character of the teaching is based on an enduring commitment of the Church to certain basic values such as human dignity, the value of the person as a worker, the right of everybody to the conditions required to be free and responsible, the importance of human community and solidarity, and the notion of the common good as meaning the welfare of all—in a way that gives priority to the person rather than the State.

These values, in turn, are based on certain fundamental truths about the human person, the nature of society, and the role of the Church. They are truths that include the following:

— Every person is called by God to share in the divine creative work, in the redemption of the world, and in the promotion of the Reign of God.

— Human cooperation in creation, redemption, and the furthering of God's Reign is brought about through an integral development which has social, economic, political, cultural, and religious aspects.

— An integral development is one where the spiritual and the temporal are not sharply opposed to each other and where the mission of the Church is not limited to purely religious matters.

John Paul's account of the continuity between *Rerum Novarum* and present teaching (CA 4–11) brings out the fact that, even a century ago, Leo XIII was defending the fundamental truths and values which lie at the heart of the Church's social teaching today. Furthermore, this continuity is not just nominal but is the basis for continuity in practical *implications*. For instance, John Paul, when defending the right of Brazilian workers to form trade unions, could present his teaching as part of a tradition stretching back to Leo XIII. Again, there is a real continuity in the misgivings expressed by Leo XIII, Pius XI, Paul VI, and John Paul II both about capitalist society and about Marxism.

The conclusion which emerges from what I have been saying is that there is a certain organic unity in Catholic social teaching, even though there has been considerable development and significant shifts of focus and emphasis over the years. It would be foolish to imagine that the Church can provide clear practical guidelines to politicians, economists or planners. But the vision of life derived from the Gospel and developed in the Church over centuries does provide Christians and all people of good will with important criteria which can be of great help in their ongoing search for ways of living in society that are truly just and humane.

However, the body of Catholic social teaching is not a single indissoluble whole. It is composed of many different strands and some of these are more developed and more valuable than others. So I move on now to explore some of the strengths and weaknesses of this tradition of social teaching.

The Strengths of Catholic Social Teaching

— The *first* and perhaps the greatest strength of the tradition of Catholic social teaching is that it is humanistic. Not, of course, humanist in the sense of excluding faith or the supernatural. I am referring to the humanistic aspect which Pope John Paul constantly emphasises—e.g. in his first encyclical (RH 14–5), in the centenary encyclical (CA 53–5) and when he was acknowledging that his Gospel message could have 'political' effects in Eastern Europe, as I noted above. In the past this was expressed mainly by saying that the Church's social teaching was founded on 'natural law'. In recent times this term 'natural law' is used more rarely; what John Paul says is that the Church's social teaching is based on a Christian anthropology.

A particular advantage of having a social teaching that is humanistic is that it aims to appeal not merely to Christians but to all people of good will. Furthermore, it means that there is room for a constant dialogue with other traditions—not merely a desire to *teach* others but also a willingness to *learn* from them. Perhaps the most obvious example of this is the way in which over the past generation the popes have taken up and used the language of human rights which was originally articulated not in the Catholic tradition but in the humanistic traditions of enlightenment France and the newly independent USA. More recently the Church has begun to make its own the moral wisdom that is emerging through the ecological movement and the feminist movement, neither of which were particularly Catholic at first.

— A *second* great strength of Catholic social teaching as it is understood today is that it is not just humanistic in a vague general sense. It focuses particular attention on two key human-istic values which serve to give content to the teaching and provide criteria which can be applied in practice. These values are participation and solidarity. Participation is crucial because it means a sharing of power; where this value is respected, people themselves can claim their rights and shape their own destiny. Solidarity is vital because it rescues people from individualism and gives them a sense of being responsible for each other and for the welfare of the community. It is a virtue which gives them the will and the energy not to be content with theory and words but to act justly and to work and struggle for justice.

— The *third* strong point of the Church's social teaching is that it is not too detailed or specific but is compatible with a certain pluralism. It is open to a variety of applications in different continents and different circumstances. Very closely related to this is the fact that, while touching on the political sphere in a general way, Catholic social teaching seeks to avoid being identified with the policies of any particular political party or movement. It claims rather to offer criteria by which such specific policies may be evaluated.

The official Church has learned how important it is to keep at a certain distance from the popular trends or preferred options of any particular era, even those which seemed very admirable to leading Christians at the time. Around the time of Leo XIII it seemed to many that the true Christian option was a revival of the guild system; in the 1930s it seemed that a 'vocational' or corporative organisation of society was the only correct Christian answer to social problems; after both World Wars there was a strong move to identify Church teaching with the policies of 'Christian Democrat' parties in many countries; in the aftermath of John XXIII's encyclicals many Christians opted for a 'Welfare State' model; in the 1960s and 1970s 'Christians for Socialism' and other New Left movements seemed to many to be the only authentic way forward; in the 1980s and 1990s some sectors of the Church came to believe that the solution lies in 'New Right' approaches.

There have been occasions when various popes have flirted to some extent with one or other of these trends—but never to the extent to which the enthusiasts would have wished. On the whole the pope and bishops have tried to keep the official Church 'above politics'; they have maintained a certain distance from specific applications of the general principles, leaving it to lay Christians as citizens to opt for one policy or another. However, they have not hesitated to suggest that some of the proposed policies (particularly left-wing ones) are not compatible with the basic principles of Catholic social teaching.

—A *fourth* strength of Catholic social teaching is that it is based on a good deal of social analysis, on a serious attempt to identify the historical, economic and cultural root causes of global poverty and inequity. Consequently it is not content with speaking out against unjust actions or people but condemns the sinful *structures* which are both the effect and the cause of acts and attitudes of social injustice.

—The *fifth* strong point about the Church's social teaching, especially as it has developed in more recent years, is that it is biblical, at least in the sense that it can find a fairly solid basis in the Bible. This means that there is ample room for ecumenical dialogue on social issues with other Christian Churches, most of whom tend to rely more on the Bible than on a 'natural law' or humanistic basis.

— A *sixth* strength of Catholic social teaching is that it is prophetic in the sense of being radically challenging and inspirational. It is uncompromising in its condemnation of oppression and exploitation, and of the consumerism and alienation which are linked to them. It is in direct continuity with the words of the Old Testament prophets in denouncing injustice and announcing new hope for all, above all for the poor and oppressed. At its best it can be experienced as a sharing in the liberating task of Jesus. It calls on Christians and all people of good will to work for a fundamental reshaping of society both at the global and the local levels. Within the past generation it has come to a deeper understanding of the Church's call to side with the poor and the powerless in working for justice; and it has found in the term 'option for the poor' a striking and effective way of expressing this call. For these reasons Catholic social teaching is inspiring and evangelical, a teaching which lies at the heart of the Christian faith.

Weaknesses in the Social Teaching Tradition

There are a number of areas in which Catholic social teaching is somewhat weak or at least insufficiently developed.

— In the *first* place, it has not yet become sufficiently eco-logical in its scope. In a sense, this is the negative aspect of its greatest strength which is its humanistic character; it has become unduly anthropocentric. In one way it was a step forward when Church leaders began to switch their emphasis from 'natural law' to 'the defence of the human'. In a similar way it was a kind of progress when, at about the same time, theologians began to replace their courses and books on 'The Theology of Creation' with 'Theological Anthropology'. But what tended to become lost as a result of these changes was a sense of the unity of creation as a whole. What is needed now is to situate the Church's social teaching and the theological anthropology on which it is based within the context of a renewed theological cosmology or theology of creation.

As I pointed out in the previous chapter, Pope John Paul affirms the integrity of creation. But Catholic teaching has not yet provided us with guidelines for knowing how to respect this integrity. We do not yet have criteria for discerning the limits of human 'interference' with Nature. There is need for serious work to be done on whether, or in what sense, animals have rights; and this should be related to study and reflection on the 'right' to continued existence of various species of living beings and even of places of natural beauty. As I noted in my commentary on *Centesimus Annus*, Pope John Paul (like many other Catholic theologians) articulates the duty of respect-ing the environment in terms of its effect on *humans*. But he supplements this by invoking as an ultimate criterion the 'prior God-given purpose' of the Earth (CA 37). An urgent task for theologians today is to find ways of discerning this 'God-given purpose'; it is not enough to rely on common sense or to expect some ecclesiastical or secular authority to decide in a volun-taristic or arbitrary manner what it is.

— A *second* weakness of Catholic social teaching is that the human values which it embodies may not be as fully transcultural as they are assumed to be. These values were articulated almost entirely in a Western context; and at present Rome seems unduly reluctant to allow the local Churches of different continents to develop their own articulations of social teaching. The present body of teaching, for all its merits, needs to be supplemented, and partially corrected, by the values that have been or will be articulated in situations where Christianity is incarnated in, say, Asian or African cultures. An example may bring out the point. At present, Catholic social teaching seems to presuppose that the family means the nuclear family; so it neglects or ignores the rich values embodied in the extended family, although this is an institution which plays a central role in the lives of most African peoples and many of the peoples of Asia (e.g. the Lebanese and the Pakistanis).

Another example raises even more far-reaching questions. Catholic social teaching now places a lot of emphasis on the right to development. But, as I pointed out towards the end of Chapter 7, it is essential to distinguish between development and *Western-style* development; and many Church leaders and theologians have not succeeded in holding on to this distinction, despite the helpful approach adopted by Paul VI in *Populorum Progressio*. Consequently, here is a real danger that the promotion of Catholic social teaching (as presently articulated) may contribute to the imposition of Western values on the peoples of other cultures. It may also lead to the neglect, in Catholic social teaching, of some of the most fundamental values of non-Western cultures e.g. serenity, respect, contemplation, a sense of oneness with Nature or with 'the All', rootedness, harmony, cooperation, and gentleness.

There are indications that when 'development' is promoted in non-Western cultures it brings with it exploitativeness, competition, and consumerism. Of course some people believe that these problems are characteristic not of European or Western culture as such but only of the 'decadent West'; and that they can be remedied by an influx of renewed faith coming from the resurgent Catholics of Eastern Europe. But one must remember that Eastern Europe was totally dedicated to 'development'; and the effects there were at least as horrifying as in the West. And, granted that communism was imposed on several East European countries from outside, it can scarcely be argued that this absolves the peoples of these countries from all complicity in the evil effects brought about by the 'development plans' of their governments.

It is quite true that the cultures of Eastern and Western Europe have been permeated at a deep level by the Christian faith. But it would be far too simple to dismiss exploitativeness as just an accidental and passing aberration of modern Western culture. Thomas Berry has put forward some strong arguments in favour of the view that insensitivity to the Earth and lack of reverence for life have very deep roots not only in Western culture but even in the Judaeo-Christian tradition. This suggests the urgent need for Catholic social teaching to be far more open than in the past to the values of non-Western cultures and of other religious visions of life.

— A *third* area in which Catholic social teaching is somewhat weak or undeveloped concerns the issue of alternatives to the present model of development. This is closely related to the topic I have just been discussing. It is understandable— though inexcusable—that *politicians* should play down the problems associated with a reliance on rapid economic Western-style development as a solution to problems of poverty, inequity, and unemployment. But it is more difficult to understand why those who articulate the Church's social teaching should fail to point out sharply and trenchantly the futility and sheer foolishness of relying on 'development' to solve such major problems. Could it be due to a desire of mainline Catholic social thinkers to be 'respectable'? Perhaps this leads them to cling on to an outdated paradigm, and prevents them from keeping in touch with the most recent advances in the earth sciences and social sciences, or gives rise to a certain lack of creativity in drawing out their implications. Of course it is true that those who cry out against 'development' are often dismissed as unrealistic cranks. But since the Church is called to be prophetic it has to be somewhat 'unrealistic' in the sense that it cannot allow the prevailing situation to be the sole determinant of what is considered realistic.

A more benign explanation for the failure to emphasise alternatives is a fear by Church leaders of falling once more into the trap of proposing an alternative 'blueprint' for society. What is required of the Church in this situation is not some particular Catholic blueprint but rather an insistence on the urgent need of a search for alternative models of living and of organising society. The Church need not claim to have the answer; but it could certainly list some of the criteria, e.g. reliance on renewable energy, technology that does not lead to mass unemployment, policies which favour public transport systems rather than private vehicles, production units that are not so big and so specialised that the workers are alienated from the products produced, reliance as far as possible on local food products and raw materials. (Some of these criteria are already implicit in the Church's traditional emphasis on the principle of subsidiarity; but the implications need to be spelled out.) It is also important to take account of a point noted as early as 1973 by Ivan Illich in his essay 'Energy and Equity'. He showed that an increased use of energy goes hand in hand with an increase in the gap between the rich and the poor; this brings out the close links between the ecological issue and the justice issue (Illich [1978] 110–43) and the urgent need for an alternative to the present dominant model of human development.

— The *fourth* and perhaps the biggest lacuna in the social teaching of the Catholic Church is its failure to provide an adequate treatment of the issue of justice for women. Amata Miller has written a striking study, the title of which sums up her main point: 'Catholic Social Teaching—What Might Have Been if Women were not Invisible in a Patriarchal Society' (A. Miller [1991]). She stresses the 'fundamental congruence' between the basic values undergirding Catholic social teaching and the values of the women's movements of the past hundred years. But she spells out a major blind spot in those who articulated Catholic teaching during that period: they did not take account of the real situation of women in the work-place during that time.

Miller documents the exploitation of women in the economic life of the nation. This is the basis for what is perhaps the most valuable aspect of her study, namely, the way in which she inserts the victimisation of women into the mainstream of social injustice, rather than allowing 'women's issues' to remain in a separate category. She brings out how the commitment of Church leaders to the ideal of 'woman in the home' prevented them acknowledging (or perhaps even seeing) the numbers of women who were going out to work; and how this caused them to overlook the gross exploitation of women's labour. Miller shows that the blindness in relation to women at work persisted during the greater part of the past century of social teaching; and she holds that even John Paul II has maintained an unrealistic approach on this issue. She goes on to bring out very effectively the gap which has been left in Catholic social teaching. She speculates shrewdly about the advances that might have been made 'if church leaders had been able to see and hear the women of their times, and if women struggling for justice had found consistent support in the official teaching of the church'. For her, what is in question is a serious sin of omission which weakens the strength of the 'exhortations to justice in the workplace' issued by Church leaders like Pope John Paul and 'makes their calls for respect of life hollow and partial to many'.

I suggested in Chapter 12 (pp. 300–2) that *Laborem Exercens* may be understood as a significant break away from previous Church teaching about women and work. But even if the official teaching on women and work has changed, the change has been so surreptitious and unheralded that it may well have been counter-productive in its effect. I suspect that it has left Church spokespersons with no clear sense of where Catholic social teaching now stands on this issue. The result is that they do not speak out strongly on the various kinds of exploitation of women which commonly occur nowadays in the work-place. This spares women from hearing the old-fashioned and patronising defence of women which they often heard from Church leaders in the past. But the resulting silence may well be even more damaging, because it makes women at work more 'invisible' than ever.

Probably the most impressive statement by the official Church on justice from the point of view of women is a short passage in the document issued in 1971 by the Bishops' Synod in Rome. In it the bishops urged that women should have a proper share of responsibility and participation both in society and in the Church (JW 42). It is time that the official Church took up this theme once again. The controversy surrounding the efforts of the bishops of the USA to prepare a document about women is a clear indication of how difficult it will be to find a way forward so long as the main articulators of Catholic social teaching are male clerics. The Church must find a means of enabling women themselves to play a more central role in formulating the social teaching and policies of the Church, especially those which concern women.

— The *fifth* area in which Catholic social teaching needs further development and clarification has to do with the role of the Church in politics. There are some general guidelines which have been developed by the Church over the past 100 years. Central to the accepted approach is a practical distinction between the area of 'politics' and that of 'religion'—even though the two overlap to some extent. Within the terms of this distinction, the Church's main concern is with 'religion'; but by its nature this includes some involvement in the social and political spheres of life. It is accepted that Church leaders are not entitled to claim any special competence in purely political matters. Lay Christians, in their capacity as citizens, are encouraged to take part in politics, even party politics. But the Church discourages priests and members of religious communities from becoming actively involved in overtly political activity, or party politics; the aim is to ensure that the Church does not compromise its basic function by becoming too closely identified with any particular party.

These guidelines have served the Church well and are not to be discarded lightly. But they still leave some awkward questions—particularly now that Church leaders are insisting so strongly on social justice and are committing the Church to the defence of the poor and oppressed. When Church leaders speak out on justice issues they enter on an area which is 'political'. The distinction between politics in a broad sense and 'party politics' is very helpful where a number of different democratic parties, sharing the same fundamental moral values, differ in regard to priorities and programmes; the Church can then maintain its neutrality in relation to all of them. But what happens if there are two major parties and the policy of one of them is to maintain an unjust and totally undemocratic social order while the other party is committed to social justice? What if a tyrannical government outlaws democratic opposition and the only effective resistance is through movements which are labelled as subversive? If Church leaders speak out clearly and specifically on issues of justice in such situations they will be understood to be taking sides on political issues, and will in fact be no longer keeping aloof from 'party politics'.

In practice, of course, Church leaders cope with the problem by speaking out on various justice issues while pointing out that they are not identifying themselves with any particular party policy. But it would be helpful if Catholic social teaching were to acknowledge more clearly the difference between this kind of situation and one where the differences between political parties are concerned not with fundamental social justice but only with the practical means of attaining it.

— The *sixth* area in which Catholic social teaching needs to be developed more fully concerns the matter of social analysis. In listing the strengths of the tradition I noted that present social teaching is based on a good deal of social analysis. But this analysis is incomplete; there is some attempt to explore the historical roots of international injustice; but there seems to be a reluctance to engage in an analysis of the root causes of social injustice at the national and local levels. In *Laborem Exercens*, Pope John Paul went some way towards closing this gap; but even his account remained rather generic and put the focus more on the past rather than the present.

It seems that the reason why Catholic social teaching is so reticent on this issue is because social analysis reveals and high-lights the extent to which most modern societies are divided into different social classes. All through the past century Church authorities have tended to shy away from the question of the class structure of society. This springs from an understandable desire not to foment class struggle. But there seems to be a failure to distinguish between acknowledging the reality and approving of it. Critics would say that Church leaders are unwilling to acknowledge the extent to which the Church is unduly 'tied' to the interests of the more powerful classes in society. There was some truth in this accusation in the past; so it is not surprising that Church people at that time tended to see social analysis as a Marxist idea.

When Church leaders in Latin America and elsewhere made 'an option for the poor' they were setting out to correct this imbalance. The sectors of the Christian community who favour such an option are also committed to serious social and structural analysis; for it is only in this way that they can discover who 'the poor' really are and what are the fundamental causes of their poverty. But the new commitment to social analysis has not yet had its full impact on the main Church documents on social justice issues.

— A *seventh* point on which the teaching of the Church remains insufficiently developed is related to the previous one; it concerns the question of confrontation and conflict. I have touched on aspects of this in various parts of this book and have discussed the topic of confrontation at some length when examining John Paul's teaching on solidarity in *Sollicitudo Rei Socialis*. It suffices to say here that the traditional social teaching put so much emphasis on harmony and consensus that it played down the fact that opposition can at times be an essential aspect of working for social justice. The teaching of John Paul on solidarity provides a partial corrective for this oversight. But, even yet, insufficient attention is paid to this question. Vatican authorities seem reluctant to say anything which might be taken as an incitement to the poor or the powerless to demand their rights; and priests or members of religious communities who help the poor in organising themselves to press for their rights are often frowned on as being too political or as being involved in a wrong form of liberation theology.

Furthermore, John Paul's concept of solidarity, though it is very valuable, seems to presuppose that there is consensus in society on fundamental social values. The fact is, however, that there is a radical pluralism in most modern societies. Many Christians find themselves in situations where society is created as much through conflict as through consensus and harmony. So there is need for more realistic guidelines to help those who are struggling for social justice in such situations; they need support and guidance in finding ways to struggle for their own basic values while respecting the views of those whose vision of life is quite different.

— An *eighth* issue on which the social teaching of the Church is in need of further development concerns the question of justice within the Church itself. The only major document in which this issue is taken up courageously is 'Justice in the World' issued by the Bishops' Synod of 1971. It recognised that if the Church's social teaching about society is to be credible and effective, then the Church itself should be a living witness to this teaching. The crucial test is whether Church leaders are prepared to take seriously the commitments made in that Synod, and ensure that the institutional Church itself gives more effective witness to justice in its structures and style of operation. Many observers of the Church accuse it of authoritarianism at every level—of not offering lay people, especially women, effective participation in decision-making. A lot of people, above all in the English-speaking world, are quite shocked at the continued use of sexist language in official documents and at other instances of sexism which they see in the Church. Some go much further and accuse it of being grossly patriarchal in its organisation and mode of acting. The most effective way of responding to these complaints will be to change the way in which the Church's social teaching is articulated; and this is the next point which I shall consider.

— The *ninth* and final lacuna in the social teaching of the Catholic Church is not a matter of its content but rather of the way in which the teaching is worked out. In recent years the Vatican has begun to consult lay experts more frequently. But private consultation with specialists is not sufficient. The US Catholic bishops and the World Council of Churches have shown that it is possible to have a much more widespread and public type of consultation. The Roman authorities must find more effective ways of listening to the *sensus fidei*. People nowadays expect to be consulted about matters which touch their own lives. Many Catholics would like to be actively involved in the formulation of the Church's social teaching. They have much to contribute.

Conclusion

I have tried to spell out as clearly as possible some areas where there is room for improvement in Catholic social teaching. But I hope that this will not give the impression that I am playing down the strengths which I outlined earlier. Despite its inadequacies, the tradition of social teaching in the Church is one of which we Christians can be proud. An awareness of the richness of this tradition should encourage us to develop it even further and to give a more effective witness to it in our lives. This tradition calls us to examine our actions, our life-styles and our structures and to make sure that there is not too wide a gap between what we are proclaiming and what we are actually doing.

The task of building a just and truly humane world is a formidable one. But those who engage in this work receive inspiration, encouragement and hope from the Catholic tradition of social teaching. It is a tradition which is long; and within the past generation the teaching has grown stronger, deeper and clearer. The Church has committed itself to the belief that working for justice in the world is an essential part of preaching the Gospel.

In recent times the full implications of this commitment have emerged more clearly. The Church now acknowledges that in preaching the Gospel and working for justice it must make an option for the poor. It must be in effective solidarity with those who are powerless and voiceless and must seek to empower them and give them back their voice. Catholic social teaching recognises that the poor and the powerless are 'God's favourites' (to use the words of Pope John Paul). They can no longer be seen as just the ones who are to be helped by others. They are called by God to be key agents, under God, in bringing justice and liberation to the world.

SUMMARY

In the seventy years between 1891 and 1961 Catholic social teaching had a high level of consistency. There was a 'Catholic ethos' which led the Church to give religious backing to conservative political groups. An important change of direction in social teaching and in the Catholic ethos began with Pope John and came to fruition at Medellín. This has led to a struggle within the Church between those who favour liberation theology and those who oppose it. Liberation theology has gradually become more acceptable. It has had a big impact at the political level and in the local Churches in many places. But those who try to live it out are still looked at with some suspicion by Rome.

Despite occasional changes of emphasis and one major change of direction there is an organic unity in the tradition of social teaching over the past century. Among the strong points of Catholic social teaching are its humanistic character, its practical emphasis on participation and solidarity, its refusal to become identified with any political party, the fact that it identifies structures of sin, its biblical aspect, and the fact that it is radical in its commitment to the poor and is therefore evangelical and inspirational.

Among the less well-developed aspects of Catholic social teaching are a failure to be adequately ecological and cosmological, an unduly Western and centralising character, a lack of emphasis on alternative models of development, an inadequate treatment of justice for women, an unduly simple distinction between politics in the broad sense and party politics, an insufficient use of social analysis to reveal the class structures of society, a playing down of the importance of contestation in the struggle for justice, a failure to focus on issues of justice in the Church, and a lack of adequate consultation processes which would enable many Christians to play a full role in articulating the teaching. Despite these inadequacies Catholic social teaching provides support and inspiration for Christians in their efforts to bring justice to the world.

Questions for review:

1. Describe 'the Catholic ethos' of about 1950.
2. What were the stages in the break-up of this outlook?
3. In what sense is there continuity in Catholic social teaching over the past hundred years?
4. What are the strong points of the Catholic social teaching tradition?
5. In what areas does it need further development?

Questions for reflection:

1. What does 'the integrity of creation' mean to you at the level of theology and in the everyday decisions of life?
2. What kind of process would be most helpful in enabling many Christians of all kinds to play a more active role in exploring and articulating Catholic social teaching?
3. Why is the Church's teaching on justice for women so under-developed and so controversial? What ways forward would you suggest?
4. Is Catholic social teaching unduly Western in its underlying values and assumptions? How can there be dialogue between it and the teachings of Islamic Fundamentalism or the vision of those who belong to the Eastern religions or to primal-traditional religions?

Issues for further study:

1. The meaning of respect for creation, including the issue of animal rights.
2. The concept of patriarchy. (Read some feminist studies of the topic.)

Notes

Chapter 1, pp. 13–34.

1. For a full account of the writing of the document and the changes in its different drafts, see Molony 64–105; cf. Duncan 69–70. It would be wrong to suggest that *Rerum Novarum* represents an entirely new beginning; for there is a good deal of coherence between it and papal teaching of the previous 150 years (see Coleman [1991] 3–4). Nevertheless it represents a significant turning-point in the tradition.

2. For a helpful account of Leo's position on the limits of the State's competence and duty of intervention in economic affairs see Murray (1953) 552–60.

3. In RN 29 Leo contrasts the 'richer class' with 'the mass of the poor' and adds that wage-earners 'mostly belong to that class' (i.e. the poor).

4. 17. E.g. RN 35: ' . . . the gulf between vast wealth and sheer poverty will be bridged over, and the respective classes will be brought nearer to one another'; RN 15: in a State it is 'ordained by nature that these two classes should dwell in harmony and agreement'.

5. In the very first sentence of the encyclical (RN 1) the pope distinguishes between 'the sphere of politics' and 'the cognate sphere of practical economics'. The Latin text reads: ' . . . ut commutationum studia a rationibus politicis in oeconomicarum cognatum genus aliquando defluerent.' The Italian draft text on which the Latin was based reads: 'Le gravi agitazioni . . . che travagliano da tempo la presente società non potevano rimanere nei soli confini dell' ordine politico, ma, come era naturale, dovevano farsi sentire anche nell' ordine economico e sociale, per la connessione che esiste tra i diversi ordini dell' umano consorzio.'—see Antonazzi 78; cf. Leo XIII, *Praeclara Gratulationis* BP IV 102 where he distinguishes between the social question and the political question and says he has treated the former in an earlier encyclical (i.e. *Rerum Novarum*) and then he goes on to speak of the political question; cf. also Leo XIII, *Graves de Communi*.

6. In the next chapter I shall examine Leo's teaching on this question of working for change by democratic means.

7. Cf. Vidler 144; also Calvez and Perrin 353: 'It would be foolish to conclude . . . that Leo XIII entertained any romantic attachment to the past. The men of the last years of the eighteenth century were blameworthy, not because they had destroyed the "ancient working-man's guilds", but because they had put no other organization in their place.'

8. For the various words used in the original Italian drafts and in successive Latin texts, see Antonazzi 157–75.

9. In an address which he gave six years before *Rerum Novarum*, Leo had followed a similar line. He called for unity—but what he had in mind was that Catholics should unite with each other rather than with others; see

Leo XIII, *C'est avec* in *Pope and People* 68–9. Some years later (in 1895) in a letter to the bishops of the USA, Leo reluctantly acknowledged that religiously neutral trade unions may sometimes be necessary—see *Longinqua Oceani* in *Great Ency.* 372: ' . . . Unless forced by necessity to do otherwise, Catholics ought to prefer to associate with Catholics . . . '

Chapter 2, pp. 35–60.

1. For an explanation of the abbreviations 'BP' and '*Great Ency*' and of the sources used see my bibliography of official documents, p. 397.
2. Cf. *Quod Apostolici Muneris* BP I, 38, *Great Ency* 32: '. . . the relations of the State and Religion are so bound together . . . that whatever is withdrawn from religion impairs by so much the dutiful submission of the subject and the dignity of authority.' In a valuable study of Pope Leo's teaching, John Courtney Murray notes that his polemical bias led him closer to absolutist conceptions than to Christian and medieval ones; so he put the stress 'on the duty of the people to consent to the king's legislation, rather than on the duty of the king to obtain the consent of the people . . . '—see Murray, (1953) 23; (1952) 546, note 50.
3. Six years later the pope followed the same line in his encyclical *Libertas Praestantissimum* (BP II, 194–6; *Great Ency* 151) where he said that since religion 'derives the prime origin of all power directly from God Himself . . . it admonishes subjects to be obedient to lawful authority as to the ministers of God . . . forbidding all seditious and venturesome enterprises calculated to disturb public order and tranquillity . . . ' It is on this basis that Leo claims that religion of its essence is wonderfully helpful to the State.
4. It should perhaps be noted that when Leo speaks of seditious activity ('religio . . . vetat . . . seditiose facere') he is using a term which has a moral judgment built into it; in Catholic tradition (and elsewhere) sedition means not just resistance to authority but unjustified resistance; on this question see Bride, especially cols. 1969–71 and 1987.
5. This is from the encyclical *Diuturnum*; cf. *Quod Apostol* (BP I, 34, *Great Ency* 28): 'But should it please legislators and rulers to enjoin or sanction anything repugnant to the divine and natural law, the dignity and duty of the name of Christian and the Apostolic injunction proclaim that one "ought to obey God rather than humans" (Acts 5:29)'; cf. *Libertas Praestantissumum* BP II, 202, *Great Ency* 156: 'But when anything is commanded which is plainly at variance with the will of God . . . it is right not to obey.'
6. Cf. also his encyclical *Graves de Communi*, issued in 1901 (BP VI, 210).
7. BP II, 210: ' . . . fas est aliam quaerere temperationem reipublicae . . . ' The common English translation says simply, 'it is lawful to seek . . . a change of government'. The French translation in the Bonne Presse edition is, 'il est permis de chercher une autre organisation politique'— see BP II, 211.
8. BP III, 118: 'Thence it follows that, in these kinds of situations, all the newness pertains to the political form of civil power, or to its mode of transmission; it in no way affects the power considered in itself . . . . in

all hypotheses, civil power, considered as such, is from God, always from God.' (*Great Ency* 257–8 translation emended).

9. It should be noted that this teaching of the pope was given in the same encyclical in which he ruled out any attempt to overthrow existing governments.

10. As an indication that Leo continued to hold this view to the end, one may note the following passage from his 1901 encyclical on Christian Democracy, *Graves de Communi*: ' . . . the mind and the action of Catholics who are devoted to the amelioration of the working classes, can never be actuated with the purpose of favouring and introducing one government in place of another.'—BP VI, 210, *Great Ency* 483 .

11. Zigliara 266–7, quoted in Bride col. 1970. According to Zigliara 'defensive resistance' in this case would not be a rejection of the authority of God since the ruler, through the abuse of power, would no longer be acting as the agent of God. For background on the traditional teaching and an account of how this teaching came to be modified in the nineteenth century see Leclercq 163–207; cf. René Coste, 'Le problème de la légitimité de principe de la guerre révolutionnaire', in Theas *et al* 191–208.

12. Cf. Encyclical *Sapientiae Christianae*, BP II, 282, *Great Ency* 196: 'The Church . . . since she not only is a perfect society in herself, but superior to every other society of human growth, . . . resolutely refuses, prompted alike by right and by duty, to link herself to any mere party and to subject herself to the fleeting exigencies of politics.'

13. For general background to the political teaching of Leo XIII, and particularly for an explanation of its polemical context, as well as a careful identification of the forces defined by the pope as 'the Enemy' see Murray (1953) 23; also Murray (1953) 145–214, 551–67; (1954) 1–33. For more general background on the period see Aubert (1963); also the early chapters of Aubert et al.; also Molony passim and Duncan 56–64.

14. On the change of approach by Leo XIII see the articles by Murray, especially (1953) 145–214. Cf. Holland and Henriot 75: ' . . . Leo XIII . . . while still a traditionalist, had switched from hostile rejection to diplomatic outreach toward the modern world.'

15. Cf. *Exeunte Jam Anno* BP II, 232, *Great Ency* 168: ' . . . rationalism, materialism, and atheism have begotten socialism, communism, and nihilism—fatal and pestilential evils, which naturally, and almost necessarily, flow forth from such principles.' In *Laetitiae Sanctae* BP III, 244–6, Pope Leo bemoans the growth of discontent and envy between the classes of society; he finds in the workers 'a tendency . . . to shrink from toil, . . . to have expectations of things above them, and to look forward with mindless hope to a future equalisation of property.' (my translation)

16. ' . . . We are alluding to that sect of people who, under the motley and all but barbarous terms and titles of Socialists, Communists, and Nihilists, . . . bound intimately together in baneful alliance, . . . strive to carry out the purpose long resolved upon, of uprooting the foundations of civil society at large.' (*Great Ency* 22 translation adapted); cf. *Diuturnum* BP I, 156: 'From this heresy there arose in the last century a false philosophy—a new right, as it is called, and a popular authority, together with an

unbridled licence which many regard as the only true liberty. Hence we have reached the limit of horrors, to wit, communism, socialism, nihilism, hideous deformities of the civil society of humanity and almost its ruin.' (Gilson 151 translation adapted).

17. ' . . . the fear of God . . . being taken away, the authority of rulers despised . . . a change and overthrow of all things will necessarily follow. Yea, this change and overthrow is deliberately planned and put forward by many associations of Communists and Socialists; and to their undertakings the sect of Freemasons is not hostile, but greatly favours their designs, and holds in common with them their chief opinions' (*Great Ency* 99).

18. Laurentin 96–7, refers to a growing misunderstanding of the teaching of St Thomas, a misunderstanding which affected the drafting of *Rerum Novarum*; cf. Camp 55.

Chapter 3, pp. 61–74.

1. In a comment on this statement Calvez and Perrin (356) say: 'If one did not take account of the polemical context, one could well be astonished at such a list, where natural and institutional inequalities are jumbled up together.'

2. A footnote in the English translation says tactfully that Leo's documents do not 'explicitly' state what Pius says—see *Pope and People* 184.

3. Indeed such a theology was put forward as late as 1963 in de Soras 64–5.

Chapter 4, pp. 75–95.

1. For some background on the encyclical and a contemporary commentary see *Action Populaire* 81–108; also Duncan 113–24.

2. Cf. DR 8; also Pius XI's encyclical *Caritate Christi Compulsi* AAS 24, 179: ' . . . that unjust distribution of goods, the effect of which is to concentrate the wealth of the nations in the hands of a small group of private citizens who . . . regulate the markets of the world according to their choice, to the great detriment of the mass of humankind' (my translation).

3. Cf. encyclical *Nova Impendat*, AAS 23, 393–7.

4. It should be noted that the paragraph numbering system used by Chenu is quite different to that used in the English translations.

5. Cf. QA 4: the open violation of justice is sometimes not merely tolerated but even ratified by legislators.

6. In reference to this development of capitalism into a system where domination replaces competition, Gudorf (10) claims that, 'Pius XI placed the blame . . . not on any natural direction of the system of capitalism, but on the lack of moral restraint of the individuals concerned.' Her remark seems to miss the point. It is true of course that the pope blamed capitalists for lack of restraint. But his main point here is the need for some limits to be imposed on free competition; and these limits are to be not merely moral but *structural*, since they are to be imposed by public authorities. It is an uncalled-for polarisation of the issue to see it simply in terms of choosing between lack of moral restraint of individuals on the one hand and the 'natural direction of the system of capitalism' on the other.

7. The phrase 'benevolent attention' was used by Pius XI two weeks after he had issued *Quadragesimo Anno*, to describe its attitude to the Italian system. See address of 31 May 1931, AAS 23, 231: ' . . . nella Enciclica *Quadragesimo Anno* tutti hanno facilmente riconosciuto un cenno di benevola attenzione agli ordinamenti sindicali e corporativi italiani.' It may be noted that Nell-Breuning, in a commentary originally written in German in 1932, gave a very different interpretation of these paragraphs—see Nell-Breuning (1936) 254–7. There he professed to see delicate irony and understated criticism in the pope's references to the Italian system. Since Nell-Breuning was the principal drafter of the encyclical, his interpretation would, in normal circumstances, have to be taken very seriously. However, nearly forty years later Nell-Breuning wrote a very revealing account of the drafting of the encyclical (see Curran and McCormick 60–2) where he acknowledged that the pope himself insisted on having these paragraphs added into the draft; the implication is that Pius XI did intend to convey some degree of approval of the Italian system. It is clear that Nell-Breuning himself strongly disapproved of such a system; so his earlier commentary on this topic might be termed an exercise in 'damage limitation', an effort to tone down the meaning of what the pope had insisted on saying.

8. For background information on the development of trade unions see Somerville.

9. A rather similar distinction between two meanings of capitalism, and a similar conclusion about the attitude of Pius XI may be found in Ryan 181.

10. In the CTS translation the Latin phrases 'oeconomica res' and 'moralis disciplina' are rendered as 'economic life' and 'moral conduct' respectively; for the translation used in the text I have taken the Nell-Breuning rendering of the first term and the Miller version of the second term—see Nell-Breuning (1936) 77 and R. Miller 42.

11. The Latin text is '*quae artis sunt*'; the CTS translation ('in matters of technique') is not satisfactory.

12. Even the balanced treatment of the topic by Ryan seems to presuppose that the pope had 'the answer' (Ryan 174–8).

13. O'Brien (20) sees the position of Pius XI as guided by 'an ideology of counterattack and Catholic restoration'. He goes on to claim that 'it was a utopia, and a dangerous one'. There is a good deal of truth in this view but it seems to me to be somewhat one-sided, playing down unduly the more modern aspects of Pius's teaching.

14. It may be noted that in this passage the pope is recounting the teaching of the Mexican bishops; but he leaves no room for doubt about his own acceptance and approval of this teaching. It is well to note also that Pius is not by any means giving a *carte blanche* for violent resistance; for in the following paragraph he adds that the means used must not be intrinsically evil and should 'not bring greater harm to the community than the harm they were intended to remedy'.

15. For a brief account of some of the earlier skirmishes (political and military) between the socialist government and Catholic resisters see Rhodes 94–102.

Chapter 5, pp. 96–112.

1. In order to avoid cumbersome references to the works of Pius XII, I have given full bibliographical references to twenty-seven of his documents (in chronological order) in my bibliography—see pp. 400–1—and have given each of them a reference number—D1, D2, D3 etc. I have used these abbreviations whenever I refer to the works of Pius XII e.g. the present reference 'D21 55–9' refers to pages 55 to 59 of Document 21 which is the official text of his Christmas Message of 1950. Part Three of this message is concerned with internal peace while Part Four deals with peace between peoples. The former treats of some economic issues while the latter refers mostly to political rather than economic matters.

2. Cf. Moody 71: 'While the attitude of neutrality to the various forms of government still stands, there is evident a pronounced papal benevolence toward the active participation of all citizens in government and a strong rejection of absolutism in all its forms.' It is clear that democracy as such was by no means an absolute for the pope; what he was concerned about was the needs of a healthy community. These, he said, can also be met under other legitimate forms of government—see D14 258.

3. For instance, at the height of the Cold War, in his Christmas Message of 1954, (D27 25) Pius found no solid basis in the communist countries for coexistence with other nations, since he saw communism as a system which is completely detached from the base provided by natural law. The implications of such a judgment are far-reaching: it could be concluded that a communist regime lacks the moral authority to command its citizens and is incapable of entering into morally binding international agreements. It is not a mere flight of fancy to suggest that such conclusions could be drawn. See, for instance, the following statement made by the well-known moralist Jacques Leclercq (182): ' . . . le gouvernement bolchevique fonde toute sa politique sur une philosophie qui va à l'encontre des exigences de la nature humaine. Il ne peut être légitime . . . '

4. ' . . . die Not des Prolitariats und die Aufgabe, diese den Zufälligheiten der wirtschaftlichen Konjuktur schutzlos preisgegebene Menschenklasse emporzuheben zu einem den anderen gleichgeachteten Stand mit klar umschriebenen Rechten. Diese Aufgabe ist, jedenfalls im Wesentlichen, gelöst . . . '

5. 'Die Überwindung des Klassenkampfes durch ein organisches Zueinanderordnen des Arbeitgebers und Arbeitnehmers.'

6. 'Che questa servitù derivi dal prepotere del capitale privato o dal potere dello Stato, l'effetto non muta . . . ';

7. On this occasion the pope made only a brief reference to the need for stability; but he developed this point more fully in later statements e.g. D4 13 and D30.

8. Pius XII had already made a briefer and vaguer statement on this question in the final section of an early encyclical (D1 642), where he said that the goods of the earth have been created by God for all people and that the basic point of the social question was that these goods should be equitably shared out with justice as the guide and charity as the support. In his 1941 radio message, however, his teaching is much more specific;

e.g. D3 221: 'Undoubtedly the natural order, deriving from God, demands also private property . . . But all this remains subordinated to the natural scope of material goods and cannot be independent of the first and fundamental right which concedes their use to all people; but it should rather serve to make possible the actuation of this right in conformity with its scope.' (translation adapted)

Chapter 6, pp. 113–48.

1. For an account of the various translations of these two documents see the bibliography of official documents, pp. 397–410. When giving references to these two encyclicals I shall use the abbreviations MM and PT followed by the paragraph number.

2. Bolté (I, 289) makes the interesting suggestion that the 'negandum' of the Latin text should be translated not as 'it will not happen' but as 'it must be resisted' i.e. not allowed to happen. This translation would certainly fit in better with what the pope says in the following two paragraphs; but neither the Italian text nor the letter of the Holy See to the French Social Week (the text of which seems to have been the original source for the passage in the encyclical) is open to this interpretation.

3. See Bolté II, 376–7 for the nuances of the translation.

4. See Calvez 64–6 on 'development' in relation to capitalism and socialism.

5. The translation of the passage is itself a matter of controversy. I have taken the phrase 'false philosophical theories' from the Waterhouse version since it is clearer than the Campion version which uses the word 'teachings' instead of 'theories'. But I have used the phrase 'historical movements' from the Campion version in preference to Waterhouse's vague phrase 'practical measures'. The translations into other European languages speak of 'movements' (see Bolté II, 613); and the latter part of the paragraph clearly refers to developments within such movements.

6. The following remark by Cronin (in John XXIII, *The Encyclicals and Other Messages* 325) sums up the position: 'It is widely held that they apply to contacts with the Communist world . . . But the principles as given in the encyclical are general in nature, and we cannot quarrel with those who also see in them reference to anti-clerical movements in Europe and Latin America, or the "opening to the left" in Italian politics, Spanish fascism or any similar accommodation with historic antagonists.'

7. My translation, with emphasis added. The sentence quoted is a summary of an important part of a Radio Message given by Pius XII in 1941 (D3 200–1).

8. Cf Bolté II, 321–5. Note that Bolté's numbering of the paragraphs of QA differs from that of the English text.

9. My translation. In order to give some approximation to what the pope had in mind I have translated *ius privatum* as 'contractual law'. For the nuances of meaning see Bolté I, 231–57; also the translator's note and publisher's note in Kirwin 90–3 and (v); also Calvez (v)–(vi) and 102 note 13.

10. 'Socialium rationum incrementa'; equivalent Latin phrases are used in each of the paragraphs from 59 to 67 inclusively; in each of these nine

cases the Italian text uses 'socializazzione'. Many translations in other European languages used words equivalent to the Italian word; but one authoritative German version and Bolté's later, careful, French text gave a more literal translation of the Latin.

11. The Gibbons version speaks of 'the multiplication of social relationships'; that of Kirwan gives 'the development of the network of social relationships'.

12. Kirwan (92) sees it as quite significant that the official Latin text 'rejected the term'; Bolté (I, 241) inclines to the opposite view—that the reason the word was omitted was simply to avoid a Latin neologism.

13. Cf. Calvez 14: 'Socialization has no meaning in reality save as . . . a "should" of personal freedom.'

14. Kirwan 93–4 points out that the terms used echo those of QA. For a careful study of the relationship between the words used in the two encyclicals see Bolté I, 317–25.

15. Bolté's very comprehensive study at times gives the impression that his discovery of such parallels has led him to play down the difference in approach between Pius XII and John XXIII; for instance, on the question of 'socialisation', Bolté I 246.

16. The Campion text quoted here is preferable to the Waterhouse version which does not bring out the contrast in the first sentence (Latin: 'tum . . . tum').

17. My translation. The phrase 'munus . . . sociale' is very difficult to translate accurately. Kirwan gives 'social function' and the Italian and French texts use a corresponding phrase. But in English this is too vague. The Gibbons text gives 'social responsibility'; this is excellent except that it only conveys one of the two aspects of the meaning of 'munus'. I have added 'role' to express the second aspect.

18. At page 118 and note 5 above. It has been noted that Pope John's 'opening to the left' was actually a belated response of the Vatican to the overtures of the Italian Communist Party, led by Gramsci and Togliatti—see Marzani 14–6.

Chapter 7, pp. 149–78.

1. In his study of papal teaching Camp does not include any serious study of the teachings of Vatican II.

2. Vatican II, *Nuntius*. For background information on this document see Marie-Dominique Chenu, 'Le Message au monde des Pères conciliaires (octobre 1962)', in Congar and Peuchmaurd (ed.), 191–3.

3. See Willem J. Schuijt's history of the text in Vorgrimmler V, 339.

4. Bishops from dioceses in Asia, Africa, and Latin America constituted about 40 per cent of the bishops at the Council—see Aubert *et al*, 627–8.

5. E.g. GS 69.2, 70. In referring to *Gaudium et Spes* I shall use the initials GS followed by numbers to designate the paragraph and, where relevant, the sub-paragraph, as given in the Latin text. In quoting in English from GS, I shall make use of whichever of the available translations seems most accurate for the particular passage; on some occasions, in the

interests of accuracy, I shall adapt the translation or give my own translation of the text.

6. For the names on the various committees see Charles Moeller's history of the text in Vorgrimmler V, 21, 39, 40, 49, 63.

7. There seems to be a patronising tone in GS 69.2 which says that customs may be useful if they are brought up to date. Even during the Council, drafts of GS were criticised as being too Western in outlook— e.g. the intervention by Bishop James Corboy from Zambia in *Acta Synodalia* Vol III, Pars V, 625–6.

8. Cf René Coste's commentary in Vorgrimmler V, 368.

9. For instance GS follows *Mater et Magistra* in what it says about the process of socialisation (GS 6, 23.1, 25.2, 75.3). It is interesting to note that the official Latin text of GS 75.3 includes the word *socializatio*, in contrast to the Latin text of *Mater et Magistra*. While GS was being drafted, Pope John issued his encyclical *Pacem in Terris* and this was so comprehensive that those who were writing GS found they had little to add to it on the more practical aspects of the question of peace and war; they did however offer a richer theology of peace as I shall point out later.

10. ' . . . the fruit of that right ordering of things with which the divine founder has invested human society . . . ' (Flannery translation) .

11. ' . . . the achievement of peace requires . . . unceasing vigilance . . . ' (Flannery translation).

12. ' . . . the common good of humankind . . . depends . . . upon circumstances which change as time goes on; consequently, peace will never be achieved once and for all, but must be built up continually.' (Flannery translation, emended).

13. For references to two addresses in which Pope John mentions the point see Bolté III, 899–90.

14. Cf. Jean-Yves Calvez's remarks in Congar and Peuchmaurd II, 502.

15. The following statement by Gamani Corea, Secretary General of the United Nations Conference on Trade and Development (UNCTAD), will indicate the close correspondence between what GS asked for and the NIEO concept: 'The theme of structural change is one of the crucial concepts of the New International Economic Order. It signifies the conviction of the developing countries that the development process . . . requires . . . changes in some of the prevailing mechanisms and systems that govern international economic relations.' (UNCTAD, 2).

16. ' . . . reformationes multae in vita oeconomica-sociali atque mentis et habitudinis conversio ab omnibus requiruntur.' The Italian translation brings out the fact that what is in question is structural reform: 'si richiedono molte riforme nelle strutture della vita economico-sociale . . . '. Chiavacci (314) understands the Council to be calling for a fundamental reform of the economic system.

17. In his commentary on this part of GS, L.J. Lebret is rather more specific; he maintains that reform of international trade requires reform of the structures of production, of the monetary systems, and of the economic regimes which actually are in force at present—see Lebret in de Riedmatten *et al*, 224.

18. The Abbott version speaks of the need for a 'reform' of the structures while the St Paul version uses the verb 'revamp'; the Flannery version is more accurate here since it uses the word 'reassess' to translate the Latin 'recognoscendi'. The Italian text has 'una revisione'. The French text speaks of a 'recasting' ('une refonte'); this was probably the working text of the drafting group; but the toning down of the phrase in the Latin text (which is of course the official one) is hardly accidental.

19. ' . . . ut distribuantur fundi non satis exculti . . . '.

20. It may be noted that this vagueness is to be found not merely in the text but also in some of the commentaries on it. For instance the lengthy commentary by Augustino Ferrari Toniolo on this section of GS does little more than repeat the words of the document itself, when treating of this delicate issue—see his commentary in E. Guano et al, 984–5.

21. Cf. Jean-Yves Calvez's remarks in Congar and Peuchmaurd II, 503; also Ermenegildo Lio, 'Povertà (Theol morale)', in Garofalo (ed.), col. 1646.

22. In QA 51, the only proviso made by Pius XI was that the work should be devoted to the production of really useful goods.

23. GS 65.3 insists that the common good is seriously threatened by those who hoard their wealth unproductively. Other statements in favour of investment can be found in GS 70 and 85.2.

24. Originally it was proposed to insert in the text of GS the passage in Pope John's *Pacem in Terris* (PT 127) which states that it is unreasonable to hold that war can any longer be seen as a means to obtain justice for violated rights. But difficulties and objections led to the passage being relegated to a footnote (at GS 80.3). (On this point see the remarks of D. Dubarle in Congar and Peuchmaurd (ed.), II, 581 note 11.) This change was obviously significant. So too was the fact that the footnote is appended to a passage in which the Council is condemning total war. In this way the authors of GS imply that Pope John was outlawing only *total* war, not all kinds of war; and there is some basis for this interpretation since the relevant passage in *Pacem in Terris* includes a reference to atomic weapons.

25. Cf. comment by D. Dubarle in de Riedmatten et al., 276–9; comment again by D. Dubarle in Congar and Peuchmaurd (ed.), II, 582; comment by Raimondo Sigmond in E. Guano et al, 1087–8.

26. A proviso is added: 'so long as there is no injury to the rights and duties of others or of the community' (my translation).

27. 'It seems proper (aequum videtur) that the law should make humane provision for those who for reasons of conscience refuse to bear arms . . . ' (my translation). This way of expressing the point allowed the Council to by-pass the question of the correctness of such a conscientious judgment.

28. Note that in GS 1 there is a certain sense of solidarity with the poor: 'The joy and hope, the grief and anguish of the people of our time, *especially of those who are poor or afflicted in any way*, are the joy and hope, the grief and anguish of the followers of Christ as well.' (Flannery translation, emended slightly and emphasis added). But this sense of solidarity is not very evident later in the document.

29. This passage may have been influenced by Paul VI's first encyclical, *Ecclesiam Suam*, which had emphasised the spirit of poverty. Various

documents of Vatican II refer to the need for Christians to follow Christ who became poor for our sake and came to bring good news to the poor, e.g. *Lumen Gentium* par. 8 and 41,; *Apostolicam Actuositatem* par. 4; *Perfectae Caritatis*, par. 1 and 13; *Ad Gentes* par. 3 and 5; *Presbyterorum Ordinis* par. 17. But none of these documents offers a developed spirituality of poverty which integrates the christological and evangelical aspects with the economic and social reality.

30. The clear recognition by the Council of the pluralist character of modern society was recognised as a significant change. See, for instance, the following statement by a Church representative at the International Labour Office (ILO): 'The impact of the Council from the point of view of society springs from the fact that in it the Church sketched the guiding lines along which it reckons to be able to play its part in a pluralistic society and that it called on its members to accept the rules laid down. The Church's message and mission remain unaltered, but the framework within which it has to deliver the one and accomplish the other has changed' (Joblin [1966] 20).

31. In this paragraph there are obvious echoes of the passage about dialogue at a variety of levels, in Pope Paul's encyclical *Ecclesiam Suam* 654–9.

32. This reference to service of the poor is especially significant; but it is weakened by the addition of the phrase 'such as works of mercy and similar undertakings'; had these instances not been given the text could more easily be taken as referring to a structural reform of society for the benefit of the poor.

33. In his commentary on this part of GS, Giuseppe Mattai calls this a truly fundamental proposition; but unfortunately he does little to explain its importance—see his commentary in E. Guano *et al*, 1049. Oswald von Nell-Breuning sees this relinquishment of privilege as the culmination of this chapter of GS and as a major challenge to the Church—a cheque that must be honoured—see his commentary in Vorgrimmler (ed.), V, 326–7.

Chapter 8, pp. 179–204.

1. It is commonly accepted that the text of *Populorum Progressio* was drafted mainly by Mgr Pavan. But it is clear that the inspiration of Lebret pervades the encyclical, and some of its statements are taken almost word for word from Lebret's writings—cf. Malley 99.

2. Cf. Cosmao (1978) 51: ' . . . ce que nous appelons le sous-développement s'explique en effet, bien plus fondamentalement, par un *processus de déstructuration des sociétés polarisées par la société dominante en expansion*'; cf. Cosmao (1979) 44–8. For a historical account of how this process took place over several centuries see Stavrianos.

3. See for instance, Elliot 228–76; also Todaro 235–65. Both of these authors show how Western schooling is used to reinforce the gap between the rich and the poor and has other damaging effects on the economic and social structures of poor countries.

4. In PP 48, however, there is reference to 'the gifts that providence has bestowed' on a country; this phrase, coupled with the general tone of the paragraph, could give the impression that the pope accepts the view

that the so-called 'underdeveloped' countries have been given less of such resource gifts. Although this may be true about some individual countries it cannot be said of the poorer countries as a whole; in fact it is a myth which people in the West often cling to—perhaps to avoid the implications about the past exploitation and present injustice that have to be drawn once the myth is challenged.

5. The standard English translation, 'innovations that go deep', does not do justice to the Latin phrase 'rerum forma penitus renovetur'.

6. One finds, for instance, a strong moralistic note in PP 66: 'The world is sick. The cause lies less in the lack of resources, or their monopolisation by a small number of people, than in the lack of brotherhood and sisterhood among individuals and peoples.'

7. Cf. Address of Pope Paul to the United Nations (880) where he spoke of the need to move progressively towards the establishment of a world authority.

8. In this final sentence of the paragraph the pope moves on to speak of what ought to be done, as distinct from what happens in fact.

9. In an article on the encyclical written shortly after its publication Joblin ([1967] 5) remarked about these words that 'those who are struggling bravely against injustices will undoubtedly interpret them as approval of their activities'.

10. The words within double quotation marks are from an earlier message of Pope Paul, which he quotes here.

11. Freire became famous for his literacy work in a national programme in Brazil in 1963–4. He was imprisoned by the new military regime in 1964 and while in detention he began to write his essay 'Education as the Practice of Freedom' (which did not appear in English until 1974, in Freire). His views would have been well known at the time of writing *Populorum Progressio* even though his better known works were not written until later. For background on Freire see Collins.

Chapter 9, pp. 205–27.

1. I know no adequate way of conveying in English the meaning of the phrase I have translated here as 'the ordinary people'. The semi-official English version translates it as 'the popular sectors'. But the word 'popular', which is widely used in translations of Latin American Church documents, is quite misleading; it does not mean 'popular' in the conventional English sense but refers rather to the masses of ordinary people; so 'the popular sectors' might be taken as the equivalent of 'the masses'—but without the heavy ideological overtones which that phrase carries in English. Similarly, the widely-used phrase 'popular religion' ought to be translated as 'the religion of the ordinary people' or even, at times, as 'folk religion'.

2. 'If it is true that revolutionary insurrection can be legitimate in the case of evident and prolonged "tyranny that seriously works against fundamental human rights, and which damages the common good of the country", whether it proceeds from one person or from clearly unjust structures, it is also certain that violence or "armed revolution" generally

"generates new injustices, introduces new imbalances and causes new disasters; one cannot combat a real evil at the price of a greater evil".' The passages within double quotation marks are taken from PP 31.

3. The option for non-violence expressed in this passage fits in with the reference in an earlier paragraph to 'the pacifist position of the Church'— 2.17 (p. 54).

4. However, there are indications that Paul VI was still influenced by this concept of development—see, for instance, his references to 'stages' in OA 2 and OA 10.

5. This sentence and the remainder of this paragraph are my attempt to paraphrase a particularly difficult and obscure passage in OA 25.

6. 'This insight will enable Christians to see the degree of commitment possible along these lines . . . '

7. Cf. OA 42: the Church 'does not intervene to authenticate a given structure or to propose a ready-made model . . . '

8. The reference to GS 43 confirms this understanding of the text.

9. The Latin and Italian versions of the text are equally vague.

Chapter 10, pp. 228–59.

1. Apart from its full-time staff the Commission could draw on the expertise of several highly competent scholars who were members of the Commission or consultants to it. One such person was Barbara Ward-Jackson, whose study, *The Angry Seventies: The Second Development Decade: A Call to the Church*, was published by the Commission in 1970.

2. For some background on the use of the phrase 'the signs of the times' see Hebblethwaite (1982) 88–9.

3. In a brief but valuable study of the Synod document Hollenbach (86–7) says: 'Lack of adequate nourishment, housing, education and political self-determination are seen as a consequence of this lack of participation'; and he maintains that for the Synod the fundamental right to part-icipation 'integrates all other rights with each other and provides their operational foundation'. Hollenbach is undoubtedly correct in holding that participation is a central issue; but the texts to which he refers are not quite so clear as he is in seeing economic and social deprivations as the consequence of lack of participation; the document seems at times to locate lack of participation alongside other lacks.

4. It is not clear whether the 'we' used in this paragraph is intended to mean 'we, the authors of this document', i.e. the Synod bishops, or whether it is a more generic 'we' meaning people who are reflecting on the world situation and committed to working for justice; but even the more generic 'we' would clearly include the bishops and other Church leaders.

5. I am indebted to Mgr Charles O'Connor for background information on this controversy.

6. For the pope's references to the request of the Synod see EN 2 and 5.

7. The document is at pains later to ensure that its teaching does not involve any playing down of the importance of the Church—e.g. EN 28; cf. McGregor, 70–1.

8. For instance in paragraph 6 of the Vatican II Decree on the Church's Missionary Activity (*Ad Gentes*) the Council says that in situations

where there is no possibility of preaching the Gospel directly, missionaries ought at least to bear witness to the love and kindness of Christ and thus prepare a way for the Lord and in some way make him present.

9. In translating the Latin in this case I have allowed myself to be influenced by the Italian text because it seems more in harmony with the dynamic quality of the relationship between the present and the future as developed in the rest of the sentence. The Dillon translation (which follows the Latin more literally) speaks of 'another life' which is 'at once connected with and distinct from' the present state.

10. It is interesting to note that in EN 32 the pope quotes from an address he gave at the opening of the 1974 Synod. He spoke then of the need to re-affirm the specifically religious purpose of evangelisation. There is a discernible shift of emphasis in the text of EN itself—an avoidance of the tendency to present the issue in terms of a sharp contrast between the 'religious' and the 'worldly'. The quotation from the earlier address may even have been included here precisely in order to ensure that it would be interpreted in the light of the more comprehensive teaching of the later document—and in this way to suggest a continuity between the two.

11. One recalls here what Pope Paul had said in *Octogesima Adveniens* about the Church not having a ready-made model for human society (OA 42).

12. There are two significantly different translations of the first sentence of EN 37. The Vatican translation reads: 'The Church cannot accept violence . . . and indiscriminate death as the path to liberation'. The Dillon translation has: 'The church cannot accept any form of violence . . . nor the death of any man as a method of liberation.' The Vatican English text may find some basis in the Italian, *'la morte di chicchessia'*, while the Dillon text is closer to the Latin *'cuiusvis mortem hominis'*. The French text is *'la mort de qui que ce soit'*, which still leaves one not quite clear about what is intended. Is the writer saying that the goal of liberation does not justify the death of even one person? Or is it simply that one must not seek liberation through a type of violence that is liable to cause the death of anybody (at random, or indiscriminately)? The former would be a strongly pacifist position, while the latter could be understood as simply a rejection of an arbitrary kind of violence. Perhaps the writer intended to leave the text somewhat ambiguous.

Chapter 11, pp. 260–87.

1. For instance the document accepts that there is need also for the Church to minister to elite groups, and that it must face difficult questions regarding evangelisation of the upper classes, military chaplaincies, etc.

2. *'Tome o 'Evangelii Nuntiandi' como documento de referencia no estilo e na forma da elaboração.'*

3. E.g. Arns, 2: 'The option for the poor is not a class option in the Marxist sense . . . '; Baum (1981), 84: 'The Marxist position is . . . quite different from the Christian option for the poor.'

4. It should be noted that at Puebla the bishops also committed themselves to a preferential option for young people (Puebla 1166–1205). This had the effect of playing down to some degree the uniqueness of the phrase

'option for the poor' and in this way making it less threatening and more widely acceptable.

5. For a helpful treatment of the concept of an 'option for the poor', based on Puebla and on Pope John Paul's addresses in Mexico, see Antoncich, 108–15.

6. An earlier English text issued by the Vatican and used in *John Paul II in Mexico: His Collected Speeches* (p. 79) omits the word 'primarily'; so too does the Italian text in, *Giovanni Paolo II alla Chiesa che é in Messico: Discorsi del primo viaggio apostolico*, Alba (Figlie di San Paolo: 1979) 37; however, the Spanish text as published in AAS 71(1979) 79, has '*sobre todo*'.

7. Cf. address of 30 November 1978, p. 4: 'Priority attention for those who are suffering from radical poverty, for those who are suffering from injustice, certainly coincides with a fundamental concern of the Church . . . '

8. Chenu (8, 88) notes angrily that the term 'social doctrine' was rein-troduced into the text of GS 76 'by an illegal intervention after its promulgation'.

9. It may be noted in passing that Chenu's case is weakened by the fact that Paul VI had not entirely abandoned the use of the term. He used it in EN 38: '*Ecclesia . . . praebet . . . doctrinam socialem . . .* '.

10. It is clear, however, that the drafters of the Puebla document preferred the term 'social teaching' to 'social doctrine'.

11. The Vatican translation reads: 'Is man, as man, developing and pro-gressing or is he regressing and being degraded in his humanity?'

12. The original Spanish text is ' . . . *tras precisar algunos conceptos*'. For a list of the modifications that were made to the Puebla text (and an angry reaction to these changes) see *Esperance des Pauvres*.

Chapter 12, pp. 288–316.

1. Cf. Schotte 31: ' . . . the pope is cautiously not suggesting any concrete formula.' Schotte 27: 'He does not propose a "third way" between liberal capitalism and Marxism . . . . In the debate between capitalism and communism, he offers elements for a critique of both systems . . . '

2. Schotte (30) makes the point that transnational enterprises should be seen as both direct and indirect employers.

3. It may be of interest here to note the way in which the issue of class warfare was treated by the Pastoral Commission of the Brazilian Bishops. The Commission states that the Church condemns the Marxist postulate of class war, in the sense that to promote such a struggle would be contrary to the Gospel and would not provide the solution to the real problems of today. But, it adds, the Church recognises realistically the existence of class conflicts—conflicts which ought to be overcome through the establishment of justice and of a spirit of brotherhood; see Bishops of Brazil (1977) 10.

4. Cf. Baum (1982) 29: 'Pope John Paul II offers . . . an imaginative rethinking of class conflict. The initiative for the struggle resides in the persons who recognise their common objective situation and freely commit themselves to solidarity in a joint struggle.'

5. On the question of motivation of the poor in Marx see Miranda, 1–28. On the question of how, in John Paul's view, the struggle to overcome oppression goes beyond narrow 'class interest' see Baum (1982) 30–1, 49, 69.

Chapter 13, pp. 317–51.

1. These have been constant themes of the pope (e.g. his Letter to the Religious of Latin America (*L'Oss. Rom.* 30 July 1990, 4) repeated above all during his visits to Latin America—for instance, during his second visit to Mexico (*L'Oss. Rom.* 14 May 1990, 3) and his second visit to Brazil (*L'Oss. Rom.* 28 October 1991, 12).

2. Cf. Land and Henriot 65–74; however, their attempt to show that the pope uses 'the pastoral cycle' seems a little contrived.

3. The pope does, however, point out that the Church feels called by the Gospel to take a stand alongside the poor in their public but non-violent demands for justice (SRS 39).

4. I accept the view of Coleman ([1991] 39 and 42) on this issue. He says: 'I agree with Dorr that some movement (at least in verbal acknowledgment) has taken place in Catholic social thought to give room to conflict models of society. I do not think, however, that Catholic social thought has really budged all that much from its historic bias toward harmony models' (42).

5. Some months later, the pope took up again the issue of human stewardship of the earth. In an address to participants in a study week on the environment he said, 'it is precisely the special value of human life that counsels, in fact compels us, to examine carefully the way we use other created species' (*L'Oss. Rom.* 28 May 1990, 5). In Comacchio in Northern Italy he said that the transformation of the environment enables people to become more human. (*L'Oss. Rom.* 8 October 1990, 4–5).

6. Section (c) of RM 37 (dealing with the 'forms of the Areopagus') is closer in style to John Paul's other encyclicals.

7. A somewhat similar process was used by the Australian bishops; and the Irish bishops also set up a series of consultations with representatives from different sectors of society in preparation for a new pastoral letter on justice.

8. The term 'Real Socialism' used in the English translation is rather misleading. Perhaps a better translation would have been '*actual* socialism' i.e. the version of socialism which actually developed in Eastern Europe, as distinct from some ideal socialism of which philosophers or politicians might speak.

Bibliography of Church Documents

Leo XIII:
    —*Actes de Leon XIII, Encycliques, Moto Proprio, Brefs, Allocutions, Actes de Dicastreres etc.*, Paris (Bonne Presse: n.d.). This seven-volume collection gives the text of the documents in Latin together with a French translation. I have used this Bonne Presse Latin-French collection as the main source for references to the writings of Leo XIII, since it is more complete and accessible than the *Acta Sanctae Sedis*; in referring to it I have cited the volume and page number, preceded by the initials BP (—for Bonne Presse).
    —*The Great Encyclical Letters of Pope Leo XIII (with a preface by John J. Wynn)*, New York (Benziger Brothers: 1903), 33. This collection is referred to as *Great Ency.*
    —*The Church Speaks to the Modern World: The Social Teachings of Leo XIII* (ed. Étienne Gilson), Garden City (Doubleday Image: 1954). This collection is referred to as Gilson.
    —Encyclical *Rerum Novarum*, 15 May 1891, *Acta Sanctae Sedis* 23(1890–1) 641–70; also available in Latin (together with a French translation) in BP III, 18–70. In neither of these texts are the paragraphs numbered. But the numbering of the paragraphs was added by the Vatican in a revised edition, issued in 1931. For the text of various drafts see Antonazzi. The official Vatican translation into English is available in Fremantle 20–56 and in *Great Ency* 207–48. A revised version of this translation was published by the Catholic Truth Society and reprinted many times under the title, *The Workers' Charter, On the Condition of the Working Classes*, London (CTS: 1960). In these two texts the paragraphs are numbered in accordance with the 1931 Vatican edition. An entirely new translation by John Molony is available in Molony 165–203. Unfortunately

the paragraphs are not numbered in this version. Partly for this reason and partly because the older version is so widely used I have quoted from the CTS version and have occasionally adapted it. References to the encyclical are given by citing the paragraph number, preceded by the initials RN.

—Encyclical *Inscrutabili*, 2 April 1878, BP I 8–25; *Great Ency*. 9–21.

—Encyclical *Quod Apostolici Muneris*, 28 December 1878, BP I, 26–41; *Great Ency*. 22–33.

—Encyclical *Humanum Genus*, 20 April 1884, BP I, 242–77; *Great Ency*. 83–106.

—'C'est avec une particulière satisfaction', 24 February 1885, translated as 'Working-Men's Clubs and Associations' in *The Pope and the People*.

—Encyclical *Libertas Praestantissimum*, 20 June 1888, BP II, 172–213; *Great Ency*. 135–63.

—Encyclical *Exeunte Jam Anno*, 25 December 1888, BP II, 226–49; *Great Ency*. 164–79.

—Encyclical *Sapientiae Christianae*, 10 January 1890, BP II, 262–97; *Great Ency*. 180–207.

—Apostolic Letter *Ad Extremas*, 14 June 1893, BP III, 204–13.

—Encyclical *Laetitiae Sanctae*, 8 September 1893, BP III, 242–55.

—Encyclical *Praeclara Gratulationis Publicae*, 20 June 1894, BP IV, 82–107; *Great Ency*. 303–19.

—Letter to Bishops of USA *Longinqua Oceani*, 6 January 1895, BP IV, 158–79; *Great Ency*. 320–35.

—Encyclical *Graves de Communi*, 18 January 1901, BP VI, 204–27; *Great Ency*. 479–94.

Antonazzi, Giovanni (ed): *L'enciclica Rerum Novarum: testo autentico e redazioni preparatorie dai documenti originali*, Roma (Edizioni de Storia e Letteratura: 1957)

Pius X:

—*Motu proprio, Fin dalla prima*, 18 December 1903, ASS 36 (1903–4) 339–45.

—Letter on *Le Sillon*, 25 August 1910, AAS 2 (1910) 613–33.

Benedict XV:
—Encyclical *Ad Beatissimi* AAS 6 (1914) 565–81.
—Letter to the Bishop of Bergamo, AAS 12 (1920), 109–12.
—Encyclical *Maximum Illud*, 13 November 1919, AAS 11(1919) 440–55.

Pius XI:
—Encyclical *Rerum Ecclesiae*, 28 February 1926, AAS 18 (1926) 65–83.
—Message to the Bishops of China, 1 August 1928, AAS 20 (1928) 245–6.
—Encyclical *Quadragesimo Anno*, 15 May 1931, AAS 23 (1931) 177–228; English translation: The Social Order, London (Catholic Truth Society) and Oxford (Catholic Social Guild). A second English translation is incorporated in R. Miller; another English translation is to be found in Nell-Breuning (1936) 401–42. The paragraphs are not numbered in the original Latin text but they are numbered in each of the above three translations. Unless otherwise stated all quotations in English are taken from the first of the three translations mentioned above. References are given by citing the number of the paragraph preceded by the initials QA.
—Address of 31 May 1931, AAS 23 (1931) 229–32.
—Encyclical *Nova Impendat*, AAS 23 (1931) 393–7.
—Encyclical *Caritate Christi Compulsi*, AAS 24 (1932) 179–94.
—Encyclical *Divini Redemptoris* AAS 29 (1937) 65–106 (Latin text) and 107–38 (Italian text); English translation in *Twelve Encyclicals*. The original Latin text does not have the paragraphs numbered, but the paragraphs are numbered in the Italian and English texts. References are given by citing the number of the paragraph preceded by the initials DR.
—Encyclical *Firmissimum* AAS 29 (1937) 189–99 (Latin text), 200–11 (Spanish text). This encyclical is also known as *No es muy*. English translation in *Twelve Encyclicals*. The paragraphs are numbered in the English text. In references to the encyclical I use the paragraph numbers.
—Encyclical *Mit brennender Sorge*, AAS 29 (1937) 143–67;

English translation in *Twelve Encyclicals*. The paragraphs are numbered in the English text. In references to the encyclical I use the paragraph numbers.

—*Twelve Encyclicals of Pius XI (with a foreword by Msgr P.E. Hallett)*, London (C.T.S.: 1943).

Action Populaire, *L'Encyclique sur la Restauration le l'Ordre Social: Texte française complet, table analytique, étude doctrinale*, Paris (Editions Spes: 1931) 81–108.

Pius XII:

(In order to avoid long and cumbersome references to the many writings and addresses of Pius XII, I have numbered the following 32 texts as D1 to D32 in chronological order; in referring to them in this book I identify them as D1, D2, etc.)

D1 = Encyclical *Sertum Laetitiae* AAS 31 (1939) 635–44.

D2 = Christmas 1939 Address, AAS 32 (1940) 6–13.

D3 = Radio Message *La sollenità della Pentecoste* 1 June 1941, AAS 33 (1941) 195–205 (Italian text), 216–27 (English text).

D4 = Christmas 1941 Radio Message, AAS 34 (1942) 10–21.

D5 = Christmas 1942 Radio Message, AAS 35 (1943) 9–24.

D6 = Address of 13 June 1943, AAS 35 (1943) 175.

D7 = Christmas 1943 Radio Message, AAS 36 (1944) 11–24.

D8 = Radio Message of 1 July 1944, AAS 36 (1944) 252–3.

D9 = Radio Message of 1 September 1944, AAS 36 (1944) 252–3.

D10 = Christmas 1944 Radio Message, AAS 37 (1945) 10–23. An English translation is available in Pius XII, *Selected Letters and Addresses* 299–318.

D11 = Address to the Nobles of Rome January 1945, Savignat II 1586.

D12 = Address of 11 March 1945, AAS 37 (1945) 68–72.

D13 = Address of 2 June 1945, *Documentation Catholique* 24 June 1945.

D14 = Address of 2 October 1945, AAS 37 (1945) 256–62.

D15 = Address to the Nobles of Rome January 1946, Savignat II 1595–6.

D16 = Address of 15 November 1946, AAS 38 (1946)

435–6

D17 = Address to the Nobles of Rome January 1947, Savignat II 1603.

D18 = Address of 1 November 1947, Savignat II, 1774.

D19 = Address of 7 May 1949, AAS 41 (1949) 283–6.

D20 = Address of 3 June 1950, AAS 42 (1950) 485–8.

D21 = Christmas 1950 Message, AAS 43 (1951) 49–59.

D22 = Address to the Nobles of Rome January 1952, Savignat II 1605.

D23 = Address of 31 January 1952, Savignat II, 1670.

D24 = Radio Message of 14 September 1952, AAS 44 (1952) 789–93.

D25 = Christmas 1952 Radio Message, AAS 45 (1953) 33–46.

D26 = Letter to Charles Flory 14 July 1954 Savignat II, 1748.

D27 = Christmas 1954 Message AAS 47 (1955) 15–28.

D28 = Address to FAO 10 November 1955, *Documentation Catholique* 52 (1955) 1488–91.

D29 = Christmas 1955 Message AAS 48 (1956) 26–41.

D30 = Address of 17 February 1956, *L'Osservatore Romano* 18 February 1956.

D31 = Encyclical *Fidei Donum*, 21 April 1957, AAS 49 (1957) 223–48. English translation in Hickey.

D32 = Address of 13 April 1958, *Documentation Catholique* 55 (1958) 543–6.

Pius XII: *Selected Letters and Addresses of Pius XII*, London (CTS: 1949)

Savignat, Alain (ed.): *Relations humaines et société contemporaine: synthèse chrétienne directives de S.S. Pie XII*, Fribourg (St Paul: 1956) (Savignat's compilation is an expanded version of an earlier compilation by Utz and Groner.)

John XXIII:

—Encyclical *Ad Petri Cathedram*, 29 June 1959, AAS 51 (1959) 497–531. English text in John XXIII, *The Encyclicals and Other Messages*.

—Encyclical *Mater et Magistra*, dated 15 March 1961 but actually issued just two months later. AAS 53 (1961) 401–64. There are at least five English versions, of which the

most widely used at present seems to be that of W. J. Gibbons
for the Paulist Press. This text is available in Gremillion
141–200; also in O'Brien and Shannon 50–123. J.R. Kirwan
made an interesting translation which often succeeds in
expressing the underlying meaning of the text much better
than the other versions, but is occasionally unacceptable.
It can be found together with some helpful comments in
Kirwan. A very careful French translation is to be found in
Bolté. As a companion to his translation, Bolté has produced
a four-volume commentary on the text (see other bibliography). References to the text of *Mater et Magistra* are
given by citing the paragraph number preceded by the
initials MM.

—Encyclical *Pacem in Terris*, dated 11 April 1963, AAS 55
(1963) 257–304. There are a number of English versions,
some of which differ from each other only in minor respects.
The easiest to read is that of Henry 0. Waterhouse, available
in *The Social Thought of John XXIII* but it seems rather less
accurate in some important places than the version of
Donald R. Campion available in Gremillion 201–41. References to the text of *Pacem in Terris* are given by citing
the paragraph number preceded by the initials PT.

—*The Encyclicals and Other Messages of John XXIII*
Washington D.C. (T.P.S. Press: 1964).

—*The Social Thought of John XXIII*, Oxford (Catholic
Social Guild: 1964)

Vatican II: (In this bibliography I have listed separately the
various documents of the Council to which I have referred
specifically).

—*Nuntius ad Universos Homines Summo Pontifice Assentiente
a Patribus Missus Ineunte Concilio Oecumenico Vaticano II*,
AAS 54 (1962) 823–4; English translation in Gremillion
351–4.

—*Gaudium et Spes* AAS 58 (1966) 1025–1115. There are
three English translations in common circulation. They
are to be found in Abbott (199–308) Gonzalez (513–624)
and Flannery 903–1001. The second of these almost always
follows the sub-paragraphing of the Latin text; the third
does so in most cases; the first does not do so.

—*Dignitatis Humanae*, AAS 58 (1966) 929–41.

—*Perfectae Caritatis*, AAS 58 (1966) 702–12.

—*Lumen Gentium*, AAS 57 (1965) 7–71.

—*Apostolicam Actuositatem*, AAS 58 (1966) 837–64.

—*Ad Gentes*, AAS 58 (1966) 947–90.

—*Presbyterorum Ordinis*, AAS 58 (1966) 991–1024.

—*Sacrosancti Concilii Oecumenici Vaticani II*, Roma (Vatican Press: 1975). This collection contains all the official documents of the Council.

Abbott, Walter M. (ed.): *The Documents of Vatican II*, New York (America Press: 1966) and London (Chapman: 1967).

Flannery, Austin (ed.): *Vatican Council II: The Conciliar and Post-Conciliar Documents*, Northport, New York (Costello: 1975, 1977).

Gonzalez, J.L. and the Daughters of St Paul: *The Sixteen Documents of Vatican II*, Boston (St Paul Editions: n.d.).

Paul VI:

—Encyclical *Ecclesiam Suam*, 6 August 1964, AAS 56 (1964) 609–59.

—Address to the United Nations AAS 57 (1965) 877–85.

—Encyclical *Populorum Progressio* 26 March 1967, AAS 59 (1967) 257–99, para. 3; English translation of Vatican Polyglot Press in Gremillion 387–415 and in O'Brien and Shannon 313–51. A slightly different (and better) version of this translation is in *Encyclical Letter of his Holiness Pope Paul VI: On the Development of Peoples (with commentary by Barbara Ward)*, New York (Paulist: 1967). Quotations from the encyclical in English are taken from this last text except in cases where I considered it necessary to adapt it or to give my own translation from the Latin.

—Apostolic Letter *Octogesima Adveniens*, 14 May 1971, AAS 63 (1971) 401–41. English translation from the Vatican Press in Gremillion 485–512 and in O'Brien and Shannon 352–83. A slightly emended version of this text is given in the booklet, *Social Problems: Apostolic Letter of Pope Paul VI: 'Octogesima Adveniens'* (No. S 288), London (Catholic Truth Society: n.d.). Quotations in English are taken from this booklet, unless otherwise stated. References are given by using the initials OA, followed by the number of the paragraph.

—Message to the United Nations International Conference on the Environment, 1 June 1972, AAS 64 (1972) 443–6.

—Apostolic Exhortation *Evangelica Testificatio*, 29 June 1971, AAS 63 (1971) 497–526.

—Apostolic Exhortation *Evangelii Nuntiandi*, AAS 68 (1976) 5–76. There are two easily available English translations: one is published by the Vatican Press and distributed by CTS, London; the other is by Dom Matthew Dillon and is published in a special issue of *Doctrine and Life*, 27 (1977) 3–52. The latter is based on the Latin text whereas the former appears to follow the Italian text. Neither translation is wholly satisfactory so in most cases I give my own translation of the official Latin text. References to the document are given by using the initials EN followed by the number of the paragraph.

John Paul II:

—Encyclical *Redemptor Hominis*, AAS 71 (1979) 257–324; English translation issued by Libreria Editrice Vaticana. References to the encyclical are given by citing the number of the 'paragraph' preceded by the initials RH. In quoting from the document I have adapted the Vatican translation and have at times used my own translation.

—Encyclical *Dives in Misericordia*, AAS 72 (1980) 1177 –1232; English translation issued by the Vatican Press. References to the encyclical are given by citing the number of the 'paragraph', preceded by the initials DM. Quotations in English are from the Vatican text.

—Encyclical *Laborem Exercens* AAS 73 (1981) 577–647; English translation issued by Vatican Press. References to the encyclical are given by citing the number of the 'paragraph', preceded by the initials LE. Quotations in English are from the Vatican text.

—Encyclical *Solicitudo Rei Socialis*, 30 December 1987, English translation, Vatican City (Libreria Editrice Vaticana: 1988). The text is divided into numbered paragraphs. References are given by citing the paragraph number, preceded by the initials SRS.

—Encyclical *Redemptoris Missio*, 7 December 1990, *L'Osser-*

vatore Romano (English edition) 28 January 1991, 5–20. References are given by citing the paragraph number, preceded by the initials RM.

—Encyclical *Centesimus Annus* 1 May 1991, Vatican City (Libreria Editrice Vaticana: 1991).

—Addresses of his Mexican visit of 1979. The official texts of the pope's addresses, in the original languages, are given in AAS 71 (1979) 164–246. The best available translation of the opening address of the pope to the conference is contained in the two English editions of the Puebla document. I have used this translation and given references by citing the numbered sections and paragraphs. In the case of all of the other addresses I have used the English text from, *John Paul II in Mexico: His Collected Speeches*, London and New York (Collins: 1979); this is the Vatican translation of *L'Osservatore Romano*. References to these addresses are given citing the page number in AAS Vol 71.

—Address to the Pontifical Commission 'Justice and Peace', in, *L'Osservatore Romano* (English edition) of 30 November 1978, p. 4.

—Address to the United Nations, AAS 71 (1979) 1153–4.

—Address to UNESCO, AAS 72 (1980) 735–52.

—Addresses of his Brazil visit of 1980. The text of the major addresses given by the pope in Brazil is available (in the original languages, Portuguese, Spanish, and French) in, AAS 72 (1980) 825–961; but not all of his addresses are given there. The full text of all of his addresses is given in the various issues of *L'Osservatore Romano* from 2 July to 13 July 1980 (inclusive), which also contain an Italian translation in a series of supplements to these issues. An English translation of all the addresses is given in the English language weekly edition of *L'Osservatore Romano* of 7, 14, 21 and 28 July, and 4, 11, and 25 August 1980. The longer addresses are divided into numbered 'paragraphs'. References are given by citing the paragraph number (where available) and the page reference to the original text as given in AAS (or, where the text is not given in AAS, to the original text as given in [the daily] *L'Osservatore Romano*). Quotations in English are from the translation referred to above unless otherwise stated.

—Addresses of his Philippines visit of 1981. The text of

the pope's addresses on this visit to the Far East is given in AAS 73 (1981) 304–429. The address at Tondo is also available in English edn. of *L'Osservatore Romano*, 23 February 1981, pp. 13–14.

—Address in Managua, Nicaragua, 4 March 1983, AAS 75 (1983) 718–23.

—Address to priests in San Salvador, 6 March 1983, *L'Osservatore Romano* (daily edition), 7–8 March 1983, 4.

—Address to American Indians at Quezaltenango, Guatemala, 7 March 1983, AAS 75 (1983) 740–4.

—Address at Port au Prince, 9 March 1983, AAS 75 (1983) 765–71).

—Address to Council of Latin American Bishops (CELAM) at Port au Prince, Haiti, 9 March 1983, AAS 75 (1983) 771–9.

—Address to educators and scientists in Seoul, Korea, 5 May 1984, AAS 76 (1984) 984–8.

—Address to Pastoral Conference, Korea, 6 May 1984, AAS 76 (1984) 994–9.

—Address to Indians and Inuit of Canada, 18 September 1984, AAS 77 (1985) 417–22.

—Address to Amerindian people at Latacunga, Ecuador, 31 January 1985, AAS 77 (1985) 859–69.

—Address at University of Yaounde, Cameroons, 13 August 1985, AAS 78 (1986) 52–61.

—Address to Aborigines of Australia at Alice Springs, 29 November 1986 AAS 79 (1987) 973–9.

—Address to Scientists and Cultural Leaders in Assuncion, Paraguay, 17 May 1988, AAS 80 (1988) 1612–8.

—Apostolic Letter *Dignitate Mulieris* On the Dignity of Women, 15 August 1988, AAS 80 (1988) 1653–729.

—Address to Bishops of Southern Africa, 2 September 1989, AAS 81 (1989) 322–34.

—Message for World Day of Peace 1990: 'Peace with God the Creator: Peace with All of Creation', Vatican City, 8 December 1989, AAS 82 (1990) 147–56. (References given are to the numbered paragraphs.)

—Address to Priests, Religious and Laity in Mexico City, 12 May 1990 *L'Osservatore Romano* (English edn.), 14 May 1990, 3–4.

—Address to Mexican Business Leaders, in Durango, Mexico, May 1990 *L'Osservatore Romano* (English ed.), 28 May 1990, 6–7.

—Address to participants in Study Week on the Environment, Vatican City, 18 May 1990, *L'Osservatore Romano* (English ed.), 28 May 1990, 5.

—Letter to the Religious of Latin America, 29 June 1990, *L'Osservatore Romano* (English ed.), 30 July 1990, 1–7.

—Address to people of Comacchio (Northern Italy), 22 September 1990 in *L'Osservatore Romano* (English ed.), 8 October 1990, 4–5.

—Address to the Diplomatic Corps 12 January 1991 in *L'Osservatore Romano* (English ed.), 14 January 1991, 1–3.

—Address to factory workers at Matelica: 'Working Woman's Dignity' in *L'Osservatore Romano* (English ed.), 25 March 1991, pp. 6–7.

—Meditation: 'Experts Contribute to Social Doctrine', on 21 April 1991, in *L'Osservatore Romano* (English ed.), 29 April 1991, 2.

—Address to Amazonian Indians at Cuiabá, Brazil, 16 October 1991, *L'Osservatore Romano* (English ed.) 28 October 1991, 10.

—Address to Laity at Campo Grande, Brazil, 17 October 1991, *L'Osservatore Romano* (English ed.) 28 October 1991, 12–3.

—Address to the shanty-dwellers of Vitória, Brazil, 19 October 1991, *L'Osservatore Romano* (English ed.) 4 November 1991, 4.

—Address to the Diplomatic Corps in Dakar, Senegal, 22 February 1992, *L'Osservatore Romano* (English ed.) 28 February 1992, 8.

Synod of Bishops: *De Justitia in Mundo*, AAS 63 (1971) 923–42. English translation: *Justice in the World*, Roma (Vatican Press: 1971); this translation is also given in Gremillion 513–29 and in O'Brien and Shannon 390–408. The paragraphing in each of these three English texts is the same; but that of the Latin text is slightly different. Only the Gremillion text actually numbers the paragraphs. References to this document are given by using the initials JW followed by the number of the paragraph, as in Gremillion. Quotations in English are from

this text unless otherwise stated.
Sacred Congregation for the Doctrine of the Faith:
   —*Instruction on Certain Aspects of the 'Theology of Liberation'*,
   Vatican City (1984), AAS 76 (1984) 876–909. (References
   are given according to section and paragraph numbers.)
   —*Instruction on Christian Freedom and Liberation*, Vatican
   City (1986), AAS 79 (1987) 554–99. (References are given
   according to the paragraph numbers.)

Pontifical Commission '*Justitia et Pax*' (name changed later to
Pontifical Council '*Justitia et Pax*'):
   —*Ways of Peace: Papal Messages for the World Days of Peace
   (1968–1986)*, Vatican City n.d.
   —'At the Service of the Human Community: An Ethical
   Approach to the International Debt Question', Vatican City
   1986. (References are given according to the paragraph
   numbers.)
   —'The Church and Racism: Towards a More Fraternal
   Society', Vatican City 1988 .
   —*The Holy See at the Service of Peace: Pope John Paul II to
   the Diplomatic Corps (1978–1988)*, Vatican City (1988).
   —*Human Rights and the Church: Historical and Theological
   Reflections*, Vatican City (1990).
   —*De 'Rerum Novarum' à 'Centesimus Annus': Textes integraux
   des deux encycliques avec deux études de Roger Aubert et Michel
   Schooyans*, Vatican City (1991).
   *Une terre pour tous les hommes: la destination universelle de
   biens* (Actes du colloque international organisé par le Conseil
   pontifical 'Justice et Paix' du 13 au 15 mai 1991), Paris
   (Centurion: 1992).

Medellín: Second General Conference of Latin American
Bishops: *The Church in the Present-Day Transformation of Latin
America in the Light of the Council*, II: Conclusions, Washington
D.C. (Secretariat for Latin America, National Conference of
Bishops: 3rd ed. 1979). There are sixteen main documents,
numbered 1 to 16. Each of these is divided into numbered
'paragraphs'. In referring to the documents I give the number
of the document, followed by the number of the paragraph
within the document, followed by a page reference, within

brackets, to the above edition.

Puebla: Third General Conference of Latin American Bishops, Puebla: *Evangelization at Present and in the Future of Latin America: Conclusions (Official English Edition)*, Middlegreen and London (St Paul Publications and CIIR: 1980). The text is also given in Eagleson and Sharper. The paragraphs of the text are numbered. References are given by citing the paragraph numbers.

Bishops of Brazil:
   —'Fraternidade no Mundo do Trabalho', in *Trabalho e Justiça para Todos, Campanha da Fraternidade* 1978, CNBB (Rio de Janeiro: 1977).
   —'*Documento: As Reflexões da Assembleia Geral Extraordinaria realizada em Itaici, de 18 a 25 de abril [1978]*', published in O São Paulo, 29 April–5 May 1978.

National Conference of Catholic Bishops [of the United States]:
   —*The Challenge of Peace: God's Promise and Our Response: Pastoral Letter on War and Peace in the Nuclear Age*, Washington D.C. and London (CTS/SPCK) 1983.
   —*Economic Justice for All: Pastoral Letter on Catholic Social Teaching and the U.S. Economy*, Washington D.C. (1986).
   —*Justice in the Marketplace: Collected Statements of the Vatican and the U.S. Catholic Bishops on Economic Policy, 1891–1984* (ed. David M. Byers), Washington D.C. (United States Catholic Conference: 1985).

Conference of European Churches: *Peace with Justice: The official documentation of the European Ecumenical Assembly, Basel, Switzerland. 15–21 May, 1989*, Geneva (Conference of European Churches: 1989). (References are given according to the paragraph numbers.)

Collections of Texts

Carlen, Claudia (ed.): *Papal Pronouncements, A Guide: 1740–1978*, Ann Arbor (Perien Press).
Carlen, Claudia (ed.): *The Papal Encyclicals 1740–1981*, Ann Arbor (Perien Press: 1990).

The Pope and the People: Select Letters and Addresses on Social Questions by Pope Leo XIII, Pope Pius X, Pope Benedict XV and Pope Pius XI, London (CTS: 1929, reprinted 1937).

Gremillion, Joseph (ed.): *The Gospel of Peace and Justice: Catholic Social Teaching since Pope John*, Maryknoll (Orbis: 1976)

Hickey, Raymond (ed.): *Modern Missionary Documents*, Dublin (Dominican Publications: 1982).

O'Brien, David J. and Shannon, Thomas A. (eds.): *Renewing the Earth: Catholic Documents on Peace, Justice and Liberation*, Garden City (Doubleday Image: 1977)

Walsh, Michael J. and Davies, Brian (eds.): *Proclaiming Justice and Peace: Documents from John XXIII to John Paul II* (new expanded edition), London (Cafod/Collins: 1991).

Bibliography of
Secondary Sources

Alix, Christine: 'Le Vatican et la décolonisation', in Merle 17–113.

Antonazzi (ed.), Giovanni: *L'enciclica Rerum Novarum: testo autentico e redazioni preparatorie dai documenti originali*, Roma (Edizioni de Storia e Letteratura: 1957).

Antonchic, Ricardo: *Los Cristianos ante la Injusticia: Hacia un lectura latinamericano de la doctrina social de la Iglsia*, Bogota (Ediciones Grupo Social: 1980).

Arns, Paulo Evaristo Cardinal: 'The Church of the Poor: A Persecuted Church', in *Center Focus: News from the Center of Concern*, July 1981.

Aubert, Roger, *et al*: *The Church in a Secularized Society* (vol. 5 of *The Christian Centuries*) London (Darton, Longman and Todd: 1978) and New York (Paulist: 1978).

Aubert, Roger: *Le pontificat de Pie IX* (vol. 21 of *Historie de l'Église*, ed. A. Fliche et V. Martin), Paris (2nd edn 1963).

Baum, Gregory: 'The First Papal Encyclical', in *The Ecumenist: A Journal for Promoting Christian Unity*, 17 (1979).

Baum, Gregory: 'Liberation Theology and "The Supernatural"', in *The Ecumenist: A Journal for Promoting Christian Unity* 19 (1981).

Baum, Gregory: 'John Paul II's Encyclical on Labor', in *The Ecumenist: A Journal for Promoting Christian Unity*, 19 (1981).

Baum, Gregory: *The Priority of Labor: A Commentary on Laborem Exercens, Encyclical Letter of Pope John Paul II*, New York /Ramsey (Paulist: 1982).

Baum, Gregory: 'Structures of Sin', in Baum and Ellsberg 110–26.

Baum, Gregory and Ellsberg, Robert (eds): *The Logic of Solidarity: Commentaries on Pope John Paul II's Encyclical 'On Social Concern'*, Maryknoll (Orbis: 1989).

Berry, Thomas: *The Dream of the Earth*, San Francisco (Sierra Club Books: 1988).

Bloch, Alfred and Czuczka, George T. (eds): *Karol Wojtyla (Pope John Paul II): An Anthology*, New York (Crossroad: 1981)

Boff, Leonardo: 'The Originality of the Theology of Liberation', in Ellis and Maduro 38–48.

Boff, Leonardo: 'Vatican Instruction Reflects European Mind-Set' in Hennelly (1990) 415–18.

Boff, Leonardo and Elizondo, Virgil: *1492–1992: The Voice of the Victims (Concilium* Special) London (SCM: 1991) (book edition of *Concilium* December 1990).

Bolté, Paul-Emile: *Mater et Magistra: texte latin, nouvelle traduction, index analytique*, Montréal (Univ. de Montreal: 1968).

Bolté, Paul-Emile: *Mater et Magistra, commentaire*, Vol I 1964, Vol II 1966, Vol III 1967, Vol IV 1968, Montréal (Univ. de Montréal).

Bonino, José Miguez: *Towards a Christian Political Ethics*, London (SCM) and Philadelphia (Fortress Press) 1984.

Bride, A.: articles 'Tyranni' and 'Tyrannicide' in *Dictionnaire de théologie catholique* XV, cols. 1969–71 and 1987.

Brookfield, Harold: *Interdependent Development*, London (Methuen: 1975).

Calvez, Jean-Yves: *The Social Thought of John XXIII: Mater et Magistra*, London (Burns and Oates: 1964).

Calvez, Jean-Yves and Perrin, Jacques: *The Church and Social Justice: The Social Teaching of the Popes from Leo XIII to Pius XII (1878–1958)*, Chicago (Regnery: 1961).

Camp, Richard L.: *The Papal Ideology of Social Reform: A Study in Historical Development 1878–1967*, Leiden (E.J. Brill: 1969).

Campaign for Human Development and the Office of Domestic Social Development: *On Human Work: A Resource Book for the Study of Pope John Paul II's Third Encyclical*, Washington D.C. (United States Catholic Conference: 1982) (contains the text of LE as well as background articles and a condensed paraphrase of the text by James R.Jennings).

Carrier, Hervé: *The Social Doctrine of the Church Revisited: A Guide for Study*, Vatican City (Pontifical Council for Justice and Peace: 1990).

Charles, Rodger: *The Social Teaching of Vatican II, its origin and development: Catholic Social Ethics, an historical and comparative study*, Oxford (Plater Publications) and San Francisco (Ignatius Press: 1982).

Charles, Rodger: 'General Introduction', in Herr 7–27.

Chenu, Marie-Dominique: *La 'doctrine sociale' de l'Église comme idéologie*, Paris (Cerf: 1979).

Chiavacci, Enrico: *La costituzione pastorale sulla Chiesa nel mondo contemporaneo: Gaudium et Spes*, Roma (Studium: 1967).

Coleman, John A.: 'The Culture of Death', in Baum and Ellsberg 90–109.

Coleman, John A. (ed.): *One Hundred Years of Catholic Social Thought: Celebration and Challenge*, Maryknoll (Orbis: 1991). As well as editing this compilation, Coleman has contributed two of the articles in it—the introduction (1–10) and 'Neither Liberal nor Socialist' (25–42).

Collins, Denis: *Paulo Freire: His Life, Works and Thought*, New York (Paulist: 1977).

Congar, Yves M.J. and Peuchmaurd, M., (eds.): *L'Église dans le monde de ce temps: Constitution pastoral 'Gaudium et Spes': Tome III, Reflections et perspectives* (Unam Sanctam 65c), Paris (Cerf: 1967).

Cosmao, Vincent: *Dossier: nouvel ordre mondial; les chrétiens provoqués par le développement* (Chalet: 1978).

Cosmao, Vincent: *Le Redempteur de l'homme: lettre encyclique de Jean-Paul II: un guide de lecture*, Paris (Cerf: 1979).

Cosmao, Vincent: *Changer le monde: une tâche pour l'Église*, Paris (Cerf: 1979).

Coste, René: 'Le problème de la légitimité de principe de la guerre révolutionnaire', in Theas *et al.* 200–1.

Cronin, John F.: 'A Commentary on *Mater et Magistra*' in John XXIII, *The Encyclicals and Other Messages of John XXIII*, Washington D.C. (T.P.S. Press: 1964).

Cronin, John F.: 'A Commentary on *Pacem in Terris*' in John XXIII, *The Encyclicals and Other Messages of John XXIII*, Washington D.C. (T.P.S. Press: 1964).

Curran, Charles and McCormick, Richard: *Readings in Moral Theology No 5: Official Catholic Social Teaching*, New York (Paulist: 1986).

Curran, Charles: *Directions in Catholic Social Ethics*, Notre Dame (Univeristy of Notre Dame Press: 1985).

de Riedmatten, H. *et al*: *La Chiesa nel mondo contemporaneo: commento alla costituzione pastorale: 'Gaudium et Spes'*, Brescia (Queriniana: 1966).
de Soras, Alfred: *International Morality (Faith and Fact Books, no 58)*, London (Burns and Oates: 1963).
Dorr, Donal: *Spirituality and Justice*, Dublin (Gill and Macmillan) and Maryknoll (Orbis Books), 1984.
Dorr, Donal: *Integral Spirituality: Resources for Community, Justice, Peace and the Earth*, Dublin (Gill and Macmillan) and Maryknoll (Orbis Books), 1990.
Dorr, Donal: *The Social Justice Agenda: Justice, Ecology, Power and the Church*, Dublin (Gill and Macmillan), Maryknoll (Orbis Books), Melbourne (Collins Dove), 1991.
Duncan, Bruce: *The Church's Social Teaching: From Rerum Novarum to 1931*, Melbourne (Collins Dove: 1991).

Eagleson, John and Sharper, Philip (eds): *Puebla and Beyond: Documentation and Commentary*, Maryknoll (Orbis: 1979).
EATWOT: 'Final Document: International Ecumenical Congress of Theology, February 20–March 2, 1980, Sao Paulo, Brazil' (EATWOT Conference), in *Occasional Bulletin of Missionary Research*, July 1980, p. 129; this document is also available in Torres and Eagleson.
Elliott, Charles: *Patterns of Poverty in the Third World: A Study of Social and Economic Stratification*, New York (Praeger: 1975).
Ellis, Marc H. and Maduro, Otto: *The Future of Liberation Theology: Essays in Honor of Gustavo Gutiérrez*, Maryknoll (Orbis: 1989).
'Esperance des Pauvres': *Revue de presse*, No. 183 (*Septembre* 1979).

Ferraro, Benedito: *A Significão Politica e Teologica da Morte de Jesus à luz do Novo Testamento*, Petropolis (Vozes: 1977).
Filochowski, Julian: 'Medellín to Puebla', in Pope John Paul Il and others, *Reflections on Puebla*, London (CIIR: 1980).
Fitzgerald, Garret: 'Encyclical is impressive but insensitive on some issues', in *Sunday Press*, 5 May 1991, 11.

Flannery, Harry W. (ed.): *Pattern for Peace: Catholic Statements on International Order*, Westminster Md. (Newman Press: 1962).

Freire, Paulo: *Education for Critical Conscioumess*, New York (Continuum/Seabury: 1974) and London (Sheed and Ward: revised edn 1985).

Freire, Paulo: *The Politics of Education: culture, power and liberation*, South Hadley MA. (Bergin and Garvey; 1985) and London (Macmillan: 1985).

Fremantle, Anne (ed.): *The Social Teachings of the Church*, New York (Mentor-Omega: 1963).

Galilea, Segundo: 'The Theology of Liberation, A General Survey', in *Liberation Theology and the Vatican Document (Vol 1)*, Quezon City, Philippines (Claretian: 1984) 1–51.

Garofalo, Salvatore (ed.), *Dizionario del Concilio Ecumenico Vaticano Secondo*, Roma (Vatican Press: 1969).

Geyer, Alan: 'Two Peace Pastorals Compared', in *The Ecumenist: A Journal for Promoting Christian Unity*, 28 (1989).

Gilson, Etienne (ed.), *The Church Speaks to the Modern World: The Social Teachings of Leo XIII* Garden City (Doubleday Image: 1954).

Gorbachev, Mikhail: article in *La Stampa*, English version in *The Irish Times*, 4 March 1992, 9.

Goulet, Denis: 'The Search for Authentic Development' in Baum and Ellsberg 127–42.

Gremillion, Joseph (ed.): *The Gospel of Peace and Justice: Catholic Social Teaching since Pope John*, Maryknoll (Orbis: 1976).

Guano, E. *et al*: *La costituzione pastorale sulla Chiesa nel mondo contemporaneo: introduzione storico-dottrinale; testo latino e traduzione italiano; esposizione e commento*, Torino-Leamann (Elle di Ci: 1966).

Gudorf, Christine E.: *Catholic Social Teaching on Liberation Themes*, Lanham (University Press of America: 1980).

Gutiérrez, Gustavo: *A Theology of Liberation: History, Politics and Salvation*, Maryknoll (Orbis: 1973) and London (SCM: 1974).

Hauerwas, Stanley: 'Work as "Co-Creation"—A Remarkably Bad Idea' in *This World*, No. 3, Fall 1982, 89–102.

Hebblethwaite, Peter: 'The Popes and Politics: Shifting Patterns in "Catholic Social Doctrine'" in *Daedalus: Journal of the American Academy of Arts and Sciences*, Winter 1982, 88–9.

Hebblethwaite, Peter: *John XXIII: Pope of the Council*, London (Chapman: 1984).

Hebblethwaite, Peter: 'Spiritual Points in Liberation Themes Basic to the Document: An Analysis', in *Liberation Theology and the Vatican Document (Vol. 3): Perspectives from the Third World*, Quezon City, Philippines (Claretian: 1987) 85–95.

Heckel, Roger: *The Social Teaching of John Paul II, Booklet I, General aspects of the social catechesis of John Paul II; the use of the expression 'social doctrine' of the Church*, Vatican City (Pontifical Commission '*Justitia et Pax*': 1980).

Hehir, J. Bryan: 'The Church in the World: Where Social and Pastoral Ministry Meet', in *Church*, Winter 1990, 17–22.

Hennelly, Alfred T.: 'A Spirituality of Work' in: Campaign for Human Development and the Office of Domestic Social Development, *On Human Work: A Resource Book for the Study of Pope John Paul II's Third Encyclical*, Washington D.C. (United States Catholic Conference: 1982).

Hennelly, Alfred T. (ed.): *Liberation Theology: A Documentary History*, Maryknoll (Orbis: 1990).

Herr, Theodor: *Catholic Social Teaching: a textbook of Christian Insights*, London, (New City: 1991).

Hickey, Raymond (ed.): *Modern Missionary Documents*, Dublin (Dominican Publications: 1982).

Hogan, Michael (ed.): *Justice Now! Social Justice Statements of the Australian Catholic Bishops. First Series: 1940–1966*, Sydney (Dept of Government and Public Administration, University of Sydney: 1990).

Hoinacki, Lee: 'Development and John Paul II', in *The Aisling Magazine* No. 3, 53–7.

Holland, Joe and Henriot, Peter: *Social Analysis: Linking Faith and Justice* (revised and enlarged edition), Maryknoll (Orbis Books), Washington D.C. (Center of Concern), Melbourne (Dove Communications), 1983.

Hollenback, David: *Claims in Conflict: Retrieving and Renewing the Catholic Human Rights Tradition*, New York (Paulist: 1979)

Illich, Ivan D.: *Toward a History of Needs*, Berkeley (Heyday Books: 1978).

Illich, Ivan D.: *Tools for Conviviality*, Berkeley (Heyday Books: 1988) and London (Marion Boyars).

Jedin, Hubert (ed.): *The Church in the Industrial Age* (*History of the Church* Vol IX), New York (Crossroad: 1981).

Joblin, Joseph: "'The Church in the World": a Contribution to Pluralism', *The International Labour Review*, Vol. 93, No. 5, May 1966, Geneva (ILO: 1966).

Joblin, Joseph: 'Towards Complete Development', booklet reprint from *The International Labour Review*, Vol. 96, September 1967, Geneva.

Kairos theologians, *The Kairos Document: A Theological Comment on the Political Crisis in South Africa* (revised edition), Braamfontein (Skotaville Publishers), Grand Rapids (Eerdmans), London (C.I.I.R.) 1986.

Kirby, Peadar: 'The Pope in Brazil', in *Doctrine and Life*, 30 (1980) 363.

Kirwan, J.R.: notes on *Mater et Magistra* in *The Social Thought of John XXIII*, Oxford (Catholic Social Guild: 1964).

La Stampa: interview with Pope John Paul II about article by Mikhail Gorbachev; English version in *The Irish Times*, 4 March 1992, 9.

Land, Philip S.: 'The Social Theology of Pope Paul VI', in *America*, 12 May 1979, 394.

Land, Philip S. and Henriot, Peter J.: 'Toward a New Methodology in Catholic Social Teaching', in Baum and Ellsberg 65–74.

Laurentin, René: *Liberation, Development and Salvation*, Maryknoll (Orbis: 1972).

Leclercq, J.: *Leçons de droit naturel, II: L'État ou la politique* (2nd edn), Namur (Wesmael-Charlier: 1934).

Lernoux, Penny: 'The Long Path to Puebla', in Eagleson and Sharper 3–27.

Lonergan, Bernard J.F.: *Insight: A Study of Human Understanding*, New York (Harper and Row: 1977) and London (Longmans: 1958).

Lonergan, Bernard J.F.: *Method in Theology*, New York (Harper and Row: 1979) and London (Darton, Longman and Todd: 1972).

Lovelock, James: *The Ages of Gaia*, Oxford (Oxford University Press: 1988).

Malley, François: *Le Père Lebret: l'économie au service des hommes*, Paris (Cerf: 1968).

Marzani, Carl: 'The Vatican as a Left Ally?', in *Monthly Review*, July–August 1982.

Masse, Benjamin L. (ed.): *The Church and Social Progress: Background Readings for Pope John's Mater et Magistra*, Milwaukee (Bruce: 1966).

McGovern, Arthur F.: *Marxism: An American Christian Perspective*, Maryknoll (Orbis: 1980).

McGregor, Bede: 'Commentary on *Evangelii Nuntiandi*', in *Doctrine and Life*, 27 (1977) 70–1.

Merle, Marcel (ed.): *Les Églises chrétiennes et la décolonisation*, Paris (Armand Colin: 1967).

Miller, Amata: 'On the side of the Poor: Evolution of a Stance', in *Shaping a New World: The Catholic Social Justice Tradition 1891–1991*, Washington D.C. (Network: 1991).

Miller, Amata: 'The Centennial Encyclical—*Centesimus Annus*, in *Shaping a New World: The Catholic Social Justice Tradition 1891–1991*, Washington D.C. (Network: 1991).

Miller, Amata: 'Catholic Social Teaching—what might have been if women were not invisible in a patriarchal society', in *Journal of Justice and Peace*, 3 (1991) 51–70.

Miller, Raymond J.: *Forty Years After: Pius XI and the Social Order: A Commentary*, St Paul, Mmn. (Radio Replies Press: 1947).

Miranda, Jose Porfirio: *Marx Against the Marxists: The Christian Humanism of Karl Marx*, Maryknoll (Orbis: 1980).

Molony, John: *The Worker Question: A New Historical Perspective on Rerum Novarum*, Melbourne (Collins Dove) and Dublin (Gill and Macmillan) 1991.

Moody, Joseph N.: *Church and Society: Catholic Social and Political Thought and Movements 1789–1950*, New York (Arts Inc.: 1953).

Murray, John Courtney: 'The Church and Totalitarian Democracy, in *Theological Studies* 13 (1952) 525–63.

Murray, John Courtney: 'Leo XIII on Church and State: The General Structure of the Controversy', in *Theological Studies* 14 (1953) 1–30.

Murray, John Courtney: 'Leo XIII: Separation of Church and State', in *Theological Studies* 14 (1953) 145–214.

Murray, John Courtney: 'Leo XIII: Two Concepts of Government', in *Theological Studies* 14 (1953) 551–67.

Murray, John Courtney: 'Government and the Order of Culture', in *Theological Studies* 15 (1954) 1–33.

Nell-Breuning, Oswald von: *Reorganization of Social Economy: The Social Encyclical Developed and Explained* (English edition prepared by Bernard W. Dempsey), Milwaukee (Bruce: 1936).

Nell-Breuning, Oswald von: 'The Drafting of *Quadragesimo Anno*', in Curran and McCormick 60–8.

Nell-Breuning, Oswald von: articles on 'Social Movements', 'Socialism', etc. in *Sacramentum Mundi* VI, New York (Herder and Herder: 1970) and London (Burns and Oates: 1970), 98–116.

Nolan, Albert: 'The Option for the Poor in South Africa', in *Cross Currents* 36 (1986) 17–27.

Novak, Michael: '"Creation Theology"—John Paul II and the American Experience', in *This World*, No. 3, Fall 1982, 71–88.

Novak, Michael: *Catholic Social Thought and Liberal Institutions*, Oxford (Transaction Publishers: 1989).

O'Brien, David J. and Shannon, Thomas A. (eds.): *Renewing the Earth: Catholic Documents on Peace, Justice and Liberation*, Garden City (Doubleday Image: 1977).

O'Brien, David J.: 'A Century of Catholic Social Teaching: Contexts and Comments', in Coleman (1991) 13–24.

Pakenham, Thomas: *The Scramble for Africa 1876–1912*, London (Weidenfeld and Nicolson: 1991).

Potter, George Ann: *Dialogue on Debt: Alternative Analyses and Solutions*, Washington D.C. (Center of Concern: 1988).

Price, Vera: 'A Feminist Look at Catholic Social Teaching', in *Doctrine and Life* 41 (1991) 123–9.

Quade, Quentin L. (ed.): *The Pope and Revolution: John Paul II Confronts Liberation Theology*, Washington D.C. (Ethics and Public Policy Center: 1982).

Rhodes, Anthony: *The Vatican in the Age of the Dictators 1922–45*, London (Hodder and Stoughton: 1973)

Robertson, James: *Future Work: Jobs, Self-Employment and Leisure after the Industrial Age*, Aldershott (M. T. Smith: 1985).

Rostow, Walt W.: *The Stages of Economic Growth: A Non-Communist Manifesto*, New York (Cambridge University Press: 1960).

Ryan, John A.: *A Better Economic Order*, New York (Harper: 1935)

Ryan, Liam: 'The Modern Popes as Social Reformers', in *The Furrow* 42 (1991) 87–100.

Sachs, Wolfgang: 'The Economist's Prejudice', in *The Aisling Magazine* 1991, No 4, 59–63.

Sandoval, Moises: 'Report from the Conference', in Eagleson and Sharper 28–43.

Savignat, Alain (ed.): *Relations humaines et société contemporaine: synthèse chrétienne directives de S.S. Pie XII*, Fribourg (St Paul: 1956).

Schotte, Jan P. (ed.): *From Rerum Novarum to Laborem Exercens: Towards the Year 2000 (Symposium)*, Rome (*Pontificia Commissio Justitia et Pax*: 1982).

Schotte, Jan P.: Reflections on 'Laborem Exercens', Vatican City (Pontifical Commission *'Justitia et Pax'*: 1982).

Schultheis, Michael J., DeBerri, Edward P., and Henriot, Peter J.: *Our Best Kept Secret: The Rich Heritage of Catholic Social Teaching* Washington D.C. (Center of Concern) and London (Cafod) 1988.

Schumacher, E. F.: *Small is Beautiful: A Study of Economics as if People Mattered*, London (Abacus: 1974) and New York (Harper and Row: 1989).

Segundo, Juan Luis: *Theology and the Church: A Response to Cardinal Ratzinger and a Warning to the Whole Church*, Minneapolis (Winston Press) and London (Chapman) 1985.

Sobrino, Jon: 'The Significance of Puebla for the Catholic Church in Latin America', in Eagleson and Sharper 289–309.

Sobrino, Jon: 'Jesus, Theology and Good News', in Ellis and Maduro 189–202.

Somerville, Henry: *Studies in the Catholic Social Movement*, London (Burns Oates and Washbourne: 1933).

Stavrianos, Leften Stavros: *Global Rift: The Third World Comes of Age*, New York (Morrow: 1981).

Tamez, Elsa: *The Bible of the Oppressed*, Maryknoll (Orbis: 1982).

Theas, Pierre Marie *et al.*, *Guerre révolutionnaire et conscience chrétienne*, Paris (Pax Christi: 1963).

Todaro, Michael P.: *Economic Development in the Third World: An introduction to problems and policies in a global perspective*, London (Longman: 1977).

Torres, Sergio and John Eagleson, eds.: *The Challenge of Basic Christian Communities*, Maryknoll (Orbis Books: 1981).

Tripole, Martin: 'A Church for the Poor and the World: At Issue with Moltmann's Ecclesiology', in *Theological Studies*, 42 (December 1981) 645–59.

UNCTAD, *Restructuring the international economic framework: Report by the Secretary-General of the United Nations Conference on Trade and Development to the fifth session of the Conference*, New York (United Nations: 1980).

Utz, Arthur Fridolin: *Die Friedensenzyklika Papst Johannes XXIII: Pacem in Terris*, Freiburg (Herder: 1963).

Vidler, Alec R.: *A Century of Social Catholicism*, London (SPCK: 1964).

Villain, Jean: *L'enseignement social de l'Église, t.I: Introduction, capitalisme et socialisme*, Paris (Spes: 1953).

von Pastor, Ludwig F.: *The History of the Popes: From the Close of the Middle Ages*, Vol XXXI, London (Kegan Paul, Trench, Trabner and Co: 1940).

Vorgrimmler, Herbert (ed.): *Commentary on the Documents of Vatican II*, Vol 5, London (Burns and Oates: 1969) and New York (Herder and Herder: 1969).

Walsh, Michael J.: Editor's Introduction xi–xxv in, *Proclaiming Justice and Peace: Documents from John XXIII to John Paul II* (new expanded edition), London (Cafod/Collins: 1991).

Ward-Jackson, Barbara: Editor's Commentary in, *Encyclical Letter of His Holiness Pope Paul VI On the Development of Peoples* New York (Paulist: 1967) 1–22.

Ward-Jackson, Barbara: 'Looking back on Populorum Progressio', in *Doctrine and Life* 29 (1978), 196–212.

Ward-Jackson, Barbara: *The Angry Seventies: The Second Development Decade: A Call to the Church*, Vatican City (Pontifical Commission '*Justitia et Pax*': 1970).

Weigel, George and Royal, Robert (eds.): *A Century of Catholic Social Thought: Essays on 'Rerum Novarum' and Nine Other Key Documents*, Washington D.C. (Ethics and Public Policy Center: 1991).

Williams, Raymond: *Keywords: A Vocabulary of Culture and Society*, Glasgow (Collins Fontana: 1976).

Williamson, Edwin: *The Penguin History of Latin America*, London (Allen Lane: 1992).

Wojtyla, Karol (Pope John Paul II): *An Anthology edited by Alfred Bloch and Ceorge T. Czuczka*, New York (Crossroad: 1981).

Zigliara, *Summa Philosophica III*, Lyon (4th edn 1882).

INDEX